ORDER NUMBER

PO NYAATP08

BOOK NUMBER

9283665

BAY NUMBER

2667-1

AUTHOR	Altmann, G (ed)

TITLE	Parsing and Interpretation (Special Issue of 'Language and Cognitive Processes')

DESCRIPTION

This is an ex-library book and may have the usual library/used-book markings inside.This book has hardback covers. Clean from markings. In poor condition, suitable as a reading copy. No dust jacket.

Special Issue of
Language and Cognitive Processes

Parsing and Interpretation

Edited by

Gerry Altmann
Laboratory of Experimental Psychology,
University of Sussex, Brighton, U.K.

Lawrence Erlbaum Associates Ltd., Publishers
27 Palmeira Mansions
Church Road
Hove
East Sussex, BN3 2FA
U.K.

British Library cataloguing in Publication Data

Parsing and interpretation.
1. Languages. Sentences. Psycholinguistic aspects
I. Altmann, Gerry T.M. II. Language and cognitive processes,
ISSN 0169-0965
401'.9

ISBN 0-86377-141-6

Typeset by Acorn Bookwork, Salisbury
Printed and bound by BPCC Wheatons, Exeter

CONTENTS

LANGUAGE AND COGNITIVE PROCESSES, 1989, *4*, (3/4) SI 1–19

Parsing and Interpretation: An Introduction

Gerry T. M. Altmann
Laboratory of Experimental Psychology, University of Sussex, Brighton, U.K.

This introduction describes a number of contemporary issues in the psycholinguistics of parsing and interpretation, and provides a context within which to view the accompanying papers in this special issue. It consists of a general overview of the major topics considered since the early 1960s, with particular emphasis on surface structure ambiguity; parsing strategies; long-distance filler-gap dependencies; the roles of subcategorisation information, thematic information and referential information during parsing and interpretation; and the immediacy of anaphoric reference resolution.

INTRODUCTION

The distinction between parsing and interpretation is far from clear-cut. One definition might be that (surface structure) parsing consists in the assignment of grammatical categories and structural relations to the constituents of a sentence (irrespective of the "meaning" of those consituents), whereas interpretation consists in the integration of the information conveyed by both the constituents themselves and the structural dependencies holding between them into some internal representation of the events depicted by the utterance. Although far too simplistic, this definition serves to illustrate some of the major topics of research into human sentence comprehension, many of which are concerned with the relationship between parsing on the one hand, and interpretation on the other. For instance, to what extent are structural assignments made independently of "meaning"? What is the nature of the information "conveyed" by the constituents of a sentence and used during interpretation? To what extent does this differ from the information used by the parsing device in order to establish the structural dependencies between the constituents in the first

Requests for reprints should be addressed to Gerry Altmann, Laboratory of Experimental Psychology, University of Sussex, Brighton BN1 9QG, U.K.
I am grateful to Alan Garnham, Mark Steedman, and Lorraine K. Tyler for their comments on an earlier draft of the manuscript.

place? And, finally, what degree of communication exists between the two classes of process?

Another perspective on these issues is to consider the following question: What information is used when, in order to arrive at what kind of new representation? In other words, what is the time-course of the perceptual process, and what kinds of information contribute at what time to the formation of the final percept? This latter approach is agnostic on the issue of whether there is in fact a real distinction to be drawn between parsing and interpretation.

The accompanying papers in the present volume all address this single issue—the time-course of sentence comprehension, and the nature of the information that is used during this process. The remainder of this introduction will consist of a brief historical overview of the development of this issue, and of recent psycholinguistic research into "parsing and interpretation".

LINGUISTIC COMPETENCE VERSUS LINGUISTIC PERFORMANCE

The advent of Chomskian linguistics in the early 1960s led to widespread attempts to validate the psychological status of syntactic processing. The emphasis at this early stage was on showing that perceptual complexity, as measured using a variety of different tasks (see Fodor, Bever, & Garrett, 1974, for a review), was related to linguistic complexity, with a presumed correspondence between the linguistic processes postulated by transformational grammar (Chomsky, 1957; 1965) and the psychological processes responsible for sentence comprehension. However, the linguistic processes which formed a part of Chomsky's theory of transformational grammar, and whose psychological validity was assumed by the Derivational Theory of Complexity (DTC: Fodor et al., 1974), were a part of a theory of linguistic *competence*, and *not* a part of any theory of linguistic *performance* (Chomsky, 1965).[1] That is, transformations were a descriptive device introduced by generative grammarians in order to capture the systematicity of natural language—they were not intended as descriptions of the steps that a processor might go through in order to assign an interpretation to an utterance. However, early theories of DTC (e.g. Miller, 1962) did assume such a correspondence, and it was only later (e.g. Fodor & Garrett, 1966)

[1]To the extent that a theory of competence necessarily constrains the range of theories of performance, it follows that there is a sense in which transformation can be considered a part of a model of performance (see Valian, 1979).

that it was suggested that only the syntactic *structures* postulated by transformational grammar had any psychological reality, and that transformations did not (see Fodor et al., 1974, and Valian, 1979, for reviews of the demise of DTC).

An influential study which explicitly addressed linguistic *behaviour* as opposed to linguistic *knowledge* was Bever's (1970). He pointed out, following Chomsky, that whereas some sentences are undeniably "grammatical" given our intuitions about grammatical structure, these sentences are perceptually unacceptable, i.e. there is a dissociation between our competence and our performance. Examples of such sentences include the multiply self-embedded sentences (cf. 1), whose perceptual complexity is apparently due only to the number of embeddings that they contain, and the "garden-path" sentences (cf. 2), whose complexity is due to an initial misinterpretation of an ambiguous structure such that subsequent structures prove incompatible with the earlier (mis)interpretation:

1. The comments which reviewers whom the editor coerced produced were often ignored.
2. a. The horse raced past the barn fell.
   b. The author read the report snarled.

While issues relating to complexity of embeddings have been studied subsequently (e.g. Frazier & Fodor, 1978; Kimball, 1973; Wanner & Maratsos, 1978), the bulk of contemporary psycholinguistic research into sentence processing, and specifically surface structure parsing, has focused on garden-path phenomena of various kinds (i.e. various kinds of linguistic misinterpretations—see below for other examples), and the question of why, and under what conditions, the Human Sentence Processing Mechanism (HSPM) adopts one analysis of an ambiguous structure rather than another.

The rationale for asking this question is that systematic preferences presumably reflect the HSPM's use of particular kinds of information at particular points in the processing sequence. Once these preferences have been identified, the nature of the biasing information can be investigated. If such identification is possible, then a further consideration is whether the use of this information is based simply on the HSPM's priorities (i.e. use one kind of information rather than another irrespective of whether the other is simultaneously available), or whether it is based on the unavailability of other kinds of potentially disambiguating information (i.e. use one kind of information simply because the other kind is as yet unavailable). The current state of research is still at the stage of identifying the nature of the information used by the HSPM to guide its processing decisions.

PARSING STRATEGIES

In distinguishing between linguistic knowledge and linguistic behaviour, Bever (1970) proposed that whereas sentence grammaticality might be defined by linguistic *rules*, linguistic behaviour is constrained by the operation of a number of general perceptual *heuristics*, or strategies. Bever argued that any explanation of the effects described above should be based not on properties of the parsing mechanism itself, but on properties of the perceptual/cognitive system as a whole. The strategies he proposed are non-linguistic, in that they are processes "in which the knowledge of linguistically defined syntactic structure is not utilized actively in actual perception" (Bever, 1970, p. 298). The role of these strategies is to map what Bever called "external sequences" on to "internal structures". Thus, it is not the linguistic representations themselves which govern the HSPM's choices, but rather the mapping by which the internal structures are derived.

In order to explain the "horse raced . . ." example, Bever suggested that the HSPM interprets any noun–verb–noun (NVN) sequence in a sentence as actor–action–object.[2] As further evidence for the existence of such a strategy, Bever pointed out that whereas the pronoun deletion in (4) leads to a perfectly acceptable sentence, the deletion in (5) leads to an *ungrammatical* sentence:

3. The financier who had financial problems was desperate.
4. The financier having financial problems was desperate.
5. *The financier had financial problems was desperate.

Valian (1979) pointed out that a major problem with this whole approach was that it failed to explain why some strategies affect the grammar, such that certain strings are rejected if they cause the strategy to be misapplied (cf. the pronoun deletion data), whereas others do not (cf. the garden-path sentences, which are perfectly grammatical). Valian attributed the pronoun data to one strategy (Bever's "strategy B") and the garden-path data to another (strategy D). Valian's criticism has all the more force when it is considered that Bever attributed *both* kinds of data to

---

[2]The full definition of this strategy is: *Strategy D*: "Any Noun–Verb–Noun (NVN) sequence within a potential internal unit in the surface structure corresponds to 'actor–action–object'" (Bever, 1970, p. 298). In addition, two related strategies are: *Strategy A*: "Segment together any sequence X . . . Y, in which the members could be related by primary internal structural relations, actor action object . . . modifier" (p. 290), and *Strategy B*: "The first N . . . V . . . (N) . . . clause (isolated by strategy A) is the main clause, unless the verb is marked as subordinate" (p. 294). It is unclear just which of these is primarily responsible for the effects described in the main text (see Frazier, 1979, for further discussion).

the *same* strategy (strategy B). Why should the same strategy shape the grammar in one instance but not in another?

Underlying this indeterminacy in the theory is the fact that Bever may not have succeeded in *explaining* these various aspects of linguistic behaviour—to say that an NVN sequence is interpreted as actor–action–object is merely to *describe* the behaviour. A more formal attempt at explanation was undertaken by Kimball (1973; 1975), who suggested that the HSPM's preferences (and processing limitations) were due not to a set of *ad-hoc* and non-generalisable heuristics, but to a set of (seven) principles of *surface structure* parsing which do actively utilise linguistically defined syntactic structure. Thus, decisions in the face of ambiguity are made on the basis of syntactic structure *per se*. This basis is exemplified by Kimball's Principle of Right Association—"Terminal symbols optimally associate to the lowest nonterminal node" (Kimball, 1973, p. 24)—which was claimed to account for the parsing preferences in materials similar to (6) and (7):

6. The forecaster said that it will snow yesterday.
7. My flatmate cooked the leftovers that I had been saving for my friend.

In (6), "yesterday" is initially misinterpreted as a modifier of "will snow", while in (7) the preferred interpretation is that "for my friend" modifies "saving" rather than "cooked". In both cases, the initial analysis is that predicted by Right Association.

Kimball's ideas were refined further by Frazier (1979), who pointed out a number of inadequacies with their original formulation. Frazier proposed two variants of principles originally formulated by Kimball: Late Closure (equivalent to Right Association) and Minimal Attachment: "Attach incoming material into the phrase marker being constructed using the fewest nodes consistent with the well-formedness rules of the language" (Frazier, 1979, p. 76). The latter is a more general version of a principle first described by Kimball in 1975,[3] and has been claimed to explain a variety of parsing preferences (see Clifton & Ferreira, this issue), including the original "horse raced . . ." example. In addition to these principles, Frazier suggested that linguistic behaviours may reflect more than just the operation of a number of processing strategies which govern the operations

[3]Kimball's formulation was in terms of duplication of nodes. If the processor could choose between a hierarchical structure of the form "A . . . B . . . C", where A dominates B, which in turn dominates C, or of the form "A . . . B . . . B . . . C", then the processor would choose the "canonical" "A . . . B . . . C". Frazier's formulation is more general in that it merely takes into account the *number* of nodes, and not their identity.

of the HSPM: They may also reflect principles which are imposed on the HSPM's workings by its own architecture.

THE ARCHITECTURE OF THE HSPM

Frazier and Fodor (1978) described a two-stage model of the human parser in which Right Association arose because of the limited "view" which the first stage had of the incoming sentence: A lexical node could not be attached to any item on its left which had passed out of this limited view window. This limited view also accounted for the difficulties associated with multiply self-embedded sentences. Minimal Attachment was proposed as an independent principle, but it was suggested that it reflected the outcome of a race: The fewer the nodes in the phrase marker, the sooner that phrase marker would be constructed, and hence the preference for minimally attached structures.

These ideas led to considerable debate, notably the interchange between Wanner (1980) and Fodor and Frazier (1980). Wanner suggested that the data were more compatible with an Augmented Transition Network (ATN) model of the HSPM (although he was careful to avoid any claim that the HSPM *is* an ATN). An important aspect of this debate is that it led to further consideration of Right Association and Minimal Attachment within the context of other computationally implementable models, including the Shift-Reduce parser (Pereira, 1985; Shieber, 1983) and a parallel version of the ATN (Wanner, 1987). In each of these cases, it was claimed that the two principles could arise very naturally from the workings of the computational mechanism. In the case of the parallel ATN, the two principles did not have to be stipulated as independent processing principles which governed the workings of the parser—it was claimed that they arose as a natural *and inevitable* consequence of the processor's architecture.

The emphasis on architecture reflects a significant departure from the kind of question posed earlier, concerning the nature of the information used to guide processing decisions, and the timing of its use. To claim that parsing strategies arise as a consequence of the parser's architecture, is to deny that they necessarily reflect the processor's reliance (for whatever reason) on a particular information source at a particular time. However, although the various computational models demonstrate that some linguistic behaviours may in principle be architectural artefacts, it is unclear whether they capture successfully the relevant behaviours—Fodor and Frazier (1980) point out that the serial ATN model of the HSPM makes incorrect predictions of certain sentences, while Altmann (1988) makes the same case against the parallel ATN, as well as pointing out the invalidity of many of the assumptions underlying this kind of model. Moreover, and as we shall see below, there is increasing evidence which is claimed to show that there are occasions when structural strategies such as Minimal Attachment *do not* guide the HSPM's decisions (cf. Tanenhaus et al., this issue; McClelland et al., this issue), and there is a considerable debate over whether Minimal Attachment *ever* guides the processor's decisions (cf. Altmann & Steedman, 1988; Clifton & Ferreira, this issue; Steedman & Altmann, this issue). If the behaviours that give rise to the postulation of parsing strategies are in fact architectural in origin (and hence "hard-wired"), then they should be immutable. Several studies have claimed, however, that this is not the case (see below).

The architectural avenue, although undeniably important, forces us to stray from the original question concerning the time-course of information use. However, it is unclear whether the available computational models provide sufficient support for the abandonment of that particular question.

FROM CONSTITUENT STRUCTURE TO LONG-DISTANCE DEPENDENCIES

Before returning to consider whether the HSPM's preferences in the face of ambiguity reflect anything more than a reliance on purely syntactic information, a second major avenue of research should be considered. Thus far, we have considered the development of ideas relating to the HSPM's treatment of ambiguous *constituent structure*—from DTC, through Bever's general perceptual strategies, to Kimball's and ultimately Frazier's specifically syntactic parsing strategies. However, the early 1980s saw the emergence of a second field of study within sentence processing, namely the study of sentences exhibiting long-distance filler–gap dependencies. Examples of such sentences are shown in (8) and (9) (from Frazier, Clifton, & Randall, 1983):

8. This is the girl$_1$ the teacher$_2$ wanted —$_2$ to talk to —$_1$.
9. This is the girl$_1$ the teacher$_2$ wanted —$_1$ to talk.

The "—" indicates the presence of a "gap", and the subscript indicates which filler constitutes the correct assignment. At issue here is how the HSPM decides which filler to associate with which gap. Frazier et al. (1983) proposed the Most Recent Filler Strategy: a gap is co-indexed with the most recent potential filler (cf. Fodor, 1978; 1979). This predicts that example (9) would be harder than (8) simply because the gap would first be co-indexed with "the teacher" (the most recent potential filler), and that this co-indexing would need to be revised when no second gap is encountered. No such reanalysis would be required of (8). Using a simple comprehension task, Frazier et al. found the expected difficulty with materials similar to (9).

A further question which Frazier et al. considered was whether verb control information could override the most recent filler strategy. In example (10), the verb "decided" forces the following gap to be filled with the most recent potential filler, whereas in (11), "forced" constrains the gap to be filled by the more distant potential filler:

10. This is the girl$_1$ the teacher$_2$ decided —$_2$ to talk to —$_1$.
11. This is the girl$_1$ the teacher$_2$ forced —$_1$ to talk.

If the potentially disambiguating information conveyed by the verb is *not* used by the HSPM in deciding which filler to use, then the difference between examples (8) and (9) should still be apparent when the unambiguous verbs "decided" and "forced" are used. If the verb control information *is* used, then the difference between the two types of material should disappear. Frazier et al. found no effect of verb control information—materials similar to (11) were still harder than materials similar to (10).

This study is significant for a number of reasons. First, it explicitly questions the role of syntactic subcategorisation information (cf. the different control properties of "forced" and "decided") during the parsing process—see also Fodor's (this issue) review of filler–gap studies, and Mitchell (this issue) for additional evidence that subcategorisation information is not used during the first-pass analysis. Secondly, and related to the first, it explicitly addresses the time-course of information-use during processing. Frazier et al. (1983) conclude that "processing operations involving constraints on the permissible indexing (or evaluation) of structures lag behind the processor's structure building operations" (p. 188), and they suggest that "the unambiguous sentences act as if they are ambiguous because they *are* effectively ambiguous due to the delayed use of semantic control information" (p. 211).

Frazier et al. (1983) proposed a number of reasons for why the use of semantic information may be delayed: Either the architecture of the processor prevents semantic control information from being accessed because of the complete autonomy of the initial syntactic processing (cf. Forster, 1979), or the use of semantic information is delayed simply because of differences in the time needed to compute the relevant information. A third possibility they consider is that if simpler strategies can, on average, lead to correct assignments, then the processing effort is optimised if they are scheduled before the more complex ones. We return to these proposals below, as well as to the consideration of the related issue of the co-indexing of overt pronominal nounphrases to their antecedents.

Frazier et al.'s (1983) study raises important questions concerning the use to which different kinds of information might be put during sentence processing, and the timing of this use. The next sections consider two important developments during the 1980s which fuelled the debate on what kinds of information are used when.

BEYOND SYNTAX: THEMATIC ROLES

Rayner, Carlson, and Frazier (1983) proposed that the HSPM's initial decisions, when faced with surface structure ambiguities, are made on the basis of purely structural criteria. If the initial decision subsequently turns out to have been wrong (as in the case of a garden path), then a *thematic processor* guides the HSPM on to the correct analysis. Let us take a concrete example. In (12), the preferred analysis, according to Rayner et al., is for the final prepositional phrase to modify the main verb. In (13), such a decision subsequently proves implausible, and reanalysis is initiated:

12. The spy saw the cop with binoculars.
13. The spy saw the cop with a revolver.

They claim that once the initial analysis fails, *thematic* information associated with the main verb, i.e. information concerning the possible arguments that the verb can take and their *roles* in the event denoted by the verb, is used to guide the processor to the correct analysis. In the case of a verb like "see", there are two thematic frames associated with the verb, one corresponding to <*experiencer, theme, instrument*> and the other to <*experiencer, theme*>. If the assignment of thematic roles to the initial analysis is implausible (so "revolver" could not fill the instrument role of the verb "see"), then the alternative analysis is selected. The *thematic selection hypothesis* appears to be an example of the kind of processing optimisation argued for by Frazier et al. (1983), with simple structural computations preceding more complex thematic ones. However, if the thematic processor must in any case consider the plausibility of the initial role assignment (where such consideration involves a *comparative* assessment across the different possible analyses: Clifton & Ferreira, this issue), and if it *can* guide reanalysis, what savings would be lost by also having it guide the *first* analysis?

Recent evidence suggests that thematic information *is* used during the first-pass analysis by the HSPM. Taraban and McClelland (1988; see McClelland et al., this issue) show that there is a class of sentence similar in structure to (12) and (13) in which the preferred interpretation is *not* the predicted one on the basis of Minimal Attachment—the preferred interpretation corresponds to the *non*-minimally attached analysis (cf. 14), and not the minimally attached one (cf. 15):

14. *Non-minimal attachment (preferred)*
    The thieves stole the paintings in the museum.
15. *Minimal attachment (unpreferred)*
    The thieves stole the paintings in the night.

They suggest that these preferences are due to thematic expectations associated with the verb which guide the processor's initial analysis.

Trueswell, Tanenhaus, and Garnsey (submitted; see Tanenhaus et al., this issue) provide additional evidence using materials similar to Bever's original "horse raced . . ." example. In (16), "the man" can either be the subject of a main verb ("recognised") or the object of a reduced relative clause. The preference according to Minimal Attachment (or Bever's NVN strategy—see below) is for the subject of a main verb. Hence the evidence that subjects garden path on the "by-clause" in such cases (cf. Ferreira & Clifton, 1986).

16. The man recognised by the spy took off.

In (17), however, the inanimate nounphrase "the van" cannot fill the *experiencer* role of "recognised", and if this information is used by the processor, then there should be no such garden-path effect:

17. The van recognised by the spy took off.

This is exactly what was found. Tanenhaus, Carlson, and Trueswell (this issue) review further evidence which suggests that thematic information plays a role in the processing of "closure" sentences (Stowe, 1986), and during the processing of long-distance filler–gap dependencies of the kind described above (see Tanenhaus, Garnsey, & Boland, in press). These findings echo Bever's (1970) observation that lexically derived information *can* override structural preferences. However, they go further by suggesting that the apparently structural preferences are *not* structural in origin (cf. Altmann, 1987; Altmann & Steedman, 1988; Crain & Steedman, 1985; Taraban & McClelland, 1988).

The shift towards thematic control is reminiscent of the suggestion by Ford, Bresnan, and Kaplan (1982) that parsing preferences are brought about by *lexical* preferences. In their formulation, these lexical preferences related to preferred *syntactic* structures associated with the lexical items. The available evidence suggests that such preferences may instead (or also) be due to preferred *thematic* structures (see Mitchell, this issue, for a review of lexical guidance effects).

BEYOND SYNTAX: REFERENTIAL CONTEXT

Rayner et al. (1983) proposed that the preferences associated with the "PP-attachment" sentences ("saw the cop with . . .") were due to the operation of Minimal Attachment. Taraban and McClelland (1988) suggest that these preferences are in fact due to thematic expectations associated with the verb. Crain and Steedman (1985) and Altmann and Steedman (1988) suggest yet another explanation. They point out that just as a simple definite NP (e.g. "the cop") presupposes the existence of a unique individual to whom the NP can refer,[4] so does a complex NP (e.g. "the cop

[4]In fact, it is not the NP which presupposes anything, but rather the speaker/writer who presupposes it.

with the revolver"). Additionally, the restrictive modification of an NP (with either a PP modifier as in the present example, or a relative clause) presupposes a *set* of individuals, exactly one of whom can be distinguished on the basis of the modifying information (see Clifton & Ferreira, this issue, for further discussion). They claim that in the absence of any explicit context (the "null" context), the complex NP violates more presuppositions than does the simple NP (which does not presuppose, among other things, the existence of a set of entities), and under a principle of "parsimony", an analysis which violates fewer presuppositions (the simple NP analysis) is preferred over the one that violates more (the complex NP analysis).[5]

Altmann (1987) reinterprets Crain and Steedman's proposal, and suggests an alternative account of the apparent preference in the null context for minimally attached structures where the choice is between a simple or complex analysis of an NP. The information conveyed by a restrictive modifier is, by definition, "given" information (cf. Clark & Haviland, 1977). In the absence of any explicit context, nothing in the incoming sentence can provide given information. Thus, if there is a choice between one analysis which presupposes given information (the restrictive NP modification) and another analysis which does not, then the analysis which does not presuppose given information will be the preferred one.

An important prediction that follows from these claims is that appropriate *referential* contexts should force the processor into selecting one analysis or another, depending on whether or not the context satisfies the presuppositions conveyed by these alternative analyses.[6] Specifically, if there is more than one individual in the preceding context, then a complex NP will be preferred, whereas if there is only a single individual to whom a target NP can refer, then the simple NP analysis will be preferred. Under a "structure-sharing" implementation of such a proposal (but see Haddock, this issue, for an alternative implementation), the analysis of an NP proceeds in exactly the same manner, *irrespective* of whether it is a simple NP or the head NP of a complex construction. The distinction between simple and complex manifests itself only *after* the processing of the initial NP. If the NP fails to refer, then the subsequent input is interpreted, if

[5]Crain and Steedman (1985) propose that their Principle of Parsimony is a special case of the Principle of A Priori Plausibility: A reading which is more plausible in terms of general world knowledge, or knowledge about the discourse, will be preferred over one that is not. Thematic information is one example of the kind of information on which basis the plausibility or otherwise of a reading might be assessed, and its role in influencing the parser's decisions is thus an example of the application of the principles put forward by Crain and Steedman.

[6]Again, an analysis does not really "convey" a presupposition. The speaker/writer presupposes something, and the hearer/reader infers what it is that is presupposed on the basis of the input string and his/her mental model of the discourse so far.

possible, as a restrictive modifier. Crain and Steedman (1985), Altmann (1988), and Altmann and Steedman (1988) provide evidence to suggest that referential information *can* influence the parser's decisions in the manner just outlined (but see Ferreira & Clifton, 1986, for contrary evidence, and Altmann & Steedman, 1988, for a critique of Ferreira & Clifton's study).

These claims have caused considerable controversy, and the debate is by no means over (see Clifton & Ferreira, this issue; Steedman & Altmann, this issue). One aspect of this debate focuses on the experimental methodologies that have been used in order to tap the operation of the human parser. There is considerable controversy surrounding the conclusions that can be drawn on the basis of data collected using different methodologies, and the evidence is equivocal: Many effects which are found using eye-movement studies are also found with phrasal or word-by-word reading times (Ferreira & Clifton, 1986; Rayner et al., this issue), although the validity of using reading time studies at all has been questioned (cf. Clifton & Ferreira, this issue). The main argument is that eye movements allow the experimenter to distinguish between first- and second-pass parsing effects in a way that reading times do not. Given that the theoretical debate focuses on exactly this distinction, it follows that a methodology that is sensitive to these different effects should be given more credence than one which is not. However, even eye-movement studies are not immune to criticism (e.g. Altmann & Steedman, 1988; Kennedy et al., this issue), and descriptions of the methodology (e.g. Rayner et al., this issue) make clear that there is no *single* eye-movement measure which unequivocally divides the movements into first- and second-pass effects.

The distinction between first- and second-pass parsing effects has also been made in respect of the role of subcategorisation information during parsing. Not only is it a strong source of disambiguating information in terms of forcing certain attachments rather than others, but certain forms of subcategorisation information (concerned with argument structure) are closely linked with thematic role information.

THE ROLE OF SUBCATEGORISATION INFORMATION DURING PARSING

In the preceding two sections we have seen that there is considerable evidence to suggest that parsing decisions take account of a variety of information sources. However, there is also evidence which has been claimed to show that not all information sources are used immediately. It has already been mentioned that subcategorisation information may not be used during initial filler–gap assignments (Frazier et al., 1983). Mitchell (1987; this issue) suggests that subcategorisation information is not even used when deciding whether a post-verbal nounphrase is the direct object of the verb, or the subject of a subsequent clause (cf. "the doctor" in 18):

18. After the child sneezed the doctor made out a prescription.

Mitchell suggests that subcategorisation information is only used during a second-pass monitoring phase: If the control properties of the verb are found to be incompatible with the initial attachment (made on the basis of Late Closure or Minimal Attachment), then the structure is reanalysed. However, there is some uncertainty concerning the interpretation of the empirical data (see Fodor, this issue). Further investigation of this issue is underway in collaboration with Don Mitchell and Anna Clarkson, using materials such as the following:

19. The fireman told the woman *that he had risked his life for* several people in the past.
20. The fireman told the woman *that he had risked his life for* to install a smoke detector.
21. The fireman asked the woman *that he had risked his life for* to install a smoke detector.

Minimal Attachment predicts that the *italicised* sequence in (19) and (20) will be interpreted initially as a complement clause, only to cause a garden-path effect on the "to . . ." phrase in (20). Mitchell predicts that the equivalent sequence in (21) will also be interpreted as a complement, *despite* the unambiguous control information carried by the verb "asked". Lexical monitoring, which takes place after the initial analysis, would cause a reanalysis of the italicised sequence in time to prevent the garden path on the "to . . ." phrase. Consequently, reading times to the final (unitalicised) phrase should be no longer in (20) than in either (19) or (21), while reading times to the italicised phrase in (21) should be longer than in (19) and (20), where the lexical monitor would not cause the initial complement analysis to be revised (as it is compatible with the control properties of "told"). A pilot study by Mitchell provided some support for these predictions, although we await the outcome of the full-scale study, using these more controlled materials.[7,8]

---

[7]Preliminary results suggest a pattern in keeping with Mitchell's predictions. However, the pattern associated with the relative/complement sequence disappears when the materials are embedded in referentially supportive contexts. These preliminary results are from a pilot study, however, and further investigations are under way.

[8]These materials are also of interest because (19) and (20) are equivalent in structure to the materials used by Crain and Steedman (1985) and Altmann (1988) in order to assess the effects of referential context on parsing ambiguous relative/complements. Neither of these two studies used unambiguous controls, as provided by example (21), and an important question is whether the disambiguating properties of a referentially supportive context will manifest themselves in the same way as the disambiguating information provided by the unambiguous verb "asked" (assuming that this information *is* used in the first-pass analysis, Mitchell's lexical monitoring hypothesis notwithstanding).

If Mitchell's hypothesis were to be confirmed, then this would have considerable implications for Frazier et al.'s (1983) view that the processor is optimised by delaying the use of complex information (this was their preferred interpretation of their results). It is hard to see how a processor which ignored subcategorisation information (with ensuing, and inevitable, reanalysis) could be considered to have optimised its processing schedule. On the other hand, it is hard to see how, within certain kinds of grammatical framework (e.g. Combinatory Categorial Grammar, e.g. Steedman, 1985; 1987), subcategorisation information *could* be ignored. In categorial grammars, subcategorisation information is encoded directly in the complex categories assigned to each lexical item.

Aside from doubts expressed elsewhere (e.g. Fodor, this issue), there is a further issue which bears on the interpretation of Mitchell's results. There appears to be an inconsistency with the claim that, on the one hand, subcategorisation information is *not* used during the initial pass, whereas on the other, thematic information *is* (cf. Tanenhaus et al., this issue). The inconsistency arises because thematic role information must *subsume* a degree of subcategorisation information, by virtue of specifying the argument structure, and associated roles, demanded by the verb—and argument structure is exactly what verb subcategorisation information provides. It is unclear, therefore, how the processor could possibly be sensitive to thematic information without also being sensitive to subcategorisation information. Further research is clearly required in order to reconcile the two views.

FROM SURFACE STRUCTURE TO ANAPHORIC REFERENCE

Thus far, the issue of timing and information use has been considered mainly from the perspective of surface-structure parsing. Recent research forces us to consider not just *what kind* of information is used *when*, but also how information from different sources *interacts* during the parsing process (and, of course, when such interactions occur). Several lines of research suggest that non-syntactic information does play an important role in influencing what would otherwise be regarded as *syntactic* decisions. The claim that referential information can influence the parser's initial processing decisions assumes that some form of internal representation of the discourse is actively used during parsing. Moreover, referential information must be available early on if it is to influence the parsing processes. If referential information were made available to the processor only *after* the onset of a potential post-nominal modifier, then either some other source of information would have to be used in order to decide how to interpret the ambiguous material, or else the decision would have to be delayed until the relevant information was available.

A number of studies demonstrate the immediacy of nounphrase evaluation (and hence the immediacy with which referential information becomes available). However, while studies have shown that in the case of pronominal anaphora, a pronoun can be co-indexed with its antecedent and a referent assigned to the pronoun immediately (cf. Marslen-Wilson & Tyler, 1987; Tyler & Marslen-Wilson, 1982), this is not always the case. Sanford and Garrod (this issue) conclude that the processes responsible for reference resolution are initiated early on for both full referring expressions (nounphrases and proper names) and pronouns, but that in the case of pronouns, these processes use information whose interpretation may only be based on *later* input. Also, Oakhill, Garnham, and Vonk (this issue) suggest that pronouns may sometimes be only partially interpreted, and that the interpretation of a text (i.e. its internal representation) may often be incomplete.

There is evidence to suggest, then, that the assignment of a referent to a nounphrase does occur, in the general case, immediately. However, there is also evidence to suggest that on occasion such assignments are either delayed or not made at all. Sanford and Garrod (this issue) distinguish between the initiation of the process of assignment, which they claim is triggered as soon as an anaphoric expression is identified in the input, and the completion of this process, which may often be delayed. The goal of much current research is to identify the determinants of processing time, and hence the time-course with which information is added to the developing discourse model.

CONCLUDING REMARKS

The emphasis of the present overview has been on the nature of the information that is used during the parsing process, and the timing of its use. A number of issues have been avoided by adopting this approach, e.g. issues concerning the autonomy of syntax (e.g. Crain & Steedman, 1985; Forster, 1979), and the modularity or otherwise of the parsing system (cf. Fodor, 1983). Despite the attention that these issues have received in the past, their popularity as theoretical tools for guiding empirical research has diminished recently. For instance, Crain and Steedman (1985) distinguished between "representational autonomy" (to do with whether the processing system includes a level of uninterpreted structure corresponding to syntax) and "formal autonomy" (to do with whether *the model* permits such structures, irrespective of whether the system being modelled does). However, more important than the issue of autonomy is *the unit of incrementation*, i.e. the size of the unit which is passed to semantics for interpretation, and *the fineness of grain* of the interaction between syntax and semantics, i.e. the size of the unit which, in the event of a choice having to be made between several possible analyses, is passed up for semantic or pragmatic *adjudication*.[9] If the semantic/pragmatic evaluation of a constituent occurs past the point at which it was built, then such a model is said to be *non*-interactive (cf. Rayner et al.'s, 1983, proposals concerning Minimal Attachment and a subsequent *thematic processor* which assesses plausibility only some time *after* the initial construction of the relevant constituents). If constituents are evaluated as they become available to semantics, i.e. if the fineness of grain of the interaction is limited only by the size of the unit of incrementation, then such a model is *interactive*.[10] In the extreme case, where the unit of incrementation corresponded to the word, and the maximum fineness of grain were exploited, then it would not be possible, empirically, to distinguish between a model which proposed an autonomous syntax, and one which did not.

Modularity is another issue that has received much attention in recent years, although once again it is unclear how it applies to theories of parsing and interpretation in terms of any empirically demonstrable distinctions. Moreover, whether or not it is desirable for a system to be "informationally encapsulated" depends in large measure on the kinds of computation being performed, and whether or not computational efficiency is at stake (Thompson & Altmann, in press). This said, there are approaches to language processing that do appear to be characterisable in terms of autonomy and modularity. McClelland, St. John, and Taraban (this issue) describe a Parallel Distributed Processing approach to sentence processing (in fact, thematic processing), which denies a formal status for uninterpreted syntactic structures, and which is, in the loose sense of the term, non-modular. However, these are properties of the theory, and it is unclear whether any empirical consequences arise from them (see Haddock, this issue, for a review of the more "traditional" approaches to the computational modelling of sentence processing).

Whereas attention to theoretical issues such as autonomy and modularity might be diminishing (and this is itself a contentious point), attention to practical issues, such as the kind of experimental method employed in empirical studies, is on the increase. We saw earlier how one aspect of the Minimal Attachment/Referential Support debate is focused on exactly this issue. However, methodological considerations are not confined solely to

[9]In principle, the unit of incrementation and the fineness of grain do not have to coincide. The fineness of grain of the interaction could be larger than the unit of incrementation—the latter could be the word, whereas the former could be the phrase.

[10]Altmann and Steedman point out that the unit of incrementation is determined by *the grammar*, under Bresnan and Kaplan's Strong Competence Hypothesis (Bresnan, 1982).

the domain of surface structure parsing. Sanford and Garrod (this issue) point out a number of problems with the various techniques associated with studies of anaphoric processing, while Oakhill et al. (this issue) suggest that task demands, as perceived by the experimental subjects, can have profound effects on the measures used, and the conclusions which are then drawn in respect of the on-line construction of discourse models. Clearly, a considerable amount of further research is required in order to validate the various techniques that are currently available, and to develop new techniques—see Tanenhaus et al. (in press; this issue) for a description of evoked potentials and their application to sentence processing research.

The state-of-the-art in research into human sentence processing has progressed significantly in the 20 years since the publication of Bever's (1970) paper on processing strategies. Bever offered a paradigm which has shaped the research of the last two decades—the study of ambiguous structures and associated perceptual preferences. Many issues remain outstanding, and the debates and controversies which have arisen in recent years are far from over. The papers in the present collection highlight many, though not all, of the current controversies and research topics. Evidence is mounting in favour of the view that sentence processing is highly interactive, with a variety of different information sources being able to contribute to the processor's parsing decisions. The task now is to study these interactions, and continue charting the flow of information through the human sentence processor.

REFERENCES

Altmann, G. T. M. (1987). Modularity and interaction in sentence processing. In J. Garfield (Ed.), *Modularity in knowledge representation and natural language understanding*, pp. 249–258. Cambridge, Mass.: MIT Press.

Altmann, G. T. M. (1988). Ambiguity, parsing strategies, and computational models. *Language and Cognitive Processes, 3*, 73–97.

Altmann, G. T. M. & Steedman, M. (1988). Interaction with context during human sentence processing. *Cognition, 30*, 191–238.

Bever, T. G. (1970). The cognitive basis for linguistic structures. In J. R. Hayes (Ed.), *Cognition and the development of language*. New York: John Wiley.

Bresnan, J. (Ed.) (1982). *The mental representation of grammatical relations.* Cambridge, Mass.: MIT Press.

Chomsky, N. (1957). *Syntactic structures.* The Hague: Mouton.

Chomsky, N. (1965). *Aspects of the theory of syntax*. Cambridge, Mass.: MIT Press.

Clark, H. H. & Haviland, S. E. (1977). Comprehension and the given-new contract. In R. O. Freedle (Ed.), *Discourse production and comprehension*. New Jersey: Ablex.

Crain, S. & Steedman, M. J. (1985). On not being led up the garden path: The use of context by the psychological parser. In D. Dowty, L. Karttunen, & A. Zwicky (Eds), *Natural language parsing: Psychological, computational, and theoretical perspectives*. Cambridge: Cambridge University Press.

Ferreira, F. & Clifton, C. (1986). The independence of syntactic processing. *Journal of Memory and Language, 25*, 348–368.

Fodor, J. A. (1983). *Modularity of mind*. Cambridge, Mass.: MIT Press.

Fodor, J. A. & Garrett, M. F. (1966) Some reflections on competence and performance. In J. Lyons & R. J. Wales (Eds), *Psycholinguistic papers*. Edinburgh: Edinburgh University Press.

Fodor, J. A., Bever, T. G., & Garrett, M. F. (1974). *The psychology of language*. New York: McGraw-Hill.

Fodor, J. D. (1978). Parsing strategies and constraints on transformations. *Linguistic Inquiry, 9*, 427–473.

Fodor, J. D. (1979). Superstrategy. In W. E. Cooper & E. C. T. Walker (Eds), *Sentence processing: Psycholinguistic studies presented to Merrill Garrett*. London: Lawrence Erlbaum Associates Ltd.

Fodor, J. D. & Frazier, L. (1980). Is the HSPM an ATN? *Cognition, 8*, 417–459.

Ford, M., Bresnan, J., & Kaplan, R. M. (1982). A competence-based theory of syntactic closure. In J. Bresnan (Ed.), *The mental representation of grammatical relations*. Cambridge, Mass.: MIT Press.

Forster, K. (1979). Levels of processing and the structure of the language processor. In W. E. Cooper & E. C. T. Walker (Eds), *Sentence processing: Psycholinguistic studies presented to Merrill Garrett*. London: Lawrence Erlbaum Associates Ltd.

Frazier, L. (1979). On comprehending sentences: Syntactic parsing strategies. Ph.D. Thesis, University of Connecticut. Indiana University Linguistics Club.

Frazier, L. & Fodor, J. D. (1978). The sausage machine: A new two-stage parsing model. *Cognition, 6*, 291–325.

Frazier, L., Clifton, C., & Randall, J. (1983). Filling gaps: Decision principles and structure in sentence comprehension. *Cognition, 13*, 187–222.

Kimball, J. (1973). Seven principles of surface structure parsing in natural language. *Cognition, 2*, 15–47.

Kimball, J. (1975). Predictive analysis and over-the-top parsing. In J. Kimball (Ed.), *Syntax and semantics*, Vol. 4. London: Academic Press.

Marslen-Wilson, W. & Tyler, L. (1987). Against modularity. In J. Garfield (Ed.), *Modularity in knowledge representation and natural language processing*, pp. 57–104. Cambridge, Mass.: MIT Press.

Miller, G. A. (1962). Some psychological studies of grammar. *American Psychologist, 17*, 748–762.

Mitchell, D. C. (1987). Lexical guidance in human parsing: Laws and processing characteristics. In M. Coltheart (Ed.), *Attention and Performance XII: The psychology of reading*. London: Lawrence Erlbaum Associates Ltd.

Pereira, F. C. N. (1985). A new characterization of attachment preferences. In D. Dowty, L. Karttunen, & A. Zwicky (Eds), *Natural language parsing: Psychological, computational, and theoretical perspectives*. Cambridge: Cambridge University Press.

Rayner, K., Carlson, M., & Frazier, L. (1983). The interaction of syntax and semantics during sentence processing. *Journal of Verbal Learning and Verbal Behavior, 22*, 358–374.

Shieber, S. M. (1983). Sentence disambiguation by a shift-reduce parsing technique. *Proceedings of the 21st Annual Meeting of the Association for Computational Linguistics*, 15–17 June, pp. 113–118.

Steedman, M. (1985). Dependency and coordination in the grammar of Dutch and English. *Language, 61*, 523–568.

Steedman, M. (1987). Combinatory grammars and human sentence processing. In J.

Garfield (Ed.), *Modularity in knowledge representation and natural language processing*, pp. 428–444. Cambridge, Mass.: MIT Press.

Stowe, L. (1986). Evidence for on-line gap location. *Language and Cognitive Processes, 1*, 227–245.

Tanenhaus, M. K., Garnsey, S. M., & Boland, J. (in press). Combinatory lexical information and language comprehension. In G. T. M. Altmann (Ed.), *Cognitive models of speech processing: Psycholinguistic and computational perspectives*. Cambridge, Mass.: MIT Press.

Taraban, R. & McClelland, J. L. (1988). Constituent attachment and thematic role assignment in sentence processing: Influences of content-based expectations. *Journal of Memory and Language, 27*, 597–632.

Thompson, H. S. & Altmann, G. T. M. (in press). Modularity compromised—Selecting partial hypotheses. In G. T. M. Altmann (Ed.), *Cognitive models of speech processing: Psycholinguistic and computational perspectives*. Cambridge, Mass.: MIT Press.

Trueswell, J. C., Tanenhaus, M. K., & Garnsey, S. M. (submitted). *Semantic influences on parsing: Use of thematic role information in syntatic disambiguation*. Department of Psychology, University of Rochester.

Tyler, L. K. & Marslen-Wilson, W. D. (1982). Processing utterances in discourse contexts: On-line resolution of anaphors. *Journal of Semantics, 1*, 297–315.

Valian, V. (1979). The wherefores and therefores of the Competence–Performance distinction. In W. E. Cooper & E. C. T. Walker (Eds), *Sentence processing: Psycholinguistic studies presented to Merrill Garrett*. London: Lawrence Erlbaum Associates Ltd.

Wanner, E. (1980). The ATN and the sausage machine: Which one is baloney? *Cognition, 8*, 209–225.

Wanner, E. (1987). The parser's architecture. In F. Kessel (Ed.), *The development of language and language researchers: Essays in honour of Roger Brown*. London: Lawrence Erlbaum Associates Ltd.

Wanner, E. & Maratsos, M. (1978). An ATN approach to comprehension. In M. Halle, J. Bresnan, & G. A. Miller (Eds), *Linguistic theory and psychological reality*. Cambridge, Mass.: MIT Press.

LANGUAGE AND COGNITIVE PROCESSES, 1989, *4*, (3/4) SI 21–49

Eye Movements and On-line Language Comprehension Processes

Keith Rayner, Sara C. Sereno, Robin K. Morris, A. Réne Schmauder, and Charles Clifton, Jr.
Department of Psychology, University of Massachusetts, Amherst, Massachusetts, U.S.A.

Eye movement records have been used profitably to study on-line comprehension processes in reading. We present some basic facts about eye movements during reading, emphasising issues concerning the use of eye movement data to infer cognitive processes that are involved in (1) word processing, (2) syntactic parsing, and (3) higher-order processes. We review research on each of these topics and present new data dealing with word processing and high-order processes. We conclude that the analysis of eye movement records provides a great deal of useful information about on-line processing and that eye movement recording is a good way to study many critical issues concerning language comprehension processes.

INTRODUCTION

In the past few years, many psycholinguists have become interested in the immediate, on-line processes that underlie sentence and text comprehension. According to some current perspectives, it is not enough to know what representation is finally given to a string of words. Such final representations can be gauged effectively by examining subjects' recall or the answers they provide to questions, or by asking them to participate in non-speeded tasks (like grammaticality or semantic judgements). However, knowing what the final representation of a sentence is does not tell us how the appropriate decisions about sentence structure and meaning are made

Requests for reprints should be addressed to Keith Rayner, Department of Psychology, University of Massachusetts, Amherst, Massachusetts 01003, U.S.A.

Preparation of this article and the research described herein was supported by Grant BNS-8510177 from the National Science Foundation and by Grant HD17246 from the National Institute of Child Health and Human Development. We thank Gerald Altmann, Alan Kennedy, Don Mitchell, and Wayne Murray for their comments on an earlier draft of this paper.

on a word-by-word basis. How and when, for example, does the parser make the decision to assign a word to the current constituent unit or to begin a new unit? Questions such as these have become increasingly important as theories of language processing have become more complex. Much of the research on sentence parsing, reference determination, and inferencing is motivated by the belief that understanding how immediate, on-line decisions are made will help us to uncover the basic structure and routines of the language processing sytsem.

To intrude on the silent, private activity of reading, cognitive psychologists have devised many clever techniques in the hope that appropriate inferences can be made about moment-to-moment language processes. These tasks include (1) word-by-word silent reading (subjects press a button to display each new word), (2) word-by-word lexical decision (subjects make a lexical decision about successively presented words by pressing a button), (3) rapid serial visual presentations (RSVP) of words (presented at a set rate in the same spatial location to subjects), and (4) fragment completion responses (subjects silently read a passage up to a target word and then make a standard word recognition response, such as naming or lexical decision, on the word). While many of these techniques and paradigms have yielded interesting findings, there are problems associated with each of them. For example, all of these tasks are somewhat unnatural in relation to the normal silent reading process (i.e. readers do not normally do such things), and the reading rate that emerges from such paradigms is often grossly different from that of silent reading. Some tasks disrupt the flow of reading, whereas others involve a secondary task in addition to reading. A fifth technique widely used to infer moment-to-moment processing involves measuring the total reading time for a larger segment of text (such as a phrase, clause, or sentence). In reality, this measure is simply a larger version of the word-by-word reading paradigm. But whereas the unit of analysis demarcated by successive button presses is a single word in the word-by-word paradigm, the unit of analysis here is enlarged to include a number of words. While this paradigm comes closer to the natural reading situation, it loses the capacity to register precisely the amount of time needed for processing individual words, and hence remains a pale reflection of moment-to-moment processes.

In this paper, we will argue that one of the best ways to study the moment-to-moment language processes that occur during reading is to engage subjects in the task of reading while recording their eye movements. It is now clear that the pattern of readers' eye movements provides insights into the nature of language processing. In comparison to most other techniques available for studying language processing, eye movements provide a relatively natural, on-line method for investigating critical issues. Eye movement data have advantages over data obtained in the other tasks mentioned above, in that eye movements do occur naturally in silent reading and a subject's normal reading rate is unperturbed when eye movements are monitored. On the other hand, it should be noted that laboratory recording of eye position generally requires a fixed head (via a bitebar or chin rest) and vertical text presentation. These constraints are sometimes viewed as introducing an unnatural component of reading when eye movements are recorded. However, Tinker (1939) demonstrated that reading rate and comprehension did not differ when subjects read text in the eye movement laboratory and when they read under normal conditions (i.e. no fixed head and the text in a non-fixed position). Our own introspections as subjects in an eye movement laboratory lead us to believe that subjects in eye movement experiments read quite normally.

We do not wish to argue that eye movements are the only way to study on-line language processes, because some of the tasks mentioned above may often yield accurate inferences about such processing. Further, converging evidence must be sought from various sources in building a theory of language processing. Eye movements are one of the *best* ways (but certainly not the only way) to study moment-to-moment language processes in reading.

BASIC FACTS ABOUT EYE MOVEMENTS

The basic facts about eye movements during reading have been well known for some time. Readers typically spend about 200–250 msec on each fixation and typically move their eyes forward about 8 character spaces during a saccade. In addition, they regress (look back in the text to reread material) on about 10–15% of the fixations. Perhaps the most important fact is that there is a considerable amount of variability in each of these measures (fixation duration, saccade length, and frequency of regressions) within subjects. A given subject may fixate from under 100 msec to over 500 msec in the same passage, and may move his or her eyes as little as 1 character space or as much as 15 or more character spaces (though such long saccades typically initiate or follow a regression). Eye movement data have become increasingly important, as it has been documented that the variability associated with each of these measures is related to cognitive processes activated during language comprehension (Rayner, 1978; Rayner & Pollatsek, 1987; 1989). It is clear that when text is difficult, readers fixate longer, move their eyes a shorter distance with each saccade, and make more regressions (Frazier & Rayner, 1982).

Whereas eye movement data are very informative with respect to understanding language processing, they are not perfect reflections of the mental activities associated with language comprehension. One reason why they are not is that there is a purely motoric component involved with fixation time (Kowler & Anton, 1987; Rayner, Slowiaczek, Clifton, & Bertera, 1983b). In addition, low-level visual and perceptual factors can also influence fixation duration and the landing position following a saccade (O'Regan & Levy-Schoen, 1987). Each of these factors distorts the signal which is being taken to reflect immediate language processes. Nevertheless, useful information can be gleaned from the resulting data.

CRITICAL ISSSUES IN USING EYE MOVEMENT DATA

In using eye movement data to investigate moment-to-moment language processes, there are a number of issues inherent in the methodology that need to be addressed. We will discuss four relevant questions: (1) What is the size of the perceptual span in reading, (2) how tight is the link between eye location and the mind's processing of information at that location, (3) what propels the eyes forward through text, and (4) what is the best measure of processing time associated with eye movements and fixation times? Each of these issues will be discussed in turn.

The Perceptual Span

The perceptual span is the region around a reader's fixation point from which useful information can be obtained. Knowing the size of this region and the type of information that can be gathered from it is important. If the region is large enough to encompass several words, eye movement data would not provide a very good measure of on-line processing because it could not be determined which word was being processed at any point in time. The ideal situation would be that the reader identifies only the fixated word and then moves to the next word on the ensuing saccade. Fortunately, it turns out that this is frequently the case.

As we noted earlier, readers typically move about 8 character spaces per saccade, which is roughly 1.5 words. Moreover, as we also pointed out, there is considerable variability in how far readers move their eyes. Practically, this means that words are skipped some of the time (i.e. they do not receive a fixation, even though they are perceived and processed). However, there are systematic differences in what kinds of words get skipped. Short words (3 or fewer letters) are much more likely to be skipped than longer words (6 or more letters). Words that are 8 letters or more are rarely skipped, and words that are 6 letters long are fixated most of the time (Rayner & McConkie, 1976). Carpenter and Just (1983) reported that content words were fixated 83% of the time, whereas function words (which are much shorter) were fixated only 38% of the time. Rayner and Duffy (1988) reported that a content word (ranging in length from 5 to 9 letters) was fixated 84% of the time, whereas the function word *the*—which preceded the content word—was fixated only 19% of the time.

The most definitive research on the size of the perceptual span has utilised the eye-contingent display change techniques introduced by McConkie and Rayner (1975) and Rayner (1975). More thorough reviews of the research can be found in Rayner (1978) and Rayner and Pollatsek (1987; 1989). The primary finding is that the perceptual span is quite limited during an individual fixation. Readers seem to extract information from a region extending from the beginning of the currently fixated word, but no more than 3 or 4 character spaces to the left of fixation, to about 15 character spaces to the right of fixation. However, information used to *identify* a word during the current fixation is generally confined to a region extending no more than about 5–7 character spaces to the right of fixation. Thus, the word identification span is smaller than the total perceptual span. Functionally, this often means that the reader is able to identify only the currently fixated word and must then make an eye movement to the next word. However, if two short words (or even three very short words) fall within the word identification span, they will all likely be identified during the single fixation. Likewise, when a reader fixates on a content word and a short function word follows the content word, the function word can be identified without a direct fixation. The region within which words can be identified is thus quite small, but it clearly is not the case that only one word is identified on each fixation.

Another important point is that when the word to the right of fixation is not identified, some processing of that word is done before the reader fixates on it. However, the processing that is done is not at a semantic level (Rayner, Balota, & Pollatsek, 1986). Indeed, a fair amount of research (see Rayner & Pollatsek, 1987) has documented a *preview effect*, in which readers process the first few letters of the word to the right of their fixation. The existence of the preview effect and the fact that more than one word can sometimes be identified on a fixation are problems that must be dealt with in interpreting the eye movement record. But neither problem is insurmountable and both are due to natural aspects of the processing activity of readers. Thus, attempts to eliminate these characteristics of processing (as is done in some of the techniques we mentioned above) will lead to unnatural strategies on the part of the reader.

The Eye–Mind Span

The eye–mind span relates to the question of how tightly linked the eyes and the mind are in reading. If the eyes lead the mind by an appreciable amount, then eye movement data would not be a particularly sensitive measure of the processing time associated with a given word (or segment of text), because the experimenter would never be sure which word was being processed during a particular eye fixation. On the other hand, if the eye–mind span is negligible, then eye movement data can provide a good reflection of the moment-to-moment cognitive processes associated with reading.

Just and Carpenter (1980) argued against the existence of an eye–mind span and in favour of what they termed the *immediacy hypothesis*. On the basis of multiple regression analyses of eye movement data, they argued that the reader completes all processing associated with a given word (or, at least all processing which can be completed) prior to moving on to the next word. However, while there is now clear evidence that the ease or difficulty of processing a word influences how long the reader looks at the word, the relationship is not perfect. There are two problems in claiming that fixation times on a word are a pure reflection of the processes associated with comprehension of the word. The first is the parafoveal preview effect discussed in the prior section: Some of the processing associated with a word is initiated on the prior fixation. The second problem has to do with *spillover* effects. Spillover effects are best exemplified in the following two sentences:

1. The shiny new gondola moved slowly.
2. The shiny new vehicle moved slowly.

These two sentences are identical except for a single content word, which differs in word frequency (*gondola* is a low-frequency word and *vehicle* is a high-frequency word). Inhoff and Rayner (1986) and Rayner and Duffy (1986) found that fixation times were 30–90 msec longer on low-frequency words than high-frequency words. However, when they examined the fixation time on the next word (*moved* in the example), they also found that its fixation time increased by 30–40 msec. It seems that the processing associated with the low-frequency word spilled over on to the processing of the next word in the text. Such spillover effects are quite pervasive and have been observed in a number of studies dealing with eye movements and language processing.[1]

On the one hand then, the Inhoff and Rayner (1986) and Rayner and Duffy (1986) studies provide clear evidence that the difficulty associated with a specific target word influences the amount of time that a word is

[1]Some portion of spillover effects are apparently due to the lack of preview effects. For example, when fixated on a word that is difficult to process (such as a low-frequency word), readers devote so much attention to processing that word that they may not pick up preview information from word $n + 1$ (Henderson & Ferreira, in press, Inhoff, Pollatsek, Posner, & Rayner, 1989; Rayner, 1986).

looked at. On the other hand, they also provide clear evidence for spillover effects. When one adds the spillover problem to the fact that some processing of the word is done prior to fixating it (the preview effect), some questions arise about the extent to which the processing time for a word can be determined from the fixation time on that word alone. Ultimately, we will need a theory of just what processing is completed during fixation on a word, and what processing is done only after the eyes have moved on. As a practical matter for the present, however, by carefully controlling the context in which the words of interest appear (for example, by keeping their preceding context identical), we can make safe conclusions when we find differences in eye movement behaviour on or after these words.

What Propels the Eyes Forward in Text?

Most of the evidence now available suggests that the two major attributes of eye movements during reading (saccade length and fixation duration) are controlled by different mechanisms. That is, *where* a reader looks next and *when* a reader makes an eye movement are largely independent decisions (Rayner & McConkie, 1976; Rayner & Pollatsek, 1981; 1987). Where a reader looks next is very much influenced by the length of words to the right of fixation (Morris, Rayner, & Pollatsek, in press; O'Regan, 1979; 1980; Rayner, 1979; Rayner & Pollatsek, 1987). The decision of when to move the eyes seems to be based on more complex processes, but it is clear that the ease or difficulty of understanding the fixated word influences when the eyes move to another word (and when the eyes remain fixated on the same word).

An important and elegantly simple model of when the eyes move in reading was proposed by Morrison (1984). According to his model, when a reader accesses the meaning of the currently fixated word (word n), attention shifts to the next word (word $n + 1$), and a saccade follows in a more or less time-locked fashion. However, Morrison also proposed that because it takes time to actually get the eyes moving from word n, the reader will sometimes be able to access the meaning of word $n + 1$ before the saccade occurs. This is particularly likely to happen when $n + 1$ is a short function word. In the situation when the meaning of word $n + 1$ is accessed before the saccade occurs, the reader may sometimes be able to cancel the currently programmed saccade and programme a new saccade, thus skipping over word $n + 1$. However, on other occasions, the programme for the next saccade may be so far along that it cannot be cancelled. In this case, the reader begins programming another saccade in parallel. The result is a short fixation on word $n + 1$, followed by a fixation on word $n + 2$, or a landing position intermediate between the two saccade targets. By this simple mechanism, Morrison was able to account for phenomena in the eye movement record that have puzzled researchers for over 100 years. For example, his account was able to explain word skipping, very short fixations (under 100 msec), and the fact that the eye sometimes lands in very uninformative locations (see Morrison, 1984, for details).

Although the Morrison model successfully accounts for a number of important characteristics of eye movements in reading, it suffers from a major problem that has been addressed subsequently (Pollatsek & Rayner, in press; Rayner & Balota, 1989; Rayner & Pollatsek, 1987). Namely, the model fails to account for the fact that readers often make more than one fixation on word *n* before moving to word $n + 1$. A related problem is that recent research clearly shows that fixation time on a word is also influenced by integration processes (Rayner & Frazier, 1989; Schustack, Ehrlich, & Rayner, 1987). Thus, lexical access cannot be the sole trigger propelling the eyes forward through the text; discourse integration processes come into play and are reflected in the amount of time that a reader spends on a word. We note two other relevant points here. First, integration time can often spill over onto the next fixation (Ehrlich & Rayner, 1983; Rayner & Duffy, 1986). Secondly, syntactic parsing effects are also reflected in the fixation times on certain words (Ferreira & Clifton, 1986; Frazier & Rayner, 1982).

It is beyond the scope of this paper to go into further detail about the exact mechanisms controlling the movement of the eyes through text. However, the prior discussion raises the following question: If eye fixations reflect sentence parsing and integration processes as well as lexical access processes, is it possible to determine exactly what fixations reveal? This question, coupled with the fact that eye movement data are more difficult to obtain than word-by-word button-press measures or global sentence reading time measures, has been put forward to suggest that eye movement data may not be particularly useful in examining sentence comprehension processes (see Altmann, 1988; Altmann & Steedman, 1988). Altmann (1988) and Altmann and Steedman (1988) used sentence reading times[2] as a preferred alternative on the grounds that eye movement data do not provide any better resolution than reading times for differentiating between these processes (and hence cannot be used to determine where parsing decisions are made). However, it seems far preferable to have the moment-to-moment record that eye movement data make available and then to examine it for evidence of difficulty in processing a sentence. For example, significant differences in any property of eye fixations that appear

[2]Altmann and Steedman (1988) used global sentence reading time in one experiment and phrase reading time in another. The arguments presented here about global sentence reading time apply to phrasal reading time.

at a certain point between the sentences of two experimental conditions indicate that the processing of the sentences differed at least as early as that point. A conclusion like this may permit the test of hypotheses that could not be tested using more global total reading time measures. Further, as we learn more about just what kinds of effects show up immediately in the eye movement record, we will be able to draw an even stronger conclusion under certain circumstances: the processing of the sentences began to differ exactly at a certain point.

Although there are cases in which we cannot accurately differentiate the processes reflected in *every* eye fixation, often we still can obtain valuable data from the eye movement record. In many studies, we are looking for ease or difficulty of processing as a function of some manipulation that has been made in the text. When we have clear hypotheses and know where to look in the eye movement record, our experience is that the eye movement record yields valuable data. Thus, while we cannot at this point firmly establish what propels the eyes through text, we will continue working on two fronts: On the one hand, investigating eye movement control in reading and, on the other, using eye movement data as an on-line measure of comprehension processes.

The Appropriate Measure of Processing Time

Another controversy we must address concerns the appropriate measure of processing time to be used with eye movement data (see Blanchard, 1985; Inhoff, 1984; Just & Carpenter, 1980; McConkie, Hogaboam, Wolverton Zola, & Lucas, 1979; Rayner & Pollatsek, 1987). The issues differ depending upon whether the unit of analysis is a single word or some larger region (such as a group of words), which we shall consider in turn.

If readers made only one fixation on each and every word, then there would be little problem. However, words are sometimes fixated more than once and sometimes words are skipped. The problem of multiple fixations (before moving on to another word) on a word has received different solutions. For example, some researchers appear to use the *first fixation duration* on a word as a measure of lexical access (Inhoff, 1984). The assumption seems to be that what occurs after the first fixation reflects higher-order processing or is noise. However, other researchers make the opposite assumption (O'Regan & Levy-Schoen, 1987), arguing that the second fixation on a word results when the reader initially lands in a "bad" place and then moves to a more informative position in the word. On this account, the second fixation on a word is more diagnostic of lexical access than the first. Whereas multiple fixations on a word may be due in part to low-level processes, such as not being in the most informative place in a word, many such cases are also clearly due to the processing difficulty associated with the word (Rayner & Pollatsek, 1987). For example, a recent study in our laboratory (Sereno & Rayner, 1989) has demonstrated that significant word-frequency effects are present in the first fixations of words receiving more than one fixation (see also Inhoff & Rayner, 1986).

A second solution to the problem of multiple fixations on a word is to use the *gaze duration* measure. Gaze duration represents the total amount of time that a reader looks at a word before moving on to another word; it is the sum of the fixations on a word excluding any that result from regressions to the word. Whereas some researchers favour it as the best measure of processing time (Just & Carpenter, 1980), others view it with scepticism (Hogaboam & McConkie, 1981; Kliegl, Olson, & Davidson, 1982). Elsewhere, the distinction between first fixation duration and gaze duration has been discussed in more detail (see Rayner & Pollatsek, 1987). Our argument is that first fixation duration and gaze duration reflect related processes; when readers have difficulty processing a word, they either maintain their initial fixation on the word or they programme a second fixation on the word (in the latter case, the second fixation has to be programmed fairly early during the first fixation given saccadic latency constraints). When readers have extreme difficulty with a word (particularly a long word) they may make three or four fixations on the word. Most of the data that we are familiar with comparing first fixation duration and gaze duration show that the measures yield similar results. For example, for the word-frequency effect discussed above (Rayner & Duffy, 1986), first fixation duration was 37 msec longer on low-frequency words than high-frequency words and gaze duration was 87 msec longer. Both effects were highly significant and support the same basic conclusion: Low-frequency words are more difficult to process in text than high-frequency words.

We will not discuss word skipping in detail here (see Rayner & Pollatsek, 1987); however, two points are important to note. First, when a word is skipped, it is most likely identified on the fixation prior to skipping; the duration of the fixation prior to skipping is inflated (Hogaboam, 1983; Pollatsek, Rayner, & Balota, 1986). Secondly, some versions of gaze duration (and also a reading time per word measure that is sometimes used) assign zero milliseconds to a word when it is not fixated (Just & Carpenter, 1980). Such a measure surely cannot yield an accurate measure of processing time. An alternative is gaze duration or reading time per word conditionalised on there being a fixation on the word (Blanchard, 1985; Carpenter & Just, 1983). However, this measure may err in the other direction. A reasonable strategy is to look for consistency across different measures. Our preference is to report first fixation and gaze duration conditionalised upon a fixation on a target word, and also to report the probability of fixating the word.

Our general conclusion is that as much information as possible should be examined in inferring cognitive activities associated with word processing. Examining first fixation duration, gaze duration, the probability of fixating a word, and the frequency of regressions to a word provides researchers with a great deal of information to use to construct a coherent explanation of how words are processed. Clearly, the ease or difficulty of word processing influences all of the measures mentioned.

When the unit of analysis is larger than a single word, it is also important to examine multiple measures obtained from the eye movement record. Under such conditions, researchers typically have divided a sentence into different target regions and examined processing times for each region. Among the measures often adopted (see Frazier & Rayner, 1982) are first pass reading times, second pass reading times, and the probability of a regression into a region.

First pass reading times are obtained by summing all left-to-right fixations in a region plus any regressions made to other points within that region. When the reader makes an eye movement out of a region (either a regression to a prior region or a forward movement to the next region), first pass reading is considered complete for that region. Second pass reading times include, in addition, all re-readings of a region. Because various experimental manipulations may result in regions with differing absolute numbers of words (and with words also differing in word length), we often divide the reading time for the region by the number of letters in the region to yield a *reading time per character* measure.

While the reading time per character measure smooths out differences due to the number of words in a region, there are potential problems associated with it. One obvious problem is that it assumes that reading time is a linearly increasing function of the number of letters in a region, and ignores such factors as the time spent making a saccade in a region whose length requires multiple fixations. Thus, it may give an inaccurate reflection of the true state of affairs if two critical regions to be compared differ widely in the number of letters in the region. Also, if the two regions to be compared have the same number of words, but the words differ widely in word frequency, there are potential problems.

Combining the reading time per character measure with the procedure of dividing sentences into different regions can also be problematic. Consider the following sentence:

3. The evidence was examined by the lawyer for the defence.

Suppose that the prepositional phrase "by the lawyer" is considered a region of analysis and the reader makes a fixation on the word *by*, and then makes a regression to an earlier part of the sentence. According to the first pass algorithm, when the reader follows the regression out of the prepositional phrase with a fixation on *lawyer*, the fixation time on *lawyer* will be allocated to second pass reading time. Thus, the first pass reading time assigned to the prepositional phrase would be quite short. An alternative to the first pass reading time measure is *summed gaze duration* for a region in which the gaze duration for each word is computed separately and then summed. In the example, the fixation time on *by* and the gaze duration on *lawyer* would be summed (and then perhaps divided by the number of letters to get the reading time per character measure) to get a summed gaze duration. In our laboratory, we now have computer programs that score the data for different regions in all of the ways that have been discussed here (reading time per character for first pass reading of a region, reading time per character for second pass reading, probability of a regression from and to a region, summed gaze duration, total reading time), as well as more standard word measures (first fixation duration, gaze duration). Our strategy is to examine *all* of the measures to ensure that they provide a consistent picture of what is happening as the sentence is read. Of course, it is preferable to match words within regions on critical variables like word length and word frequency and to match the number of words (and number of letters in the words) in regions as well as possible. However, given various experimental questions, this is not always possible. But, the goal should be to control for as many things as possible.

Having discussed some critical issues related to using eye movements to study on-line language processing, we now turn to research on language processing. In our review, we will focus primarily (though not exclusively) on studies conducted in our laboratory. We will discuss evidence that eye fixations reveal a considerable amount of information about (1) word processing, (2) syntactic parsing, and (3) higher-order processes. By so doing, we will thus focus on research dealing with word processing, and we will then move up a level to research dealing with how words (once having been recognised) are parsed into appropriate constituent units, and then finally we will discuss how text information is integrated during on-line comprehension processing.

WORD PROCESSING AND EYE FIXATIONS

A number of variables that are thought to influence lexical access for a word have been examined in recent eye movement studies. Some of these variables, such as word frequency (Rayner & Duffy, 1986), letter bigram and trigram frequency (Lima & Inhoff, 1985), and whether a word has a prefix or a pseudoprefix (Lima, 1987) significantly influence fixation times, whereas others, such as verb complexity (Inhoff, 1985; Rayner & Duffy, 1986; Schmauder, 1989), do not. For any given study, there can always be questions about whether appropriate controls were used and good experimental manipulations were employed. However, the general pattern of results that has emerged is quite interesting.

It is now an uncontroversial fact that the ease or difficulty of processing a word is reflected in the fixation time on that word. As we just indicated, the amount of time that a reader looks at a word is influenced by the frequency of the word (Inhoff, 1984; Inhoff & Rayner, 1986; Just & Carpenter, 1980; Kliegl et al., 1982; Rayner, 1977; Rayner & Duffy, 1986). Although early demonstrations of this finding tended to confound word length (which has a powerful effect on the amount of time that a reader looks at a word) and word frequency, the most recent experiments have controlled for word length and number of syllables. Fixation time on a word is also influenced by the predictability of the word (Balota, Pollatsek, & Rayner, 1985; Ehrlich & Rayner, 1981; Inhoff, 1984; Schustack et al., 1987; Zola, 1984). We have already discussed the basic finding from the word frequency studies: low-frequency words yield longer fixations than high-frequency words. In the predictability studies, readers have typically read passages in which fixation time on a target word has been measured when the word is or is not predictable in the passage. The general finding is that readers tend to look at the unpredictable word longer than the predictable word and they tend to skip over the predictable word more frequently than the unpredictable word. Finally, it has also been found that priming from semantically related earlier-occurring words reduces fixation time on a target word. Carroll and Slowiaczek (1986) reported that such priming effects occurred primarily when the related words were within the same clause. However, more recently, Duffy and Rayner (submitted) obtained priming effects across sentences when the priming word and the target word were coreferential.

Results such as these make it very clear that the ease or difficulty of processing a word greatly influences the amount of time that a reader looks at that word. What is less clear is whether these effects should be attributed to lexical access processes or to text integration processes. According to the lexical access account, high-frequency words, predictable words, and primed words are looked at for less time because they are easier to access in the lexicon: high-frequency words because we look them up more frequently than low-frequency words; predictable and primed words because the combination of contextual constraint and parafoveal preview (Balota et al., 1985) allows us to get to the lexicon more quickly.[3] According to the text integration account, high-frequency words, predict-

[3]It is also possible that sub-lexical processes are involved with the word frequency effect; low-frequency words are often orthographically irregular. However, Rayner and Duffy (1986) controlled for digram and trigram frequency and still obtained significant frequency effects.

able words, and primed words are easier to integrate into the discourse representation that the reader is building.

In an attempt to determine how much of fixation time on a word is related to lexical access processes versus integration processes, we recently completed an experiment on this issue. The test sentences in the study contained an initial noun phrase whose characteristics were manipulated with respect to word frequency and the presence or absence of a modifier. We examined sentence initial phrases because processing load is light and sentence wrap-up effects are minimal at this point in a sentence. There were three types of experimental sentences:

4a. The *tiger* started to growl.
 b. The *fierce tiger* started to growl.

5a. A *theory* will explain the facts.
 b. A *simple theory* will explain the facts.

6a. Jerry's *acoustic guitar* needs new strings.
 b. Jerry's *electric guitar* needs new strings.

Each of 12 subjects read one version (i.e. either an a or b version) of each of the three types (sentence 4, 5, or 6) of the noun phrase constructions. For reasons unrelated to the experimental manipulations, one subject's data were eliminated from some of the analyses reported here.

In sentences like (4), the target nouns were of low frequency (less than 10 occurrences per million), and in sentences like (5), they were of high frequency (more than 50 occurrences per million), according to the word frequency norms of Francis and Kučera (1982). The adjectives in sentences like (4b) and (5b) had frequencies that matched the noun they modified. Sentences like (6a) and (6b) contained low- and high-frequency adjectives, respectively, followed by the same noun (whose frequency was not systematically controlled). Low- and high-frequency words were matched on word length.

Subjects' eye movements were monitored by a Stanford Research Institute Dual Purkinje Eyetracker, which was interfaced with a Hewlett Packard 2100 computer. The computer in turn was interfaced with a Hewlett Packard 1300 Cathode Ray Tube (CRT), which was used to present the sentences. Three characters equalled 1 degree of visual angle on the CRT and subjects' heads were immobilised by a bitebar during the experiment (further details about the apparatus can be found in Rayner & Duffy, 1986).

Fixation durations were recorded while the subjects read the sentences. Both first fixation duration and gaze duration measures were calculated, and are summarised in Table 1. Subjects fixated on both the adjective and the noun 98% of the time and the data reported here are only from trials

TABLE 1
Mean First Fixation Duration (FFD) and Gaze Duration (GD) for all Conditions

Sentence Type	*Word Frequency* Adj.	*Word Frequency* Noun	*FFD (msec)* Adj.	*FFD (msec)* Noun	*GD (msec)* Adj.	*GD (msec)* Noun
4a		L		251		308
4b	L	L	245	283	335	360
5a		H		220		274
5b	H	H	221	276	284	323
6a	L	mixed	255	273	345	346
6b	H	mixed	233	270	272	317

on which both target words were fixated (or only the noun in the unmodified condition). The data from sentences like (4) and (5) will be discussed first. An examination of the fixation times on the adjectives in sentences like (4b) and (5b) revealed a 24-msec difference between low- and high-frequency adjectives on first fixation duration [$F1(1,10) = 6.24$, $P < 0.05$; $F2(1,28) = 5.83$, $P < 0.05$]. For gaze duration, this difference increased to 51 msec [$F1(1,10) = 6.06$, $P < 0.05$; $F2(1,28) = 9.61$, $P < 0.01$]. Because frequency effects on the modified nouns were confounded by the fact that they were preceded by adjectives of similar frequency, a 2 (low-frequency *vs* high-frequency noun) × 2 (modified *vs* unmodified) ANOVA was performed on the nouns. Effects of both word frequency and "modification" were found. For first fixation duration, low-frequency nouns were fixated for 19 msec longer than high-frequency nouns [$F1(1,10) = 15.97$, $P < 0.01$; $F2(1,28) = 2.03$, $P < 0.165$]. Similarly, the gaze duration on low-frequency nouns was 36 msec longer than that of high-frequency nouns [$F1(1,10) = 4.52$, $P < 0.057$; $F2(1,28) = 11.60$, $P < 0.01$]. This finding replicates the frequency effects found by Rayner and Duffy (1986) that were discussed earlier. Unmodified and modified nouns were also compared. For first fixation duration, there was a 44 msec "modification" effect (nouns preceded by an adjective were fixated longer than nouns with no preceding modifier)—$F1(1,10) = 11.41$, $P < 0.01$; $F2(1,28) = 32.98$, $P < 0.001$. Likewise, for gaze duration, modified nouns were fixated 50 msec longer than unmodified nouns [$F1(1,10) = 5.03$, $P < 0.05$; $F2(1,28) = 7.01$, $P < 0.05$]. There was no interaction between frequency and modification, either for first fixation or gaze duration (all Fs < 1).

Because sentences like (6) juxtaposed low- and high-frequency adjectives with the same noun, integration effects other than that of modification could be observed. Once again, there was an effect of frequency (though it was not significant for first fixation). On first fixation duration, low-frequency adjectives were fixated for 22 msec longer than high-frequency ones [$F1(1,11) = 4.04$, $P < 0.07$; $F2(1,17) = 2.39$, $P < 0.14$]. For gaze duration, the difference was 73 msec [$F1(1,11) = 10.96$, $P < 0.01$; $F2(1,17) = 6.89$, $P < 0.05$]. The noun that followed the adjective showed a "spillover" effect (though it was only significant in the item analysis), a 29-msec increase on nouns following a low-frequency adjective on gaze duration [$F1(1,11) = 2.52$, $P < 0.14$; $F2(1,17) = 5.58$, $P < 0.05$].

Spillover from a word (e.g. the adjective) on to the following word (e.g. the noun) can be attributed either to its incomplete access or to its subsequent integration with the next word. It could be that these two effects are inseparable if low-frequency words *per se* are more difficult to integrate. Assuming this is not the case, it seemed possible to distinguish between the two accounts of spillover. Difference scores between the means of the low- and high-frequency adjectives were correlated with the difference scores between the means of the associated noun. Because the same noun was modified both by a low- and high-frequency adjective, the difference in fixation time on the noun in the two contexts should correlate positively with the differences in time spent on its preceding low- or high-frequency adjective, if the spillover on the noun was primarily lexical in nature. By items, there was no significant positive correlation ($r = +0.16$, $P > 0.25$). This seems to rule out spillover due to access as a major cause, and suggests an account whereby any lexical effects (frequency) are masked by larger integration effects (conjoining concepts, meaning integration).

It thus appears that fixation times on a word reflect both lexical access processes and integration processes. Certainly, the data that we have just discussed suggest that conclusion. Recent studies dealing with lexical ambiguity (Duffy, Morris, & Rayner, 1988; Rayner & Frazier, 1989) and a study reported by Schustack et al. (1987) also lead to this conclusion.

SYNTACTIC PARSING PROCESSES

Eye movement research, beginning with Mehler, Bever, and Carey (1967), and continuing since then, both in our laboratory (Ferreira & Clifton, 1986; Frazier & Rayner, 1982; 1987; Rayner, Carlson, & Frazier, 1983a; Rayner & Frazier, 1987) and other laboratories (Holmes & O'Regan, 1981; Kennedy & Murray, 1984), has led to sharp insights into the initial stages of language comprehension. Many of our studies of sentence parsing have used the eye movement record to determine when the parsing of a sentence is disrupted. Evidence from a variety of sentence constructions points to the conclusion that a reader initially assigns a *single* syntactic analysis to an ambiguous (or temporarily ambiguous) portion of a sentence. If later information shows that the initial analysis is wrong, it is revised, often disrupting the normal progression of fixations through the text (Frazier, 1987; Frazier & Rayner, 1982). The initial analysis is often chosen on the basis of psychologically motivated principles—in particular, Minimal Attachment and Late Closure (Frazier, 1979; Frazier & Rayner, 1982). These principles entail, for example, an initial analysis of the noun phrase (NP) "John" as object of the verb, not subject of a complement sentence, in a string like "We knew John . . .". If the string turned out to be

7. We knew John left.

in which *John* begins a sentence complement rather than being an object NP, this analysis would have to be revised at some cost in processing.

The most persuasive evidence in favour of this position comes from the long duration of the initial fixation made in the region of a sentence that indicates the initial analysis to be wrong. In example (7), the initial fixation on *left* (the critical word which indicates the preferred analysis to be wrong) would be long, compared to an appropriate baseline. The earliest eye movement study of Late Closure and Minimal Attachment reported such an immediate disruption effect (Frazier & Rayner, 1982), and similar results have been obtained in subsequent studies.

The choice of an appropriate baseline against which to compare fixations on critical words can be aided by what we know about the factors controlling eye movements. Many studies compare fixation times on the critical word to fixation times on the previous word, or to fixation times on words that are consistent with the presumed initial analysis, such as *well* in

8. We knew John well.

Such comparisons may confound perceptual and lexical factors with parsing factors, and must be made with caution. More recent research has compared fixation times on identical words, when they occur following ambiguous *vs* unambiguous contexts. Rayner and Frazier (1987), for example, found longer initial fixations on *would* in sentences like the temporarily ambiguous

9. The contestant imagined the small tropical islands would be completely deserted.

than in the corresponding sentence with a disambiguating *that* inserted after *imagined*. Ferreira and Henderson (in press) have obtained similar data, using short sentences that were presented on a single line of the CRT, and went further to show that similar effects were found even with verbs like *hope* that take only a sentence complement.

No individual study, it seems, is perfectly free of extraneous factors that could affect the eye movement record. Rayner and Frazier's (1987) study has been criticised (Kennedy, Murray, Jennings, & Reid, this issue) because its sentences spanned more than one line on the CRT, and the return sweeps needed to move the eye from one line to the next could affect the pattern of eye movements. A line break may provide an occasion for the reader to complete interpreting a phrase earlier than normal. If it occurred at the end of the ambiguously attached NP, the line break could encourage the reader to interpret the NP as a complete direct object, not as the beginning of a new clause. However, each of Rayner and Frazier's sentences had a line break in the middle of the ambiguous NP, and in only 2 of their 24 sentences could the NP possibly have been taken to be complete at the line break. Further, Ferreira and Henderson's (in press) study is not subject to this criticism, because in their study all sentences appeared on a single line. However, their study is subject to the criticism that the "ambiguous" regions in the disambiguated sentences were preceded by a short function word (*that*), whereas this was not the case in the ambiguous sentences. Because word frequency and word length affect eye fixations, and sometimes have spillover effects, the difference between ambiguous and disambiguated sentences could, in principle, be attributed to such effects rather than to syntactic reanalysis. We do not believe, though, that these *ad hoc* criticisms of individual experimental conditions have much force. We would argue that the consistency of the effect of syntactic reanalysis across a variety of different conditions should be given primary weight in choosing a theoretical account of these phenomena.

Data other than first fixation durations can provide useful evidence to support claims that parsing is disrupted. Frequent regressions from disambiguating regions, or lengthened reading times in disambiguating regions, indicate disruption. But such evidence, like evidence from such commonly used tasks as self-paced reading, is not maximally diagnostic about just where and when a sentence misanalysis is noted. It aggregates effects that arise during the reading of several different words and may arise from different causes. It could reflect not only the existence of an erroneous initial analysis, but also the relative plausibility of competing analyses, the syntactic differences between the initial and the revised analysis, and so on. Such other factors could even obscure the underlying disruption effect.

The studies discussed so far have emphasised the role eye movement measurements play in identifying the ways temporary ambiguities are resolved in parsing. Another question that the eye movement methodology may be able to address concerns the effect that syntactic complexity in the absence of ambiguity has on parsing difficulty. Here the evidence is less clear. Holmes, Kennedy, and Murray (1987; Kennedy et al., this issue) claimed that the differences we have analysed as indicating disruption and reanalysis actually indicate differences in complexity. According to their argument, a sentence complement, for example, is more complex than a

NP object, and therefore more difficult to process. However, a good deal of other evidence (Ferreira & Henderson, in press; Mitchell & Holmes, 1985; Rayner & Frazier, 1987) indicates that sentences with unambiguous sentence complements are easier to process than those with temporarily ambiguous sentence complements. Further, Rayner and Frazier (1987) found no evidence that sentences with unambiguous sentence complements were more difficult to process than sentences with direct object NPs. This finding of equality should be given rather little weight because it requires comparing reading times on different words; it should not be taken as definitive evidence against the claim that structural complexity *per se* contributes to processing difficulty. However, it certainly provides no support for the claim (Holmes et al., 1987; Kennedy et al., this issue) that such structural complexity is responsible for the processing difficulty of sentence complement sentences.[4]

The question of whether syntactic complexity, as opposed to garden-pathing disruptions, affects the eye movement record is still an open one (cf. Carroll & Slowiaczek, 1987; Frazier, 1985; 1988; Frazier & Rayner, 1988). Deciding this question is important. It may be the case that eye movements are primarily controlled by perceptual and lexical factors, and secondarily by disruptions of comprehension as well as general interpretive processes (see the next section). The eye movement record, in this event, would not directly reflect the normal operation of the presumably modular and automatised process of parsing. It could be used, as described above, to determine when these processes lead a reader down a garden path, and thus to infer some of their characteristics, such as the degree to which they are informationally encapsulated (Ferreira & Clifton, 1986; Fodor, 1983; Forster, 1979; Rayner et al., 1983a). However, if eye movements directly reflect the complexity of the structures being built during parsing, then eye movement techniques can be used to measure the moment-to-moment demands of routine syntactic parsing processes and to analyse in fine detail the inner workings of these processes.

HIGHER-ORDER PROCESSES

We turn now to a discussion of the extent to which eye movement data can reflect higher-order comprehension processes in reading. The basic question here is: Can effects associated with these processes be localised in

[4]We are at a loss to account for the Holmes et al. (1987) and the Kennedy et al. (this issue) reports of no differences between the complements with and without complementisers. Most of their data come from self-paced reading tasks, which we have argued (see also Clifton & Ferreira, this issue) can distort the reading process. However, some of their data came from eye movement monitoring. Thus, methodological factors apparently do not account for the differences between their studies and ours; nor does the line break manipulation that Kennedy et al. use to explain the differences.

specific eye fixations? That is, can we pinpoint specific locations in text where higher-order processes begin to have an effect? Here, we will briefly discuss experiments undertaken in our laboratory dealing with three different issues: (1) sentence and clause wrap-up, (2) antecedent search, and (3) elaborative inferences. In each case, fixation times on a target word have been examined where some higher-order manipulation has occurred earlier in a passage of text. If fixation times on a target word vary, it is most likely because readers will have integrated information they obtained earlier in the text, which allows them to process the target word more efficiently (or with more difficulty if they have not integrated the prior material).

Sentence and Clause Wrap-up

Just and Carpenter (1980) reported that fixation times on words occurring at the end of a sentence were unusually long. However, in their study, fixation times on words that ended a sentence were compared with fixation times on different words that did not end a sentence. In a recent study in our laboratory, the same target word occurred either at the end of a sentence or at the end of a clause. Table 2 shows such an example. Note that the target word *Boston* occurs at the end of a sentence in the first example in the table, but in the second example it does not. Sixteen subjects read 12 passages like those in Table 2. On half of the trials, the target word was the last word in a sentence and the other half of the time it was not. Appropriate counterbalancing measures were taken to ensure that each target word occurred equally often in each condition. Our primary finding was that gaze durations on target words ending a sentence (315 msec) were longer than those on the target word when it did not end the sentence (267 msec)—$F1(1,15) = 24.49$, $P < 0.001$; $F2(1,11) = 11.38$, $P < 0.01$. This result replicates the effect reported by Just and Carpenter, although the magnitude of the effect was not nearly as large as they found.

TABLE 2
Examples of Paragraphs for the Sentence Wrap-up Study

Sentence end condition
The chairman told Hoffman to take his time in deciding. Hoffman made his decision about the new offer later, after he had returned to Boston. He explained the possibilities to his wife. She agreed that it was probably for the best.

Sentence not-end condition
The chairman told Hoffman to take his time in deciding. Hoffman made his decision about the new offer later. After he had returned to Boston, he explained the possibilities to his wife. She agreed that it was probably for the best.

In a second experiment, subjects read sentences where a target word either ended a clause or did not. For example, in sentence (10), the target word *planet* occurs at the end of a clause, whereas in sentence (11) it does not:

10. Before the large and impressive dinosaurs which we see preserved in museums ruled the planet, tiny primitive mammals called therapsids had already been present for a long time.
11. Before the large and impressive dinosaurs which we see preserved in museums ruled the planet billions of years ago, tiny primitive mammals called therapsids had already been present for a long time.

Fourteen subjects participated in the experiment. We found that subjects fixated longer on the target word (277 msec) when it ended a clause than when it did not (251 msec)—$F1(1,13) = 8.41$, $P < 0.02$; $F2(1,11) = 7.15$, $P < 0.05$. In both experiments, the target word was fixated 97% of the time and the probability of fixating the target word did not differ across conditions.

These experiments provide clear evidence that additional processing occurs at the end of a clause or sentence as the reader apparently integrates information from within that clause or sentence. However, in order to comprehend written discourse successfully, readers must also integrate current information with information that occurred earlier in the passage. We will now discuss several studies that have been undertaken to investigate when and where such connections are made.

Antecedent Search

Antecedent search is the process of establishing a connection between two concepts that are explicitly stated in the text. Two situations in which such a connection is required in order for the reader to understand the text are pronominal reference and noun-to-noun reference. In the case of pronominal reference, when a pronoun like *she* is encountered in the course of reading a passage, the reader must identify its antecedent. Sometimes this process is trivially easy, resulting in no disruption in the eye movement record (Blanchard, 1987). Clifton and Ferreira (1987) presented data suggesting that the process becomes substantially more difficult when the antecedent is not the sentence topic or, perhaps more accurately, not an argument of the main clause of the previous sentence (cf. Graesser, 1981; Sanford & Garrod, 1981).

Eye movement data can be used to determine how this extra difficulty appears in reading. Ehrlich and Rayner (1983) varied the distance between the mention of the antecedent and the occurrence of the pronoun. They found evidence to suggest that when the distance was large (resulting, in their materials, in a change of topic between antecedent and pronoun), the reader must initiate a search of the earlier text for the mention of the antecedent that is appropriate in gender, number, and plausibility for the pronoun. Such an antecedent search process is initiated immediately upon encountering the pronoun; the fixation on which the pronoun was encoded was significantly longer (about 20 msec) than the previous fixation. However, they also found evidence indicating that such processing was not always completed while the reader fixated the pronoun; that is, there was clear evidence of spillover effects. Thus, they concluded that antecedent search is initiated while the reader is fixating the pronoun, but may not be completed until one or two fixations following the pronoun.

Just as a pronoun requires an antecedent, a definite noun phrase (which does not directly refer to something outside the text) requires a coreferring antecedent in the text. For example, if a reader encounters *the bird*, and the current topic sentence is not about a bird, a search for the previous mention of an appropriate bird may be initiated. A recent study by Duffy and Rayner (1989) used anaphoric noun phrases to investigate antecedent search. Pronouns are special lexical items which carry very little semantic information beyond gender and number, and therefore they may elicit an extensive antecedent search, which under some conditions extends over several fixations. In contrast, nouns typically have more semantic content, presumably making the immediate search for an antecedent much easier. Indeed, Duffy and Rayner found evidence that with anaphoric noun phrases the antecedent search time was for the most part localised on the target noun (i.e. there were no major spillover effects).

Elaborative Inferences

So far we have discussed the simplest kind of connection in which a word refers back to a single word (with both words explicitly stated in the text). However, readers may also infer information that has not been explicitly stated in the text up to that point. Many current models of discourse comprehension assume that readers activate relevant world knowledge in order to comprehend text, and that this results in a text representation that incorporates what the reader infers or "fills in", as well as information that is explicitly stated in the text. The critical difference between the elaborative inference process and antecedent search processes is that an elaborative inference involves generating information on-line that has not been explicitly stated in the text up to that point. Evidence for on-line elaborative inferences is relatively weak, because the data used to demonstrate such activities are open to the alternative explanation that the inference is made only when it is probed for. Because so many investigators assume

TABLE 3
Examples of Passages from O'Brien et al.'s (1988) study

High context explicit condition
All the mugger wanted was to steal the woman's money. But when she screamed, he stabbed her with his knife in an attempt to quiet her. He looked to see if anyone had seen him. Then he threw his knife into the bushes and ran away.

High context implicit condition
All the mugger wanted was to steal the woman's money. But when she screamed, he stabbed her with his weapon in an attempt to quiet her. He looked to see if anyone had seen him. Then he threw his knife into the bushes and ran away.

Low context explicit condition
All the mugger wanted was to steal the woman's money. But when she screamed, he assaulted her with his knife in an attempt to quiet her. He looked to see if anyone had seen him. Then he threw his knife into the bushes and ran away.

Low context implicit condition
All the mugger wanted was to steal the woman's money. But when she screamed, he assaulted her with his weapon in an attempt to quiet her. He looked to see if anyone had seen him. Then he threw his knife into the bushes and ran away.

that on-line inferences are important in reading comprehension, it is important to demonstrate their existence empirically.

Eye movements have been used to demonstrate that elaborative inferences do occur on-line and to differentiate between conditions in which an inference is made and conditions in which the reader waits for more explicit information and then constructs a connection between the two concepts. O'Brien, Shank, Myers, and Rayner (1988) used passages such as those in Table 3 to determine whether readers were in fact making elaborative inferences before they reached the target word *knife* in the final sentence. They found no difference in gaze durations on *knife* when the second sentence explicitly mentioned *knife* and when it did not mention it but strongly suggested the concept knife (i.e. when the verb *stabbed* was used along with *weapon*). It thus appears that the concept knife was inferred from the phrase "stabbed her with his weapon". In contrast, when the second sentence did not strongly suggest the concept knife (i.e. "he assaulted her with his weapon"), gaze duration on *knife* in the final sentence was longer than when *knife* was explicitly mentioned earlier in the passage. This finding indicates that the longer gaze duration on *knife* resulted because subjects were searching memory for an antecedent for *knife*. The finding also demonstrates that the process of searching for the antecedent begins immediately.

Although the study of O'Brien et al. (1988) provides evidence for on-line elaborative inferences, other studies reported by O'Brien et al. clearly demonstrated that such inferences occur only under rather restricted circumstances. They found evidence for elaborative inferences only when the context was sufficiently constraining or when there was a "demand sentence" (which invited the reader to make the inference) just prior to the sentence containing the target word. A subsequent study by Garrod, O'Brien, Morris, and Rayner (in press) further constrained the conditions under which evidence for elaborative inferences will be obtained. Garrod et al. found evidence for elaborative inferences only when there was an anaphoric relationship between two nouns, such as *weapon* and *knife* in our example. They found that gaze durations on the target word (*knife*) were equivalent in explicit and implicit conditions (in terms of prior mention of the target word) when there was an anaphoric relationship, but longer in the implicit condition than explicit condition when there was not.

The research we have described dealing with clause and sentence wrap-up, antecedent search, and elaborative inferences, shows quite clearly that fixation times on a target word can be influenced by higher-order processes. In all three cases, fixation times on target words could only be influenced (given various control conditions in the experiments) if readers were using information obtained earlier in the text to process the target word.

SUMMARY

The studies that we have reviewed here lead us to believe that eye movement data are a good way to study word processing, syntactic parsing, and higher-order processes in reading. The primary characteristic of most of the work reviewed is that we have been able to identify in advance specific locations in the text where processing should be more difficult (or easier), depending upon the underlying relationships existing in the text. In effect, this research has indicated that the cognitive processing load is reflected in the pattern of eye movements, particularly the fixation times. The advantage of the method is that the data can be collected on-line as subjects read text; it is not necessary to draw inferences about comprehension processes using data from end-of-sentence tasks or using global measures such as total reading time where one is not sure which part of the sentence actually led to changes in reading time. Subjects can read at their own pace, secondary tasks need not be employed, and the situation is relatively normal.

This is not to say that eye movements are a perfect reflection of cognitive processes in reading. There are many serious problems that need to be addressed and we have touched on some of them here (see also Rayner &

Pollatsek, 1987). In addition, there are some inconsistent results in the literature. Some of this inconsistency is undoubtedly due to characteristics of the particular studies and methods of data scoring and analysis. Further, some processes at the syntactic, semantic, or discourse level may not be confined to single fixations in the eye movement record, but rather may extend across a number of fixations. We have had the experience of producing what seemed like perfectly good passages to examine a certain type of comprehension process, only to find no obvious or immediate effect in the eye fixation times. In such cases, the overall reading times generally reveal the processing complexity.

We suggest that one goal of research using eye movements to study comprehension processes ought to be the delineation of conditions under which individual fixation times do and do not reflect such processes. In cases in which processing difficulty is not expressed in individual fixations, we need theories that make strong predictions about when and where the processing difficulty is likely to occur allowing us to interpret the data at a level of detail that goes beyond global reading time measures. Nevertheless, recent research using eye movement data to investigate comprehension processes has been very informative, and we suspect that answers to many questions about on-line language processing will be unveiled by examining in greater detail the spatial and temporal record left by the eyes during reading.

REFERENCES

Altmann, G. (1988). Ambiguity, parsing strategies, and computational models. *Language and Cognitive Processes*, *3*, 73–97.

Altmann, G. & Steedman, M. (1988). Interaction with context during human sentence processing. *Cognition*, *30*, 191–238.

Balota, D. A., Pollatsek, A., & Rayner, K. (1985). The interaction of contextual constraints and parafoveal visual information. *Cognitive Psychology*, *17*, 364–390.

Blanchard, H. E. (1985). A comparison of some processing time measures based on eye movements. *Acta Psychologia*, *58*, 1–15.

Blanchard, H. E. (1987). Pronoun processing during fixations: Effects of the time course information utilization. *Bulletin of the Psychonomic Society*, *25*, 171–174.

Carpenter, P. A. & Just, M. A. (1983). What your eyes do while your mind is reading. In K. Rayner (Ed.), *Eye movements in reading: Perceptual and language processes*. New York: Academic Press.

Carroll, P. & Slowiaczek, M. L. (1986). Constraints on semantic priming in reading: A fixation time analysis. *Memory & Cognition*, *14*, 509–522.

Carroll, P. & Slowiaczek, M. L. (1987). Modes and modules: Multiple paths to the language processor. In J. L. Garfield (Ed.), *Modularity in knowledge representation and natural-language understanding*. Cambridge, Mass.: MIT Press.

Clifton, C. & Ferreira, F. (1987). Discourse structure and anaphora: Some experimental results. In M. Coltheart (Ed.), *Attention and performance XII*. London: Lawrence Erlbaum Associates Ltd.

Clifton, C. & Ferreira, F. (1990). Ambiguity in context. *Language and Cognitive Processes*, *4*, 77–103.

Duffy, S. A. & Rayner, K. (submitted). Eye movements, lexical access, and antecedent search: The effect of antecedent typicality and distance.

Duffy, S. A., Morris, R. K., & Rayner, K. (1988). Lexical ambiguity and fixation times in reading. *Journal of Memory and Language*, *27*, 429–446.

Ehrlich, K. & Rayner, K. (1983). Pronoun assignment and semantic integration during reading: Eye movements and immediacy of processing. *Journal of Verbal Learning and Verbal Behavior*, *22*, 75–87.

Ehrlich, S. F. & Rayner, K. (1981). Contextual effects on word perception and eye movements during reading. *Journal of Verbal Learning and Verbal Behavior*, *20*, 641–655.

Ferreira, F. & Clifton, C. (1986). The independence of syntactic processing. *Journal of Memory and Language*, *25*, 348–368.

Ferreira, F. & Henderson, J. M. (in press). The use of verb information in syntactic parsing: Evidence from eye movements and word-by-word self-paced reading. *Journal of Experimental Psychology: Learning, Memory, and Cognition*.

Fodor, J. A. (1983). *Modularity of mind*. Cambridge, Mass.: MIT Press.

Forster, K. I. (1979). Levels of processing and the structure of the language processor. In W. E. Cooper & E. Walker (Eds), *Sentence processing: Psycholinguistic studies presented to Merrill Garrett*. Hillsdale, N.J.: Lawrence Erlbaum Associates Inc.

Francis, W. N. & Kučera, H. (1982). *Frequency analysis of English usage: Lexicon and grammar*. Boston: Houghton Mifflin.

Frazier, L. (1979). *On comprehending sentences: Syntactic parsing strategies*. Bloomington, Ind.: Indiana University Linguistics Club.

Frazier, L. (1985). Syntactic complexity. In D. Dowty, L. Karttunen, & H. Zwicky (Eds), *Natural language parsing*. Cambridge: Cambridge University Press.

Frazier, L. (1987). Sentence processing: A tutorial review. In M. Coltheart (Ed.), *Attention and performance XII*. London: Lawrence Erlbaum Associates Ltd.

Frazier, L. (1988).. Grammar and language processing. In A. Davison & G. M. Green (Eds), *Linguistics: The Cambridge Survey. II. Linguistic theory: Extensions and implications*. Cambridge: Cambridge University Press.

Frazier, L. & Rayner, K. (1982). Making and correcting errors during sentence comprehension: Eye movements in the analysis of structurally ambiguous sentences. *Cognitive Psychology*, *14*, 178–210.

Frazier, L. & Rayner, K. (1987). Resolution of syntactic category ambiguities: Eye movements in parsing lexically ambiguous sentences. *Journal of Memory and Language*, *26*, 505–526.

Frazier, L. & Rayner, K. (1988). Parameterizing the language processing system: Left- vs. right-branching within and across languages. In J. A. Hawkins (Ed.), *Explaining language universals*. Oxford: Basil Blackwell.

Garrod, S., O'Brien, E. J., Morris, R. K., & Rayner, K. (in press). Elaborative inferencing as an active or passive process. *Journal of Experimental Psychology: Learning, Memory and Cognition*.

Graesser, A. C. (1981). *Prose comprehension beyond the word*. New York: Springer-Verlag.

Henderson, J. M. & Ferreira, F. (in press). The effects of foveal processing difficulty on the perceptual span in reading: Implications for attention and eye movement control. *Journal of Experimental Psychology: Learning, Memory and Cognition*.

Hogaboam, T. W. (1983). Reading patterns in eye-movement data. In K. Rayner (Ed.), *Eye movements in reading: Perceptual and language processes*. London: Academic Press.

Hogaboam, T. W. & McConkie, G. W. (1981). The rocky road from eye fixations to comprehension. Technical Report 207, Center for the Study of Reading, University of Illinois.

Holmes, V. M. & O'Regan, J. K. (1981). Eye fixation patterns during the reading of relative clause sentences. *Journal of Verbal Learning and Verbal Behavior, 20*, 417–430.
Holmes, V. M., Kennedy, A., & Murray, W. S. (1987). Syntactic structure and the garden path. *Quarterly Journal of Experimental Psychology, 39A*, 277–294.
Inhoff, A. W. (1984). Two stages of word processing during eye fixations in the reading of prose. *Journal of Verbal Learning and Verbal Behavior, 23*, 612–624.
Inhoff, A. W. (1985). The effect of factivity on lexical retrieval and postlexical processing during eye fixations in reading. *Journal of Psycholinguistic Research, 14*, 45–56.
Inhoff, A. W. & Rayner, K. (1986). Parafoveal word processing during eye fixations in reading: Effects of word frequency. *Perception & Psychophysics, 40*, 431–439.
Inhoff, A. W., Pollatsek, A., Posner, M. I., & Rayner, K. (1989). Covert attention and eye movements during reading. *Quarterly Journal of Experimental Psychology, 41A*, 63–89.
Just, M. A. & Carpenter, P. C. (1980). A theory of reading: From eye fixations to comprehension. *Psychological Review, 87*, 329–354.
Kennedy, A. & Murray, W. S. (1984). Inspection times for words in syntactically ambiguous sentences under three presentation conditions. *Journal of Experimental Psychology: Human Perception and Performance, 10*, 833–849.
Kennedy, A., Murray, W. S., Jennings, F., & Reid, C. (1990). Parsing complements: Comments on the generality of the principle of minimal attachment. *Language and Cognitive Processes, 4*, 51–74.
Kliegl, R., Olson, R. K., & Davidson, B. J. (1982). Regression analysis as a tool for studying reading processes: Comment on Just and Carpenter's eye fixation theory. *Memory & Cognition, 13*, 107–111.
Kowler, E. & Anton, S. (1987). Reading twisted text: Implications for the role of saccades. *Vision Research, 27*, 45–60.
Lima, S. D. (1987). Morphological analysis in reading. *Journal of Memory and Language, 26*, 84–99.
Lima, S. D. & Inhoff, A. W. (1985). Lexical access during eye fixations in reading: Effects of word-initial letter sequence. *Journal of Experimental Psychology: Human Perception and Performance, 11*, 272–285.
McConkie, G. W. & Rayner, K. (1975). The span of the effective stimulus during an eye fixation in reading. *Perception & Psychophysics, 17*, 578–586.
McConkie, G. W., Hogaboam, T. W., Wolverton, G. S., Zola, D., & Lucas, P. A. (1979). Toward the use of eye movements in the study of language processing. *Discourse Processes, 2*, 157–177.
Mehler, J., Bever, T. G., & Carey, P. (1967). What we look at when we read. *Perception & Psychophysics, 2*, 213–218.
Mitchell, D. C. & Holmes, V. M. (1985). The role of specific information about the verb in parsing sentences with local structural ambiguity. *Journal of Memory and Language, 24*, 542–559.
Morris, R. K., Rayner, K., & Pollatsek, A. (in press). Eye guidance in reading: The role of parafoveal letter and space information. *Journal of Experimental Psychology: Human Perception and Performance.*
Morrison, R. E. (1984). Manipulation of stimulus onset delay in reading: Evidence for parallel programming of saccades. *Journal of Experimental Psychology: Human Perception and Performance, 10*, 667–682.
O'Brien, E. J., Shank, D. M., Myers, J. L., & Rayner, K. (1988). Elaborative inferences during reading: Do they occur on-line? *Journal of Experimental Psychology: Learning, Memory, and Cognition, 14*, 410–420.
O'Regan, J. K. (1979). Eye guidance in reading: Evidence for the linguistic control hypothesis. *Perception & Psychophysics, 25*, 501–509.

O'Regan, J. K. (1980). The control of saccade size and fixation duration in reading: The limits of linguistic control. *Perception & Psychophysics*, *28*, 112–117.

O'Regan, J. K. & Levy-Schoen, A. (1987). Eye-movement strategy and tactics in word recognition and reading. In M. Coltheart (Ed.), *Attention and performance XII*. London: Lawrence Erlbaum Associates Ltd.

Pollatsek, A. & Rayner, K. (in press). Eye movements and lexical access in reading. In D. A. Balota, G. B. Flores d'Arcais, & K. Rayner (Eds), *Comprehension processes in reading*. Hillsdale, N.J.: Lawrence Erlbaum Associates Inc.

Pollatsek, A., Rayner, K., & Balota, D. A. (1986). Inferences about eye movement control from the perceptual span in reading. *Perception & Psychophysics*, *40*, 123–130.

Rayner, K. (1975). The perceptual span and peripheral cues in reading. *Cognitive Psychology*, *7*, 65–81.

Rayner, K. (1977). Visual attention in reading: Eye movements reflect cognitive processes. *Memory & Cognition*, *4*, 443–448.

Rayner, K. (1978). Eye movements in reading and information processing. *Psychological Bulletin*, *85*, 618–660.

Rayner, K. (1979). Eye guidance in reading: Fixation locations within words. *Perception*, *8*, 21–30.

Rayner, K. (1986). Eye movement and the perceptual span in beginning and skilled readers. *Journal of Experimental Child Psychology*, *41*, 211–236.

Rayner, K. & Balota, D. B. (1989). Parafoveal preview and lexical access during eye fixations in reading. In W. Marslen-Wilson (Ed.), *The lexicon and language processing*. Cambridge, Mass.: MIT Press.

Rayner, K. & Duffy, S. A. (1986). Lexical complexity and fixation times in reading: Effects of word frequency, verb complexity, and lexical ambiguity. *Memory & Cognition*, *14*, 191–201.

Rayner, K. & Duffy, S. A. (1988). On-line comprehension processes and eye movements during reading. In M. Daneman, G. E. MacKinnon, & T. G. Waller (Eds), *Reading research: Advances in theory and practice*, Vol. 6. London: Academic Press.

Rayner, K. & Frazier, L. (1987). Parsing temporarily ambiguous complements. *Quarterly Journal of Experimental Psychology*, *39A*, 657–673.

Rayner, K. & Frazier, L. (1989). Selection mechanisms in reading lexically ambiguous words. *Journal of Experimental Psychology: Learning, Memory and Cognition*, *15*, 779–790.

Rayner, K. & McConkie, G. W. (1976). What guides a reader's eye movements? *Vision Research*, *16*, 829–837.

Rayner, K. & Pollatsek, A. (1981). Eye movement control in reading: Evidence for direct control. *Quarterly Journal of Experimental Psychology*, *33A*, 351–373.

Rayner, K. & Pollatsek, A. (1987). Eye movements in reading: A tutorial review. In M. Coltheart (Ed.), *Attention and performance XII*. London: Lawrence Erlbaum Associates Ltd.

Rayner, K. & Pollatsek, A. (1989). *The psychology of reading*. Englewood Cliffs, N.J.: Prentice-Hall.

Rayner, K., Carlson, M., & Frazier, L. (1983a). The interaction of syntax and semantics during sentence processing: Eye movements in the analysis of semantically biased sentences. *Journal of Verbal Learning and Verbal Behavior*, *22*, 358–374.

Rayner, K., Slowiaczek, M. L., Clifton, C., & Bertera, J. H. (1983b). Latency of sequential eye movements: Implications for reading. *Journal of Experimental Psychology: Human Perception and Performance*, *9*, 912–922.

Rayner, K., Balota, D. A., & Pollatsek, A. (1986). Against parafoveal semantic preprocessing during eye fixations in reading. *Canadian Journal of Psychology*, *40*, 473–483.

Sanford, A. J. & Garrod, S. C. (1981). *Understanding written language: Explorations in comprehension beyond the sentence*. New York: John Wiley.

Schmauder, A. R. (1989). Argument structure frames: A lexical complexity metric? Unpublished Master's thesis, University of Massachusetts.

Schustack, M., Ehrlich, S. F., & Rayner, K. (1987). The complexity of contextual facilitation in reading: Local and global influences. *Journal of Memory and Language*, *26*, 322–340.

Sereno, S. C. & Rayner, K. (1989). First fixations in refixated words: Why are they shorter? Presented at the Midwestern Psychological Association meetings, Chicago.

Tinker, M. A. (1939). Reliability and validity of eye-movement measures of reading. *Journal of Experimental Psychology*, *19*, 732–746.

Zola, D. (1984). Redundancy and word perception during reading. *Perception & Psychophysics*, *36*, 277–284.

LANGUAGE AND COGNITIVE PROCESSES, 1989, *4*, (3/4) SI 51–76

Parsing Complements: Comments on the Generality of the Principle of Minimal Attachment

Alan Kennedy, Wayne S. Murray, Francis Jennings, and Claire Reid
Department of Psychology, University of Dundee, Dundee, U.K.

Two experiments are described in this paper, which examine the processing of English sentences containing "complement" verbs, and which may be followed either by a nounphrase, as a direct object, or by a complement clause. It has been claimed by Frazier and Rayner (1982) that subjects are "garden-pathed" when reading reduced complements (lacking the overt complemetiser), and that this fact is strong evidence in support of the application of the principle of "Minimal Attachment" as a universal property of the human parser. Holmes, Kennedy, and Murray (1987) questioned this conclusion by providing evidence that full and reduced complements present equivalent problems, probably because of their greater structural complexity. Rayner and Frazier (1987) disputed this conclusion, ascribing it to an artefact resulting from the use of a self-paced reading task. The first experiment examines this controversy with a replication of the study by Holmes et al., measuring eye movements as the sentences are processed. The results replicate those of the original study and further show that the effects cannot be attributed to lexical preferences associated with the verb. The second experiment examines the format of the displayed text as one possible reason for the discrepancy between the two sets of results. When sentences are displayed across several lines, the line breaks are interpreted by subjects as signals for potential clause endings, "garden-pathing" the reader. However, misparsings induced in this way cannot be used to support the claim that readers are generally garden-pathed by the temporary ambiguity of reduced complement sentences.

INTRODUCTION

In a recent paper, Frazier (1987) contrasts two separate approaches to the derivation of a performance model of the human parser. The first, which she characterises as most popular among experimental psychologists,

Requests for reprints should be addressed to Alan Kennedy, Department of Psychology, University of Dundee, Dundee, U.K.

emphasises the diversity of processing mechanisms. From this point of view, sentences are parsed (if at all) by the relatively unconstrained use of a variety of heuristics and *ad hoc* strategies. The second approach can be traced to recent developments in linguistic theory. From this perspective, subjects are seen as deploying, in a systematic fashion, certain invariable principles of syntactic analysis. The "Garden Path Model" (e.g. Frazier & Fodor, 1978; Frazier & Rayner, 1982) belongs to this second class. It encompasses three essential features: (1) words in a sentence are incorporated into complete syntactic structures at the earliest possible opportunity (i.e. the structural description is developed "on-line", word-by-word); (2) attachment of words within a structure is invariably achieved in a way which minimises the number of nodes demanded (the principle of *Minimal Attachment*); (3) new words are incorporated, wherever this is possible grammatically, into the current clause or phrase being processed (the principle of *Late Closure*). This paper focuses on the degree to which the principle of Minimal Attachment can be seen, as Frazier suggests, as a general rule of cognition, invariably applied in appropriate linguistic environments.

The most clear-cut evidence on this question is found in a study by Frazier and Rayner (1982), which examined readers' eye movements as sentences like (1) and (2) were read:

1. The city council argued the mayor's position *forcefully*.
2. The city council argued the mayor's position *was wrong*.

Average reading time per character was longer in (2) than in (1), the focus of disruption being the (italicised) disambiguating phrase. This result is consistent with the application of the Minimal Attachment rule, which in (2) would assign the second nounphrase as a direct object rather than the subject of a sentential complement. The lack of the overt complementiser ("that") leads to a temporary structural ambiguity which is only resolved when the verbal auxilary is encountered. Frazier and Rayner attribute the additional processing time to the fact that the initial structural decision (determined by application of the principle of Minimal Attachment) must be revised. The pattern of readers' eye movements is consistent with this view, with subjects more likely to make reinspections in (2) than in (1).

There are, however, good reasons to question the validity of the conclusion that these data provide *conclusive* support for the principle of Minimal Attachment. First, while application of the strategy to reduced complements should certainly lead to a misparsing and consequent processing difficulty, it is less clear how this could be remedied. Intuitively, it may seem obvious that the reader should reassign the words to a new structure. This is precisely what Frazier (1987) claims, contrasting, for example, the relative ease with which a new S node may be introduced into the structure in a reduced complement with the greater difficulty posed by structural revision in reduced relative constructions, such as (3):

3. The boat sailed on the pond sank.

The principle of Minimal Attachment does not *itself*, however, lead to any such conclusion. On the contrary, it suggests that the reader would become trapped in a cycle of misperception in which each re-reading arrives at the same faulty construction. Formally, therefore, the principle requires rather careful modification to avoid this problem. There are a number of routes such modifications might follow (see Altmann, 1988, for a brief review), but all have the effect of diminishing somewhat the force of the claim that readers make a *single* initial structural assignment. For example, Wanner (1980) showed that minimal attachment arises as a consequence of adopting a simple set of priority rules governing the ordering of arc choices within an ATN. A parser of this form would not need to maintain a record of the outcomes of previous (unsuccessful) parses, but it *would* need to know which parse it is currently on if it is to avoid a cycle of misperception.[1] Alternatively, minimal attachment can be demonstrated as a consequence of parallel exploration of arcs (Wanner, 1987), although in this context the notion of a single initial structural assignment loses much of its meaning. For this reason we assume that, in postulating Minimal Attachment as a universal principle, Frazier has in mind a performance model within which psychological constraints on processing must be taken into account. Were this not the case, the analogy proposed between strategies of reanalysis and patterns of reinspection (indexed by eye movements) when reading sentences (Frazier & Rayner, 1982) would be difficult to understand. However, if processes underlying reinspection (i.e. defined by the eye movement control system and governing the allocation of attention to different parts of a displayed sentence) are to be seen as mirroring the processes of reanalysis (i.e. operations defined within the parser), it is worth making explicit the paradoxical conclusion which follows. Selective reinspection of regions of a sentence previously read is only possible if the reader knows *where* potential targets lie. This involves a memory representation: It cannot be achieved by the physical identification of words which may lie well into peripheral vision (Kennedy & Murray, 1987a). The paradox is, of course, that such a memory record suggests a reading strategy sensitive *on the first pass* to possible alternative structural analyses.

Another difficulty arising from the argument that Minimal Attachment and Late Closure are general principles with universal applicability, is that

[1]A referee has pointed out that this is, in any case, a requirement if the parser is to decide on a single pass *which* attachment is, in fact, minimal.

they sometimes lead to conflicting parsing decisions (Wilks, Huang, & Fass, 1985). The argument that Minimal Attachment takes precedence does not solve the problem, however. Consider, for example, (4) and (5):

4. She positioned the dress on the rack.
5. She wanted the dress on the rack.

The preferred assignment appears to differ for these two examples. However, because Minimal Attachment and Late Closure lead to conflicting assignments of the prepositional phrase in *both* cases, a simple precedence mechanism cannot solve the problem. Mitchell (this issue) considers means whereby this problem can be resolved.

The most direct empirical challenge, however, is provided by the results of Holmes, Kennedy, and Murray (1987). They pointed out that the processing difficulty of sentences like (2) relative to (1) may relate to the fact that complement structures are, in any case, structurally more complex, containing two clauses. The appropriate contrast to secure the claims of Frazier and Rayner is between structures like (1) and (2) and those like (6), where the presence of the complementiser will have the effect of cancelling the application of the principle of Minimal Attachment (at least on encountering the following definite article):

6. The city council argued that the mayor's position *was wrong*.

Holmes et al. (1987) showed that, in fact, (2) and (6) posed virtually identical difficulties, *both* leading to slower processing than (1), and concluded that the difficulty in processing reduced complements was due to their greater structural complexity, rather than to "garden-pathing". Obviously, such a finding seriously weakens the idea of Minimal Attachment as a generally applicable strategy. The result shows readers are more cautious than the theory suggests or that they handle any reanalysis at no measurable cost.

In a later paper, Rayner and Frazier (1987) take issue with this conclusion on both theoretical and empirical grounds. First, they argue that the self-paced reading task used by Holmes et al. (1987), while sometimes sensitive to processing load (e.g. Ferreira & Clifton, 1986; Kennedy & Murray, 1984; Mitchell & Holmes, 1985), is not invariably so. Inter-response times, in contrast to fixation durations, are relatively long, and for this reason the task may be insensitive to the processes of initial structural assignment. This is an ingenious objection, as it leaves open the possibility that "later" processes (e.g. semantic effects) may be reflected in measured inter-response time and that it is these which Holmes et al. may be reporting. Secondly, they note that the word-by-word cumulative display mode employed (in which successively displayed words remain on view), is peculiarly susceptible to a strategy whereby the reader's button presses become "de-coupled" from the display itself. For example, Just, Carpenter, and Woolley (1982) found that subjects in this presentation mode would run off a rapid series of responses to display a large segment of text and only then pause to read it. Clearly, this objection is weakened by the observation of systematic differences in inter-response time in the data, but it stands as a possible reason why the task may not adequately reflect early processes "on-line". The empirical evidence produced by Rayner and Frazier (1987) is more persuasive. An eye movement study was carried out using materials based on those of Holmes et al. (1987), comparing performance on the three structures (1), (2), and (6), with the addition of a fourth condition employing an infinitival clause like (7):

7. The city council argued the mayor's position to be wrong.

The crucial results[2] are shown in Fig. 1(a) as reading times per character in the three "zones" they defined. Figure 1(b) shows for comparison the equivalent data from Holmes et al. (1987). It is obvious that a major discrepancy exists: The results in Fig. 1(a) are consistent with the application of Minimal Attachment, and Rayner and Frazier (1987) feel justified both in reasserting the generality of this parsing principle and in dismissing the data of Holmes et al. as arising artefactually from the use of an inappropriate task. However, this conclusion, while plausible, is not entirely immune from criticism. First, there is ample evidence of the sensitivity of self-paced reading tasks to a variety of processing strategies. In fact, the results reported by Kennedy and Murray (1984) showed that, with sentences containing "garden paths" of the type predicted by Late Closure, the results from inter-response time mirrored the results from eye movement analyses. Relatively long times *per se* do not preclude the use of inter-response times as an index of "early" effects—although it is conceivable that they may be somewhat diluted. Secondly, the objections posed by Just et al. (1982) to the cumulative display appear to arise only when display changes are not tightly coupled to the button press. We find that when they are tightly coupled there is no tendency for subjects to "press ahead". Thirdly, in the replication of Holmes et al.'s study, the inclusion of the infinitival complement condition represented a complication whose effects on the material set as a whole are difficult to assess. Their subjects clearly found this condition considerably more difficult than any of the others and there is the possibility, at least, that this may have given rise to some carry-over effects. Further, almost all the sentences as presented by Rayner and Frazier (1987) were altered to some degree, frequently by

[2]That is, the results from the reduced and unreduced complements and the simple transitive construction.

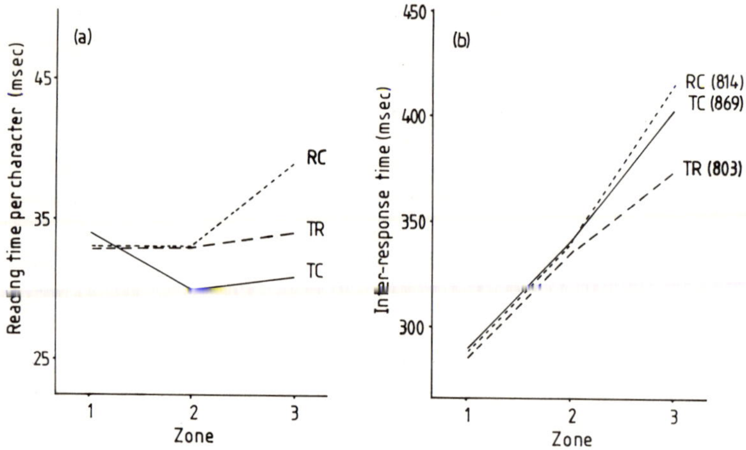

FIG. 1 (a) First-pass reading time per character (from Rayner and Frazier, 1987) and (b) inter-response time per word (from Holmes et al., 1987) for the initial region (zone 1), the ambiguous NP (zone 2), and disambiguating region (zone 3) of transitive (TR), that-complement (TC), and reduced-complement (RC) sentences. Final word times (from Holmes et al., 1987) are shown in parentheses.

lengthening the final segment. The reason for these changes related to intuitions that those sentences containing a tensed complement but no overt complementiser appeared somewhat unnatural. Nonetheless, the manipulation of this variable produced no statistically significant effects and the changes served to make comparisons between the two studies problematic, because length is known to influence the application of parsing strategies (Frazier & Rayner, 1982; Kennedy & Murray, 1984). Finally, the materials as presented by Rayner and Frazier were spread over several lines of the display, in contrast to the single-line format used by Holmes et al. Line breaks, like punctuation, may have quite profound effects on the reader's segmentation strategies (Mitchell, 1987). In any case, the use of a measure of average time across "zones" becomes difficult to defend if large right-to-left saccades, relating to line-ends, appear *within* a zone. Clearly, a more convincing rebuttal of Holmes et al. would involve a direct replication of their study, preserving as many features of the materials and mode of presentation as possible, and measuring eye movements directly. The first experiment reported here set out to achieve this end. However, before reporting the outcome, another line of theoretical argument must be considered.

Holmes (1987) attempts to short-circuit the claims and counterclaims outlined above by introducing into the debate the possibility that lexical preference (i.e. verb subcategorisation frames) may determine whether a "direct object" or "complement" strategy is applied in a given sentence. Such a proposal obviously strikes at the root of Minimal Attachment as a *general* parsing principle. To achieve her argument, Holmes (1987) subcategorised the verbs originally employed by Holmes et al. (1987) into those with a structural bias (as assessed by subject ratings) towards taking a clausal complement (e.g. "believe", "claim", "deny", etc.) and those with a NP bias ("accept", "check", "consider", etc.). A *post hoc* item analysis revealed that reading times for sentences with "NP bias" verbs in the reduced complement constructions were *relatively* slower than those with "complement bias" verbs. Unfortunately, the interpretation of this result is greatly complicated by the observation that sentences with "complement bias" verbs were processed *more slowly* when the complement was actually present. It is, in fact, not possible logically to offer a coherent account of the three contrasts in Fig. 1(b) (RC *vs* TR, RC *vs* TC, and TC *vs* TR) in terms of the operation of a single variable. Thus, reference to lexical preference obscures rather than clarifies the discrepancy between Fig. 1(a) and 1(b). Nonetheless, Holmes raises an important issue if, as seems to be the case, differences in processing strategy may attend different verb forms. At the very least it becomes necessary to control for these subjective preferences systematically. For this reason, Experiment 1 not only comprised a complete replication of Holmes et al.'s (1987) study in terms of materials and display structure (i.e. each sentence presented as a single line of text) using eye movement measures, but also attempted to balance verb types as closely as possible using the rated materials provided by Holmes (1987). This involved minor changes to four of the original sentences.

EXPERIMENT 1

Method

Subjects. A total of 24 unpaid student volunteers from the University of Dundee took part. All had normal, or corrected-to-normal, vision. The subjects had not previously participated in eye movement studies.

Materials and Design. The experimental sentences were, with four exceptions, those used by Holmes et al. (1987). Each was produced in three versions: (1) TR, in which the verb was followed by a direct object; (2) TC, in which the verb was followed by a complement clause introduced by the complementiser "that"; and (3) RC, a "reduced" complement construction, lacking the complementiser. For the purposes of later analysis, the sentences were considered to contain four "zones": an initial region, up to and including the first verb; the temporarily ambiguous nounphrase (but excluding the "that" in the TC condition); a disambiguating region; and the final word. These zones are marked by slashes in examples (8)–(10):

8. The workers considered / the last offer from the management / of the / factory.
9. The workers considered / (that) the last offer from the management / was an / insult.
10. The workers considered / the last offer from the management / was an / insult.

The endings of the TR and complement sentences were matched for length and frequency. Of the original set of 24 sentences employed by Holmes et al., 20 contained verbs which appeared on the list of complement verbs compiled by Holmes (1987). These provided 10 NP-bias verbs and 10 complement-bias verbs. To complete the full set of 24 base sentences for the present study, those with unlisted verbs were replaced by four new sentences (two NP-bias and two complement-bias verbs), also matched for length and frequency. Within the constraints imposed by the verb change, these sentences were as similar as possible to the ones they replaced. Each of the 24 sentences had an associated question. These were balanced for "yes" and "no" correct responses. Following Holmes et al., the questions were equally divided between those that focused on the early part of the sentence, prior to the disambiguation, and those that focused on the disambiguating region. For this reason, late focus questions relating to TR versions differed from their complement equivalents. The materials are reproduced in the Appendix. Included with the experimental sentences were 60 fillers, each with associated questions, again balanced for "yes" and "no" answers. The fillers comprised a range of simple and embedded-clause constructions comparable in length to the experimental sentences.

Three counterbalanced sets of experimental items were derived from the total set of sentences. Each contained eight TR, eight TC, and eight RC constructions, with four sentences of each type containing an NP bias verb and four a complement bias verb. No more than one version of the same base sentence occurred in any set. Twelve of the fillers were used for initial practice on the task; the remaining 48 fillers and 24 experimental items were presented in a pseudo-random shuffled sequence, which ensured maximal spacing between experimental items. A different sequence was used for each subject. Three groups of eight subjects each received one of the three sets. In both subject (*F*1) and item (*F*2) analyses, sentence type and zone were repeated-measures factors. Verb type was a repeated-measures factor in the subject analysis and a between-groups factor in the item analysis. Item set was treated as a between-groups dummy variable in all analyses.

Apparatus. Eye movements were recorded using a conventional infrared limbus-tracking device mounted on spectacle frames. Subjects viewed the display binocularly, and the horizontal displacement of their right eye was sampled every 10 msec using a 12-bit A-D device interfaced to a Cromemco computer. The apparatus was calibrated using an array of five numbers across the display screen. Analysis of eye movement data was carried out off-line. Overall accuracy of the system was approximately plus or minus one character position.

The stimulus materials were presented under computer control on the "green-screen" monitor of an Apple IIe computer linked via "hand-shaking" software to the Cromemco. The sentences appeared on a single line (max. 80 characters) in normal upper and lower case. Subjects were seated 0.7 m from the screen, at which distance 4.2 character spaces subtended 1° of visual angle.

Procedure. Each subject sat with their head fixed by means of a dental composition bite-bar and with the index finger of each hand over a response button. The sentences were displayed centred on the screen. Preceding each presentation, an arrow appeared for 500 msec at a point two character positions to the left of the position where the first character of the sentence would be displayed. After reading the sentence, the subject's button press terminated its display and the question appeared after a 1-sec delay. Subjects responded "yes" or "no" by pressing buttons using their right or left hands. Feedback about the accuracy of their response was provided. Calibration of the eye movement system took place every three sentences, ensuring that each experimental sentence was associated with a fresh calibration.

Results

Total Pass per Word. Because the experiment was designed to replicate that of Holmes et al. (1987), the first analysis attempted to provide a measure, derived from the obtained eye movement data, which would be equivalent to the obtained inter-response times in the original study. To do this, a measure of *total pass per word* was calculated. Total pass for a given zone was defined as the sum of all initial fixations arising from left-to-right saccades, plus all regressions (i.e. to another point within the same zone or to a prior zone) launched from that zone. Total time was scaled to the number of words in the zone. This measure reproduces inter-response times well for the first three zones as defined by Holmes et al., but presents difficulties for the fourth zone (the final word). In their study, zone 4 was analysed separately and revealed inter-response times which were both more variable and much longer than those in other zones. This was probably the result of re-readings initiated after the final word had been inspected. It is, however, difficult to treat the final word as a separate zone in an eye movement analysis, because in many cases the disambiguating zone itself was only two words long. Treating the final word separately would, in these cases, leave a zone 3 comprising a single short word, which was not invariably fixated. Because the focus of discussion is on the relative duration of times in zones 2 and 3, it was decided to incorporate the final word into zone 3, but to exclude all regressions made after the rightmost fixation. This provides a good approximation to the inter-response times over the first three zones reported by Holmes et al. (1987). The results are shown in Fig. 2.

Comparing Fig. 2 with Fig. 1, it is apparent that the outcome is remarkably close to the original result of Holmes et al. This conclusion is supported statistically. Over zones 1 and 2 there is no indication of any differences in the way the three sentence types are read, with no interaction between sentence type and zone ($F1$ and $F2$ both <1). In zone 3, however, the reading times for the three sentence types diverge from the baseline set in zone 2. The overall interaction between zone and sentence type was significant by subjects [$F1(2,42) = 3.71$, $P < 0.05$], although it failed to achieve significance over items [$F2(2,36) = 1.83$] (it should be noted that the inclusion of bias as a between-items factor reduces the power of the item analysis). However, the theoretically important pairwise comparisons at this point do show clear differences between the conditions. Reading time increased more in going from zone 2 to zone 3 for TC

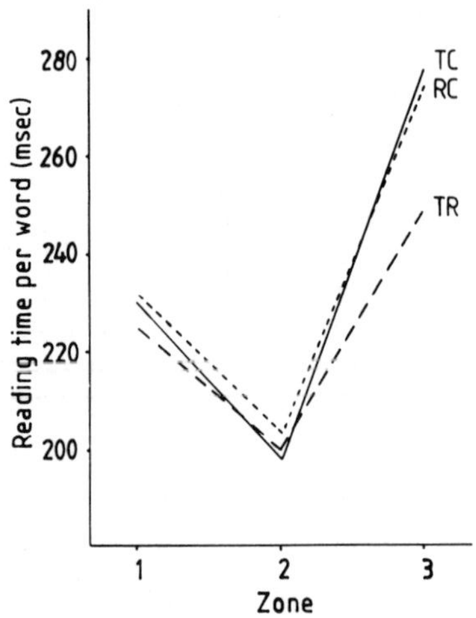

FIG. 2 Total pass reading time per word for TR, TC, and RC sentences over the three zones.

than for TR sentences, with a significant interaction between sentence type and zone [$F1(1,21) = 7.16$, $P < 0.05$; $F2(1,18) = 5.01$, $P < 0.05$]. TR and RC conditions showed a similar pattern of differences, although in this case it did not achieve statistical significance [$F1(1,21) = 3.24$, $P = 0.08$; $F2(1,18) = 1.84$], whereas TC and RC conditions clearly did not differ ($F1$ and $F2$ both <1).

Table 1 shows the effects of bias in the verbs on total pass reading times. It is clear that no support can be recruited for Holmes' (1987) claims. Bias affects all three sentence types in the same way, with NP-bias producing a larger increase in time moving from zones 2 to 3 than complement bias. There were no hints of a significant interaction between bias and sentence type and no three-way interactions (all Fs <1). It follows that the interactions apparent in Figs 1(b) and 2 cannot arise as a result of strategies based on lexical preference. It is equally apparent that the results are embarrassing for the interpretation offered by Rayner and Frazier (1987), because use of the eye movement measure effectively answers their most powerful criticism. But before commenting on this discrepancy it is necessary to analyse the data using measures more directly related to those they employed.

First Pass per Character and per Word. Both Frazier and Rayner (1982) and Rayner and Frazier (1987) measured processing time across a zone in terms of average fixation duration per character. This is presumably intended as a control for variable word length, but whether it is adequate in this respect is rather doubtful. As O'Regan (1989) points out, whether or not an increment in fixation duration is found as word length increases, depends on the *location* of the initial fixation. Further, the use of a measure of reading time per character involves the highly questionable assumption

TABLE 1
Mean Total Pass per Word Reading Time (msec) for each Sentence Type and Verb Bias

Sentence type	*Bias*	*Zone* 1	2	3
TR	Comp.	220	201	227
	NP	232	201	283
TC	Comp.	236	198	263
	NP	225	198	293
RC	Comp.	222	209	267
	NP	240	199	283

that one long fixation is equivalent in processing terms to two or more shorter ones (Blanchard, 1985). The issue is not, of course, of critical importance (save possibly as a source of unwanted variability) if stimulus materials are identical across conditions. Unfortunately, this cannot be the case for the stimuli we are considering here: TR sentences, of necessity, end in a different way from their TC and RC counterparts. In fact, inspection of the sentences constructed by Rayner and Frazier suggests that they were *not* particularly well-matched. For example, in (11) and (12) the number of words comprising zone 3 differs:

11. The singer demonstrated / her vocal range in difficult arias / and / duets.
12. The singer demonstrated / her vocal range in difficult arias / was absolutely / amazing.

Similarly, although it is well-known that word frequency affects fixation duration (Kliegl, Olson, & Davidson, 1982), the words in the "disambiguating" region of TR and complement sentences were not well matched.

For these reasons, two complementary analyses were carried out, the first using a measure of reading time per character (as used by Rayner and Frazier) and the second a measure of reading time per word. Scaling to the "number of words" is more consistent with the argument that, in reading, the primary perceptual segmentation is in terms of "word objects" (McConkie, Kerr, Reddix, & Zola, 1988). In employing this measure we chose not to incorporate the complementiser "that" into zone 1. There is little linguistic justification for doing this and it has the disadvantage of producing an imbalance in length. Thus, in the per-word analyses here, we treated the word "that" separately.

Rayner and Frazier (1987) define "first-pass" reading as the sum of all first-pass fixations (left-to-right saccades) within a specified zone, plus any within-zone regressions prior to the disambiguating zone. Our definition of first-pass reading time for the "per word" analysis was very similar: the sum of all first-pass within-zone fixations plus any within-zone regressions, prior to the final fixation. It should be noted that this measure includes regressions within zone 3, while excluding all "second-pass" reading. Results for both measures are shown in Fig. 3.

Analysis of variance of the data in Fig. 3(a) revealed an overall interaction of sentence type and zone [$F1(4,84) = 2.86$, $P < 0.05$; $F2(4,72) = 2.55$, $P < 0.05$]. Separate analyses were carried out for the critical comparisons involving zones 2 and 3 for the three pairs of sentence types. There was a significant interaction of sentence type and zone for the TR–TC contrast [$F1(1,21) = 6.96$, $P < 0.05$; $F2(1,18) = 4.59$, $P < 0.05$], with reading times again showing a greater increase in the TC conditions. The results for the RC condition lay between these two extremes, and did

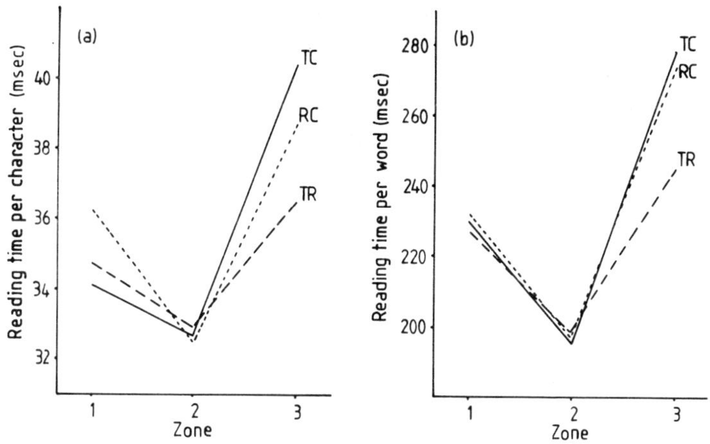

FIG. 3 (a) First-pass reading time per character and (b) first-pass reading time per word, for TR, TC, and RC sentences over the three zones.

not differ reliably from either of them [TR–RC: $F1(1,21) = 2.62$, $F2 < 1$; TC–RC: $F1 < 1$, $F2(1,18) = 2.07$].

Analysis of the data in Fig. 3(b) showed similar, but somewhat clearer, results. Overall, the interaction in first-pass reading time per word between sentence type and zone was significant by subjects [$F1(4,84) = 2.58$, $P < 0.05$], but not by items [$F2(4,72) = 1.36$]. Separate analyses over zones 2 and 3 again revealed a significant interaction of sentence type and zone for the TR–TC contrast [$F1(1,21) = 8.46$, $P < 0.01$; $F2(1,18) = 5.26$, $P < 0.05$], and a marginal effect for TR–RC [$F1(1,21) = 5.16$, $P < 0.05$; $F2(1,18) = 2.44$], whereas there was no evidence at all of any difference between the TC and RC conditions ($F1$ and $F2$ both <1).

Even allowing for the lack of power in the item analyses, all of these results stand in marked contrast to those of Rayner and Frazier (1987). In the only measure which shows even a hint of a difference between TC and RC conditions, the results go in the opposite direction to that predicted by the operation of the principle of Minimal Attachment. Similarly, application of the principle could not explain an increase in processing time in the TC condition relative to TR.

The analysis of bias throws very little light on these discrepant results. Table 2 shows the mean first-pass reading time per word for the two types of verb across the three zones for each sentence type separately. Analysis of these data showed no significant sentence type × bias interaction [$F1(2,42) = 1.66$; $F2(2,36) = 1.17$], and no three-way interaction [$F1(4,84) = 2.03$; $F2(4,72) = 1.08$]. Verb type has equivalent effects in all

TABLE 2
Mean First Pass per Word Reading Time (msec) for each Sentence Type and Verb Bias

Sentence Type	Bias	Zone 1	Zone 2	Zone 3
TR	Comp.	220	197	224
	NP	232	195	268
TC	Comp.	236	196	263
	NP	225	192	289
RC	Comp.	222	203	267
	NP	240	187	277

sentence types: Sentences with complement-bias verbs (as defined by Holmes) appear overall to be slightly easier to process, but obviously this outcome provides no support for the notion that lexical preference determines the form of the interactions present in Fig. 3.

Regressions. Table 3 shows the frequency of occurrence (as percentages) of regressions from zone 3 to earlier zones in the sentences. There were too many missing cases to justify item analyses, but subject analyses were possible (although they should be interpreted with caution). The TR–TC contrast showed a significant effect of sentence type [$F1(1,21) = 5.58$, $P < 0.05$], with a greater number of regressions launched in TR sentences. There were no effects of bias and no interactions with this variable (all Fs < 1). In the comparison of TR and RC items, there was no reliable effect of sentence type [$F1(1,21) = 2.13$], and again no effect of bias ($F1 < 1$) and no interaction ($F1 = 1.46$). In the TC—RC contrast, there was no effect of sentence type [$F1(1,21) = 1.57$], bias [$F1(1,21) = 2.00$], and no interaction ($F1 < 1$). These results are not consistent with the pattern of reinspections reported by Rayner and Frazier

TABLE 3
Mean Frequency of Occurrence (Percentages) of Regressions from Zone 3 to a Prior Zone in the Sentence

Sentence Type					
TR		*TC*		*RC*	
Comp.	*NP*	*Comp.*	*NP*	*Comp.*	*NP*
67.3	62.3	36.8	40.5	42.8	61.1

(1987, table II). In particular, the principle of Minimal Attachment obviously does not predict a greater number of regressions (which, it will be recalled, were taken to index reanalysis) in TR sentences.

Discussion

One outcome is completely clear-cut: Lexical preference plays no part in determining parsing strategies for complement structures of the form used here. We can safely dismiss the idea that knowledge of case information influences the ease with which complement clauses or direct objects can be attached. It can also be safely asserted that the data provide no support for the operation of the principle of Minimal Attachment and, in large measure, confirm the original findings of Holmes et al. (1987). The form of Figs 1(b) and 2 show remarkable similarity. It is clear that there is no evidence of the longer reading times predicted by Minimal Attachment in the disambiguating region of reduced complements compared to the same region in the unambiguous version containing the overt complementiser.[3]

It is particularly worrying that Figs 1(a) and 3 should be so discrepant, because they involve near-identical methods of analysis and very similar materials. Because this discrepancy is of such theoretical significance, it is clearly necessary to ask why it might arise. Suspicion falls on the only remaining major source of difference between the two studies—this concerns the *format* of the displays used. The experiment reported here measured horizontal eye movements only and, consequently, restricted the length of materials to no more than 80 characters, presented on a single line. It will be recalled that Rayner and Frazier (1987) were able to increase the length of several of the sentences to greater than 80 characters, because the apparatus they used permitted accurate registration of vertical position. In fact, they displayed the sentences with up to 42 characters per line over several lines. The possibility must be considered that line breaks themselves influence parsing strategy. This would be unwelcome news to adherents of the principle of Minimal Attachment, but it would help to resolve the otherwise inexplicable differences between two sets of data collected over similar materials using comparable methodology.

It is not difficult to imagine that line breaks might yield powerful, if misleading, clues to the reader. For example, intuitively, sentences (13)

---

[3]A referee has pointed out that, while it is true that TC sentences should not be harder to process than RC sentences, predictions regarding the TR–TC comparison are less clear-cut. Both may be parsed correctly on the first pass, but the TC tree, being more complex, may take longer to build.

and (14) appear to pose quite different processing problems:

13. The maid disclosed the safe's location
    had been changed.
14. The maid disclosed the safe's location had
    been changed.

The most direct approach to the question would be to reanalyse the data of Rayner and Frazier with position of line-break as a factor. Detailed information on this was not available when the present study was conducted, although it was known that a general rule was applied which stipulated that for a given base sentence, line breaks always fell in the same position (Rayner, personal communication). It is, in fact, difficult to explore this issue in detail, because the range of possible break positions within a given sentence is large. Mitchell (1987, p. 615) offers a way out, suggesting that at potential clause boundaries, one consideration determining whether additional information is added, may be whether the display ". . . ends at this point, i.e. if there is no further unprocessed parafoveal information to the right of the potential clause boundary". This suggests that, for the materials under consideration here, the most informative manipulation would be to construct line breaks which either do, or do not, segment the disambiguating phrase, as in (13) and (14). It should be emphasised, however, that no claim is made that Rayner and Frazier employed line breaks at either of these points.[4] However, if line breaks *per se* can be shown to alter the reader's parsing strategy, we shall have moved a significant way towards reconciling the highly discrepant results discussed in Experiment 1.

Experiment 2 examined performance on the materials used in Experiment 1, again using a self-paced reading task, with a single line break segmenting the display, either before the disambiguating phrase (an early break) or after the initial word of the disambiguating phrase (a late break). That is, the break was either at the zone 2/3 boundary shown in examples (8)–(10) or one word later.

It is clear that the principle of Minimal Attachment makes no predictions in this situation: The subjects' parsing strategy is determined by the application of a general rule in which display format plays no part, and

---

[4]Further details on the position of line breaks in Rayner and Frazier's (1987) study have since become available. In only 2 of the 24 cases could the NP have possibly been taken to be complete at the line end. In all 24 cases, the line break fell in the middle of the ambiguous NP, but in all but 2 cases there were words at the end of the line making it clear that the NP was not complete. Thus, for almost all trials, unprocessed parafoveal information was to the right of the potential clause boundary (Rayner, personal communication; see also Rayner et al., this issue).

indeed would have been applied to the ambiguous NP long before the line end in both cases. If, on the other hand, subjects make use of a range of strategies or heuristics, drawing on whatever evidence is available, predictions can be made. In particular, following Mitchell (1987), the break in (14) should be more "informative" (in the sense of giving early notice of the inapplicability of the direct object strategy) than the break in (13). On these grounds, subjects may find late-break sentences more costly in processing terms. In contrast, the presence of the overt complementiser in TC constructions, prior to the break, should act to minimise (or even eliminate) differences due to format. With regard to TR sentences such as (15) and (16), the situation is more complicated, and predictions are difficult to make:

15. The witness denied the lawyer's claims about her motives
    for the crime.
16. The witness denied the lawyer's claims about her motives for
    the crime.

It will be noted that the pre-break segment in (15) is a complete sentence and, in the absence of other information, the second line in this case could be taken to begin a new sentence (although lacking an initial upper-case letter). If the reader segments in this way, then (15) will present severe processing problems. On the other hand, the first line of (16) does not *definitely* flag a direct object ending (as in 17, for example, in which the possibility of a TR "garden path" is raised):

17. The witness denied the lawyer's claims about her motives for
    the crime were valid.

For reasons of this kind, it is not possible to make strong predictions regarding the effects of line-break on the TR constructions employed.

EXPERIMENT 2

Method

Subjects. A total of 30 unpaid student volunteers of the University of Dundee took part. All were naive with regard to the purpose of the study and had not participated in Experiment 1.

Materials and Design. The experimental sentences were identical to those used in Experiment 1. For the purposes of Experiment 2, verb bias was not considered as a separate factor, although the two verb types were balanced in the design. Six counterbalanced sets of experimental sentences were derived, each containing eight sentences of the three constructions

TR, TC, and RC, and within each construction four contained an early break and four a late break. As before, each base sentence was found only once in each set. In both subject ($F1$) and item ($F2$) analyses, sentence type, zone, and break (early *vs* late) were treated as repeated-measures variables. Item set was a between-groups dummy factor in all analyses.

Procedure. The materials were presented on a "green-screen" monitor connected to an Apple IIe computer. For each item, the subject's initial button-press resulted in the display of a series of dashes and spaces, corresponding to the characters in the sentence to be displayed. In this way, the position of each word and the overall format and length of the sentence to be displayed was evident to the subject. Subsequent button-presses replaced sets of dashes with individual words. The button-press following display of the final word erased the sentence from the screen. Following a 1-sec delay, a question appeared, centred on a single line. This was answered in the usual way using right- and left-hand buttons for "yes" and "no" responses.

Results and Discussion

The inter-response times obtained were used to compute average reading time across the four zones identified by Holmes et al. (1987): (1) the beginning of the sentence, up to and including the verb; (2) the temporarily ambiguous nounphrase; (3) the disambiguating region prior to the final word; and (4) the final word. The results are shown in Fig. 4, in which the data for early and late breaks are plotted separately. Overall, there was a significant three-way interaction involving sentence type, zone, and break [$F1(6,144) = 3.08$, $P < 0.01$; $F2(6,108) = 2.78$, $P < 0.05$]. In view of this, separate analyses were carried out on the results from early- and late-break conditions. Over zones 1 and 2, early-break items showed a hint of an interaction between zone and sentence type in the subject analyses [$F1(2,48) = 3.04$, $P > 0.05$], but this was not reliable over items [$F2(2,36) = 1.69$], whereas for late-break items there was no sign of any interaction ($F1$ and $F2 < 1$). Over zones 2, 3, and 4 there was no evidence of an interaction between sentence type and zone for early-break items [$F1 < 1$, $F2(4,72) = 1.01$], but this interaction was significant for items containing late breaks in the subject analysis [$F1(4,96) = 3.94$, $P < 0.01$], and approached significance in the items analysis [$F2(4,72) = 2.40$, $P = 0.06$]. Separate analyses of the data for zone 4 alone show similar results: no significant effect of sentence type for early-break sentences [$F1(2,48) = 1.37$; $F2(2,36) = 1.79$], but a significant effect for late-break sentences [$F1(2,48) = 5.76$, $P < 0.01$; $F2(2,36) = 3.60$, $P < 0.05$].

It is apparent from Fig. 4 that the line break has quite different effects

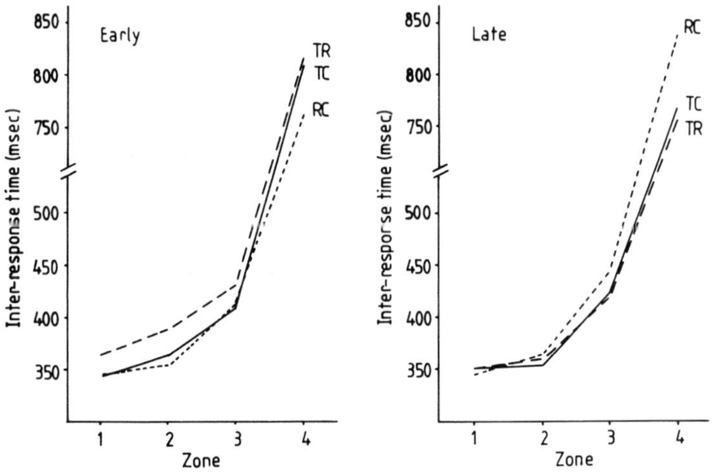

FIG. 4 Mean inter-response times for (a) early-break and (b) late-break versions of TR, TC, and RC sentences over zones 1–3 and zone 4 (the final word).

for the three sentence types. For RC sentences, reading times on the final word are significantly slower following a late break [$F1(1,24) = 4.43$, $P < 0.05$; $F2(1,18) = 8.46$, $P < 0.01$]. The apparent effect in the reverse direction for TR sentences narrowly fails to achieve significance [$F1(1,24) = 3.49$, $P = 0.07$; $F2(1,18) = 3.20$, $P = 0.09$]. But, as predicted, for TC sentences, there is no effect of break [$F1(1,24) = 1.65$; $F2 < 1$].

Although the experiment was not designed to examine the effect, it appears plausible that the marginally significant effect of break for the TR constructions relates to the fact that, in the vast majority of cases, in the early-break condition the initial words on the second line can be treated as the start of a new sentence. A line break in an "unnatural" position (before the available space to the right of the line has been exhausted), is possibly construed by the subject as indicative of a significant division in the materials. This hypothesis will apparently be confirmed if the new line appears to begin a new sentence, notwithstanding the absence of an initial capital letter. We presume it is the later disconfirmation of this hypothesis which leads to the increase in processing time when the final word appears.

GENERAL DISCUSSION

The pattern of results shown in Fig. 4 for late-break presentation provides a fair approximation to the pattern shown in Fig. 1(a). It is worth noting that the line breaks in the late-break condition in Experiment 2 resemble the breaks employed by Rayner and Frazier (1987) in one important regard—in both there were words at the end of the line which effectively inhibited the subject from treating the constituent under analysis as complete at that point (see footnote 4). For example, for sentences (8)–(10), the late-break condition produced a line ending ". . . management of". The equivalent break in the presentation conditions employed by Rayner and Frazier produced a line ending ". . . offer from". Obviously, the absolute position of break differs, but its effect in signalling that the structure is incomplete at that point is very similar. We may conclude, therefore, that the *form* of the data produced by Rayner and Frazier is capable of replication, but it would be unwise to draw the same conclusions from this pattern of differences that they do, because the form of the results from the early-break condition is quite different and, furthermore, neither outcome closely resembles the results obtained when a single-line presentation is employed. Thus, while we do not wish to claim that Rayner and Frazier's results arise necessarily as a consequence of the effects of a particular (accidental) pattern of line breaks, it must be accepted that line breaks do exert a powerful influence on the reader's behaviour. To the extent that reading time represents a window on parsing strategy, it appears clear that the apparent application of Minimal Attachment, at least for complement sentences of this form, may be a consequence of the presence of non-linguistic cues to segmentation. When sentences were presented (as in Holmes et al., 1987) on a single line, and such cues were not present, we found that both full and reduced complement structures were more difficult to process than direct objects, but there was no evidence of the *additional* difficulty which the principle of Minimal Attachment predicts for the reduced form.

We can now return to the distinction drawn by Frazier (1987) between approaches to performance models of the human parser. The choice she proposes is between the systematic application of invariable principles of syntactic analysis, on the one hand, and the use of heuristics and *ad hoc* strategies, on the other. The results reported here suggest that we need to follow the second course, but this does not necessarily constitute an admission of defeat in the search for parsing principles which are securely based in psycholinguistic processes. Thus, although we argue here that presentation format influences parsing decisions, we do not believe that the influence is either unsystematic or incapable of principled explanation.

The starting point for a theoretical account is the observation (Kennedy & Murray, 1984) that readers' reanalysis strategies vary as a function of two factors: whether previously read material remains visible and available for reinspection, and whether material is presented in a "spatialised" form (i.e. each word occupying a distinct spatial location on the display screen). The results were open to the interpretation that having material visible, in a spatially extended format, facilitates the processes of reanalysis because reinspection is available to the reader as a strategy. There is, however, an additional possibility: At the time of presentation, differential spatial location *per se* may assist the reader in computing syntactic relations. For the hearer, word order is an essential index to syntax; but for the reader, "order" must be interpreted in both temporal and spatial terms. As a result, because the normal presentation of text allows for free inspection, one of the processing demands placed on the reader is to arrive at a mapping between a temporal order of inspection and the necessary (speech-equivalent) order of words to which a structural description must be attached. In fact, when these two processes are dissociated experimentally, it is strongly suggested that the removal of cues to spatial adjacency disrupts syntactic operations. For example, Pynte, Kennedy, Murray, and Courrieu (1988) contrasted the presentation of segments of a sentence in a spatially extended format with a non-spatialised presentation in which each segment displayed occupied the same physical location on the display. The crucial dependent measure was the pattern of inspection over a whole-sentence display which followed the two different forms of segment presentation. Differences were apparent in the pattern of eye movements which led Pynte et al. to conclude that "subjects in the non-spatialised mode were apparently unable (or, at least, unwilling) during the initial segment-by-segment presentation to compute relationships demanding positional information". That is, spatial extension in the presentation of text appears to aid the reader, in the sense that word-order can be coded in spatial terms.

Obviously, this spatial coding is a processing option denied to the listener, and there is, in fact, evidence that sentences of the type considered here are processed differently when presented in the auditory modality (Kennedy & Murray, 1987b; Murray & Kennedy, 1988). With auditory presentation, there is, again, no evidence that full and reduced complements pose different processing demands. However, both appear *easier* than the equivalent TR constructions. At least one plausible interpretation of this outcome is that, for the hearer, adopting a single structural analysis is too risky. The TR constructions employed have in common the property that, until the sentence end has been identified, they may be parsed either as a direct object construction or as the initial clause of some more complex structure. This possibility imposes a processing penalty on the hearer, suggesting that the alternative options may be entertained in parallel. The reader avoids this cost because the physically present page permits a process of rapid reinspection. The page, or screen boundary, in this sense, provides a local co-ordinate system which underlies a "spatially addressed" memory. Whether or not the reader can safely adopt a single syntactic analysis when faced with ambiguity, depends on the relative cost of reanalysis. We assume this is high if the operations involve computations over a speech-based memory record. On the other hand, this cost may be reduced if the reader has access to a form of representation which can capitalise on the stability and permanence of spatially extended text.

These observations provide an important gloss on the notion of reanalysis. At a linguistic level, it is entirely consistent that subjects, having been garden-pathed, should make eye movements back to the point in a sentence where an incorrect attachment had been made. But psychologically, this phenomenon demands an explanation in terms of the representation preserved by the reader which *allows for* accurate reinspection (as distinct from, for example, backtracking or re-reading). We believe that there is a convincing case that this representation involves a spatial code and, from this perspective, the results summarised in this paper reflect differences in the ease with which such a code can be developed and used.

With regard to the proposed principle of Minimal Attachment, it seems that subjects are both more cautious and more perceptive than the model advanced by Frazier (1987) suggests. They are cautious in the sense that they do not appear to attach incoming material *at the time of reading* into a *complete* structural description; but, rather, the results suggest that this attachment is frequently delayed until the apparent end of the current constituent. That is, while subjects may reveal in their performance a sensitivity to left brackets, this has relatively few consequences for the processing of subsequent words until a corresponding right bracket has been located. It seems, therefore, that they are inclined to attach constituents rather than words. However, in arriving at a structural description, subjects are sensitive to a variety of cues, not all of which may be strictly linguistic. Punctuation or line format are as likely to cause the parser to adopt a premature closure as are the linguistic confusions caused by inconsiderate reductions of complement structures. The reader makes use of the information available, and whether or not this leads to a "garden path" will depend on both the nature of the structure and the manner in which it is presented.

REFERENCES

Altmann, G. (1988). Ambiguity, parsing strategies, and computational models. *Language and Cognitive Processes*, *3*, 73–97.

Blanchard, H. E. (1985). A comparison of some processing time measures based on eye movements. *Acta Psychologia*, *58*, 1–15.

Ferreira, F. & Clifton, C. (1986). The independence of syntactic processing. *Journal of Memory and Language*, *25*, 384–386.

Frazier, L. (1987). Sentence processing and text integration. In M. Coltheart (Ed.), *Attention and performance XII*. London: Lawrence Erlbaum Associates Ltd.

Frazier, L. & Fodor, J. D. (1978). The sausage machine: A new two-stage model of the parser. *Cognition*, *6*, 291–325.

Frazier, L. & Rayner, K. (1982). Making and correcting errors during sentence comprehension: Eye movements in the analysis of structurally ambiguous sentences. *Cognitive Psychology*, *14*, 178–210.

Holmes, V. M. (1987). Syntactic parsing: In search of the garden path. In M. Coltheart (Ed.), *Attention and performance XII*. London: Lawrence Erlbaum Associates Ltd.

Holmes, V. M., Kennedy, A., & Murray, W. S. (1987). Syntactic structure and the garden path. *Quarterly Journal of Experimental Psychology*, *39A*, 277–294.

Just, M. A., Carpenter, P. A., & Woolley, J. D. (1982). Paradigms and processes in reading comprehension. *Journal of Experimental Psychology: General*, *11*, 228–238.

Kennedy, A. & Murray, W. S. (1984). Inspection times for words in syntactically ambiguous sentences under three presentation conditions. *Journal of Experimental Psychology: Human Perception and Performance*, *10*, 833–847.

Kennedy, A. & Murray, W. S. (1987a). Spatial coordinates and reading: Comments on Monk (1985). *Quarterly Journal of Experimental Psychology*, *39A*, 649–656.

Kennedy, A. & Murray, W. S. (1987b). Revisiting the garden path. *Experimental Psychology Society/Canadian Psychological Association Meeting*, July, Oxford.

Kliegl, R., Olson, R. K., & Davidson, B. J. (1982). On problems of unconfounding perceptual and language processes. In K. Rayner (Ed.), *Eye movements in reading: Perceptual and language processes*. London: Academic Press.

McConkie, G. W., Kerr, P. W., Reddix, M. D., & Zola, D. (1988). Eye movement control during reading: I. The location of initial eye fixations on words. *Vision Research*, *10*, 1107–1118.

Mitchell, D. C. (1987). Lexical guidance in human parsing: Locus and processing characteristics. In M. Coltheart (Ed.), *Attention and performance XII*. London: Lawrence Erlbaum Associates Ltd.

Mitchell, D. C. & Holmes, V. M. (1985). The role of specific information about the verb in parsing sentences with local structural ambiguity. *Journal of Memory and Language*, *24*, 542–559.

Murray, W. S. & Kennedy, A. (1988). Garden paths and other side tracks. *Sixth Australian Language and Speech Conference*, August, Sydney.

O'Regan, J. K. (1989). Eye movements and reading. In E. Kowler (Ed.), *Eye movements and their role in visual and cognitive processes. Reviews of oculomotor research*, Vol. 4. Amsterdam: Elsevier.

Pynte, J., Kennedy, A., Murray, W. S., & Courrieu, P. (1988). The effects of spatialisation on the processing of ambiguous pronominal reference. In G. Luer, U. Lass, & J. Shallo-Hoffmann (Eds), *Eye movement research: Physiological and psychological aspects*. Gottingen: Hogrefe.

Rayner, K. & Frazier, L. (1987). Parsing temporarily ambiguous complements. *Quarterly Journal of Experimental Psychology*, *39A*, 657–673.

Wanner, E. (1980). The ATN and the sausage machine: Which one is baloney? *Cognition*, *8*, 209–225.

Wanner, E. (1987). The parser's architecture. In F. Kessel (Ed.), *The development of language and language researchers: Essays in honour of Roger Brown*. Hillsdale, N.J.: Lawrence Erlbaum Associates Inc.

Wilks, Y., Huang, X., & Fass, D. (1985). Syntax, preference and right attachment. *Technical Report MCCS-85-5*, Computing Research Laboratory, New Mexico State University.

APPENDIX

The sentence triples used in Experiment 1, together with associated questions, are listed below. The first of the alternative endings is for the transitive version and the second for the complement. Where two questions are given, these are "late focus" questions: the first is associated with the transitive version and the second with the complement. Where a single question is given, it is an "early focus" question. Complement- and NP-bias sentences are listed separately.

NP-bias

1. The child accepted (that) her aunt's death at the hospital (with great sorrow) / (might soon occur).

   Was the death received with indifference?
   Was the death unlikely to happen shortly?

2. The customs man checked (that) the documents we were carrying (very suspiciously) / (were authentic).

   Were the papers examined somewhat casually?
   Were the papers examined for our nationality?

3. The workers considered (that) the last offer from the management (of the factory) / (was an insult).

   Did the workers make an offer?

4. The maid disclosed (that) the safe's location within the house (to the officer) / (had been changed).

   Did the maid keep the safe's location a secret?

5. My neighbour found (that) his small son and the dog (at our house) / (had gone home).

   Was my neighbour's child at our place?
   Had my neighbour's child departed?

6. The students heard (that) the lecture series by Professor Green (on nutrition) / (was cancelled).

   Were the lecture series concerned with hygiene?
   Were the lectures likely to take place?

7. The zoologist observed (that) the behaviour of the animals (in several settings) / (had become abnormal).

   Was the behaviour studied only once?
   Was the behaviour quite commonplace?

8. The senator proposed (that) some changes in the procedures (of the administration) / (should be introduced).

   Were alterations to be made in the buildings?
   Were alterations to be completely avoided?

9. The attendant remembered (that) the main exit of the building (near the railway) / (had been blocked).

   Was there an exit near the railway?
   Was there an exit which was obstructed?

10. The singer showed (that) her vocal range in difficult solos (and duets) / (was amazing).

    Was the singer's voice suited to duets?
    Was the singer's voice considered remarkable?

11. The tutor understood (that) the problems the student was having (with his work) / (were not new).

    Were the difficulties experienced by a student?
    Were the difficulties being experienced again?

12. The journalist wrote (that) the inquest's findings on the murder (in today's paper) / (was very wrong).

    Were the conclusions published yesterday?
    Were the conclusions probably justified?

Complement-bias

1. The jury believed (that) the testimony of the last witness (for the prosecution) / (was very misleading).

   Was the testimony heard by the jurors?

2. The woman claimed (that) the profits from the sale (of the paintings) / (had been spent).

   Was the woman interested in the distribution of the money?

3. The witness denied (that) the lawyer's claims about her motives (for the crime) / (had upset her).

   Did the lawyer make assertions about the witness?

4. The astronomer discovered (that) the orbit made by the satellite (around Jupiter) / (was erratic).

   Was the orbit around a planet?
   Did the orbit seem irregular?

5. The commentator doubted (that) the decision the referee made (about the incident) / (would be accepted).

   Was the decision obviously correct?

6. The politicians explained (that) their new scheme for taxation (in great detail) / (is very fair).

   Was the politician's proposal rather specific?
   Did the politician's proposal seem reasonable?

7. The doctor forgot (that) his initial diagnosis of lung cancer (very swiftly) / (was incorrect).

   Was the doctor forgetful?
   Was the doctor sure of his diagnosis?

8. The pupils knew (that) several solutions and explanations (of the problem) / (would be possible).

   Was there only one answer to the questions?

9. The girl learned (that) the beautiful poem she was reading (with no difficulty) / (was quite famous).

   Did the girl think the poem was terrible?

10. The teacher noticed (that) only one girl from her class (in the group) / (was not present).

    Was the teacher observing the children?

11. The clairvoyant predicted (that) the effects of the earthquake (on the township) / (would be minimal).

    Did the clairvoyant deny that there would be consequences?

12. The scientist proved (that) the new theory about proteins and enzymes (in rabbits) / (had faults).

    Was the scientist dealing with a novel hypothesis?

LANGUAGE AND COGNITIVE PROCESSES, 1989, *4*, (3/4) SI 77–103

Ambiguity in Context

Charles Clifton, Jr. and Fernanda Ferreira
Department of Psychology, University of Massachusetts, Amherst, Massachusetts, U.S.A., and Department of Psychology, University of Alberta, Canada

We discuss theories of sentence parsing, paying particular attention to claims about how context may affect the resolution of syntactic ambiguities. We defend the garden-path theory, arguing that it accounts for a wide range of data that other theories do not account for. The theory proposed by Crain, Altmann, and Steedman is taken as the most attractive alternative, but we argue that its underlying semantic claims are questionable, and we suggest that the data that have been presented in its support are not inconsistent with the garden-path theory.

INTRODUCTION

The central goal of current theories of sentence comprehension is to identify the types of information people use when they hear or read sentences, and to identify the principles language users follow in using the information at their disposal. Adopting the hypothesis that knowledge of language is used in a "modular" fashion (Fodor, 1983), has led to substantial advances in our understanding of some of these principles (e.g. Forster, 1979: Frazier, 1987a; Rayner, Carlson, & Frazier, 1983; Tanenhaus, Carlson, & Seidenberg, 1985). However, it is clear that *all* relevant information can be used at some point in language comprehension. Therefore, adopting a modular position requires one not only to specify what the modules are and how each of them functions, but also how the distinct modules are co-ordinated. Meaning, discourse context, and world knowledge are generally thought to be used by modules other than

Requests for reprints should be addressed to Charles Clifton, Department of Psychology, University of Massachusetts, Amherst, Massachusetts 01003, U.S.A.

This research was supported by NIH Grant HD-18708 to C.C. and Lyn Frazier, and by NSERC Grant OGP–37323 to F.F. We would like to thank Gerry Altmann, Steve Crain, Lyn Frazier, Don Mitchell, Keith Rayner, Paul Portner, René Schmauder, Sara Sereno, Shari Speer, and an anonymous reviewer for their helpful criticisms on earlier drafts of this manuscript (not all of which, they will recognise, we heeded). We would especially like to thank Paul Portner for allowing us to describe some aspects of his research on definiteness.

the module(s) that use syntactic and lexical information (but, cf. Marslen-Wilson & Tyler, 1987). Even within such a position, though, there is room for a wide variety of claims about the behaviour of each of the modules, individually and in concert with each other.

We will focus on one modular theory that makes particularly simple claims about the operation of the modules, and see whether the claims it makes are justified. The theory we focus on is the "garden-path" theory of sentence comprehension, proposed by Frazier (1978; cf. Ferreira & Clifton, 1986; Frazier & Rayner, 1982; Frazier, 1987a,b; in press).[1] We will later contrast this theory with the "incremental-interactive" theory of Altmann and Steedman (1988), which (despite its name) is a modular theory that permits a far more intimate and elaborate interaction between the syntactic and the semantic/referential modules.

THE GARDEN-PATH THEORY

The basic claims of the garden-path theory are that (a) the sentence processing mechanism (the "parser") uses a portion of its grammatical knowledge, isolated from world knowledge and other information, in initially identifying the relationships among the phrases of a sentence; (b) the parser is sometimes confronted with an uncertain choice in how to relate a new phrase to the existing structure, and when it is, it initially commits itself to a single structure; and (c) the parser follows a very general and psychologically motivated principle in choosing the structure it builds. The principle is "choose the first available analysis" (Frazier, 1987a), and is based on the presumed functional value (given the severe limitations of human short-term memory for unstructured material) of structuring incoming information as soon as possible. This principle is realised as the parsing strategies of Minimal Attachment ("do not postulate any unnecessary nodes" or, equivalently for present purposes, "use the smallest possible number of phrase structure rule applications to attach each incoming word into the structure currently being built") and Late Closure ("if consistent with the rules of the grammar, attach each incoming word into the phrase currently being analyzed").

Frazier and her colleagues have provided substantial evidence that Minimal Attachment and Late Closure account for the ease or difficulty of comprehending a wide variety of sentence forms (Ferreira & Clifton, 1986;

[1]A garden path, within this theory, does not necessarily result in the state of eternal damnation in which the parser is "unable to arrive at *any* grammatical analysis for a perfectly grammatical and otherwise acceptable sentence", for which Altmann and Steedman (1989) want to reserve the term (attributing the usage to Bever). In our theory, virtue can be regained.

Frazier, 1978; Frazier & Rayner, 1982; Rayner et al., 1983; Rayner & Frazier, 1987; cf. Kennedy & Murray, 1984; Mitchell & Holmes, 1985; Warner & Glass, 1987). A far-from-exhaustive list includes the following contrasts:

1. NP *vs* S complement (Minimal Attachment)
   a. I knew the answer very well.
   b. I knew the answer was right.
2. S complement *vs* relative clause (Minimal Attachment)
   a. Tom told the man that he had given him.
   b. Tom told the man that he had fired.
3. VP *vs* NP attachment of prepositional phrase (Minimal Attachment)
   a. The cop saw the man with the binoculars.
   b. The cop saw the man with the revolver.
4. Main clause *vs* reduced relative clause (Minimal Attachment)
   a. The horse raced past the barn and fell.
   b. The horse raced past the barn fell.
5. NP *vs* S conjunction (Minimal Attachment and Late Closure)
   a. I saw the girl and her sister.
   b. I saw the girl and her sister laughed.
6. NP complement *vs* main clause subject (Late Closure)
   a. Because Maria knitted her sweater it kept her warm.
   b. Because Maria knitted her sweater kept her warm.
7. Low *vs* high attachment of relative clause (Late Closure)
   a. The doctor called in the son of the pretty nurse who hurt herself.
   b. The doctor called in the son of the pretty nurse who hurt himself.
8. Low *vs* high attachment of adverbials (Late Closure)
   a. Martha will say that it rained yesterday.
   b. Martha said that it will rain yesterday.

In each case, the (a) form is disambiguated by world knowledge or by syntax towards the preferred minimal attachment or late closure reading, whereas the (b) form is disambiguated towards the unpreferred non-minimal attachment or early closure reading.

There is substantial evidence in favour of the late closure and minimal attachment strategies, but some recent evidence questions their generality and even existence. Cuetos and Mitchell (1988) argue against the universality of late closure, presenting evidence that suggests it fails to apply in Spanish relative clause attachment. Frazier (1990) and Clifton (1988) present some reasons, both methodological and substantive, to question Cuetos and Mitchell's conclusions, but it is clear that additional experimentation is needed to determine whether the parsing strategies hold across all constructions in all languages, as they are claimed to. Taraban and McClelland (1988) present evidence that one kind of evidence for minimal attachment, the preference to attach a prepositional phrase to a VP rather than an NP, actually depends on semantic biases (see also Speer, Foss, & Smith, 1987; Speer, 1988, for research leading to a similar conclusion). They show faster reading times in a self-paced reading task for sentences like "The thieves stole all the paintings in the museum while the guard slept" than "The thieves stole all the paintings in the night while the guard slept." The former, of course, is a non-minimal attachment sentence, and the latter a minimal attachment sentence, but the words before *museum* or *night* semantically bias them toward the non-minimal attachment reading. This finding directly and sharply challenges Rayner et al.'s (1983) claim that the syntactic strategies operate even in the face of semantic factors.

The exact force of findings like Taraban and McClelland's is not yet clear. One possible response is to suggest that the minimal attachment strategy simply does not apply to the prepositional phrase attachment construction that Taraban and McClelland used, and therefore their findings are irrelevant to the evaluation of minimal attachment (Abney, 1989; cf. C. Smith, discussed in Frazier, 1990). The minimal attachment analysis assumes that a post-nominal prepositional phrase attaches to an NP only by introducing another NP node above the initially constructed NP node. Abney and Smith suggest that the linguistically motivated analysis of post-nominal modifiers does not require such a node to be introduced. We are not willing to accept this suggestion. Frazier (1990) provides some compelling arguments for the appropriateness of the analysis which makes the minimal attachment strategy viable. Another possible response to Taraban and McClelland's data, is to suggest that their self-paced reading technique may be insensitive to initial parsing decisions, and instead primarily reflects the ease of making semantically based reanalyses of initial analyses. There are some reasons to entertain such a response seriously. As noted by M. DeVincenzi (personal communication), a small effect of an initial minimal attachment preference might be obscured by some minor biases that exist in Taraban and McClelland's materials involving differences in the possibility of lexical priming effects between their minimal and non-minimal attachment sentences. Further, it is interesting to note that, in order to create an NP attachment bias, it is usually necessary to use a disambiguating phrase that is anomalous or very strange on the VP attachment reading (examples from Taraban and McClelland's non-minimal attachment sentences include "The couple admired the house with a garden" where "with a garden" cannot plausibly modify "admire", and "The Vietnam veteran identified his old buddy from the war"). On the other hand, most VP attachment sentences that have appeared in the literature contain disambiguating phrases that are not anomalous as NP modifiers, but are simply more plausible as VP modifiers (examples include "The couple admired the house with a friend" and "I read the magazine in the bathtub").

Still, at the very least, Taraban and McClelland's findings raise questions about the integration of various sources of information that garden-path theory has not yet adequately dealt with.

AN INCREMENTAL-INTERACTIVE THEORY

Among the most interesting of the alternatives to the garden-path theory are the claims advocated by Crain and Steedman (1985), Altmann and Steedman (1988), and Altmann (1987; 1988). These workers (whom we will refer to as "Altmann and Steedman", as their 1988 article is the primary focus of the discussion in this paper) chose to isolate a subset of the wide range of phenomena accounted for by the garden-path theory, some constructions involving post-nominal modifiers, and to account for them in terms of referential processes.

Altmann and Steedman note that several of the ambiguities (e.g. 2–4 above) resolved by the Minimal Attachment principle involve contrasts between NP modification and other structures. In these examples, NP modification is the unpreferred alternative. Altmann and Steedman suggest that this is the case not because of syntactic structural facts, but because of referential facts: the modification of the NP is not licensed by the discourse context. In most existing demonstrations of a minimal attachment advantage, either the discourse context provides a single, unique referent for the unmodified NP, or it provides no referent whatsoever for the NP, modified or not. Altmann and Steedman suggest that comprehension is disrupted when a text requires inappropriate reference relations.

The crucial principle advanced by Altmann and Steedman is the "Principle of Referential Support" (Altmann & Steedman, 1988, p. 201):

9. An NP analysis which is referentially supported will be favoured over one that is not.

An NP is taken to be referentially supported when "all its referential presuppositions are satisfied by the context". Altmann and Steedman assume that a simple definite NP ("the book") presupposes the existence of a unique book in the relevant discourse model, and that a modified NP (e.g. an NP with a relative clause or a prepositional phrase, e.g. "the book that I bought" or "the book on the table") "presuppose[s] that there is a *set* of entities of the type denoted by the head noun, which the modifier restricts over" (Altmann & Steedman, 1988, p. 199).

We will return shortly to an evaluation of these claims about presuppositions. First, though, we will review briefly how the principle of referential support is taken to account for some garden-path effects. According to Altmann and Steedman (1988, p. 208), processors like theirs "propose syntactic alternatives for semantic and pragmatic adjudication *in parallel*" [their emphasis]. Presumably, when the beginning of a definite NP is identified, each of its possible analyses is built and semantically evaluated on a word-by-word basis. Choice among the alternative analyses is made on the basis of principles like the Principle of Referential Support. If, for example, a context provides a single entity of a type (e.g. a book), and a sentence includes the string of words "the book on the table", the phrase "the book" is taken to refer to the previously introduced book, and the phrase "on the table" is not taken to modify "the book" but rather to play some other role, e.g. VP modification (as was illustrated in 3a). If, on the other hand, the context had introduced two books, one of which was on a table, then the phrase "on the table" would have been taken to restrict the NP referent, leading to a preference for sentences with NP modification, like (3b).[2]

The Principle of Referential Support just discussed is actually a special case of a very general principle, the "Principle of Parsimony" (Altmann & Steedman, 1988, p. 203):

10. A reading which carries fewer unsupported presuppositions will be favoured over one that carries more.

This principle applies in a null context (e.g. a sentence presented in the absence of any discourse model), as well as when a discourse context exists. A modified NP, according to Altmann and Steedman, carries more presuppositions than an unmodified one. The bare NP, with no relative clause, prepositional phrase, or other such modifier, will therefore be the preferred reading when a string presented out of context is ambiguous between a modified NP reading and some other reading.

Let us return to an assessment of the assumptions Altmann and Steedman make about presuppositions. The first assumption, that a definite NP presupposes a unique referent, seems to be correct. The notion of presupposition being used here appears to be the commonly used notion of logical

[2]We assume that a simple NP and an NP modified by a relative clause have distinct syntactic structures (the latter consists of an NP that includes the simple NP as a constituent). It is not certain that Altmann and Steedman assume such an analysis, or even that they assume that such syntactic structures are computed during parsing (cf. Steedman, 1987). If, however, our structural assumption accurately represents Altmann and Steedman's claim about syntactic alternatives being proposed in parallel, the question arises, why stop with one level of embedding of NPs, within NPs? Why would a third level of embedding not be proposed for semantic adjudication as well? Or a fourth? We suspect that Altmann and Steedman have implicitly made a minimal-attachment-like assumption, according to which unnecessary structure is not built. But if they have in fact made such an assumption, it may prove hard for them not to apply it in the general case.

or semantic presupposition (cf. Kempson, 1977), dating back to Russell (1905) and Strawson (1950). A presupposition of a sentence is something that must obtain in order for the sentence or its negation to have any truth value (or, following Russell, to be true). A sentence with a definite NP presupposes that the NP picks out a unique individual. The standard example of a presupposition failure, "The present King of France is bald", fails to have a truth value because there is no unique referent for "the present King of France".

The second assumption, that definite NPs with post-modifiers presuppose a set of referents, one of which is picked out by the modification, is simply wrong under this meaning of "presupposition". Portner (1989) demonstrates that the use of an NP post-modifier, such as a relative clause, does not carry presuppositions in the same sense that a definite NP does. A sentence with a post-modified NP can have a truth value even if there is not a set of referents that the modifier restricts over. Portner offers (11) as illustration:[3]

11. The unicorn that Richard saw was the only unicorn there ever was.

If the modified NP, "the unicorn that Richard saw", semantically presupposes the existence of a set of unicorns, then the sentence would have to lack truth value. It does not.[4]

Altmann and Steedman presumably have in mind a less restrictive notion of presupposition, "pragmatic presupposition" (Levinson, 1983), which permits presuppositions to be cancelled. However, as Levinson (1983) suggests, this notion of presupposition may not be distinct from the notion of a conversational implicature. A conversational implicature is an uncertain inference that requires the assumption that a speaker is following a conversational convention such as Grice's (1975) Maxim of Quantity (12):[5]

---

[3]We assume that this sentence is being uttered in a world, beloved of certain schools of semanticists, which is inhibited by at least one unicorn.

[4]As Altmann and Steedman clearly recognise, non-restrictive modifiers (e.g. "My mother, whom I dearly love, drives too fast") do not presuppose a set of possible referents. However, all the modifiers we discuss in the body of this paper are to be taken as restrictive modifiers, as should be clear from the intonational phrasings that are appropriate for them.

[5]Another very interesting example of conversational implicature arises when a maxim is blatantly violated, or "flouted". The listener infers whatever is needed to maintain the belief that the speaker is in fact being cooperative. Kempson's (1977) example of a violation of the Maxim of Relevance is:

The police came in and everyone swallowed their cigarettes.

The interpretation of this sentences relies on the hearer being sensitive to the apparent irrelevance of the second clause to the first. This irrelevance invites the implicature that the cigarettes must somehow be illegal, presumably marijuana.

12. Make your contribution as informative as required (for the current purposes of the exchange); do not make your contribution more informative than is required.

An example (Levinson, 1983) of an implicature that comes from following (12) is (13):

13. "Nigel has 14 children" implicates that Nigel has only 14 children.

To have made the utterance in (13) if Nigel in fact has 20 children, would have violated the Maxim of Quantity, even though the utterance would, strictly speaking, be true if Nigel has 20 children.

Portner (1989) argues explicitly that a restrictive relative clause in an NP conversationally implicates the existence of other members of the head noun's category, rather than semantically presupposing them. Indeed, NP modifiers are commonly used to allow a reader or listener to choose among several possible referents. However, there are other common uses of restrictive relative clauses and other NP modifiers. For example, one frequently uses them to help guide a listener to the intended referent (e.g. "please hand me that pencil on the table" in a context with only a single pencil).

Faced with a post-nominal modifier, a listener/reader might reason, "following Grice's (1975) principle of quantity, the speaker/writer would not be giving me more information than necessary; therefore, the modifier is probably needed to pick out the relevant item, so there are probably other such items or s/he may think I will have some other source of difficulty in identifying the intended referent". Perhaps Altmann and Steedman would claim that conversational implicatures do play a role in initial parsing decisions. We consider this unlikely. Conversational implicatures are not made available by linguistic form. As Grice says, conversational implicatures are "non-detachable"; they are not tied to the linguistic form of what is said, but rather, to its semantic content. To make a conversational implicature, a listener must have already parsed the sentence, assigned it its literal interpretation, realised that additional inferences must be added to make it conform to the Gricean maxim, and determined what these inferences are. Such activity could not reasonably affect the initial steps of parsing.

It would take strong evidence to convince us that referential factors play a role in initial sentence parsing if they must play their role *via* conversational implicature. This belief, combined with our preference for accounting for a wide variety of garden-path phenomena with a uniform processing principle like the "first available analysis" principle (Frazier, 1987a), rather than accounting for some of them by appeal to discourse processes and presumably leaving the rest for other principles, encourages us to examine the existing evidence to see whether it is strong enough to compel one to give up the more coherent and unified account.

We will present some new evidence that indicates that it is not. First, though, we will attempt to pinpoint just what is at stake by analysing the differences that really underlie the contrast between the garden-path and the incremental-interactive theories.

ARCHITECTURAL AND PROCESSING ASSUMPTIONS

Although the differences between the garden-path and the incremental-interactive theories are substantial, the theories share more underlying assumptions than might at first be apparent. As Altmann and Steedman (1988) make clear, modularity is not an issure. Both theories assume architectures in which different information sources are used independently, respecting information encapsulation and the other criteria of modularity (Fodor, 1983). Strong *vs* weak interaction (Altmann & Steedman, 1988; Crain & Steedman, 1985) is not an issue, either. Both theories deny a form of strong interaction by which information about the plausible message guides the operation of the module that uses syntactic information, and both acknowledge that weak interaction—in which discourse structure, plausibility, semantics, etc., filters or corrects independently constructed alternatives—is the likely state of affairs.

The "grain of interpretation" is not a crucial issue, either, from our perspective. Altmann and Steedman (cf. Ades & Steedman, 1982; Steedman, 1987) make much of their proposal that semantic evaluation is done incrementally, word-by-word, a proposal that clearly is consistent with our intuitions of understanding a sentence as we hear or read it. This proposal does contrast sharply with older theories, such as the "clausal model" (Fodor, Bever, & Garrett, 1974) that was forced on early processing theories by the transformational grammars of the time. But it does not contrast with contemporary syntactic parsing theories. Nothing in garden-path theory is inconsistent with word-by-word semantic interpretation and, in fact, such immediate interpretation is demanded by the "thematic processor" invoked by garden-path theorists to account for effects of plausibility (Frazier, 1985; 1987a,b; in press; Rayner et al., 1983). There is, however, one difference here: The incremental-interactive theory offers a hint of a mechanism for immediate interpretation, whereas the garden-path theory has not explicitly addressed the problem. The incremental-interactive theory claims the following:

> [The] process of incremental evaluation involves having available representations of "partially evaluated" referents. These are simply the members of the

> set of referents which satisfy the available constraints. This set gradually becomes more and more refined as the analysis proceeds, until just one candidate referent remains (Altmann & Steedman, 1988, p. 196).

We doubt that Altmann and Steedman's suggestion will prove to be adequate. It may be attractive to think in terms of progressively narrowing sets of referents for NPs with possible post-nominal modifiers. However, referential narrowing is far less plausible for other syntactic categories. To make just one argument, consider adjectival modifiers. The interpretation of an adjective (e.g. "red") generally depends upon its head noun (compare "red hair" and "red truck") (Halff, Ortony, & Anderson, 1976; Morrow & Clark, 1988). As an extreme case, consider the adjectives "good", "big", and "fake". These adjectives do not permit narrowing of the set of referents prior to the receipt of their head noun. Because they probably do receive some kind of semantic interpretation on a word-by-word basis, it follows that the mechanism for incremental semantic evaluation proposed by Altmann and Steedman is not adequate for all cases. We suggest that it is worthwhile to continue searching for a more generally adequate principle of incremental semantic evaluation.

There *is* a crucial difference between the theories: The garden-path theory claims that a single analysis of a syntactic structure ambiguity is initially constructed,[6] whereas the incremental-interactive theory claims that the syntactic component of the processing system offers all grammatical alternatives to the semantic component, in parallel, to be evaluated (as does Forster, 1979). There is evidence that is favourable to both sides of this issue. The mere fact of garden-pathing favours the single analysis position (Frazier, 1978; 1987a). If all possible analyses are constructed, one has the task of explaining why some are harder to arrive at than others. Conversely, the fact presumed by many workers (Altmann & Steedman, 1988; Frazier, 1987a) that we arrive at the most plausible grammatically licensed interpretation of a sentence can be taken to support a parallel analysis position. If all analyses are not considered, how can the best one be chosen?

Both of these arguments have been countered by appealing to the operation of processes outside the realm of syntactic parsing. Altmann and Steedman make such an appeal when they suggest that considerations of reference and discourse coherence lead readers or listeners down the garden path. Rayner et al. (1983) and Frazier (1987a) do it by introducing the "thematic processor" to account for the fact that people do seem to

[6]It may be that the process of adding a new word to an existing structure involves the parallel access of several phrase structure rules and, accordingly, the construction of several partial analyses. But purely syntactic considerations, in combination with syntactic processing principles, determine which single analysis is chosen and offered for semantic interpretation.

arrive at the most plausible interpretation. The thematic processor is a postulated mechanism, whose principles are just beginning to be explored (Frazier, 1985; 1987a,b; in press; cf. Carlson & Tanenhaus, 1988 and Stowe, 1989 for contrasting discussions of the use of thematic information and world knowledge). The thematic processor presumably uses thematic role preferences, discourse context, and world knowledge to choose the preferred analysis of a sentence. It considers, in parallel, all possible assignments of arguments and adjuncts to syntactic positions within syntactic domains defined by the syntactic processor, and proposes attractive alternative assignments to the syntactic processor.

Altmann (1988) offers a functional argument against a system in which choices are initially made by a syntactic processor, and later corrected by appeal to meaning and context. He says that if referential or discourse information is available, only a strange processor would make decisions without appealing to it. However, a garden-path theorist could respond, syntactic information is *always* available and *always* informative. Informative semantic and discourse information is not always available. Even if it is available in a specific instance, it can be overridden by syntactic information. An argument from "good design" might well conclude that a processor would do well to make whatever decisions it can on the basis of syntactic information before consulting other, less certain, types of information.

We doubt that such logical arguments will carry the day. We believe instead that it is an empirical question whether the constraints assumed by the thematic processor position (single initial syntactic analysis, semantic evaluation only within the domain of this analysis) actually are constraints observed by the parser, or whether a less-constrained mechanism that makes appeal to context and meaning at the earliest stages of sentence comprehension is a more adequate description of the true state of affairs. We turn now to a consideration of the evidence most relevant to such a question.

EMPIRICAL EVIDENCE

Let us turn to a discussion of the empirical evidence bearing on how context is used in sentence processing. Does it strongly support the claims of a parallel, interactive, incremental processor, as Altmann and Steedman suggest? Or is it more consistent with the serial, garden-path processor?

A variety of kinds of evidence support the garden-path model. We will focus specifically on the question of whether semantic and referential information constrain the initial choice of a syntactic analysis. Ferreira and Clifton (1986, experiment 1) presented an experiment that measured eye fixations during reading, contrasting sentences like (14a) and (14b):

14a. The evidence (that was) examined by the lawyer was unreliable.
b. The defendant (that was) examined by the lawyer was unreliable.

The experiment supported the position that the meaning inconsistency of sentences like (14a) did not block the garden-pathing found in sentences like (14b) when they lacked the relative pronoun, contrary to Bever's intuitively based claim (cited in Altmann & Steedman, 1988, p. 198). The sentences were read more slowly in the region that followed the first verb (and presumably disambiguated the sentence) when the relative clause was reduced, than when it was unreduced.

Ferreira and Clifton's claim has been criticised by several researchers, including Altmann and Steedman. There are, in fact, good reasons to question the generality (perhaps even the accuracy) of the main claim Ferreira and Clifton were making, i.e. that meaning does not block garden paths but only speeds recovery from them. In several self-paced reading experiments that used sentences much like Ferreira and Clifton's, Stowe and Cupples (1989) found that meaning could prevent garden paths. In an experiment that measured eye movements and that was modelled closely on Ferreira and Clifton (1986, experiment 1), but which used more sharply disambiguated materials, Trueswell, Tanenhaus, and Garnsey (1989) showed that garden paths which would result in anomalous meanings were largely non-existent (see also Tanenhaus, Carlson, & Trueswell, this issue). It may turn out that the influence of meaning on parsing depends on strategic factors. Stowe and Cupples (1989) found the effect of meaning only under some conditions for presenting text on the video screen (see below) and, for some presentation conditions, only when the ambiguity occurred at the beginning of a sentence. Trueswell et al.'s (1989) reading times prior to any disambiguating information were 20% slower than Ferreira and Clifton's (we estimate about 260 words per minute, as opposed to 315 words per minute), but was otherwise closely comparable. It may prove possible to maintain the position that initial parsing decisions are made by the syntactic parsing module, uninfluenced by semantic considerations, and to claim instead that apparent semantic effects appear only when strategic factors permit the thematic processor to effect reanalysis within the resolution of the reading measures that are used. Still, it is hard to resist the conclusion that some semantic factors can, in fact, block the construction of some syntactic analyses (see also Stowe, 1989; Tanenhaus, Carlson, Boland, & Garnsey, 1989).

Even if one reaches such a conclusion, one need not agree with Altmann and Steedman that referential and discourse information is used in making initial structural decisions. The most direct evidence in support of the claim that such factors do not affect initial parsing decisions was presented by Ferreira and Clifton (1986, experiments 2 and 3). These experiments (particularly experiment 2) were the focus of much of Altmann and Steedman's (1988) discussion. Ferreira and Clifton demonstrated, using eye movement and self-paced reading techniques to study the reading of sentences in story-like contexts, that garden-pathing effects are found even in contexts that provide appropriate referential support for the actual reading of a sentence. Ferreira and Clifton used sentences like (15), which are ambiguous between matrix clauses and reduced relatives, and (16), which are ambiguous between NP and VP modification:

15a. The man expected to die but would not give up easily.
b. The man expected to die would not give up easily.
16a. The clerk put the saleslip in the bag after taking her money.
b. The clerk put the saleslip in the bag into her hand.

They found, consistent with the Minimal Attachment principle of the garden-path theory, that the (a) forms were read faster in the disambiguating regions than the (b) forms. Their experiments embedded these sentences in paragraph-long discourse contexts that were designed to support the form of the sentence that was used or to be neutral between the two possible forms. The neutral contexts were designed following the only discussion of the incremental-interactive theory available at the time the experiments were conducted (Crain & Steedman, 1985), and the experiments were presented as a test of this version of the theory. Ferreira and Clifton found that initial reading times were not affected by whether context supported the interpretation, or was merely neutral between the interpretations; garden-pathing occurred to an equal degree in both contexts. The contextual difference did affect final question-answering performance, and it certainly affected intuitions of comprehension difficulty; but it did not seem to affect initial parsing decisions.

This finding explicitly contradicted a prediction made by Crain and Steedman (1985). However, later refinements of incremental-interactive theory made it clear that no context could be truly neutral, according to the theory. A context will either support the presuppositions of a modified NP, or it will not. Altmann and Steedman (1988; cf. also Altmann, 1988) argued that it was necessary to give up the logic of comparing biased contexts to a neutral context, and instead to compare positively biased with negatively biased contexts. They presented some self-paced and whole-sentence reading experiments that made such a comparison and, in doing so, led them to the conclusion that discourse context can guide parsing decisions (cf. also Perfetti, 1990, for some similar experiments). Below, we question the logic of their experiments. We suggest that *all* theories under consideration predict the effects they obtained, given the design they used, and we argue that a design like that used by Ferreira and Clifton (1986, experiments 2 and 3) provides a test that discriminates between theories, even if the idea of a truly neutral discourse context is given up. But before raising this and other concerns about the Altmann and Steedman experiments, we will briefly describe the experiments.

Altmann and Steedman compared prepositional phrases that were temporarily ambiguous between VP and NP attachment (17a and b, respectively), and that were disambiguated eventually by factors of plausibility:

17a. The burglar blew open the safe with the dynamite and made off with the loot.
b. The burglar blew open the safe with the new lock and made off with the loot.

Altmann and Steedman used a different type of construction than Ferreira and Clifton, but the theoretical analysis remains the same: Minimal Attachment would predict an initial analysis of the preposition phrase ("with the dynamite" or "with the new lock") as modifying the VP, with time-consuming reanalysis to NP modification in the case of the non-minimal attachment sentence (17b). Altmann and Steedman presented these sentences as the last sentence of a paragraph context that was either appropriate to the minimal attachment VP modification sentence (mentioning just one safe, which had a new lock), or a context that was appropriate to the non-minimal NP modification sentence (mentioning two safes, one of which had a new lock). They found long reading times when the context and the sentence were inconsistent compared to when they were consistent (especially long in the case of a non-minimal attachment context with a minimal attachment sentence). They further found a small but significant advantage for the *non*-minimal over the minimal attachment sentence when each occurred in its appropriate context. Altmann and Steedman's results appear to support the position that referential factors are all-important in the resolution of temporary ambiguities, and to give no support whatsoever for a preference for a minimal attachment analysis of a temporarily ambiguous sentence.

We have three methodological concerns to raise about Altmann and Steedman's experiments. One concern involves the sorts of influences that can safely be drawn from self-paced reading tasks like the tasks they used. The second involves the appropriateness of the experimental design Altmann and Steedman used, as compared to the design Ferreira and Clifton used. The third concerns a potential problem with Altmann and Steedman's materials, a problem which they themselves noted.

Concern 1: Self-paced Reading

Measuring how long people take to read sentences, whose presentation they control using push-buttons, has proven to be a valuable way of comparing the ease of comprehending various types of sentences and discourses. However, it does have some limitations as an analytic tool for determining the fine-grain details of how the human sentence parser works. First, it is a task at which subjects are unpracticed, compared to the task of moving their eyes across a printed page. The resulting lack of skill makes it likely that reading rate will be relatively slow, and that a subject may try out different reading strategies during an experimental session. Thus, self-paced reading may be particularly sensitive to task requirements, e.g. what kinds of questions the reader expects to be asked. Because of this, the time a reader is observed to examine a particular word or phrase in self-paced reading may reflect the influences of factors that might not come into play during normal fluent reading.

Secondly, the presentation requirements of the self-paced task actively encourage the invention of special-purpose strategies. In self-paced reading, the experimenter must divide the text into presentation regions, e.g. words or phrases. The segmentation used can influence the reading process. For instance, subjects in the self-paced reading task may engage in the strategy of attempting to interpret fully each successive region they see before moving on. Further, the mode in which words are presented on the video screen (cumulatively or non-cumulatively, centred or moving across the screen, etc.) may well affect what kinds of new strategies the reader devises to cope with the unfamiliar reading task.

These concerns about self-paced reading are not mere abstractions. Concrete data back each of them up. Aaronson (1976) demonstrated major effects of type of memory test on self-paced reading. The effects of syntactic structure were greatly reduced when question-answering rather than verbatim recall was required. Just, Carpenter, and Woolley (1982) and Kennedy and Murray (1984) showed substantial differences among the various modes of presentation. Stowe and Cupples (1989) found that garden paths in sentences with reduced relative clauses were prevented by meaning when the display was cumulative and when it moved across the screen in a non-cumulative fashion, so long as the ambiguity was sentence-initial. However, they found that initial sentence parsing was unaffected by meaning (as was reported by Ferreira & Clifton, 1986, experiment 1) when all the words appeared in the same position and when the display moved non-cumulatively across the screen, if there was an introductory phrase before the ambiguity.

In ongoing work being conducted by the first author, in collaboration with S. Speer, S. Abney, and M. Slowiaczek, the presence or absence of a minimal attachment garden-path effect in sentences like (18) appears to depend on how the sentences are segmented into presentation regions:

18a. The baby disgusted the woman with its dirty diapers.
b. The baby disgusted the woman with the red hair.

c. The woman expressed her disgust with the dirty diapers.
d. The woman expressed her disgust with a quick glance.

Presenting the entire clause shown in (18) (as the first clause in a two-clause sentence), or presenting the preposition separated from its complement, reduces or eliminates the preference for VP modification expected on the basis of Minimal Attachment. Only when medium-sized presentation regions are used (so that a prepositional phrase constitutes a single presentation region), or when eye-tracking measures were taken on whole-sentence presentations, was a robust minimal attachment effect observed.

Ferreira and Henderson (in press) compared self-paced reading and eye-movement measurements using sentences such as (19):

19a. Pam guessed / Chris / bakes / tasty cakes.
b. Pam guessed that / Chris / bakes / tasty cakes.

The slash marks indicate presentation regions for the self-paced version of the study. In the eye-movement version, the sentences were visible in their entirety. Ferreira and Henderson found standard garden-pathing effects in the eye-movement experiment and in a non-cumulative self-paced reading experiment. Subjects spent longer on the word *bakes* in (19a) than (19b), indicating that they had initially interpreted *Chris* as the direct object of guessed, and then had to revise their analysis upon receipt of the lower verb. However, in the cumulative presentation version of the study, no effects of the absence of a complementiser were found in this same disambiguating region. It appears that subjects may adopt a strategy of calling material up on the screen before they are ready to read it when presentation is cumulative.

The measurement of eye movements during normal reading has some marked advantages over self-paced reading techniques (see Rayner et al., this issue). It relies on highly practised skills, and is unlikely to be as easily modified by unusual task demands as self-paced reading is. However, eye-movement measurements do not provide a direct window into the operation of the mind. Eye movements are certainly sensitive to the goals of reading. Because reading speed is sensitive to the division of phrases across lines (at least using an experimenter-paced procedure: Graf & Torrey, 1966), eye movements may be expected to reflect how lines are broken. As Altmann and Steedman (1988, esp. pp. 214–215 and footnote 18) note, eye movements reflect a variety of processes, from lexical access through text integration. A long fixation cannot always unambiguously be attributed to a single cause, any more than a long presentation in self-paced reading can be. But the recording of eye movements has one great advantage in providing an undistorted measure of when a factor first has its influence. The fact that eye-movement records can be divided into initial and later fixations in a given region, permits the researcher to hone in on just what information has what effect and when, much more finely than self-paced reading allows. Effects that appear on the earliest fixations after some critical information is read can quite safely be attributed to that information, and such effects can in general be expected to occur as soon as the information is read.[7] No measures in self-paced reading tasks can so unambiguously be attributed to such early stages of comprehension; initial comprehension processes and the processes of revising initial analyses are inextricably confounded in the measurement of self-paced reading rates.

Let us summarise our first concern. Self-paced reading tasks are demonstrably sensitive to many factors that affect reading (as Ferreira & Clifton, 1986, experiment 3, argued when they showed minimal attachment effects in and out of context using a self-paced reading task). However, until we have a better understanding of just how self-paced reading measures are affected by factors that do not play a role in normal reading, it is risky to rely on self-paced reading data to argue for major theoretical conclusions about details of the normal flow of information in reading.

Concern 2: Experimental Design

Altmann and Steedman (1988) used a crossover design, in which the time to read a sentence in a supportive context is compared to the time to read it in an inappropriate context. They predicted, and observed, slower reading times in the latter than in the former conditions. They further claimed that the comparison Ferreira and Clifton (1986) attempted to make between a supportive context and a neutral context was impossible, because no context is truly neutral.

We accept that the "neutral" context we used was only neutral according to the specifications of Crain and Steedman (1985), and that no context is neutral in any absolute sense. However, there is still good reason to prefer the design using a "neutral" context compared to a crossover design. The basic problem with a crossover design is that *all* theories—garden-path or incremental-interactive—make the same predictions, at least for measures (like self-paced reading) that conflate initial analysis time and reanalysis

[7]As Altmann and Steedman (1988, p. 215; cf. Altmann, 1988, p. 84) note, the effects of some factors on eye movements persist beyond the region in which the effects begin. However, in general, it appears that such high-level factors as inferencing and anaphoric reference determination begin to affect the eye-movement record immediately at the word that brings the factor into play (cf. Rayner et al., this issue). Thus, it is probably incorrect to argue (as Altmann and Steedman do) that the effects Ferreira and Clifton observed to begin in the syntactic disambiguating region were really the delayed effects of a requirement to make an inference in an earlier region (cf. also, Clifton & Ferreira, 1987b). Such effects should have been apparent in the earlier region if they were the basis of the effects in the disambiguating region. They were not.

time. One cell of the crossover design places a minimal attachment sentence in a non-minimal attachment context. With the present types of sentences (17; repeated below), a non-minimal attachment context introduces two entities of a given type (e.g. two safes).

17a. The burglar blew open the safe with the dynamite and made off with the loot.
b. The burglar blew open the safe with the new lock and made off with the loot.

The minimal attachment sentence uses an unmodified definite NP ("the safe"). Such a sentence violates the presupposition that definite NPs have a unique reference. Any theory that says reference is computed quickly admits the possibility that such a reference violation will slow reading time. The garden-path theory is such a theory (at least given a context in which antecedent reference is computed at all, which may not hold for all experimental settings). In fact, the garden-path theory claims that the simple NP—which fails to refer—is the initially computed analysis, and is therefore an analysis whose failure to refer will be detected, slowing processing time. Because both the garden-path theory and the incremental-interactive theory predict that reading time will be slow for a minimal attachment sentence in a non-minimal attachment context, this cell of a crossover design provides no evidence relevant to the choice between theories.

The remaining cell—a non-minimal attachment sentence in a minimal attachment context—is hardly more relevant. The incremental-interactive theory predicts that this condition will be difficult for the same reasons the minimal attachment sentence/non-minimal attachment context condition is difficult. Under the analysis offered in the present paper, the garden-path theory does not have the same reasons for predicting processing difficulty in this condition (compared to the non-minimal sentence/non-minimal context condition). No presuppositions are violated. However, given that one felicitous use of a post-nominal modifier is to pick among several similar alternative referents, the non-minimal attachment context (which provides such alternative referents) can facilitate the process of reanalysing an initial erroneous analysis, compared to a non-minimal attachment context. Given a measure that provides no way of distinguishing between initial analysis and reanalysis processes, the garden-path theory can easily predict somewhat slowed reading times in the minimal/context/non-minimal sentence condition. We believe that Altmann and Steedman's finding of a relatively small (25-msec) reading time effect in comparing this condition to the non-minimal context/non-minimal sentence condition is perfectly consistent with the garden-path theory.

The design used by Ferreira and Clifton, especially when coupled with a measure that can reflect initial parsing processes, can distinguish between the garden-path and the incremental-interactive theories, even without making the assumption that the "neutral" conditions are truly neutral. Consider the following argument, which amounts to the claim that the design used by Ferreira and Clifton actually has the virtues of the crossover design pointed out by Altmann and Steedman, without its disadvantages. The argument is cast within a position like Altmann and Steedman's, in which multiple-sentence analyses are simultaneously evaluated in terms of how well each is supported by context, and is designed to show that the incremental-interactive theory does make a clear prediction for Ferreira and Clifton's design. Any context will provide some degree of referential support for each analysis—in the present case, the minimal and non-minimal attachment analyses. Ferreira and Clifton's (1986) minimal attachment contexts, non-minimal attachment contexts, and neutral contexts, each provide their own degree of support for each analysis. Assume, following Altmann and Steedman, that referential contexts determine sentence parsing decisions, so that sentences are read more rapidly to the extent that context supports their referential presuppositions. Assume further that if a context provides a greater amount of support for one analysis, it will necessarily provide a lesser amount of support for the other analysis. Assume finally that the "neutral" context provides some degree of support for one analysis that falls somewhere between the minimal and non-minimal attachment contexts (perhaps equal to one of them), and a complementary degree of support or non-support for the other analysis.

Under these assumptions, whatever degree of support the neutral context provides, one analysis or the other (or both) will be less referentially appropriate for the neutral context than for its own favoured context. Therefore, either the minimal attachment sentence, or the non-minimal attachment sentence, or both, will be read more slowly in the neutral context than in its own favoured context. If research fails to confirm this prediction (as Ferreira and Clifton's experiments did, when they found evidence for garden-pathing in all contexts), then we must reject at least one of the assumptions that led to it. The only contentious assumptions seem to be that multiple analyses are evaluated simultaneously with respect to context, and that such evaluations determine parsing decisions.

The one kind of evidence that Altmann and Steedman provide which appears to be inconsistent with the garden-path theory, is their finding that non-minimal attachment sentences are read *faster* than minimal attachment sentences, even in their respective supporting contexts. However, our third and final methodological concern involves just this contrast.

Concern 3: Order of Mention of Antecedents

Altmann and Steedman's contexts all had a common structure. First, an agent was introduced in possession of a possible instrument ("A burglar broke into a bank carrying some dynamite"). Then, after some intervening material, two objects were introduced, of one type or two (". . . he saw that there was a safe with a new lock and a safe/strongbox with an old lock"). Finally, there was a minimal attachment or a non-minimal attachment sentence ("The burglar blew open the safe with the dynamite/new lock and made off with the loot"). Reading times were generally found to be slower for the minimal than the non-minimal attachment sentence.

As Altmann and Steedman (1988) note, attributing the observation to J. D. Fodor (their footnote 19), the antecedent of the definite NP within the critical prepositional phrase is introduced further away from its use in the prepositional phrase in the case of minimal attachment sentences ("the dynamite") than in the case of non-minimal attachment sentences ("the new lock"). While they consider it unlikely, they acknowledge the possibility that this difference in distance could affect their results. We consider it very likely that it did affect their results. Several researchers have reported longer reading times for definite NP anaphors as the distance between them and their antecedents becomes greater (Clark & Sengul, 1979; Clifton & Ferreira, 1987a). If this is so, then Altmann and Steedman's materials are systematically biased against minimal attachment sentences, and the one result in their research that is problematic for garden-path theory may be an experimental artefact. The experiment reported below was designed to test this possibility. Because the experiment uses a self-paced reading measure, we do not wish to present it as crucial evidence regarding the early stages of integrating syntactic and discourse information. In fact, because it deliberately made the antecedent of an anaphoric NP more recent in the minimal attachment than in the non-minimal attachment sentences (just the opposite of Altmann and Steedman's experiment), we do not even want to present it as evidence for a minimal attachment advantage. We merely want to present it in support of our suggestion that the non-minimal-attachment advantage reported by Altmann and Steedman should not be taken as evidence against the garden-path theory.

NEW EVIDENCE

Method

We modified 30 of Altmann and Steedman's 32 paragraphs so that the referent of the instrument NP ("the dynamite") was initially introduced shortly before its use in the minimal attachment sentences, and the referent

TABLE 1
Sample Passages from the Present Study and from Altmann and Steedman (1988)

Passage as used in the present study

A burglar planned * to blow open * a safe. * Once inside the bank * he saw that * there was a safe * which had a new lock * and a safe/strongbox which had * an old lock. * The burglar was carrying some dynamite. * He blew open * the safe * *with the dynamite/new lock* * and made off * with the loot. * He escaped * in a stolen car. *

Passage as used by Altmann and Steedman (1989)

A burglar broke into a bank carrying some dynamite. * He planned to blow open a safe. * Once inside * he saw * that there was * a safe * which had a new lock * and a safe/strongbox * which had an old lock. * The burglar * blew open * the safe * *with the dynamite/new lock* * and made off * with the loot.

of the modifier NP ("the new lock") was introduced somewhat earlier.[8] We adopted Altmann and Steedman's crossover design, presenting both minimal and non-minimal attachment sentences in both minimal and non-minimal attachment contexts.

An example of a passage we used appears in Table 1 (with presentation regions indicated by *, options indicated by /, and the critical region italicised). It is contrasted with the version of the same passage used by Altmann and Steedman (1988). We added some extraneous material to the end of eight of the passages to disguise the critical material, and segmented the introductory region into smaller regions than Altmann and Steedman used in their experiment 2 (while retaining their segmentation for the sentence with the critical region in it). Finally, we constructed a pair of wh-questions for each paragraph, one for the minimal attachment sentence and one for the non-minimal attachment sentence ("What did the burglar blow the safe open with?" and "What did the safe that the burglar blew open have?"). In addition, we constructed 24 filler passages which were generally similar to the experimental passages, but which did not have the temporary ambiguity that marked the experimental passages.

A total of 40 University of Massachusetts undergraduates were tested on the materials described above. Each read all 54 passages in an individually randomised order, verbally answering a wh-question after each passage. The experiment was controlled by a microcomputer which presented the phrases in a non-cumulative (as opposed to cumulative, as used by Altmann and Steedman) moving window fashion. The experimenter (who was informed of the correct answer by the microcomputer) typed in a code after each answer to indicate its correctness. The time taken to read each region, and the accuracy of the answers, were recorded.

[8]Only 30 passages were used, because a clerical mistake resulted in errors in the remaining two.

Results

The mean reading times for the region before the critical region and each region after that appear in Table 2. No effects approached significance in any region before the critical region. In the critical region, reading time for the minimal attachment sentence was less than for the non-minimal attachment sentence—740 *vs* 783 msec [significant by subjects: $F1(1,39) = 8.15$, $P < 0.01$; nearly significant by items: $F2(1,29) = 3.48$, $P < 0.07$]. The main effect of context (780 msec for the minimal attachment context, 745 msec for the non-minimal attachment context) was significant in the subjects analysis [$F1(1,39) = 4.61$, $P < 0.05$], but not in the items analysis [$F2(1,29) = 1.89$, $P > 0.10$]. The theoretically crucial interaction between context and sentence form did not approach significance ($F < 1$). The regions after the critical region produced no significant differences among any of the conditions. Performance on the wh-questions asked after each passage was quite good (88% correct overall). However, performance was lower on questions of non-minimal attachment sentences than of minimal attachment sentences [84 *vs* 91% correct overall: $F1(1,39) = 11.31$, $P < 0.01$; $F2(1,29) = 8.04$, $P < 0.01$], whereas the effect of context and the context × sentence interaction were not significant.

TABLE 2
Mean Reading Times by Segment (msec) and Proportion Correct

Context Bias	*Test Sentence*	*Region*				*Proportion Correct*
		Critical − 1 ("the safe")	*Critical ("with the dyamite/ new lock")*	*Critical + 1 ("and made off")*	*Critical + 2 ("with the loot")*	
MA	MA	560	762	702	752	0.92
MA	NMA	547	798	709	716	0.83
NMA	MA	532	721	710	722	0.90
NMA	NMA	549	770	710	701	0.85

Discussion

The experiment just reported found an apparent minimal attachment advantage, when one compares minimal and non-minimal sentences to each other in the same context. We do not want to take this finding at face value, because the passages were biased toward a minimal attachment preference: The antecedent of the minimal attachment NP occurred more recently in the passage than the antecedent of the non-minimal attachment

NP. However, we do take this finding to indicate that the concern raised about Altmann and Steedman's (1988) passages, that they were biased toward a non-minimal attachment preference, is a legitimate one. We believe that it is safe to conclude that Altmann and Steedman have no good evidence for a non-minimal attachment advantage.

We found no evidence for an interaction between context and sentence form, although the passages we used should have been equivalent to those used by Altmann and Steedman. We are puzzled by this; we had expected to find slow reading times for minimal attachment sentences in a non-minimal attachment context.[9] The fact that the distance between the introduction of the two antecedents in the non-minimal context condition and the critical region was greater in our materials than in Altmann and Steedman's, may have made the contrast between the two antecedents less salient to our subjects than to Altmann and Steedman's. Conversely, information about the instrument was less salient to Altmann and Steedman's subjects than to ours, and the unavailability of this information may have amplified the referential clash between non-minimal attachment context and minimal attachment sentences for Altmann and Steedman's subjects. This suspicion receives some support from the fact that question-answering accuracy was lower in our study for the non-minimal attachment sentences than for the minimal attachment sentences. Questions about non-minimal attachment sentences always required as an answer the information that potentially contrasted the two possible antecedents, whereas questions about minimal attachment sentences required the information about the instrument. We note further that we used a non-cumulative mode of presentation, whereas Altmann and Steedman used cumulative presentation. However, we do not pretend to have a coherent account for how differences such as these could have resulted in our finding of pure syntactic effects and Altmann and Steedman's findings of pure contextual effects. We can only reiterate our concerns that self-paced reading is disturbingly sensitive to task differences, and that it is probably unwise to make major theoretical conclusions based on the results of self-paced reading studies alone.

---

[9]In fact, we did find such an effect in a preliminary study conducted at the University of Alberta, although the effect appeared only in the final presentation region of the passages, two regions after the critical disambiguating region. This study used materials similar to those used in the study reported here, but (a) used the Altmann and Steedman-type segmentation for the sentences before the critical one; (b) ordered the use of proper names, definite NPs, and pronouns to refer to the main protagonist of the story differently, so that a proper name or a definite NP rather than a pronoun was used in the critical sentence; and (c) required the subjects to paraphrase each passage rather than answering a wh-question.

CONCLUSIONS

We have argued that a wide variety of phenomena supports the operation of syntactic processing strategies like Minimal Attachment and Late Closure. We further argued that very strong evidence would be needed to support the claim that some of these phenomena actually reflect referential processes, as Altmann and Steedman and their colleagues have proposed. Such a claim would leave the bulk of the syntactic garden-path phenomena unaccounted for (unless one is willing to claim that syntactic strategies that would logically result in all the phenomena, are actually the source of only some of them).

We believe that we have demonstrated that no such strong evidence exists. Instead, the most adequate evidence (especially Ferreira & Clifton, 1986) argues against Altmann and Steedman's claims. The arguments against the design that Ferreira and Clifton used, and in favour of a crossover design (Altmann & Steedman, 1988) are invalid, and much of the data presented by Altmann and Steedman as evidence against a single-analysis, garden-path theory, are actually consistent with such a theory. The only evidence that seemed to be inconsistent with such a theory now appears to have been an artefact of the order of mention of various NPs in Altmann and Steedman's materials.

We do acknowledge the possibility that contexts may exist that are strong enough to affect sentence parsing so quickly that it is difficult or impossible to distinguish between initial analysis decisions and reanalysis. We even acknowledge the possibility that some contexts may be strong enough to guide initial parsing decisions.[10] We do not think, though, that good evidence for either of these possibilities exists at the present time.

We suggest that, while it is worthwhile to continue to search for such contexts, an even more important task is to refine our theoretical analyses of how context and meaning generally might be used in sentence comprehension. From our immediate perspective, this means developing the analysis of a presumed thematic processor, a mechanism which we claim integrates syntactic and semantic/pragmatic analyses and provides the proper amount of limited parallelism in the sentence comprehension system (cf. Frazier, 1985; 1987a,b). More generally, it means developing new analyses of the role semantics and semantic interpretation might play in sentence comprehension. Altmann, Steedman, and their colleagues

[10]The contexts used by Perfetti (1990) may fall into one of these categories. One of two self-paced reading experiments Perfetti reported, had reading rates too slow (nearly 1 sec/word) to make any conclusions from. The other experiment resulted in reading rates that appear to have approximated 200 words/min, which is slower than normal reading but well within the range commonly reported for self-paced reading.

have made interesting contributions in this vein, but we believe that we have shown that their efforts presuppose a questionable semantic analysis and are based on empirical data that are less than definitive. We believe that, contrary to their arguments, there is good reason to develop models that assume a serial syntactic analyser, working in the first place quite independently of the systems responsible for processing truth, reference, and pragmatic relations.

REFERENCES

Aaronson, D. (1976). Performance theories for sentence coding: Some qualitative considerations. *Journal of Experimental Psychology: Human Performance and Perception*, *2*, 42–55.

Abney, S. (1989). A computational model of human parsing. *Journal of Psycholinguistic Research*, *18*, 129–144.

Ades, A. & Steedman, M. (1982). On the order of words. *Linguistics and Philosophy*, *4*, 517–558.

Altmann, G. (1987). Modularity and interaction in sentence processing. In G. Garfield (Ed.), *Modularity in knowledge representation and natural language processing*. Cambridge, Mass.: MIT Press.

Altmann, G. (1988). Ambiguity, parsing strategies, and computational models. *Language and Cognitive Processes*, *3*, 73–98.

Altmann, G. & Steedman, M. (1988). Interaction with context during human sentence processing. *Cognition*, *30*, 191–238.

Carlson, G. N. & Tanenhaus, M. K. (1988). Thematic roles and language comprehension. In W. Wilkins (Ed.), *Syntax and semantics. Vol. 21: Thematic relations*. London: Academic Press.

Clark, H. H. & Haviland, S. (1977). Sharing information between speaker and listener. In R. Freedle (Ed.), *Discourse comprehension and production*. Norwood, N.J.: Ablex.

Clark, H. H. & Sengul, C. J. (1979). In search of referents for nouns and pronouns. *Memory & Cognition*, *7*, 35–41.

Clifton, C., Jr. (1988). *Restrictions on late closure: Appearance and reality*. Paper presented at 6th Australian Language and Speech Conference, Sydney, August 1988.

Clifton, C., Jr. (in press). Syntactic modularity in sentence comprehension. In R. R. Hoffman & D. S. Palermo (Eds), *Cognitive psychology: The state of the art*. Hillsdale, N.J.: Lawrence Erlbaum Associates Inc.

Clifton, C., Jr. & Ferreira, F. (1987a). Discourse structure and anaphora: Some experimental results. In M. Coltheart (Ed.), *Attention and performance XII*. Hillsdale, N.J.: Lawrence Erlbaum Associates Inc.

Clifton, C., Jr. & Ferreira, F. (1987b). Modularity in sentence comprehension. In J. Garfield (Ed.), *Modularity in knowledge representation and natural language understanding*. Cambridge, Mass.: MIT Press.

Crain, S. & Steedman, M. (1985). On not being led up the garden path: The use of context by the psychological syntax processor. In D. R. Dowty, L. Karttunen, and A. M. Zwicky (Eds), *Natural language parsing*. Cambridge: Cambridge University Press.

Cuetos, F. & Mitchell, D. C. (1988). Cross-linguistic differences in parsing: Restrictions on the use of the Late Closure strategy in Spanish. *Cognition*, *30*, 73–105.

Ferreira, F. & Clifton, C., Jr. (1986). The independence of syntactic processing. *Journal of Memory and Language*, *25*, 348–368.

Ferreira, F. & Henderson, J. M. (in press). The use of verb information in syntactic parsing: A comparison of evidence from eye movements and segment-by-segment self-paced reading. *Journal of Experimental Psychology: Learning, Memory and Cognition.*

Fodor, J. A. (1983). *Modularity of mind.* Cambridge, Mass.: MIT Press.

Fodor, J. A., Bever, T. G., & Garrett, M. F. (1974). *The psychology of language: An introduction to psycholinguistics and generative grammar.* New York: McGraw-Hill.

Forster, K. I. (1979). Levels of processing and the structure of the language processor. In W. E. Cooper & E. C. T. Walker (Eds), *Sentence processing*, pp. 27–86. Hillsdale, N.J.: Lawrence Erlbaum Associates Inc.

Frazier, L. (1978). On comprehending sentences: Syntactic parsing strategies. Unpublished doctoral dissertation, University of Connecticut.

Frazier, L. (1985). Modularity and the representational hypothesis. *Proceedings of NELS 15*. Amherst, Mass.: GLSA (University of Massachusetts).

Frazier, L. (1987a). Sentence processing. In M. Coltheart (Ed.), *Attention and performance XII.* Hillsdale, N.J.: Lawrence Erlbaum Associates Inc.

Frazier, L. (1987b). Theories of sentence processing. In J. Garfield (Ed.), *Modularity in knowledge representation and natural language understanding.* Cambridge, Mass.: MIT Press.

Frazier, L. (1990). Parsing modifiers: Special purpose routines in the HSPM? In D. A. Balota, G. B. Flores d'Arcais, & K. Rayner (Eds), *Comprehension processes in reading.* Hillsdale, N.J.: Lawrence Erlbaum Associates Inc.

Frazier, L. (in press). Exploring the architecture of the language system. In G. Altmann (Ed.), *Cognitive models of speech processing: Psycholinguistic and computational perspectives.* Cambridge, Mass.: MIT Press.

Frazier, L. & Rayner, K. (1982). Making and correcting errors during sentence comprehension: Eye movements in the analysis of structurally ambiguous sentences. *Cognitive Psychology*, *14*, 178–210.

Gibbs, R. W., Jr. (1986). What makes some indirect speech acts conventional? *Journal of Memory and Language*, *25*, 181–196.

Graf, R. & Torrey, J. W. (1966). Perception of phrase structure in written language. *American Psychological Association Convention Proceedings*, 83–84.

Grice, H. P. (1975). Logic and conversation. In P. Cole & G. Morgan (Eds), *Syntax and semantics III.* London: Academic Press.

Halff, H. M., Ortony, A., & Anderson, R. C. (1976). A context-sensitive representation of word meanings. *Memory & Cognition*, *4*, 378–383.

Haviland, S. E. & Clark, H. H. (1974). What's new? Acquiring new information as a process in comprehension. *Journal of Verbal Learning and Verbal Behavior*, *13*, 512–521.

Just, M. A., Carpenter, P. A., & Woolley, J. D. (1982). Paradigms and processes in reading comprehension. *Journal of Experimental Psychology: General*, *111*, 228–238.

Kempson, R. M. (1977). *Semantic theory.* Cambridge: Cambridge University Press.

Kennedy, A. & Murray, W. S. (1984). Inspection times for words in syntactically ambiguous sentences under three presentation conditions. *Journal of Experimental Psychology: Human Perception and Performance*, *10*, 833–847.

Levinson, S. C. (1983). *Pragmatics.* Cambridge: Cambridge University Press.

Marslen-Wilson, W. & Tyler, L. K. (1987). Against modularity. In J. Garfield (Ed.), *Modularity in knowledge representation and natural language understanding.* Cambridge, Mass: MIT Press.

Mitchell, D. C. & Holmes, V. M. (1985). The role of specific information about the verb in parsing sentences with local structural ambiguity. *Journal of Memory and Language*, *24*, 542–559.

Morrow, D. G. & Clark, H. H. (1988). Interpreting words in spatial descriptions. *Language and Cognitive Processes*, *3*, 275–292.

Murphy, G. L. (1984). Establishing and accessing referents in discourse. *Memory & Cognition*, *12*, 489–497.

Perfetti, C. A. (1990). The cooperative language processors: Semantic influences in an autonomous syntax. In D. Balota, G. B. Flores d'Arcais, & K. Rayner (Eds), *Comprehension processes in reading*. Hillsdale, N.J.: Lawrence Erlbaum Associates Inc.

Portner, P. (1989). Processing indefinite noun phrases in quantified sentences. Unpublished paper, Department of Linguistics, University of Massachusetts.

Rayner, K. & Frazier, L. (1987). Parsing temporarily ambiguous complements. *Quarterly Journal of Experimental Psychology*, *39A*, 657–673.

Rayner, K., Carlson, M., & Frazier, L. (1983). The interaction of syntax and semantics during sentence processing: Eye movements in the analysis of semantically biased sentences. *Journal of Verbal Learning and Verbal Behavior*, *22*, 358–3.

Russell, B. (1905). On denoting. *Mind*, *14*, 479–493.

Speer, S. (1988). Syntactic and thematic contributions to on-line sentence comprehension. Unpublished doctoral dissertation, University of Texas.

Speer, S., Foss, D., & Smith, C. (1986). Syntactic and thematic contributions to sentence complexity. *Paper presented at the Annual Meeting of the Psychonomic Society*, New Orleans.

Steedman, M. (1987). Combinatory grammars and human sentence processing. In J. Garfield (Ed.), *Modularity in knowledge representation and human sentence processing*. Cambridge, Mass.: MIT Press.

Stowe, L. (1989). Thematic structures and sentence comprehension. In G. N. Carlson & M. K. Tanenhaus (Eds), *Linguistic structure in language processing*. Dordrecht: Kluwer Academic.

Stowe, L. & Cupples, L. (1989). Animacy and reduced relative clauses. *Paper presented at Second Annual CUNY Sentence Processing Conference*, New York City, March.

Strawson, P. F. (1950). On referring. *Mind*, *59*, 320–344.

Tanenhaus, M., Carlson, G., & Seidenberg, M. (1985). Do listeners compute linguistic representations? In D. R. Dowty, L. Karttunen, & A. M. Zwicky (Eds), *Natural language parsing*. Cambridge: Cambridge University Press.

Tanenhaus, M., Carlson, G., Boland, J., & Garnsey, S. (1989). Parsing dative questions: Lexical projection and the interaction of syntax and semantics in parsing. *Paper presented at Second Annual CUNY Sentence Processing Conference*, New York City, March.

Taraban, R. & McClelland, J. R. (1988). Constituent attachment and thematic role assignment in sentence processing: Influences of content-based expectations. *Journal of Memory and Language*, *27*, 597–632.

Trueswell, J. C., Tanenhaus, M. K., & Garnsey, S. M. (1989). Immediate thematic influence in sentence processing. *Poster presented at Second Annual CUNY Sentence Processing Conference*, New York City, March.

Warner, J. & Glass, A. L. (1987). Context and distance-to-disambiguation effects in ambiguity resolution: Evidence from grammaticality judgements of garden path sentences. *Journal of Memory and Language*, *26*, 714–738.

LANGUAGE AND COGNITIVE PROCESSES, 1989, *4*, (3/4) SI 105–122

Ambiguity in Context: A Reply

Mark Steedman and Gerry Altmann
Department of Computer and Information Science, University of Pennsylvania, Philadelphia, U.S.A., and Laboratory of Experimental Psychology, University of Sussex, Brighton, U.K.

This paper shows that models of sentence comprehension based on "weak interaction" between syntax and interpretive processes are theoretically well-founded. According to this theory, local syntactic ambiguities can be resolved as soon as they are encountered in a single left-to-right pass through the sentence, by distinguishing the alternative partial analyses on the basis of their semantic and referential appropriateness to the context of utterance. This "incremental–interactive" theory is compared with an alternative serial structural strategy-based model proposed by Frazier and others, including Clifton and Ferreira. Particular attention is paid to a component of this theory that has been called the "Thematic Processor". This component has hitherto remained somewhat under-specified, but we examine a number of possible interpretations. We argue that the only reasonable interpretation of the thematic processor is as a mechanism identical in every respect with the incremental weakly interactive processor that we ourselves propose. We conclude that the additional postulation of parsing strategies, in particular Minimal Attachment, may be unnecessary.

INTRODUCTION

Clifton and Ferreira (this issue; henceforth "C & F") address claims that we and our colleagues have made in a number of earlier papers [Crain, 1980; Crain & Steedman, 1985 (written and presented in 1981); Altmann, 1987, 1988; Altmann & Steedman, 1988; Steedman, 1989; henceforth collectively "we", and occasionally "C & S", "A & S", etc.]. These claims concern the nature of the information used by the human sentence proces-

We thank Chuck Clifton and Fernanda Ferreira for agreeing to the publication of this reply to their paper in this volume.
Requests for reprints should be addressed to Mark Steedman, Department of Computer and Information Science, University of Pennsylvania, 200 South 33rd Street, Philadelphia, Pennsylvania 19104–6389, U.S.A.

sing mechanism in order to resolve local syntactic ambiguity during parsing. We argued that human processors resolve syntactic attachment ambiguities by comparing the rival syntactic analyses in terms of the referential properties of their interpretations with respect to the discourse context, represented as a model. We further argued that this process could occur at or very soon after the point of local ambiguity, i.e. that it could be carried out on the basis of *partial* syntactic analyses and interpretations, "more or less word by word".[1] We offered empirical support for this claim for the class of attachment ambiguities that Frazier called "Minimal Attachment Ambiguities", illustrated by the following (globally) ambiguous sentence:

1. The teacher told the girl that the boy liked the story.

To do this, we considered sentences which were globally *un*-ambiguous, but which included the same local ambiguity between a simplex and a complex NP following the word *girl* as in the following (simplified) example:

2a. The teacher told the girl that the boy kissed to feed the gerbils.
b. The teacher told the girl that the boy kissed the gerbils.

Frazier (1978, *passim*) argued, following Bever and Kimball, that the ambiguity between the simplex (NP plus S′) and complex (NP plus NP) analyses of such sentences was resolved on the basis of the "Minimal Attachment" parsing strategy, which disfavours analyses involving adjunction. She thus claimed to account for the fact that when such sentences are presented in isolation, the simplex NP analysis is preferred.

In contrast, we argued that the ambiguity between the rival readings was resolved on the basis of the degree to which they were "referentially supported" by the context. We defined referential support in terms of the concept of presupposition, arguing that definite NPs presuppose the presence in the discourse model of a uniquely identifiable entity having certain properties. When definite NPs include restrictive modifiers, as does the complex NP *the girl that the boy kissed*, we argued that they further presuppose the presence in the model of a *set* of entities, girls in the case to hand, for the modifier to restrict *over*, one being uniquely identifiable by virtue of the property denoted by the modifier. We argued that in the context of prior discourse establishing a unique girl in the model, the simplex NP analysis would be preferred. Of course, this prediction also follows from the minimal attachment strategy. However, we also argued that in contexts in which prior discourse had established more than one

[1]We were careful to distinguish attachment ambiguities from certain lexical subcategorisation ambiguities in this respect (cf. Steedman, 1989, p. 492 and note 22).

girl, and which thus supported the presuppositions of the complex analysis and not those of the simplex analysis, it would be the former analysis that would be supported, contrary to the minimal attachment proposal. We further argued that the so-called "null" context, in which there was no prior discourse at all, was a context in which any presuppositions had to be accommodated by the addition of further information to the model. In such a context, we argued that the simplex analysis would be favoured under a "Principle of Parsimony", because it carried fewest presuppositions, and therefore required fewest changes to the model.

Among a number of further specifications of the mechanism involved, we made the following specific points:

1. The influence of interpretation and reference upon syntactic processing was strictly limited to the "weak" process of evaluating the relative fit to the context of the interpretations of autonomously produced syntactic analyses.
2. The rival analyses must be presented for adjudication by this process *in parallel*.
3. The interpretations in question could be constructed "incrementally, more or less word by word". That is, interpretations could be constructed and evaluated, and the corresponding analyses favoured or disfavoured, well before the constituents in question were syntactically complete.[2] In the case of nominal modifiers, for example, we argued that this might happen as soon as a potential relative pronoun or preposition revealed the possibility of a modifier analysis. It followed that the process of weeding out pragmatically disfavoured analyses could proceed with great fineness of grain, again more or less word by word, and that the time for which the rival attachment analyses had to be maintained in parallel could be strictly circumscribed, as it must be to explain garden-path effects.[3]

As under this account there is no such thing as a truly neutral context, we also pointed out that the only way in which the predictions of the incremen-

---

[2]See Steedman (1989) for a discussion of the implications of this proposal for the theory of grammar.

[3]We shall use the term "garden path" strictly in its original sense to refer to the situation in which the processor can find no syntactic analysis whatever for a grammatical sentence, as a result of misresolving an early local syntactic ambiguity. Unlike C & F, we distinguish this eventuality from the case in which the processor merely shows evidence of increased difficulty due to local ambiguity, but does arrive at an analysis. We shall argue that the former phenomenon provides very strong information concerning the activities of the processor, and can be distinguished experimentally from the latter.

tally interactive theory could be empirically distinguished from the predictions of the structural strategy was to create minimal pairs of contexts differing only in the number of referents and their properties, and to use the target sentences like (2) as their own controls by *crossing* context and targets. The investigation of felicitous contexts and targets was not enough.

We have presented several experiments constructed on this basis, involving a number of different constructions, and using a number of different response measures. All of these experiments support the incremental–interactive hypothesis, and fail to support the Minimal Attachment hypothesis.

C & F criticise these proposals on three grounds. First, they criticise our definition of referential support in terms of the concept of presupposition. Second, they argue that our claim for very fine grain incremental interpretation and parallel adjudication is equally incoherent, and that the "thematic processor" with which the structural-strategy based theory has recently been enriched provides a better account of the effects of interpretation in parsing. Third, they offer experimental evidence which is claimed to show that our own results are contaminated by an artefact. They concede that this does not show our result to be invalid, but argue that the serial processor using structural strategies, when augmented with a "thematic processor", provides a better explanation. We will examine these three criticisms and their alternative proposal in turn.

THE CONCEPT OF PRESUPPOSITION

The term "presupposition" is notoriously fraught with different meanings and different theory-dependent technical definitions. For example, Soames (1989) ends his review of the question for the *Handbook of Philosophical Logic* (by which we are guided in this note) by remarking that "presupposition may not be a single phenomenon with a unitary explanation, but rather a domain of related issues involving the interaction of several semantic and pragmatic principles". It is for that reason that we have always been very careful (1) to be clear that we use the term simply because it has a common language use that we feel makes our theory intuitively easy to grasp, (2) to avoid nailing our colours to any particular one of the available formalisms, and (3) to ground the notion in a completely explicit, though informal, model-based account of the changing context of discourse and the particular varieties of reference that we are concerned with (cf. Crain & Steedman, 1985, p. 352, note 1; Altmann & Steedman, 1988, p. 199, note 2).

The first part of C & F's critique can be summarised as the following argument.

1. C & F set up Frege's notion of "logical" of "semantic" presupposition, claiming that this is the notion that we have in mind for the definiteness presupposition.
2. They then show that the entailments of restrictive modifiers in definites are not presuppositions in this sense, because they can be cancelled. Their example is the following sentence:

   iii. The unicorn that Bill saw was the only unicorn there ever was.

   According to our account, the use of restrictive relative modifiers presupposes the existence in the context of a set of unicorns, one of which is uniquely identifiable by virtue of Bill seeing it. C & F claim that the supposed presupposition is denied by the predicate, which asserts that the cardinality of the set of unicorns is one. Because the sentence does not lack a truth value, the presupposition in question cannot be a logical presupposition.
3. We therefore must have in mind a different notion of presupposition, namely "pragmatic presupposition".
4. Pragmatic presupposition "may not be distinct from" the notion of conversational implicature, a claim attributed to Levinson.
5. Conversational implicatures are non-detachable, i.e. they are not tied to linguistic form but to semantic content, a claim attributed to Grice. C & F claim that it follows that such implicatures cannot be acccessed until the listener has completed the parse, contrary to the incremental interactive hypothesis.
6. C & F conclude that it is unlikely that referential factors play a part in parsing.

The introduction of the Fregean concept of logical presupposition is something of a red herring. The fact that our theory is phrased in terms of a *changing* model-based discourse context, and in particular that in our discussion of the uniqueness presupposition of the definite we explicitly invoke the Stalnaker/Lewis/Heim concept of "accommodating" presuppositions, seems to us to make it obvious that our notion of presupposition is pragmatic, and that this notion applies to the definite itself, not merely to the modifier (Altmann & Steedman, 1988, pp. 203–204). C & F's unicorn sentence merely serves to emphasise the point: The predicate does not deny the (pragmatic) presupposition of the relative clause that there is a set of unicorns *in the discourse*. In the absence of any more specific information about the context of utterance, the set in question is something like the denotation of the word "unicorn"—roughly, the set of unicorns in all possible worlds, if that is how you happen to conceive your model theory. The set of unicorns in the predicate is clearly a quite different set, namely the set of unicorns in (what the speaker regards as) the *real* world. We did not commit ourselves to any particular formalisation of the pragmatic notion, or indeed to the existence of a fundamental distinction between pragmatic and logical presupposition, because we regard the jury as still out on this question, as Soames' remark suggests is only prudent. However, we do not think that there is anything in our theory that could not be directly expressed in terms of such alternatives as possible worlds (Stalnaker, 1973) or conventional implicatures (Karttunen & Peters, 1979), or the discourse representations offered by Kamp (1968) and Heim (1982). For that matter, we interpret Stalnaker (1973, p. 452; cf. Soames, 1989, p. 568) as indicating that such semantics are in turn ultimately reducible to the notion of logical presupposition, via the enriched notion of model offered by concepts such as possible worlds.

What we do *not* believe is that the notion of presupposition shoud be subsumed under the notion of conversational implicature. We are not alone in this opinion, as Karttunen and Peters' recourse to a quite opposite component of Grice's theory should already have suggested. Even the cited authority (Levinson, 1983, cf. pp. 217–225) is singularly tentative in making this suggestion, and notes a number of potential objections. Perhaps the most serious from C & F's perspective, since they make so much of the non-detachability of conversational implicature, is that presuppositions *do* seem to be detachable in Grice's terms. To use Levinson's (1983, p. 223) own example of the cleft construction, the pragmatic presupposition (b) of sentence (a) seems precisely to depend on the construction in question. The truth-conditionally equivalent (c) does not *presuppose* (b), any more than it presupposes that *Harry ate something*:[4]

4a. It was Harry who ate the beans.
b. Someone ate the beans.
c. Harry ate the beans.

Even if we were to be persuaded by this extremely questionable proposal to subsume the notion of pragmatic presupposition under the notion of conversational implicature, and to come to believe, contrary to all appearances and most received opinion, that presuppositions like the above were in fact non-detachable, none of the consequences claimed by C & F would follow. Speech Act Theory does indeed claim that conversational implicature proceeds from literal meaning to implicature via inference. But there is nothing in the concept of literal meaning that restricts it to the meanings of *sentences*, preventing conversational inference from acting until after

[4]Levinson offers a counterargument for some other factive varieties of presupposition, but he himself concludes that "it is too early to know whether or not this approach, or something similar, is ultimately viable" (1983, p. 225).

parsing is complete. There is therefore nothing in our conception of presupposition *or anyone else's* that makes referential factors unlikely *a priori* to play a part in processing.

In fact, this whole argument is quite orthogonal to the question at hand. We wrote at some length on how our concept of presupposition was grounded in the process of reference to the discourse model, for the class of referring expressions with which we were concerned. To question whether this class of presuppositions could be considered as a subset of some *other* class of phenomena, and whether the mechanism we describe will generalise to the larger class, may be an amusing intellectual exercise. But it is to mistake our purpose in advancing the mechanism in the first place. That purpose was to provide a simple and intuitively clear exemplar of how a weakly interactive processor could in principle be instantiated. The important question is not whether our mechanisms are a special case of conversational implicature, conventional implicature, or anything else, but whether they demonstrate that our concept of a weakly interactive processor is coherent. Because C & F also call this matter into question, we will turn to that part of their argument next.

THE ARCHITECTURE OF A WEAKLY INTERACTIVE PROCESSOR

There are three strands to this part of the critique. Because these strands are essentially unrelated, we will simply take them in turn.

The first charge is that our mechanism for the incremental evaluation of definite NPs will not generalise to other syntactic categories. We discuss this process in terms of the incremental narrowing of "partially evaluated referents", represented as sets of entities in the domain which satisfy the constraints imposed by the part of the expression so far encountered. The example that is offered concerns adjectives like "good", "big", and "fake", which are asserted not to permit narrowing of the set of referents in advance of the head noun.

We agree that semantics is complicated, and that there are all kinds of intensional phenomena which require more elaborate semantic structures than the primitive extensional models that we invoke. There is even less of a consensus as to which if any of the many available alternative semantic formalisms does the best job overall than in the earlier case of the nature of presupposition. However, we note that it is not uncommon for such semantics to be grounded in some form of set-theoretically founded model theory. The reason that we confined our claims to the phenomenon of Minimal Attachment (although we have always made it clear that we believe that the same explanation applies to Frazier's other major domain of attachment phenomena, i.e. Right Association/Late Closure) was partly because it was a domain in which we could demonstrate our theory with a simple and uncontroversial notion of model.[5] We do not believe that our semantics for this limited domain is incompatible with *any* of the many rival proposals for formalising natural language semantics, or that the problem of large or infinite sets that seems to worry C & F is any more serious for us than it is for any of them. We have to agree that it is "worthwhile to continue searching for more generally adequate principles of incremental semantic evaluation" by investigating such questions. Meanwhile, our intention was the more modest one of providing an existence proof for such principles, and to illustrate their use in weakly interactive parsing, *without* having to solve every problem in model-theoretic semantics as well.

C & F's second charge is directed against our claim that (the interpretations of) rival partial syntactic analyses are evaluated in parallel. We made this claim on the grounds that semantic and referential plausibility are not all-or-none properties like syntactic well-formedness, but are relative. We also made it clear that the theory allowed the discrimination of the alternatives to occur very rapidly, more or less at the point of ambiguity itself (Altmann & Steedman, 1988, pp. 202 and 208, and note 5). C & F claim in a footnote that this proposal "implicitly [contains] a minimal-attachment-like assumption, according to which unnecessary structure is not built". They appear to suggest that, if our processor can at the point of ambiguity in sentences like (1) consider in parallel the interpretations of a simplex NP *the girl* and an NP with a modifier *the girl* . . ., then it is only via an arbitrary restriction that it does not consider an NP with a modifier that contains an NP with a modifier *the girl that the boy that* . . . .

Such is not the case. Our claim has always been the one reiterated in the introduction to this paper as the third property of our model (see, e.g. Altmann & Steedman, 1988, p. 201 for a discussion of the "Principle of Referential Support"). We argue for a theory of grammar in which fragments like *the girl* . . . are syntactic entities complete with interpretations. We have argued at length on purely linguistic grounds for this theory of syntax, which is lexicalist in flavour, and is based on a generalisation of Categorial Grammar (cf. Steedman, 1987, 1989 and references therein). According to this theory, such entities are, both syntactically and semantically, *functions*. For example, the interpretation of *the girl* . . . is a function over properties, like $\lambda x.likes'(boy', x)$. Some of our colleagues have gone a long way towards providing a computable semantics to represent such interpretations, using the incremental assembly of constraint-satisfaction

[5]The reason that we have not applied our claims to Late Closure, is that the central examples frequently involve intensional complements.

networks as a vehicle (see Haddock, 1987, and references therein). According to these theories, the (complete) interpretation of the complete simplex NP *the girl* and the (incomplete) interpretation of the incomplete complex NP *the girl* . . . are compared on the basis of the Principle of Referential Support *as soon as they are built, before the string is analysed any further*. These interpretations amount to the rival claims that there is either exactly one entity in the model which is a girl, or that there is exactly one entity in the model which is a girl and which has some other property which is currently unbound, or unknown. If the constraints imposed by one analysis are not supported, whereas those of the other are supported, or if one requires more elaborate changes to accommodate the model to it than the other, then the less supported analysis will be discontinued, under the aforesaid principle. The remainder of the string will then be analysed. If it is not consistent with the earlier ambiguity resolution, then a garden-path effect may result. In A & S, we suggest that such a system can be implemented as a network constraint-satisfaction system of the kind proposed by Haddock (1987; this issue) with structure-sharing between alternative analyses.

Because the ambiguity is resolved on the basis of *partial* analyses, as soon as the locally ambiguous word *that* is encountered, and before the modifier itself is fully processed, the question of whether the modifier contains an NP at all, let alone a modified one, does not arise. Of course, in sentence (1) there *is* a local ambiguity as to whether *the boy* . . . is simplex or complex, and that too will eventually have to be resolved by the same referential criteria. But this is an incremental left-to-right processor. It simply has not got there yet.

Having claimed that our proposal for incremental interpretation and parsing via the weak interaction is semantically ill-motivated, and that our proposal for parallel consideration of alternatives is unsound, C & F somewhat surprisingly go on to make the further claim that both of these properties are anyway characteristic of the serial-strategic processor. This claim makes appeal to a component of their theory called the "thematic processor". It is a comparatively late addition to the model, and we think it deserves a section all to itself.

THE THEMATIC PROCESSOR

The empirical problem for the structural strategic model has always been the existence of true garden-path effects, in the traditional sense of the term, coupled with the steady growth of evidence that semantics and especially referential context could control them. The evidence from experiments like the one sketched at the start of this paper suggests that manipulations of referential context cannot only prevent the classic garden-path effects, but can create garden-path effects where there are not classically supposed to be any, that is where the minimal attachment strategy would yield a parse if it were followed. Even though the long-suffering jury is arguably still out on this question as well, for once a verdict seems in sight.

The problem that these data pose for the original structural strategic account proposed by Frazier (1978) is the following (cf. Altmann & Steedman, 1988, pp. 210–212; Steedman, 1989, pp. 496–497): The structural-strategic processor itself is by definition serial, and must always blindly produce the minimal attachment analysis in its first pass. On occasion, a garden path will result from which the parser will be unable to recover. If manipulations of referential context can *prevent* this effect, then the only way that this can happen is by re-starting the parser, and looking for an alternative analysis, at a cost in processing that we might expect to show up on some appropriate response measure.

The problem for the original serial non-interactive processor is that this explanation of the contextual effect now fails to explain why such sentences *ever* garden path, in the strict sense of failing to produce any analysis. At the end of the first (minimally attaching) pass, the syntax blocks, and presumably the processor has access to the fact that the NP it has produced fails to refer. But how can we explain the fact that it will *only* be able to find the alternative syntactic analysis *in those contexts in which the resulting NP will in fact refer*, and will fail to find that syntactic analysis *at all* if the analysis is not in fact referentially supported by the context? As we have noted before, it is a strange serial non-interactive processor indeed that has foresight about the compatibility with the context of an analysis which it has not yet built because it is serial, and that allows the success of such purely syntactic processes as reanalysis to be determined by referential effects to which it can have no access because it is non-interactive.

It is presumably in direct response to this problem that the advocates of the structural-strategic model have included the thematic processor in the structural-strategic model.

The discussion in Frazier (1987, pp. 301–302) makes it clear that this device works by accessing the thematic frames that are associated with verbs and other heads of phrases via their lexical entries. The thematic processor selects the most plausible thematic assignment of arguments such as nounphrases, with the benefit of discourse and real world knowledge. If the most plausible frame is not consistent with the first-pass syntactic analysis, then the thematic processor "can alert the syntactic processor to the presence of a potentially more plausible analysis". This prescription is somewhat unspecific. It is compatible with a number of interpretations, some of which strike us as very dangerous. It could be taken as claiming that such assignments can be made entirely independently of syntax.

However, such a claim would clearly go against the modularity hypothesis of Fodor (1983).[6] The proposal could also be interpreted as meaning that the thematic assignments, however they are made, can affect the priorities of the parser, making it find analyses that it would otherwise miss. However, such a proposal amounts to postulating the *strong* interaction, and therefore also compromises modularity. C & F are clearly aware of these dangers, and describe the device as follows (the italics are ours):

> The thematic processor presumably uses thematic role preferences, discourse context, and world knowledge to choose the preferred analysis of a sentence. *It considers, in parallel, all possible assignments of arguments and adjuncts to syntactic positions within syntactic domains defined by the syntactic processor*, and proposes attractive alternative assignments to the syntactic processor.

C & F further claim that "nothing in [their theory] is inconsistent with word-by-word interpretation, and in fact such immediate interpretation is demanded by the thematic processor".

We can see only one way to interpret this admirably explicit proposal. It stems from the observation that "thematic frames" are simply the semantic correlates of syntactic subcategorisations. Such frames, therefore, collectively constitute what we and other adherents to the broad church of the lexicalist hypothesis would call (the language-specific component of) *the grammar of the language*. Once that is understood, a major problem with the above proposal is resolved. C & F imply in the passage quoted above that the syntactic domains for the assignment of thematic arguments can be defined by the serial strategic processor. But of course that is impossible, because by definition it can only deliver *one* analysis at a time. It must be that the syntactic alternatives that they refer to are defined *via the grammatical information implicit in the subcategorisation frames in the lexicon*. If so, it is clear that the thematic processor has the following characteristics:

1. It is confined to the weak interaction.
2. It considers possible assignments of function–argument relations in parallel and subject to syntactic domains permitted by the grammar, which is lexically-based, *contra* Frazier (1989).
3. It demands incremental interpretation.

This prescription has a familiar sound to it. It is in fact exactly the processor outlined at the beginning of this paper, the one that we have argued for all along.

---

[6]Similar claims from within the AI literature of the early 1970s were in fact the central target of Fodor's tract.

This observation provokes the following reaction: If *that* is what the thematic processor is, who could want anything *more*? Who needs the serial strategic processor? What is the point of proposing "attractive alternative assignments" to the thing, when those assignments are apparently already available, both syntactically and semantically? It has been argued in the past that the serial syntactic analyser is there to provide a fast and computationally cheap first guess. However, recent studies suggest that at least some kinds of non-syntactic information become available and are used very early on during processing (Stowe, 1988; Taraban & McClelland, 1988, Trueswell et al., submitted). In particular, there is abundant evidence to suggest that the referential process is initiated as soon as a nounphrase is encountered. As Sanford and Garrod (this issue) put it, "evidence is also strong for a rapid completion of [this] process, whose results feed into the interpretation of subsequent material in the sentence . . . there is no evidence to suggest that a full nounphrase ever receives delayed interpretation" (see also Fodor's review, this issue, which describes a number of studies using the cross-modal priming technique to demonstrate the rapid reactivation of antecedents to empty NP categories). If the effects of semantics and context are this fast, the strategy-based first-pass parser seems entirely redundant. Because the involvement of a thematic processor leaves it unclear that there remains any imaginable empirical result that would falsify the theory as a whole, we suggest that the first-pass serial-strategic parser should now be quietly retired, under the usual procedure for under-employed theoretical assumptions.

EMPIRICAL EVIDENCE

C & F also offer three criticisms of our experimental findings. The first concerns the use of self-paced reading times as a response measure by A & S. The second concerns our insistence on crossing contexts and targets. The third concerns the possibility that the results in A & S are contaminated by a recency-of-mention effect.

We freely acknowledge that self-paced reading times have serious limitations as a measure of real-time processing load. We have an open mind on the question of whether eye-movement measures are much better, but then so do C & F. There seems to be substantial agreement here that all of our experiments so far must be regarded as pilots, and must be redone with refinements in design and measures on all sides. We would point out, however, that in C & S we used a different measure in the central experiment, namely real-time grammaticality judgements. While grammaticality judgements are comparatively slow, and do not yield information about the locus of processing effects, they do distinguish two different *consequences* of such effects, in that they do distinguish between mere processing difficulty and true garden paths, i.e. *unrecoverable* difficulties arising from the processor's first choice of analysis. While we note that C & F and their colleagues tend to conflate these two phenomena (cf. their note 2), it will be clear from our earlier discussion that we regard the difference as bearing crucial information. If the processor is unable to find *any* analysis for a sentence for which the minimal attachment strategy would find an analysis, just in case that sentence is preceded by a non-minimal attachment context, then that fact provides rather strong evidence against the strategy.

We are less impressed by C & F's argument against crossing contexts and targets. It is true that, for measures like self-paced reading that could be argued under their assumptions to "conflate analysis time and reanalysis time", it can be claimed that crossed contexts do not crucially distinguish the two theories. However, this is not true for the grammaticality judgements used in C & S. Nor, if their claims are to be believed, is it true of C & F's own measure of choice, eye movements. Because we all agree that there is no such thing as a truly neutral context, we can see no other way to investigate contextual effects than by contrasting facilitatory with inhibitory effects. We cannot understand C & F's reluctance to do such experiments themselves, given the properties that they claim for their measure.

Our perplexity is only deepened by their argument in favour of the experimental design that they regard as an alternative to crossing contexts and targets, which uses what they call a "neutral" context. While conceding our point that *no* context is referentially neutral with respect to attachment ambiguities (see Altmann & Steedman, 1988, pp. 202–204, esp. note 8), they offer the following argument in support of their design:

1. Since there is no such thing as a neutral context, the "neutral context" will either be similar to the MA-supporting context, or to the NMA-supporting context, or will be somewhere intermediate between the two. In the extreme, it may have the same effect, in terms of referential support, as either the MA- or NMA-supporting context. Or it may have an intermediate effect.
2. Consequently, we can predict that the "neutral context" should have *some* effect on the targets, in comparison with the MA- and NMA-supporting contexts: either the MA target, or the NMA target, or both, should be inhibited, although we can't predict *which*.
3. The experiments of Ferreira and Clifton (1986) fail to show such an effect of the "neutral context" on *either* target.

We have two reactions to this argument. The first is a theoretical point: If there were such an effect, what *else* could it be but an effect of crossing context with one or both of the targets? To the extent that this design is valid at all, it is simply a very weak version of the crossed context design. So why use a weak design when a strong one is available? But we also seriously question whether the design *is* in fact valid. The weakness of Ferreira and Clifton's instantiation of the context-crossing paradigm is precisely that *we know nothing about the effect of the so-called "neutral context"*. We argued (Altmann & Steedman, 1988, pp. 203–204; cf. footnote 8) that any given context can only support *either* the MA analysis *or* the NMA analysis of a given NP. We further argued that so-called neutral contexts were simply contexts which individual subjects could take either way. Under this interpretation, Ferreira and Clifton's neutral context conditions are simply conditions under which an unknown proportion of the subjects have established an MA-supporting model, while the rest have set up an NMA-supporting model. To the extent that Ferreira and Clifton succeed in devising materials that are neutral in the sense of making the alternatives equally likely, it is true that we would expect an inhibitory overall effect for both targets (albeit a weaker one than we could have obtained by *really* crossing the contexts). However, we do not know anything about the way the subjects *actually* took the contexts. In particular, we have no reason to suppose that the proportion of those interpreting neutral contexts as NMA supporting to those interpreting them as MA supporting was constant across the NMA and MA targets. The result is that we simply do not know where on the dimension from totally crossed to totally uncrossed these materials taken as a whole lie.

Some of our favourite experiments report null results. But any experiment claiming that manipulation of an independent variable fails to affect a dependent variable must show that the manipulation was successful. It follows that the "neutral context" design is only meaningful if there is adequate pre-testing or post-testing to determine which choice subjects are making. This has not typically been done. The reason is that it is very hard. We think that the obvious way to make it easier is to find some contexts which *force* one interpretation or the other. But that of course is the whole point of crossing contexts and targets. In such a design, a context which is *known* to have a consistent facilitative effect on one target is shown to have an inhibitory effect on another, where the targets differ only in their requirements for contextual support.

C & F's third point concerns the possibility, which we ourselves acknowledged in A & S, and which was first pointed out to us by Janet Fodor, that our results there could be contaminated by the following fact. The antecedent to the NP in the disambiguating prepositional phrase (PP) was further away in contexts supporting attachment of the PP as a verb modifier than in those supporting attachment as an NP modifier. If distance between antecedent and NP affects reading time, then the NP attachment would be advantaged by this arrangement, and the VP attachment disadvantaged.

This could then explain why the non-minimal attachment target was read faster than the minimal attachment target when each was preceded by its respectively felicitous context. C & F report an experiment in which they attempt to reverse this effect, modifying the context materials we used, so as to make the antecedent to the critical NP nearer in the case of contexts supporting (minimally attached) VP modifier targets than it would for those supporting (non-minimally attached) NP modifier targets. If there were such a facilitating effect, it should now work in favour of minimal attachment (MA) targets, rather than non-minimally attached ones (NMA). They report that in this case, reading times to the critical disambiguating PP were no faster for the non-minimal (NP) attachment than for the minimal (VP) attachment. C & F claim that this finding calls into question the results we reported in A & S.

The experiment C & F describe is interesting. We would not be surprised were it demonstrated that such effects exist, and if our original finding of an advantage of NMA–NMA conditions over MA–MA conditions were an artefact. (Such a demonstration would not of course in itself show our major claim to be untrue, as that claim depends upon the comparison of these two uncrossed conditions with the corresponding *crossed* conditions.) However, C & F themselves comment on a number of problems with the results. Not least among these is the finding that the (marginally) *fastest* condition was the one in which a minimally attached target sentence was preceded by the context supporting *non*-minimal attachment (which we refer to as the NMA–MA condition). This context is the one in which the narrative (cf. C & F, table 1) includes a phrase like "there was a safe which had a new lock and a safe which had an old lock", and thereby introduces two possible referents for the crucial nounphrase, such as "the safe" in the familiar example:

5. The burglar blew open the safe with the dynamite and made off with the loot.

We find this result particularly strange, because this context leaves the simplex NP "the safe" in the target with no unique referent. In A & S, we found that this condition was the *slowest*, our explanation being that of all four conditions (two contexts crossed with two targets) this was the only one in which "the safe" remained unresolved (i.e. no unique referent could be identified). It is interesting to ask why in C & F's experiment this condition was actually slightly faster than the MA–MA condition, in which the same target was preceded by a felicitous context in which only one safe was introduced. Why should the referential difficulty associated with the infelicitous NMA–MA condition make this marginally the fastest? C & F themselves explicitly state that according to both their theory and our own, this condition should be reflected in *slower* reading times. The most obvious explanation is that the subjects are not paying any attention to the contextual materials.

There is good reason to suppose that such may be the case. The experiment reported by C & F differed in one crucial respect (other than distance of antecedent to the disambiguating NP) from the description we gave of our experiment in A & S. In the phrasal experiment reported there, we asked two yes/no questions. The first question asked for information which was contained *only* in the context, and the second asked for information contained only within the target, so we could be quite sure that context had been attended to. By contrast, C & F had subjects answer a single wh-question at the end of each text. In order to answer correctly, however, it was not necessary that the subject retain *any* information contained within the context. The nature of each question may have thus led subjects to adopt a strategy in which only the target sentences were attended to. Such an experiment amounts to putting the subjects in the so-called "null" context, where all of us predict an MA advantage. The experiment therefore does not show how much, *if any*, of that overall MA advantage stemmed from the manipulation of recency.

If the subjects *were* attending to the context, C & F's data seem to us to raise more problems for their own theory than for ours. By C & F's own admission, their manipulation of recency in the materials should work in favour of the minimally attached analysis. According to the strategy-based theory, there should thus be an unusually large effect of attachment in the case of the two targets (MA and NMA) *even when preceded by their respective felicitous contexts*. The MA target should be read faster not only because the initial MA strategy works to the disadvantage of the NMA target (even in the NMA context), but also because the recency advantage is in its favour. We note that the actual difference between reading times in the critical segment for the felicitous MA–MA and NMA–NMA conditions (8 msec) is small, and unlikely to be statistically significant; indeed, the overall effect of attachment seems to be due in large part to the paradoxical advantage of MA targets embedded in the NMA context. It follows that any claim that this experiment proves the existence of a recency effect must necessarily constitute a claim that it provides evidence *against* the minimal attachment first-pass strategy.

CONCLUSIONS

The debate between advocates of structure-based parsing strategies on the one hand, and interactive processing on the other, operates on two levels. On one level are the theoretical distinctions between the two positions. At another level are the empirical data which have been collected in pursuit of a definitive answer to the debate. At the level of theory, the "incremental parallel weak interactive" processor for which we argue seems to us to have the advantage of parsimony. Why advocate two mechanisms working almost independently (a syntactic processor adhering to Minimal Attachment, and a thematic processor accessing a combination of lexical information, discourse information, and general world knowledge), when there is an alternative explanation in terms of a single mechanism? This question becomes more pressing as the thematic processor comes to bear more and more of the burden of explaining the data, and, as it becomes more explicitly specified, acquires more and more of the characteristics of the incremental weakly interactive processor itself.

At the level of the data, we have all had to come to the painful realisation that reading times (and by association, eye movements; see Rayner, this issue) are sensitive to many different contaminating factors. Our task now is to develop ways of factoring out the potential contaminants to reading time and eye-movement data, leaving a measure which reflects only whether or not a processing difficulty has been induced or avoided. On this latter point, we again insist that it is a prediction of our theory that garden paths (of the NP-attachment kind) can be induced or avoided by appropriate manipulation of the referential context. There is no other way to test this prediction than to attempt to induce garden paths where there were thought to be none before, and to overcome garden paths whose prevention has hitherto been assumed impossible.

We believe, like C & F, that it is important to develop better theories of the use of meaning and context in sentence comprehension. We do not agree that our own efforts in this vein have been based on either inadequate semantic analysis or on inadequate data; indeed, we claim to have accounted for our data more completely than C & F have for their own. However, it is clear to all of us that much further experimentation is required before we can agree that the debate between the strategy-based theory on the one hand and the incremental-interactive theory on the other is settled.

REFERENCES

Altmann, G. (1987). Modularity and interaction in sentence processing. In J. Garfield (Ed.), *Modularity in knowledge representation and natural language processing*, pp. 428–444. Cambridge, Mass.: MIT Press.

Altmann, G. (1988). Ambiguity, parsing strategies, and computational models. *Language and Cognitive Processes*, *3*, 73–98.

Altmann, G. & Steedman, M. (1988). Interaction with context during human sentence processing. *Cognition*, *30*, 191–238.

Crain, S. (1980). Pragmatic constraints on sentence comprehension. Unpublished Ph.D. dissertation, University of California at Irvine.

Crain, S. & Steedman, M. (1985). On not being led up the garden path. In D. Dowty, L. Karttunen, & A. Zwicky (Eds), *Natural language parsing: Psychological, computational and theoretical perspectives*. Cambridge: Cambridge University Press.

Ferreira, F. & Clifton, C. (1986). The independence of syntactic processing. *Journal of Memory and Language*, *25*, 348–368.

Fodor, J. (1983). *The modularity of mind*. Cambridge, Mass.: MIT Press.

Frazier, L. (1978). On comprehending sentences: Syntactic parsing strategies. Unpublished Ph.D. dissertation, University of Connecticut, Indiana University Linguistics Club.

Frazier, L. (1987). Theories of sentence processing. In J. Garfield (Ed.), *Modularity in knowledge representation and natural language processing*, pp. 291–308. Cambridge, Mass.: MIT Press.

Frazier, L. (1989). Against lexical generation of syntax. In W. Marslen-Wilson (Ed.), *Lexical representation and process*, pp. 505–528. Cambridge, Mass.: MIT Press.

Haddock, N. (1987). Incremental interpretation and combinatory grammar. *Proceedings of the Tenth International Joint Computer Conference on Artificial Intelligence*, pp. 661–663, Milan.

Heim, I. (1982). The semantics of definite and indefinite noun phrases. Unpublished Ph.D. dissertation, University of Massachusetts, Amherst.

Kamp, H. (1968). Tense logic and the theory of linear order. Unpublished Ph.D. dissertation, University of California, Los Angeles.

Karttunen, L. & Peters, S. (1979). Conventional implicature. In Ch.-K. Oh & D. Dineen (Eds), *Syntax and semantics 11: Presupposition*, pp. 1–56. London: Academic Press.

Levinson, S. (1983). *Pragmatics*. Cambridge: Cambridge University Press.

Soames, S. (1989). Presupposition. In D. Gabbay & F. Guenthner (Eds), *Handbook of philosophical logic*, Vol. IV, pp. 553–616. Dordrecht: Reidel.

Stalnaker, R. (1973). Presuppositions. *Journal of Philosophical Logic*, 2, 447–457.

Steedman, M. (1987). Combinatory grammars and parasitic gaps. *Natural Language and Linguistic Theory*, *5*, 403–439.

Steedman, M. (1989). Grammar, interpretation and processing from the lexicon. In W. Marslen-Wilson (Ed.), *Lexical representation and process*. Cambridge, Mass.: MIT Press.

Stowe, L. A. (1988). Thematic structures and sentence comprehension. In G. Carlson & M. Tanenhaus (Eds), *Linguistic structure and language processing*, pp. 319–356. Dordrecht: Reidel.

Taraban, R. & McClelland, J. L. (1988). Constituent attachment and thematic role assignment in sentence processing: Influences of content-based expectations. *Journal of Memory and Language*, *27*, 597–632.

Trueswell, J. C., Tanenhaus, M. K., & Garnsey, S. M. (submitted). Semantic influences on parsing: Use of thematic role information in syntactic disambiguation.

LANGUAGE AND COGNITIVE PROCESSES, 1989, *4*, (3/4) SI 123–154

Verb Guidance and Other Lexical Effects in Parsing

Don C. Mitchell
Department of Psychology, University of Exeter, Exeter, U.K.

The process of sentence parsing is clearly influenced by the detailed information recovered from the lexicon for each successive word that appears in the sentence. This information may be used to *guide* or *direct* the assembly of new syntactic structures during the initial phases of parsing. Alternatively, it may be used to *check* or *monitor* the internal consistency of syntactic frameworks constructed on some other basis. This paper first describes a range of different models in each of these two categories and then reviews the empirical evidence bearing on the alternative models. Overall, it is concluded that current findings are most compatible with structure-checking models. The data are discussed in terms of a model based on a symbol-processing formalism (unification grammar) and the outline of a parser based on a connectionist processing system.

INTRODUCTION

People use a variety of different types of information to make their decisions about the syntactic structure of sentences. Some of these cues are non-lexical. Examples include the use of layout and punctuation to parse written texts, the role of intonation to derive the structure of spoken material, and the influences brought to bear by pragmatic and other information derived from previous sentences. However, most of these features are likely to be of secondary importance when compared with the central source of information—the words of the sentence themselves. This paper focuses on the way in which lexical information is introduced into the parsing process.

It is easy to demonstrate that lexical information influences the structures that people assign to sentences. In some cases, these effects are based on fairly subtle linguistic distinctions and, indeed, because of the theoreti-

Requests for reprints should be addressed to Don C. Mitchell, Department of Psychology, University of Exeter, Exeter, Devon EX4 4QG, U.K.

I am grateful to Gerry Altmann, Wayne Murray, and Janet Nicol for their helpful comments on an earlier draft of this paper.

cal ramifications of these phenomena, much of the recent work has concentrated on variables of this kind. A few examples will serve to demonstrate the major effects. In each case, the syntactic structure of a sentence is changed by altering a single word. In the examples given below, the alterations are relatively minor and do not involve changing the major syntactic category (i.e. N, V, ADJ) of any word.

In example (1), the head of the relative clause varies according to whether the second verb (in brackets) is singular or plural:

1. The police recovered the photographs of the painting which (was/were) stolen last week.

Similar effects occur with gender and number changes in nouns. In addition to lexical information concerning agreement, there is a good deal of evidence that parsing is influenced by the detailed properties of verbs and, in particular, by the kinds of arguments they can take (i.e. their *subcategorisation* properties). Example (2) is acceptable with "saluted", but not with "fainted":

2. After the private had (saluted/*fainted) the sergeant he requested permission to end the exercise.

The subcategorisation features of "saluted" allow it to be used either transitively or intransitively, whereas "fainted" can only be used without a direct object. With some forms of subcategorisation, the verb imposes detailed constraints on the structure of certain other parts of the sentence. For example, with verbs that can take an infinitival complement, detailed features of the verb sometimes specify that the subject of the subordinated infinitive verb must be the same as that for the "controlling" verb. This occurs with the verb "started"—making a sentence like (3) anomalous. However, the problem disappears when the verb is replaced by one which allows either subject or object control (like "begged"). For differences of this kind to occur, clearly the detailed features of the verb must play a role in determining the structure of the sentence.

3. Everyone liked the woman who the little girl (begged/*started) to sing those stupid French songs (Frazier, Clifton, & Randall, 1983).

Sentences (4) and (5) are further examples of the same phenomenon (Tanenhaus & Carlson, 1988):

4. John promised Mary to wash (himself/*herself).
5. John persuaded Mary to wash (*himself/herself).

In extreme cases, like examples (2)–(5), detailed lexical information dictates whether or not a string of words is grammatical. However, in other cases (e.g. 1) the information may simply be used to resolve what would otherwise be some structural ambiguity within the sentence. This paper is mainly concerned with *guidance* effects of the second kind.

There is good evidence that detailed lexical information can be used to resolve such ambiguity. In a questionnaire study, Ford, Bresnan, and Kaplan (1982) presented subjects with a series of sentences including potential structural ambiguities. Immediately after each sentence, a pair of probe sentences provided unambiguously rephrased versions of the first sentence.

Subjects had to mark one or other of the sentences to indicate which of the senses had occurred to them first. The sentences were designed so that the verbs could be interchanged, as in (6):

6. The woman (positioned/wanted) the dress on the rack.

The results provided clear evidence that the structural preferences associated with one verb could be modified or even reversed when this word was replaced by another. This result was subsequently extended to a different range of sentence structures (Mitchell & Holmes, 1985), and comparable, but more immediate lexical effects have been demonstrated in on-line studies by Clifton, Frazier, and Connine (1984) and by several other investigators. From a different perspective, McCarthy and Warrington (1985) have described a severely agrammatic patient whose comprehension problems can be traced in part (the authors argue) to impairments in the representations of some of the verbs in his lexicon. Thus, taking the evidence together, there is little question that detailed lexical information has *some* influence on parsing processes. What these studies fail to clarify, however, is the precise mechanism by which this information plays its role in guiding the analysis of the sentence.

In order to elaborate on the role that detailed lexical information might play in processing, it is first necessary to outline some critical characteristics of human parsing. The first important feature is that observations with structurally ambiguous sentences have consistently shown that people tend to rely on parsing strategies in which there are uneven commitments to different syntactic analyses. It has sometimes been suggested that this commitment is complete and that people devote all of their processing resources to one of the structural alternatives (as in the "garden-path" theory of Frazier & Rayner, 1982). Recent research (e.g. Frazier & Rayner, 1987; Perfetti, in press) suggests that there may be exceptions to such singular commitment. However, even if this is so, there is little question that initial processing biases are quite widespread. A great deal of work has focused on how the initial choice is made (see Frazier, 1987a, for a review). One important feature of the selection process is that the choice has often to be made in the absence of full information, and this means that there is always a small, but unavoidable possibility that the first analysis will turn out to be wrong. It follows that there must be a facility for monitoring or reassessing the initial hypothesis in the light of later information.

A considerable amount of recent work has focused on the distinction between the processes used in *selecting* the initial interpretation and those used later to *monitor* or check these choices (e.g. Clifton & Frazier, 1988; Frazier, 1987a; Mitchell, 1987a; Rayner, Carlson, & Frazier, 1983). A major purpose of the present paper will be to discuss whether detailed lexical information of the kinds referred to above is used in one or other (or both) of these kinds of operation. A second aim will be to consider *how* such information plays its role in each case. In the sections that follow, it will be useful to have a framework for discussing the various computational hypotheses. Following an earlier discussion of "psychologically realistic parsing" (Mitchell, 1987b), I shall refer to the first set of procedures as *structure-assembly* processes and the second set of procedures as *structure-checking* or *monitoring* processes. On some analyses, the second class of procedures may also involve rejecting the initial structure, backtracking, and reassembling a new structure.

Detailed lexical information could potentially play a role at either stage of processing and the major hypotheses are described in the next section. However, before embarking on this, it may be worth mentioning ways in which the outcome of the debate might impinge upon lingusitic discussions in a wider context.

According to the structure-checking account, it is necessary to suppose that the parser incorporates machinery which enables it to assemble structures which are not sanctioned by the (full) grammar of the language. As Frazier (1988) and Fodor (1988) have pointed out, this capacity to build ungrammatical structures may be more immediately compatible with some grammars or linguistic theories than it is with others. In such cases, there may be circumstances in which "we can reasonably infer a grammatical distinction from a processing distinction" (Fodor, 1988, p. 127). To the extent that this is possible, the issues addressed here will be germane to researchers with a wider interest in linguistic analysis.

MODELS OF LEXICAL EFFECTS

Let us first consider models in which the lexical information is used to guide the initial assembly of syntactic structures. These will be referred to as *assembly-directing* models. This class of models can be subdivided into two groups: those in which two or more structural hypotheses are processed simultaneously (parallel versions of the model) and those that restrict all analysis to a single preferred structure (serial versions). Detailed specifications of these models are given in the next two subsections.

Lexically Directed Assembly: Parallel Version

To reiterate, the fundamental assumption for this class of model is that lexical information is used to *guide* the process of building syntactic structures. It is also assumed that where there is local structural ambiguity, both (or all) of the alternative analyses are pursued in parallel. The best known version of this model is the *lexical analysis strategy* put forward by Fodor, Garrett, and Bever (1968; see also Fodor, Bever, & Garrett, 1974). According to this proposal, the parser retrieves lexical information—particularly the subcategorisation properties of verbs—and uses it to explore and develop all lines of analysis that are consistent with this information. Thus, in a sentence based on a simple, transitive verb, the parser would use the verb-information to rule out complement and other complex argument structures, and in this way it would in effect focus the analysis on direct-object constructions. With other verb-types, two or more alternative structures might be developed and tested in parallel. In situations of this kind, Fodor et al. (1968) assumed that there would be some kind of cost associated with sustaining multiple analyses, and on this basis they predicted that sentences with less constraining verbs would somehow be more "difficult" to process than those with verbs which are only compatible with (say) just one structural continuation. Notice that this prediction is not a strict consequence of the verb-guidance hypothesis itself. If one assumes that two or more analyses can be developed without mutual interference or cost, then the directive effects of different verbs would not manifest themselves as differences in processing load. The crucial feature of the model, then, is not that there may be differences in processing load, but that lexical information is held to sanction or control all structural hypotheses that are entertained (in parallel) at later stages in the analysis of the sentence. In such accounts, it follows that any potential structure which is incompatible with the information will simply be eliminated from consideration.

Lexically Directed Assembly: Serial Version

As with the previous model, it is assumed that the detailed lexical information is used to guide the structural analysis in the remainder of the sentence. However, instead of simultaneously setting up *all* the syntactic structures that are compatible with the lexical information, it is assumed that the parser uses the information to select the single, most probable analysis. If this later turns out to be incompatible with other information, then the lexical selection procedures may be used to propose a second legitimate structure and so on until the parsing process eventually either works adequately or fails completely. Because the structural hypotheses are considered serially, this version of the model does not predict that the processing load will be reduced in regions immediately after words which impose tight structural constraints on subsequent material. The first analysis should be elaborated at a rate which is independent of the number of alternatives which were potentially available at the choice point. In this sense, the model differs from parallel versions of the assembly-directing hypothesis. However, both kinds of model share the assumption that lexical information has a *directing* role. In the case of the serial model, this information may determine both the range of potential structures and the order in which the various alternatives are considered.

The best-known model in this category is that proposed by Ford et al. (1982). A central premise of this model is that certain words have different "lexical forms", each of which can be used in sentences with different argument structures. All of the forms are stored in the lexical representation for the word. However, within this representation, there are variations in status. Each lexical form has a different "strength" or "salience", and Ford et al. (1982) propose that this information plays an important role in the parsing process. Specifically, they postulate that on encountering words with multiple lexical forms, the parser selects the one marked as being most salient, and uses this particular form as the framework for the syntactic analysis of the following few words. If the preferred lexical frame turns out to be incompatible with the subsequent input, then the parser moves on to the next form in the representational hierarchy and repeats the process until the match is successful or until the entire range of options has been exhausted. An important feature of this model is that the lexical information plays an explicit role in allocating priorities *within* the class of legitimate analyses. Its role is not merely restricted to *rejecting* ungrammatical analyses and *permitting* the remainder to proceed.

Structure-checking Models

In this class of models, it is assumed that structural hypotheses are initially set up *without any reference at all* to detailed lexical information. Instead, they are assembled by making use of the major syntactic categories of successive words, simple parsing strategies and conventions, etc. The structures are submitted to monitoring or checking procedures—to see whether they conform to all of the detailed requirements of the grammar. It is assumed that detailed lexical information is drawn upon exclusively during this second (monitoring) stage of the parsing process. For example, there may be procedures which are used to check that the proposed structure is compatible with the subcategorisation or "control" properties of the verb which governs it. Similarly, there may be operations which check that the structure is coherent with respect to number, gender, case agreement, and so on.

Variants of this model have been proposed by Frazier et al. (1983), Clifton et al. (1984), Frazier (1987a,b), Clifton and Frazier (1988), Mitchell (1987a,b), and Nicol (in press). Within the general class of models, different versions may vary with respect to the *type* of preassembled structure which can be passed over to the monitor for checking. At one extreme, it might be assumed that only completed sentences or clauses can be submitted to detailed consistency checking. A model of this kind would predict that detailed lexical information should have no influence on processing at any point before the end of the sentence (or clause). A second possibility is that phrases (such as nounphrases, prepositional phrases, adverbial phrases, etc.) might be considered complete enough to be subjected to detailed checking. This would lead to a more fine-grained interaction in which lexical effects might show up at the ends of individual phrases, rather than at the ends of completed clauses. Thirdly, it is possible to propose variants of the model in which consistency checks are initiated after each new word has been taken in.

In this final case, it should be clear that this proposal becomes very difficult to distinguish empirically from certain versions of the assembly-directing models. According to the fine-grained structure-checking model, consistency effects can show up as soon as the new word has been passed to the monitor and evaluated by the checking procedures. Because we have no way, in principle, of knowing how quickly this might occur, we cannot easily rule out the possibility that *any* lexical effect might have originated in this way. This might be considered to be a weakness of this version of the model and it should, perhaps, be taken into account in any comparison between the models. Fortunately, however, it is possible to make at least one differential prediction for the structure-checking models and the serial version of the assembly-directing model. On the checking model, the parser will frequently assemble structures which are illegitimate in the light of detailed lexical information. Such structures will initially have to be checked in exactly the same way that any others are, but when they fail there will be processing delays as new proposals are assembled and checked until one of them eventually works. According to the serial version of the assembly-direction model, however, illegitimate or impossible structures should never be assembled, and so it follows that no time should be wasted in considering such options. Evidence bearing on this issue will be considered on pp. 139–142.

EMPIRICAL EVIDENCE

Studies Relating to the Parallel Version of the Assembly-directing Model

Let us first consider the variants of the model based on the premise that alternative structural hypotheses somehow compete or interfere with one another. These models predict that the processing load associated with parsing will be reduced when lexical information places tight constraints on subsequent syntactic structures. As mentioned above, this prediction depends crucially on the assumption that processing load is increased whenever there is local structural ambiguity. If this assumption is incorrect, then there is no direct way of testing the proposal that lexical information is used to eliminate or reduce structural ambiguity. Unfortunately, there are strong grounds for doubting the validity of the premise. In particular, there is no evidence that reading time is increased in regions of local structural ambiguity using either eye-tracking tasks (e.g. Frazier & Rayner, 1982, p. 200; Kennedy & Murray, 1984) or self-paced reading tasks (e.g. Cuetos & Mitchell, 1988, p. 89; Holmes, Kennedy, & Murray, 1987; Kennedy & Murray, 1984). Because reading time is generally extremely sensitive to variations in processing load, this casts considerable doubt on the prospects of making effective use of on-line measures to test the model in the manner proposed by Fodor et al. (1968).

Given these doubts about the premises of the model, it is perhaps not surprising that the predictions have not generally been borne out in the literature. Using a phoneme-monitoring task, Hakes (1971) found no evidence that processing load is greater immediately following complex verbs than it is after simple transitive verbs. Similarly, Mitchell and Green (1978, experiment III) found no effect in a subject-paced reading task, even though the verbs employed in this study were taken from the list compiled by Fodor et al. (1968). More recently, Frazier et al. (1983) similarly found no processing differences between ambiguous and unambiguous words in sentences like (14) and (15), discussed at length below (and reproduced here for the reader's convenience):

14. Everyone liked the woman who the little child (begged/forced) to sing those stupid French songs.
15. Everyone liked the woman who the little child (begged/started) to sing those stupid French songs for.

In contrast with these findings, a small number of studies *have* reported evidence that verb-complexity may play a role in certain aspects of processing (e.g. Fodor et al., 1968; Holmes & Forster, 1972; Shapiro, Zurif, &

Grimshaw, 1987; 1989). However, it is not at all clear that any of these investigations demonstrate that there are influences on the procedures which guide the initial *parsing* decisions (as the hypothesis requires). The first two studies involved paraphrasing or repeating entire sentences, and therefore the effects could have occurred at any one of a number of different stages of processing—not merely during assembly operations. The more recent experiments by Shapiro et al. (1987; 1989) used a dual-task technique. Sentences containing verbs of differing (argument-structure) complexity were presented in the auditory modality and processing load was monitored by means of a secondary lexical decision task presented in the vicinity of the verb. Although these authors found that lexical decision latencies were longer immediately after the more complex verbs, it is not certain whether this result should be interpreted as a *parsing* effect or as a *lexical activation* effect. The authors appear to favour an explanation of the second kind (see abstracts of both papers), arguing merely that all argument structures for a verb are momentarily activated immediately following its presentation. Certainly, as they stand, these results cannot be taken as definitive support for the proposal that detailed lexical information guides the assembly of new structures within the parsing process.

In short, then, there is no clear-cut support for versions of the assembly-direction model in which lexical information is used to guide the parsing process by reducing the number of parallel structures in competition with one another. It should be reiterated, however, that this does not rule out the possibility that lexical information directs the parsing process in exactly the way proposed by Fodor et al. (1968). It merely argues against the proposal that such hypothetical structures necessarily *interfere* with one another.

Unfortunately, it becomes relatively difficult to test the model if we abandon the assumption that there is an increased processing load associated with considering alternative structures simultaneously. We need to look for evidence that the *content* of the analysis has been influenced by the lexical information. In fact, as with the "interfering" version of the model, the evidence is not particularly supportive.

A fundamental feature of the model is that lexical information is supposed to be used to *eliminate* analyses that are incompatible with it. It follows that the model would be severely compromised by evidence that people actively consider "impossible" structures when they are reading material in the region following the ostensibly guiding word. This would suggest that the controlling function of the lexical information had not yet been implemented at this stage in the process (on pp. 139–142 we present detailed evidence that precisely this kind of effect does occur). In particular, Mitchell (1987a) reported data which suggest that in certain circumstances people try to interpret a nounphrase following an intransitive verb as the direct object of this verb (for details, see p. 140). Clearly, it would have been impossible for this to happen if the verb-lexical information had been used immediately to eliminate the transitive clause-structure as required by the model.

To summarise, then, there is little support for the parallel versions of the assembly-directing model. We now proceed to consider the serial version of the model.

Studies Relating to the Serial Version of the Assembly-directing Model

According to this version of the model, the processing time for different regions of a sentence should not be systematically influenced by the presence of structural ambiguity in those regions. As outlined before, it is assumed that lexical information is used to select the initial interpretation, but that the material is subsequently processed *as if* it were unambiguous. In other words, the influence of lexical information is restricted to this preliminary choice.

Evidence on this model has recently been reviewed in detail by Mitchell and Zagar (1986). Among the earlier studies, Ford et al. (1982) interpreted their questionnaire data (described in the Introduction) as evidence in favour of this model. However, it is clear that in making judgements about the preferred interpretations of sentences, subjects could have used the detailed lexical information at any of the stages of processing considered in earlier sections of this paper. In other words, the data are equally consistent with all of the models considered here.

More recently, Holmes (1984) and Mitchell and Holmes (1985) have reported experimental findings which they took as support for the model. However, in retrospect, it now seems clear that these conclusions were not strictly warranted by the data. Holmes' findings were based on the speed or accuracy with which subjects responded to comprehension questions *following* sentences with different verb biases. As before, the lag before testing was sufficiently long to reflect checking effects as well as assembly effects, and the data are therefore compatible with all the versions of the model. Mitchell and Holmes (1985) examined various structures—including sentences as in (7)—and showed that the viewing time for the test display (italicised in 7) was longer following optionally transitive verbs like "phoned" than it was following intransitive verbs like "arrived":

7. As soon as he had (arrived/phoned) his wife / *started to prepare* / for the journey.

This is sufficient to demonstrate that the lexical effect comes into play before the end of the sentence. However, it fails to establish that it is an immediate assembly-directing effect. In most of the materials employed in the study, the test display included a potential boundary for the clause incorporating the verb, and so it follows that the data are just as compatible with the clause-, phrase- or word-by-word checking versions of the structure-checking model.

In a more recent study, Holmes (1987, experiment II) examined local processing effects in sentences based on verbs with different subcategorisation preferences. All of the verbs in the study were capable of taking both a direct object and a complement structure. However, preliminary work had shown that the direct object interpretation was preferred for some, whereas the complement reading dominated in others. The experimental materials were all complement sentences like (8) and (9). In each case there is local structural ambiguity *vis-à-vis* the role of the NP following the first verb. However, the following (italicised) word ensures that this is always resolved in favour of the complement structure.

8. The reporter saw her friend *was* not succeeding ("saw": direct object preference).
9. The candidate doubted his sincerity *would* be appreciated ("doubted": complement preference).

The subjects read the sentences in a cumulative word-by-word, self-paced grammatical-decision task. Viewing time for each successive word was compared with that in a control condition in which the complement interpretation was cued immediately after the main verb by inserting a relative pronoun at this point. The results showed that with the first kind of verb (as in 8), the reading time for the disambiguating word was about 400 msec longer than that in the control condition. This suggests that the ambiguous NP was initially misinterpreted following verbs in the first category. With the second kind of verb (as in 9), the difference was reduced to 110 msec, suggesting that verb-bias information might have been used at an early stage to modify the interpretation of the ambiguous NP. Unfortunately, Holmes (1987) did not report whether this reduction was statistically reliable, and so we cannot be confident that the lexical information had a genuine effect on parsing. This may have been a critical omission, because both Ferreira and Henderson (in press) and Kennedy, Murray, Jennings, and Reid (this issue) have recently failed to replicate important aspects of Holmes' findings, even though they used techniques similar to those employed in the earlier study. In fact, even if the result had been substantiated, it would not have provided unequivocal support for the assembly-directing model because, as Frazier (1987a) has pointed out, a finding of this kind could in any case readily be interpreted within the framework of the structure-checking model. One simply needs to propose that the ambiguous NP is initially interpreted as the direct object of the first verb, and that this structure is handed over to the monitor for consistency checking. We then posit that information about lexical bias becomes available at this stage of the operation, and the assumed effect can be explained simply by postulating that the initial structure is rejected on a higher proportion of trials with the second kind of verb than it is with the first.

More recently, Tanenhaus and Carlson (1988) have reported a series of experiments which appear to provide stronger support for the model. The materials were filler/gap sentences like (10):

10. The district attorney found out which (filler noun: witness or church) the reporter asked (gap 1) anxiously about (gap 2).

The filler noun was changed from sentence to sentence, but in all cases the structure dictated that it eventually had to be assigned to the gap at the end of the sentence (gap 2). In addition to this gap, there was always a *potential* gap earlier in the sentence (marked here as gap 1), and the authors set out to show that the subjects tried to fill this gap when it followed a transitive-biased verb like "asked" in (10), but that they *avoided* filling the gap when it followed an intransitive-biased verb like "hurried" in (11):

11. The physical therapist wasn't sure which (filler noun: doctor or bed) the orderly hurried (gap 1) rapidly toward (gap 2).

To determine whether they posited and filled a gap in the first position, subjects were required to read sentences containing nouns that were either *plausible* (e.g. "witness" for 10, "doctor" for 11) or *implausible* ("church", "bed") fillers for gap 1. The task was a self-paced, word-by-word reading task and the results showed that plausibility had a significant effect on the viewing time for transitive-biased verbs, but not for the others. At first sight, this result seems to suggest that readers' gap-positing strategies were controlled by the detailed features of the verb just before the gap. However, closer examination of the data throws up certain difficulties for this interpretation of the findings. If the plausibility effect for transitive-favouring verbs were genuinely due to the fact that plausible nouns (like "witness" in 10) were more readily placed in the first gap, then subjects should have been garden-pathed by making this (incorrect) decision. In other words, there should have been complications in processing materials *at some later point* in such sentences. In fact, there was no evidence of the anticipated differences between the viewing times for the plausible and implausible filler conditions. Moreover, for the word immediately following the potential gap (i.e. "anxiously" in 10), the viewing time for *both* conditions was about 100 msec less than that in the two corresponding times for the intransitive-verb condition, so if anything it appears that the garden-path effect was occurring with the "wrong" set of materials. Clearly, these phenomena will have to be examined in greater detail before they can be used as evidence in favour of one or other of the models of lexical effects in parsing.

Tanenhaus, Boland, Garnsey, and Carlson (1989) have reported one further study which seems to support the model. As in the study just described, the evidence seems to suggest that readers' gap-filling strategies may be influenced by the control properties of the verb immediately before the gap. In this experiment, half of the critical sentences were anomalous and the subjects' task was to read through the sentence in a single-word, self-paced task, pressing a "yes" button as long as the sentence continued to make sense. As soon as the sentence *stopped* making sense, they were required to press a "no" button. The critical sentences were like (12) and (13):

12. Which (customer/article) did your brother call (gap) on the office phone?
13. Which (child/movie) did your brother remind (gap) to watch the show?

In both cases, the first part of the sentence is similar to the materials used earlier (as in 10). Some of the materials used verbs (like "remind") which can either take a direct object or an infinitival complement. Others used verbs which cannot take such a complement (e.g. "called"). As in the study described above, one of the filler nouns was plausible as a direct object for the verb and the other was not. With materials of the first kind (i.e. with "call"-type verbs), the results showed that in the *implausible filler* condition people started noticing problems as soon as they read the verb. That is, at this point they pressed the "no" button more frequently than they did in the *plausible filler* condition, and even when they selected the "yes" button, their responses were slower in the anomalous condition. With the other kind of verbs, however, the pattern of results was different. With sentences like (13), there was no special tendency for subjects to *reject* the implausible filler or to respond more slowly to it when it turned up. All plausibility effects were postponed until the word *after* the test verb, or even to other words beyond that. These results suggest that detailed properties of verbs have some influence on readers' tendencies to posit and fill gaps immediately after the verb. (Tanenhaus et al. suggest that a gap is *not* posited after "remind"-type verbs because the detailed lexical information for these verbs somehow conveys to the parser the information that there will be further potential gaps later in the sentence.)

Again, however, these results do not provide conclusive evidence in favour of the model. An examination of the graph of the data (Tanenhaus et al., 1989, fig. 2A) reveals that over 40% of the subjects were still pressing the "yes" button after they had read the sequence—"Which article did the secretary call on the . . .". At the very least, this suggests that the task is somewhat insensitive to anomalies, and this raises the possibility that it simply failed to pick up genuine effects in the immediate region of the "remind"-type verbs. Of course, this would not explain why the effect *did* occur for the other verbs. Here we need to ask, however, whether the two classes of verb were fully matched in terms of the plausibility of the supposedly anomalous fillers. Is it as difficult to process sentences which involve "reminding" a "movie" as those which entail "calling" an "article"? Clearly, if there are differences here, they would be sufficient to account for the data without postulating any differential verb-control effects. Criticisms of this kind could have been deflected by demonstrating that the two sets of materials behave equivalently in structures without gaps (e.g. "The secretary called the article . . ." or "Your brother reminded the movie . . ."). However, the authors did not report having carried out such a test, and so it remains uncertain for the present whether the gap-filling effects are genuinely controlled by the preceding verb.

Finally, we consider some evidence that, whatever the status of this proposal in *English*, it is not possible to maintain the suggestion that detailed lexical information provides the only source of assembly-guidance in certain other languages. These languages employ structures in which the verb comes *after* the phrase which expresses its arguments. On a strict interpretation of the assembly-directing hypothesis, without first processing the verb, it would not be possible to make even tentative decisions about the dependency relationships between the phrases and clauses it dominates. All structural decisions would have to be postponed until the end of the clause, so that before this there should be no sign of any commitment to one syntactic reading rather than another. Evidence against this has been reported by Frazier (1987b) in a study using Dutch readers. The critical linguistic structure was the relative clause—in which the subordinate verb appears in the final position. Prior to the verb, the constituent can be interpreted either as a subject- or as an object-relative clause. Sentences were presented in two segments in a subject-paced reading task and the data showed clear evidence that the readers initially committed themselves to the former interpretation (i.e. they took the string of words to be a subject-relative clause). Because the verb occurred too late to influence this choice, it is clear that in this case the detailed information recovered from the lexicon can only have been used to check or revise structures generated on the basis of a different set of principles. Of course, this does not rule out the possibility that there are circumstances, even in Dutch, where lexical guidance might play a role. It merely serves to show that effects of this kind cannot provide a full account of the way in which detailed lexical information is used in parsing.

Evidence Relating to the Structure-checking Model

We now turn to evidence that detailed lexical information may play a role in some of the operations which are used to *monitor* or *check* the internal consistency of structures assembled by the device responsible for making the initial choice. As mentioned above, this type of account presupposes that this device is capable of generating ungrammatical structures. Work by Freedman and Forster (1985) suggests that there are at least some circumstances in which such structures can be derived, represented, and used in psycholinguistic tests. However, these investigators used a task (sentence-matching) which may have encouraged subjects to use strategies that are not normally employed in comprehension, and so it is important to consider evidence from other sources.

Some of the earlier work on structure-checking in comprehension was based upon gap-filler sentences similar to those discussed above. For example, Frazier et al. (1983) used sentences like (14) and (15):

14. Everyone liked the woman (filler 1) who the little child (filler 2) (begged/forced) (gap) to sing those stupid French songs.
15. Everyone liked the woman (filler 1) who the little child (filler 2) (begged/started) (gap 1) to sing those stupid French songs for (gap 2).

When the verb "begged" is used in these sentence-frames there is a region of structural ambiguity which lasts for several words. Specifically, the gap immediately following the verb may be filled by either of two preceding nouns (i.e. "woman" or "child" in this example). In (14), the first filler ("woman") turns out to be correct, whereas in (15), filler 2 ("child") has to go into gap 1 while filler 1 goes into gap 2 (for a full analysis of these structures, see Frazier et al., 1983). Frazier et al. (1983) argue that subjects handle this ambiguity by using exactly the same initial strategy with both kinds of sentence. Specifically, they suggest that readers employ a general procedure known as the *most recent filler strategy*—whereby the gap following the verb is initially filled with the second (i.e. most recent) filler. In line with this proposal, Frazier et al. (1983) reported that subjects took longer to report that they understood sentences like (14) even though they actually contained *fewer* words than sentences like (15).

For the next step in the argument, consider the same sentences with "begged" replaced by "forced" in (14) and by "started" in (15). The control properties of these verbs place different constraints on the complete structure, with the result that neither type of sentence remains ambiguous with these new verbs. In (14), the gap following "forced" *has* to be filled by the first filler ("woman"), whereas in (15) the alternative ("child") becomes obligatory. If this information were used at the time when the initial structures were being assembled, then the effects associated with ambiguous words like "begged" should be eliminated, or at least reduced. In fact, Frazier et al. (1983) found that the magnitude of the effect was unaffected by the change of verb. They therefore inferred that subjects must always have followed the *most recent filler* strategy, irrespective of the detailed properties of the verb. From this they concluded that the lexical information had no influence at all on the procedures which were used to assemble preliminary structures for the sentences. Comprehension data for a sample of the sentences revealed that it did *ultimately* influence the interpretation of the material, and so it seems that the detailed (verb-control) information must have been brought to bear on processing at a later, checking stage of the parsing operation.

Ford and Dalrymple (1988) have recently queried the basis for this general interpretation of the data. They claim that there are inconsistencies between the account put forward by Frazier et al. (1983) and the assumptions that the same authors had made in earlier papers. Specifically, they point out that:

> The only way in which the sentences with verbs such as *forced* could be initially processed in the same way as sentences with verbs such as *begged* would be if *subcategorization* information was ignored during initial sentence analysis and this is something that Frazier et al. do not wish to maintain (Ford & Dalrymple, 1988, p. 69).

However, this seems to be a straightforward misinterpretation of what Frazier and her colleagues have said in the past. They have certainly made statements like "verb subcategorization information is consulted early in sentence comprehension" (Clifton & Frazier, 1986, p. 213). However, the fact that the information may be used "early" obviously does not imply that it is used in the *initial* sentence analysis. Indeed, in a more recent analysis of the phenomenon, Frazier (1988, section 1.2) has made it clear that she endorses the view that verb subcategorisation information as well as verb control information might be ignored during the first pass through the sentence.

This undermines the major objection that Ford and Dalrymple (1988) raise in relation to the proposal that verb-control information is predominantly used during structure *checking* rather than structure assembly. However, there are reasons for retaining a degree of scepticism about the chain of reasoning used to support Frazier et al.'s (1983) case. Even if we go along with Frazier and her colleagues and assume that verb-control effects are predominantly (or exclusively) consistency-checking phenomena, there is a good deal of evidence that such effects can be implemented well before the end of the sentence (see pp. 132–136). This means that it is not at all self-evident that the most viable forms of the checking model would have predicted the pattern of results that occurred. If the detailed lexical information were used for structure checking at *any* point before the end of the sentence, then reanalysis and recovery from the garden-path should presumably have been triggered at this point rather than on the final word. Because recovery time generally increases with the "length" of the garden-path (Frazier & Rayner, 1982), it follows that the difference in comprehension time for unambiguous sentences—e.g. (14) with "forced" and (15) with "started"—should have been *less* than that for ambiguous sentences (e.g. those with "begged"). If Frazier's account is correct, then it is difficult to see why the difference was equivalent in the two conditions, and it may be more appropriate to seek alternative explanations for the data (as proposed by Crain & Fodor, 1985, and others).

We have already seen from Frazier's (1987b) Dutch data, that at least in the case of verb-final structures, there must be procedures that are capable of assembling syntactic units without drawing upon detailed lexical information. This study also showed that, with constituents of this kind, there must be a facility for using verb-information to *revise* the structures that are put together in this way. The question we need to ask next is whether the use of such information is restricted to this checking function, even when there is a realistic opportunity for it to be employed in other ways. In particular, does the parsing mechanism allow inappropriate hypotheses to be generated (and tested) even when it could, in principle, be in possession of lexical information which would rule such hypotheses out of consideration? An experiment by Mitchell (1987a) suggests that it does. Preposed sentences like (16) and (17) were used:

16. After the child visited the doctor prescribed a course of injections.
17. After the child sneezed the doctor prescribed a course of injections.

In (16), the phrase "the doctor" is temporarily ambiguous: It could either be the object of the verb in the subordinate clause (i.e. "visited") or else it could be the subject of the verb in the main clause ("prescribed"). Previous work by Frazier and Rayner (1982) and others has shown that in sentences of this kind readers show a strong tendency to interpret such phrases in the former way—leading to garden-path effects later in the sentence. Now, verbs like "visited" are optionally transitive and so such an interpretation is at least compatible with the subcategorisation properties of the verb. But what happens when the verb is replaced by one which is strictly intransitive (like "sneezed" in 17)? If the detailed (subcategorisation) information is used during the first pass, then the "direct object" interpretation should not be generated, because it clearly involves creating an impossible argument for an intransitive verb. In this case, the nounphrase should immediately be interpreted as the subject of the main verb and no further processing difficulties should ensue. On the other hand, if the lexical information is ignored at first, and the initial structure is generated by other means, then the nounphrase will presumably first be interpreted as a direct object, as it is with other verbs. The sequence of events after this would depend upon whether this newly assembled structure is left unchecked while further material is processed, or whether it is quickly submitted to a consistency check. In the first case, analysis (and garden-pathing) would proceed as it does with sentences like (16). However, in the second case, the parser should quickly detect the incompatibility between the tentative structure and the lexical information from the intransitive verb, and there should presumably be a pause as the misparse is corrected and a new structure is generated to replace it.

In order to test these predictions, Mitchell (1987a) conducted an experiment in which subjects were required to read sentences in a clause-by-clause, subject-paced reading task. In the main experimental condition, the string of words up to "doctor" appeared in the first display and the rest replaced this when subjects pressed the key to read on. (In addition, there were control conditions using different sentence segmentations, and using prepositional phrases to mark clause boundaries—see Mitchell, 1987a, for details.) The results showed that the first display of sentences like (17) took longer to read than the corresponding portions of sentences with optionally transitive verbs (like "visited" in 16). This result is compatible with the view that the ambiguous NP is initially assigned a role as the direct object of the first verb, but that this decision is quickly checked and, in the sentences with intransitive verbs, reconsidered before the subjects move on to new materials. It is difficult to see how the result could have occurred if the initial structural decisions had been based on detailed lexical information. On this hypothesis, the intransitive properties of a verb like "sneezed" should have ruled out the construction of a clause with a direct object, and if this *had* happened there would have been no difficulty with strings like "sneezed the doctor". Thus the results suggest that detailed lexical information may be ignored not only when the verb turns up late in the sentence (as in the study reported by Frazier, 1987b), but also when the information is potentially made available *before* the relevant structural decisions are first made. This strongly suggests that verb-subcategorisation information is used to check the internal consistency of clauses constructed using other material. Moreover, there is no need to postulate that it plays any role at all in *guiding* the assembly process.

Of course, these conclusions may be criticised in various ways. It could be that subjects took longer to read strings like "sneezed the doctor", because within such displays they were forced to end the preposed clause and engage in all the normal kinds of boundary processing associated with such points. Operations of this kind might be expected to increase latency relative to that for displays in which the words themselves do not signal the presence of a clause boundary (as in "visited the doctor"). However, this is unlikely to be the explanation, because an earlier study (Mitchell, 1986) showed that the prolonged viewing time for displays of the first kind was evident even when the latencies were compared with those for control conditions in which clause boundaries were marked explicitly by commas following the verb. If the effect had simply been associated with boundary processing, then the viewing time for "sneezed the doctor" would have been no longer than that for "sneezed, the doctor". A second possible criticism of the Mitchell (1987a) study is that "normal" parsing processes may somehow have been distorted by the effects of segmenting the sentences into different displays. For example, the "<verb>–<direct object>" parse may have been strongly facilitated by ending the display with a verb followed by a NP. Unfortunately, it is difficult to evaluate this objection properly, because at present there is no well-articulated model of how segmentation might influence the parsing process. However, there is some evidence to suggest that this factor is unlikely to be of overriding importance. Notably, verb-NP interference effects seem to occur in single-word versions of the subject-paced reading task. The data come from two experiments reported by Stowe (1989). The first study employed sentences similar to those described above. However, in this case, the experimental and control conditions were created by varying the first noun (as in 18) rather than by changing the verb, which in this case was always an ergative, causative verb like "stopped":

18. Before the (police/truck) stopped the driver was already getting nervous.

A critical point for this study is that ergative, causative verbs can readily take a direct object if the agent is animate (e.g. "police"), but "prefer" to assume a passive form without a direct object if the agent is inanimate (as with "truck"). Thus, the combined information from the noun and the verb can be used to decide whether the ambiguous NP ("the driver", in this case) should be interpreted as the object of the first verb or as the subject of the main verb. The first experiment reported by Stowe (1989) confirmed that something like this does occur on-line. Subjects spent longer viewing the verb after the ambiguous NP in the "animate" condition than in the "inanimate" condition. This indicates that detailed information about the verb (and about the noun) must have been used to influence parsing decisions at some point before the second verb appeared on the screen. On the evidence presented so far, this could have occurred either because the lexical information played a role in selecting the initial interpretation of the ambiguous NP, or because it was used to run a quick check on a decision made on some other grounds. However, a follow-up study suggested that the second explanation was closer to the truth. This time the materials included sentences like (19):

19. When the truck stopped the (driver/silence) became very frightening.

If the properties of the first noun and the verb between them had dictated in advance that the verb should have no direct object, then *any* noun would be an acceptable follow-on at the beginning of the main clause. However, it turned out that there was some evidence that processing was slower when the second NP was an *implausible* object for the subject–verb combination (e.g. "truck stopped the silence") than when it was *plausible* ("truck stopped the driver"). This suggests that the second noun was assessed for its acceptability as an object for the first verb, and it therefore implies that the non-object interpretation cannot have been selected in advance. This parallels the result reported by Mitchell (1987a), and provides some evidence that this finding was not simply generated by some artefact of segmentation.

Before leaving this issue, it should be stressed that, contrary to suggestions made by Fodor (1988, p. 137), the argument for lexical checking does not depend on any demonstration that the interference effect re-emerges when the materials are segmented in different ways. Even if the effect is associated only with certain forms of segmentation, the evidence outlined above is still sufficient to rule out extreme forms of the model in which structures are generated using information from the lexicon. On such hypotheses, intransitive verbs should simply be *incapable* of generating the kind of structure which could later benefit from such segmentation effects. The point is that no amount of pressure from extraneous cues can induce a parser to build structures that it is not in some sense *equipped* to build. If there are circumstances in which the mechanism assembles an S-V-O structure using an intransitive verb, then this clearly establishes that the device has the *potential* to assemble such objects. This is difficult to reconcile with accounts in which structures are generated exclusively on the basis of information recovered from the lexicon. It suggests that the initial structure is derived from an alternative (i.e. non-lexical) source, and that the use of the detailed lexical information is confined to the subsequent checking process.

To complete this section, let us now turn to two further studies which take different views concerning the proposal that detailed lexical information is used for consistency checking rather than for generating new structures. The first is an eye-tracking experiment carried out by Ferreira and Henderson (in press) using materials similar to those used by Holmes (1987) (e.g. 20):

20. He (wished/forgot) Pam needed a ride with him.

With some verbs (e.g. "forgot" in this case), it is not immediately clear whether the following NP should be treated as the direct object of the verb or as the subject of a reduced complement clause. It has previously been shown that such sentences are interpreted in different ways depending on which verb is used in the initial slot (e.g. Mitchell & Holmes 1985). In support of this, Ferreira and Henderson (in press) found that there were differential effects in some of their data on regressive eye movements. However, there was no evidence at all of processing differences for the two verbs when they examined the data for the first fixation on either the noun or the verb that appeared within the complement structure. In other words, as before, there was no reason to believe that the subjects' tendency to assemble a complement structure during the first pass through the sentence was influenced in any way by the detailed lexical information about the first verb. The only effects that occurred were those involved in later stages of processing—consistent with the view that the verb-information was being used to check a structure derived on some other basis.

The second study is one that has been used to argue *against* the proposal that subcategorisation information is initially ignored by the parser. In this experiment, Nicol and Osterhout (reported in Nicol, in press) used sentences like (21) (see also Nicol & Osterhout, 1988):

21. That's the actress that the dentist from the new medical center in town had (invited/hesitated/planned) to # go to the (party./party with./party with.)

In such sentences, strictly intransitive and optionally intransitive verbs can be interchanged with one another in the main verb position. In the experiments, subjects were required to listen to sentences including experimental materials of this kind, and at the moment in the tape marked #, a string of letters was displayed on a screen. Here, subjects were required to press a button to indicate whether this string was an English word. In the critical condition, the probe stimulus was a word that was closely related to the first noun in the sentence (i.e. "actress" in this example). On other trials, there were control stimuli which matched this probe in length and frequency and probes related to other words in the sentence (e.g. "dentist"). The latency data showed that people responded faster to targets related to the first noun than to matched control words. This was true following all three types of verb.

However, the priming effect only reached statistical significance with the first and third cases: a 39-msec effect following intransitive verbs (like "hesitated") turned out to be unreliable (Nicol, in press). On the basis of these data and the results of a similar study by Nicol and Osterhout (1988), Nicol (in press) suggested that the parser postulates (and fills) a gap after transitive verbs (thus producing a reliable priming effect). However, she took the reduced priming effect following *in*transitive verbs as evidence that such a trace is *not* postulated in this case. Given this assumption, she argued that subcategorisation information must have been used immediately to influence the parser's gap-positing operations.

Clearly, this interpretation of the finding is difficult to reconcile with the conclusions drawn from the studies outlined above. However, it would be premature to take these findings as decisive evidence against the structure-checking model. First, whereas the priming effect following intransitive verbs failed to reach significance, we do not have sufficient evidence to show that the priming value in this condition comes from a different population from those in the other two conditions. In a statistical sense, the results were just as compatible with the assumption that the priming effect (and hence gap-filling strategies) are equivalent in all three cases. This, of course, is precisely what would have been expected on the structure-checking model. A second point worth making is that the structure-checking model would not necessarily be compromised even if there were statistical differences in the priming effects in the two conditions. With such a pattern of results, it could still have been argued that the gap-positing processes are equivalent for all types of verb, but that once filler information has been activated, this can be suppressed more rapidly when *filtering* operations reveal that the gap is ungrammatical. In short, Nicol's (in press) results as they currently stand do not force us to qualify the claim that verb subcategorisation information is used to filter out ungrammatical constructions rather than to propose new structures in the first place.

THEORETICAL ACCOUNTS OF LEXICAL EFFECTS IN PARSING

A Two-stage Unification Model

This section provides a more detailed account of the way in which lexical information might contribute to parsing. A review of the literature shows that there is no need to postulate any role for lexical information in the initial *assembly* of syntactic structures. All of the major findings can be accounted for by supposing that this information is engaged at a later stage of processing when these structures are checked for internal consistency. We need to be more precise about what is involved in this checking process. As a step in this direction, it is useful to express the notions in terms of some of the constructs used in unification-based descriptions of grammar (Kay, 1985; Shieber, 1986). (It should be stressed that the account is somewhat speculative at the moment, and while it borrows some of the theoretical constructs of unification grammars, it makes no attempt to remain faithful to the precepts of UGs as linguistic theories.)

In unification grammars, the basic representational units are highly organised frame-like descriptions known as "feature structures" (Shieber, 1986) or "functional structures" (Kay, 1985). These may represent either individual words or larger linguistic units such as NPs, PPs, complement structures, and sentences. Each feature structure consists of a labelled set of slots which are filled in such a way that they specify properties such as number and gender of Ns and NPs, the arguments (subcategorisation properties) and "control" properties of verbs, and so on. In certain circumstances, feature structures can be combined to form new and more complex structures, which retain much of the information from the original elements. This process is known as *unification*. Unification can only succeed if the initial structures have properties which are mutually consistent. Thus, structures for "a" and "horses" could not unify to form a NP structure for "a horses", because the two initial structures have conflicting information about number. Similar problems would occur if verbs appeared in inappropriate sentence frames, or if there were other inconsistencies within the sentence.

A considerable amount of effort is currently being devoted to developing ways of handling different forms of linguistic regularity within this general framework. A long-term goal for psycholinguists is to relate this work to existing and new bodies of empirical data. However, at present I merely propose to use some of the conventions and formalisms of unification grammars to describe a limited set of processing operations in parsing.

Let us suppose, then, that parsing consists of a series of unification operations. Let us assume also that "garden-path" effects are triggered when a unification attempt fails at some point in this sequence, and that the additional processing time generated by such effects is associated primarily with "dismantling" unifications inappropriately constructed beforehand and with reassembling new ones. (Such an assumption is attractive because it correctly predicts, for example, that processing delays will be correlated with the "length" of the ambiguous sentence in the garden path; cf. Frazier & Rayner, 1982.) Next, suppose that the feature structures for individual words are held in the lexicon in a pre-assembled form, and that once the word is recognised the entire structure is passed into a buffer store where it can either be stored intact or combined with other units to yield new, more complex feature structures.

To account for the findings outlined earlier, I propose that unification takes place in two stages. At the end of a successful cycle, the initial structures will have been linked by the application of a (reverse) phrase-structure rule which dictates, among other things, which features have to match across different units. The first operation specifies *which* unification rule is to be applied in the new phase of processing.

In stage 2, all of the checks associated with this rule are run, and if the results are positive the initial elements are restructured, using procedures specified by the rule. Eventually, this produces a new unified structure. If the check uncovers inconsistencies, the unification fails and the elements are returned to their original discrete forms. At this point, a new rule can act as a potential unifying agent. In more detail, the types of processing envisaged in the two stages of analysis are as follows:

Stage 1: determining *which* unification routine is put into effect. Assume that a rule qualifies to act as a unifying agent if it satisfies a very simple "triggering condition" which is based (exclusively) on the general category labels of the structures present in the buffer. For example, if structures labelled DET, ADJ, and N appear in a string (in this order), then a rule summarised by unification (22) might be activated (stage 1). This in turn would allow the parser to proceed to stage 2 and unify the three separate feature structures for DET, ADJ and N, thereby forming a single, complex structure representing a NP:

22. DET + ADJ + N => NP

When the material in working memory is consistent with two or more potential unifications, conflict-resolution principles would have to be used to establish priorities. I assume that Frazier's (1987a) Minimal Attachment and Late Closure preferences (as well as other special-purpose strategies; Cuetos & Mitchell, 1988) are brought into effect during this stage of processing.

If at any stage the material turns out to be incompatible with the entire range of "triggering conditions" specified by the grammar, then there must presumably be ways of halting the operation and checking the input for errors (e.g. misprints, misidentification of words, etc.). However, events of this kind should be rare with clearly presented materials, and most word-strings would be assembled into at least some kind of tentative structure.

Stage 2: checking the unification. A unification rule specifies a set of constraints or conditions that have to be satisfied before the unification process can run through to completion. Once a rule is activated in stage 1, I assume that the initial, unintegrated feature structures are brought together in a partially assembled canonical form and the requisite checks are run as stage 2 of the unification process. To illustrate, in unification

(22) above, two conditions might be: (i) that the feature structures representing the elements of a nounphrase should all share the same markers for number, i.e. number (DET) = number (ADJ) = number (N); and (ii) that the feature structures should agree in their gender making, i.e. gender (DET) = gender (ADJ) = gender (N). (In other instances, the conditions might be based on semantic and pragmatic principles, as well as on numerous other grammatical constraints, including verb-subcategorisation, verb-control, and so on.)

If all the conditions are met, procedures for implementing the unification can be set in train. These procedures build a new unified structure which incorporates all of the features that it is required to introduce from the original elements, and *eliminates* features which have no place in the final "confirmed" structure. Thus, in the NP example, number (NP) is set to number (N), and gender (NP) is set to gender (N), and so on. Similarly, if an optionally transitive verb is unified with a NP as its direct object (as with "visited the doctor" in 17), then features for the NP and features associated with the transitive form of the verb are retained, whereas intransitive features are removed from the newly unified structure.

If the detailed conditions are *not* met, then the unification fails. In this case, the separate feature structures are returned to their initial, unintegrated states. At this point, the whole procedure might be repeated with an alternative rule which satisfies the preliminary (triggering) conditions of stage 1.

The process is eventually completed when the feature structures for all of the words of the sentence have been unified into a single entity representing the entire sentence. Among other things, this description indicates exactly how the sentence has been parsed.

On present evidence, there are no grounds for being very specific about the nature of the intermediate or tentative representation between the end of stage 1 and the end of stage 2. On the one hand, a new "target" structure may be synthesised as soon as stage 1 has been completed, in which case some of the implications or consequences of this tentative structure might begin to emerge even before its preconditions have been fully tested. Alternatively, the intermediate representation may take on few, if any, of the structural features of the representation destined to emerge following successful testing. For instance, it is possible that the feature structures to be integrated at this juncture are simply placed in marked "slots" within a loose framework which represents none of the consequences or implications connected with the target structure. In such a state, it may be possible for the individual argument values (e.g. for number, gender, etc.) to be read off and compared, even though the target structure has not yet been assembled. On this account, the intermediate representation would carry no information which is derived from the final structure. For example, in unification (22), the information represented would not code the fact that the ADJ modifies the N and therefore alters its semantic properties. Further work will need to be carried out before we can say which of these alternatives appears to be the more viable.

Accounting for the Data

This general framework can be used relatively easily to explain the lexical effects described in the previous sections. It was concluded that there was no need to postulate that detailed lexical information plays any role in the processes initially used to assemble structures. This amounts to claiming that such information is not used in the selection or execution of the first stage of the unification operation (i.e. selecting the unification procedure and co-ordinating the arguments and slots for the consistency checks to be run in stage 2). Instead, I propose that the effects are introduced during the second stage when the tests are actually run.

To use specific examples, let us suppose that information about subcategorisation or control properties of verbs is not scrutinised or evaluated until the second stage of the unification process. This would explain why inappropriate structures may be built (and destroyed) when lexical information is delayed until the end of the clause as in Frazier's (1987b) work on Dutch. It also explains how inappropriate structures might come to be partly built and evaluated, even when the lexical information is available at the time of construction (cf. Mitchell, 1987a; Stowe, 1989). It is worth pointing out that there is no difficulty in explaining how lexical effects can be introduced before the end of the sentence. There is no reason why the unification check in stage 2 should not be carried out a very short time after the constituent words have been read, and a failure at this point would quickly lead to a revision of the parsing process.

According to this account of the parsing process, there are always prerequisites for setting up any tentative unification. It follows that there may be circumstances in which no set of conditions is met, even though two or more feature structures co-exist in working memory. On current assumptions, there is no way in which structures can be passed on for consistency checking when this happens. Within the theoretical framework, therefore, it is possible to use data about inconsistency or implausibility effects to draw inferences about the types of structure which are capable of being generated by the first stage in the process. For instance, if it is possible to demonstrate that there are inconsistency effects which people can detect before the end of a *clause* (say), then this implies that the parser is capable of assembling (and therefore testing) feature structures that represent units smaller than clauses. Similarly, if there are inconsistencies which can be detected before the end of a *phrase*, this implies that subphrasal units can be passed from the assembler to the checker. Up to now, no one has reported any experiment in which there is a pause at a point which could not (at least potentially) be the end of a clause, and so at present we do not need to postulate that there are "transfer units" smaller than clauses. However, it seems likely that it will prove possible to demonstrate interactions which are more fine-grained than this. Such observations may have interesting implications for the kinds of feature structures that can be manipulated. For instance, if it is possible to test a nounphrase for consistency before the noun itself becomes available (e.g. in testing gender/number consistency in the incomplete phrase "la petite . . .", in French), then this would imply that the assembler is capable of passing incomplete structures over to the checker. Operations of this kind would be described more readily by some grammatical formalisms than by others. In the categorial grammar of Ades and Steedman (1982), there is a symbol (NP/N) for an incomplete nounphrase of the kind described, and it is not difficult to see how such a formalism could handle a finding of the kind mooted above. On the other hand, an observation of this kind would not be easy to reconcile with a grammar without any kind of symbols for representing incomplete structures. For a more extensive discussion of the relationship between "incremental interpretation" and different grammars, see Altmann and Steedman (1988, pp. 193–196).

A Connectionist Model

In the previous section, lexical structure-checking effects were accounted for in terms of a relatively serial symbol-manipulating model. However, this does not imply that this kind of approach has the monopoly on explanations of these data. Equivalents of these checking operations can be implemented quite effectively within the framework of "massively parallel" connectionist models of parsing of the kind outlined by Waltz and Pollack (1985), McClelland and Kawamoto (1986), St John and McClelland (in press), and others.

Suppose that the parser is a Parallel Distributed Processing (PDP) system in which the input units represent individual words (and their ordinal position within the sentence). Assume that the output units correspond to linguistic units which represent the different potential structural interpretations of the sentence. Imagine that, following extensive training, all interconnections between input, output, and any hidden units have stabilised in such a way that the system is capable of parsing any legitimate sentence. (The parsing solution might consist of the set of mutually compatible output units that are activated when the sentence is fed into the system.)

In a fully tuned form of such a system, there would presumably be inhibitory connections between units representing mutually incompatible structures. This would ensure, for example, that all structures based on intransitive verbs would be in competition with those incorporating transitive verbs in the same position in the sentence. As a consequence of this, one or other would end up being eliminated from consideration in the final parse of the sentence.

Suppose that during training, some of the "hidden" units specialise in such a way that they become active when any verb is presented in the sentence, and that others are even more specifically tuned so that they respond to particular verb forms (e.g. intransitive verbs, verbs with an infinitival complement, etc.). It is easy to see that structural decisions could be mediated by units of this kind. For example, units representing intransitive verbs could have strong excitatory links with output units representing sentences or clauses in which the verb is used intransitively. Similarly, such verb units might have *inhibitory* links with output units standing for transitive, complement, and other structures. In principle, it seems likely that network arrangements of this kind could be used to account for any evidence that detailed lexical information has an influence on the way in which sentences are parsed.

In a PDP system of this kind, "garden-path" effects could occur if the activation set up by the first few words of the sentence favoured an output unit which ultimately turned out to be inappropriate. In this case, the "correct" unit would have to compete with the "wrong" one in later stages of processing, and it could take a large number of cycles before the correct unit eventually prevailed (see Waltz & Pollack, 1985, for an illustration of such a competition effect in a connectionist parser). An account of this kind offers a ready explanation for findings in which the critical disambiguating information becomes available relatively late in the sentence. In these circumstances, it is easy to imagine inappropriate structural units first becoming active and subsequently being suppressed during competition with units that become strongly activated towards the end of the sentence.

There remains a problem of explaining why garden-path effects seem to occur even when there is no obvious opportunity for the "wrong" units to get a head-start in building up their level of activation. For example, in processing the segment ". . . sneezed the doctor . . ." in (17), it might have been expected that the unit representing "sneezed" would immediately activate a range of output units with intransitive structures and *inhibit* units taking in transitive structures. On the face of it, it is not easy to see why there should have been any competition of the kind required to explain the reading data. However, it turns out that it is not particularly difficult to handle this result within the PDP framework. Suppose that verbs like "sneeze" are connected both to units representing the general class of intransitive verbs, and also to units standing for the wider class of *all* verbs. Suppose also that these different types of unit have different patterns of connections, with the output units representing the competing structures. Imagine, in particular, that the V units have strong excitatory links with output units in which a NP after the verb is taken as its direct object (presumably because most verbs are transitive, and this is therefore the most likely interpretation of such an input). In such a situation, the <"sneezed">–<"general verb"> path will have a built-in advantage over the alternatives, and the output unit for the direct object interpretation will quickly reach a high level of activation. However, the <"sneezed">–<"intransitive verb"> path will persist in trying to build up competing the intransitive output. Eventually, it will prevail, but not without a lot of adjustment (i.e. reversals of relative levels of activation). The data can then be explained if we assume that in on-line reading studies the signal to proceed (i.e. the button-press or the eye movement) is triggered when the system reaches a critical level of stability.

This connectionist account clearly bears a resemblance to the unification model described above. The process of building up the activation in a connectionist unit corresponds to that of selecting a tentative structure in the first stage of the earlier model. Similarly, reducing unit activation in the face of competition from other units corresponds to breaking up a partly assembled structure following an unsuccessful consistency check. There are conceptual differences between the two frameworks, in that the constructs of "assembling", "checking", and "breaking up" structures are bound to the symbol-processing metaphor. (And this is the reason why we distinguish between the current model and the parallel symbol-processing models introduced on p. 127.) It is not yet clear whether there are any testable differences between the models.

CONCLUSIONS

This paper has reviewed evidence that detailed information from the lexicon is intimately involved in the process of assigning syntactic structure to a sentence. These influences have been demonstrated repeatedly with the subcategorisation and control properties of verbs and they presumably also extend to verb tenses, to animacy, number and gender of nouns, and to a variety of features of the other word classes. There is good evidence that at least some of these features are taken into consideration within a short time after the word has been processed. However, there is no definite evidence that subcategorisation features are drawn upon by the parser when it makes its initial structural decisions. On the contrary, the data show evidence of "late" structure-checking effects, and it is argued that these effects alone are sufficient to account for the data. Because it would be unparsimonious to postulate two different kinds of lexical effect when only one is needed, I have highlighted a model in which detailed lexical information is used exclusively during the checking stage. This model (the two-stage unification model) provides a satisfactory account of all existing data and suggests ways in which work on lexical effects could be developed. A second hypothesis, based on a connectionist parser, also offers an adequate, though rather general, account of the data. It remains to be seen whether an explanation of this kind can be used to generate testable predictions. Whichever model proves to be more productive, it is clear that future research will have to pay a great deal more attention to apparently minor lexical features and the way they exert their influence on the course of parsing.

REFERENCES

Ades, A. & Steedman, M. (1982). On the order of words. *Linguistics and Philosophy*, *4*, 517–558.

Altmann, G. & Steedman, M. (1988). Interaction with context during human sentence processing. *Cognition*, *30*, 191–328.

Clifton, C. & Frazier, L. (1986). The use of syntactic information in filling gaps. *Journal of Psycholinguistic Research*, *15*, 209–224.

Clifton, C. & Frazier, L. (1988). Comprehending sentences with long-distance dependencies. In G. Carlson & M. K. Tanenhaus (Eds), *Linguistic structure in language processing*. Dordrecht: Reidel.

Clifton, C., Frazier, L., & Connine, C. (1984). Lexical and syntactic expectations in sentence comprehension. *Journal of Verbal Learning and Verbal Behavior*, *23*, 696–708.

Crain, S. & Fodor, J. D. (1985). How can grammars help parsers? In D. R. Dowty, L. Karttunen, & A. M. Zwicky (Eds), *Natural language parsing: Psychological, computational and theoretical perspectives*. Cambridge: Cambridge University Press.

Cuetos, F. & Mitchell, D. C. (1988). Cross-linguistic differences in parsing: Restrictions on the use of the Late Closure strategy in Spanish. *Cognition*, *30*, 73–105.

Ferreira, F. & Henderson, J. M. (in press). The use of verb information in syntactic parsing: a comparison of evidence from eye movements and segment-by-segment self-paced reading. *Journal of Experimental Psychology: Learning, Memory and Cognition*.

Fodor, J. D. (1988). On modularity in syntactic processing. *Journal of Psycholinguistic Research*, *17*, 125–168.

Fodor, J. A., Garrett, M. F., & Bever, T. G. (1968). Some syntactic determinants of sentential complexity. II. Verb structure. *Perception of Psychophysics*, *3*, 453–461.

Fodor, J. A., Bever, T. G., & Garrett, M. F. (1974). *The psychology of language: An introduction to psycholinguistics and generative grammar*. New York: McGraw-Hill.

Ford, M. & Dalrymple, M. (1988). A note on some psychological evidence and alternative grammars. *Cognition*, *29*, 63–71.

Ford, M., Bresnan, J. W., & Kaplan, R. M. (1982). A competence based theory of syntactic closure. In J. W. Bresnan (Ed.), *The mental representation of grammatical relations*. Cambridge, Mass.: MIT Press.

Frazier, L. (1987a). Sentence processing: A tutorial review. In M. Coltheart (Ed.), *Attention and performance XII*. Hillsdale, N.J.: Lawrence Erlbaum Associates Inc.

Frazier, L. (1987b). Syntactic processing: Evidence from Dutch. *Natural Language and Linguistic Theory*, *5*, 519–560.

Frazier, L. (1988). Against lexical generation of syntax. In W. Marslen-Wilson (Ed.), *Lexical representation and processes*. Cambridge, Mass.: MIT Press.

Frazier, L. & Rayner, K. (1982). Making and correcting errors during sentence comprehension: Eye movements in the analysis of structurally ambiguous sentences. *Cognitive Psychology*, *14*, 178–210

Frazier, L. & Rayner, K. (1987). Resolution of syntactic category ambiguities: Eye movements in parsing lexically ambiguous sentences. *Journal of Memory and Language*, *26*, 505–526.

Frazier, L., Clifton, C., & Randall, J. (1983). Filling gaps: Decision principles and structure in sentence comprehension. *Cognition*, *13*, 187–222.

Freedman, S. E. & Forster, K. I. (1985). The psychological status of overgenerated sentences. *Cognition*, *19*, 101–131.

Hakes, D. T. (1971). Does verb structure affect comprehension? *Perception and Psychophysics*, *10*, 229–232.

Holmes, V. M. (1984). Parsing strategies and discourse context. *Journal of Psycholinguistic Research*, *13*, 237–257.

Holmes, V. M. (1987). Syntactic parsing: In search of the garden path. In M. Coltheart (Ed.), *Attention and performance XII*. Hillsdale, N.J.: Lawrence Erlbaum Associates Inc.

Holmes, V. M. & Forster, K. I. (1972). Perceptual complexity and underlying sentence structure. *Journal of Verbal Learning and Verbal Behavior*, *11*, 148–156.

Holmes, V. M., Kennedy, A., & Murray, W. S. (1987). Syntactic structure and the garden path. *Quarterly Journal of Experimental Psychology*, *39A*, 277–294.

Kay, M. (1985). Parsing in functional unification grammar. In D. R. Dowty, L. Karttunen, & A. M. Zwicky (Eds), *Natural language parsing: Psychological, computational and theoretical perspectives*. Cambridge: Cambridge University Press.

Kennedy, A. & Murray, W. S. (1984). Inspection times for words in syntactically ambiguous sentences under three presentation conditions. *Journal of Experimental Psychology: Human Perception and Performance*, *10*, 833–847.

Kennedy, A., Murray, W. S., Jennings, F., & Reid, C. (1990). Parsing complements: Comments on the generality of the principle of minimal attachment. *Language and Cognitive Processes* (this issue).

McCarthy, R. & Warrington, E. K. (1985). Category specificity in an agrammatic patient: The relative impairment of verbal retrieval and comprehension. *Neuropsychologia*, *23*, 709–727.

McClelland, J. L. & Kawamoto, A. H. (1986). Mechanisms of sentence processing: Assigning roles to constituents. In J. L. McClelland, D. E. Rumelhart, & the PDP Research Group (Eds), *Parallel distributed processing: Explorations in the microstructure of cognition*. Cambridge, Mass.: MIT Press.

Mitchell, D. C. (1986). On-line parsing of structurally ambiguous sentences: Evidence against the use of lookahead. Unpublished paper, University of Exeter (available from author).

Mitchell, D. C. (1987a). Lexical guidance in human parsing: Locus and processing characteristics. In M. Coltheart (Ed.), *Attention and performance XII*. Hillsdale, N.J.: Lawrence Erlbaum Associates Inc.

Mitchell, D. C. (1987b). Reading and syntactic analysis. In J. Beech & A. Colley (Eds), *Cognitive approaches to reading*. Chichester: John Wiley.

Mitchell, D. C. & Green, D. W. (1978). The effects of context and content on immediate processing in reading. *Quarterly Journal of Experimental Psychology*, *30*, 609–636.

Mitchell, D. C. & Holmes, V. M. (1985). The role of specific information about the verb in parsing sentences with local structural ambiguity. *Journal of Memory and Language*, *24*, 542–559.

Mitchell, D. C. & Zagar, D. (1986). Psycholinguistic work on parsing with lexical functional grammars. In N. E. Sharkey (Ed.), *Advances in cognitive science*. Ellis Horwood.

Nicol, J. (in press). What the parser knows about the grammar: Psycholinguistic evidence. In *Conference Proceedings of WCCFL VIII*.

Nicol, J. & Osterhout, L. (1988). Reactivating antecedents of empty categories during parsing. Unpublished manuscript, University of Arizona.

Perfetti, C. A. (in press). The destabilized language processor: Semantic influences in an autonomous syntax. In D. Balota, G. B. Flores d'Arcais, & K. Rayner (Eds), *Comprehension processes in reading*. Hillsdale, N.J.: Lawrence Erlbaum Associates Inc.

Rayner, K., Carlson, M., & Frazier, L. (1983). The interaction of syntax and semantics during sentence processing: Eye movements in the analysis of semantically biased sentences. *Journal of Verbal Learning and Verbal Behavior*, *22*, 358–374.

Shapiro, L. P., Zurif, E. B., & Grimshaw, J. (1987). Sentence processing and the mental representation of verbs. *Cognition*, *27*, 219–246.

Shapiro, L. P., Zurif, E. B., & Grimshaw, J. (1989). Verb processing during sentence comprehension: Contextual impenetrability. *Journal of Psycholinguistic Research*, *18*, 223–243.

Shieber, S. M. (1986). *An introduction to unification-based approaches to grammar*. Center for the Study of Language and Information.

St John, M. F. & McClelland, J. L. (in press). Learning and applying contextual constraints in sentence comprehension. *Artificial Intelligence*.

Stowe, L (1989). Thematic structures and sentence comprehension. In G. N. Carlson & M. K. Tanenhaus (Eds), *Linguistic structure in language processing*. Dordrecht: Klower Academic.

Tanenhaus, M. K. & Carlson, G. N. (1988). Lexical structure and language comprehension. In W. Marslen-Wilson (Ed.), *Lexical representation and processes*. Cambridge, Mass.: MIT Press.

Tanenhaus, M. K., Boland, J., Garnsey, S. M., & Carlson, G. N. (1989). Lexical structure in parsing long-distance dependencies. *Journal of Psycholinguistic Research*, *18*, 37–50.

Waltz, D. L. & Pollack, J. B. (1985). Massively parallel parsing: A strongly interactive model of natural language interpretation. *Cognitive Science*, *9*, 51–74.

LANGUAGE AND COGNITIVE PROCESSES, 1989, 4 (3/4) SI 155–209

Empty Categories in Sentence Processing

Janet Dean Fodor
Graduate Center, City University of New York
33 West 42 Street, New York, NY 10036

An empty category is an inaudible/invisible constituent of a sentence, postulated by linguists to account for certain regularities of sentence structure. To identify an empty category and associate it with an antecedent that will determine its interpretation, a sentence processing device must apply considerable linguistic knowledge, both universal and language-particular. Experiments show that human processing of empty category constructions is efficient and linguistically informed.

Different linguistic theories postulate different empty categories. Recent and ongoing experiments by several researchers attempt to determine which kinds of empty categories are recognised by the human processor. Assuming a transparent relationship between the parser and the grammar, the results of these studies could contribute to the evaluation of competing linguistic theories.

THE EMPTY CATEGORY PROBLEM

In one guise or another, empty categories have been a central topic of sentence processing research since the beginning of "generative" psycholinguistics, some 20 years ago. The reason for studying them in the early days was that they seemed to bode nothing but trouble for any sensible—indeed, any imaginable—processing routines. By watching the human sentence processing mechanism struggle with this problem, we could hope to be able to find out how it works, and to uncover properties that were not

---

Requests for reprints should be addressed to Janet Dean Fodor, Graduate Center. City University of New York, 33 West 42 Street, New York, NY 10036.

This paper was written at the urging of the special editor for this volume. I am grateful to Gerry Altmann for his encouragement, but I am embarrassed that there are no new results reported here, and far too many references to incomplete experiments. I hope that it will at least be useful as a review article, though it is not a research paper of the kind this journal usually publishes. The comments I received from Gerry Altmann, Mark Steedman, and an anonymous reviewer were extremely helpful, and I have done my best to respond to them within the bounds of time and space available.

revealed in the processing of less challenging structures. Furthermore, the nature of the processor's difficulties with these constructions promised to provide, as I will explain later, some very general conclusions about natural language design.

An empty category creates two kinds of problems for a processor. First, it does not manifest itself in the input signal, and therefore its existence has to be inferred indirectly. Secondly, in order to receive an interpretation it has to be associated with an antecedent phrase in the sentence, which is usually not adjacent to it and is often quite distant; this spoils the strictly local character of the processes that are otherwise sufficient to build up a structural representation for a sentence. In this first section, I will set out some of the details of these problems. In the next section, I will review some experiments which show how the human sentence processor copes with them. Then I will discuss general theoretical implications, and finally bring the discussion up to the minute by describing a recent line of experimental research on empty categories which may possibly help to select among competing linguistic theories.

An empty category (as is not altogether clear from its name) is a constituent that has no phonological substance associated with it; it is inaudible in speech, and invisible in the standard orthography.[1] Linguistics has not always recognised empty categories. But at least within the generative tradition, it has always recognised the phenomena which current theory accounts for by means of empty categories. For instance, in the Standard Theory of Chomsky's *Aspects* (Chomsky, 1965), there were deletion transformations to account for "missing" pieces of sentences, as in (1) and (2) (where what is missing is a verb and a verbphrase, respectively):

1. John fried the eggplant and Bill __ the tofu.
2. Sam won't eat the eggplant but Susan will __.

To delete something is to remove it completely: it was there in the deep structure of the sentence, and gone in the surface structure. Nowadays, it is widely assumed instead that something is present at all levels of derivation. The verb or verb phrase or other "missing" constituent is generated at deep structure, as any constituent is, and merely happens to be phonologically "empty".

A variety of different empty categories are assumed in current linguistic theory, and I will discuss them below. For the first part of this paper, however, the only one of concern will be what is called wh-trace. Wh-trace

---

[1]For most linguists, though not all, another difference between empty categories and overt constituents is that an empty category cannot have any internal phrase structure.

is created by the wh-movement transformation, which moves a wh-phrase (e.g. *who, which, which of the books, how many of the children*) into a clause-initial position in a question or a relative clause, in English and other languages. Nowadays, wh-movement is subsumed under a more general transformation, *move* α, but it can still be discussed as a separate phenomenon because constructions in which the variable α corresponds to a wh-phrase have their own characteristic properties, different from those of other instances of *move* α. In the early days of transformational grammar, moving a wh-phrase left nothing at the pre-movement position, just as in the case of deletion. In current theory, a "trace" of the wh-phrase is left at the pre-movement position. This trace is an empty category, which is co-indexed with the wh-phrase now at its new position.[2] Thus in (3), the wh-phrase *which of the books* has been moved into clause-initial position within the question clause, which is embedded as the object of *wonder*. There is a wh-trace after the subordinate verb *read*, co-indexed with the moved wh-phrase. As a result of this co-indexing, the wh-phrase will be assigned the thematic (semantic) role that is normally assigned to a phrase in the position of the trace (in this case the role of object or "patient" of *read*); in effect, the trace passes on the thematic role to the wh-phrase, which is no longer in a position to be assigned it directly.

3. I wonder [which of the books]$_i$ John has actually read *wh-trace*$_i$.

Now let us suppose (as we surely should, until or unless the facts dictate against it) that the human sentence processing routines compute for a sentence the very structure that is assigned to it by the mental "competence" grammar. Then the processing routines must construct a trace after the subordinate verb in (3). But consider what this involves. The processor must somehow identify one of the word boundaries in (3) as the position of the trace, while all the other word boundaries in the sentence harbour no trace. There is no quick and simple algorithm that will tell it which boundary contains the trace. The trace is not always at the end of the sentence, as is shown by (4); it is not always the object of a verb, as shown by (5) (where it is the subject of *were*) and (6) (where it is the object of a preposition). As shown by (7) and (8), the trace may immediately follow its

[2]It is this co-indexing relation which motivated the shift from the earlier theory without traces, to the current theory with traces. It was observed that the pre-movement position of a phrase and its post-movement position must stand in a certain structural relationship to each other, similar to the structural relationship that must hold between a pronoun and the antecedent with which it is co-indexed. These two separate facts could be recognised as the same fact once movement was assumed to leave a trace co-indexed to the moved phrase as antecedent (see Chomsky, 1976; Fiengo, 1977).

antecedent, or it may be separated from it by several intervening clauses:[3]

4. I wonder [which of the books]$_i$ John had read *wh-trace*$_i$ before class.
5. I wonder [which of the books]$_i$ John thought *wh-trace*$_i$ were unreadable.
6. I wonder [which of the books]$_i$ John lit the fire with *wh-trace*$_i$ yesterday.
7. I wonder [which of the books]$_i$ *wh-trace*$_i$ were unreadable.
8. I wonder [which of the books]$_i$ Mary thinks John confided to Sarah that he had read *wh-trace*$_i$.

The only way for the processor to find the trace position is to find a position that "needs" a phrase of the kind that has been moved (in these examples, a noun phrase, though in other cases it might be a prepositional phrase, an adverb, or so forth).[4] If the processor is lucky, there is just one

---

[3]According to GB theory (see below), when the moved phrase and its trace are separated by one or more clause boundaries, there must also be an intermediate wh-trace in the clause-initial position of every intervening clause, as in (i) (this is a *very* approximate statement; it is not true of all such constructions in all languages. For more details see van Riemsdijk and Williams, 1986, chs 4, 9, and 18):

i. I wonder [which of the books]$_i$ Mary thinks *wh-trace*$_i$ John confided to Sarah *wh-trace*$_i$ that he had read *wh-trace*$_i$.

I will not discuss these intermediate traces further. It would be interesting if their presence could be confirmed by psycholinguistic experiments, and some attempts have been made (see Frazier & Clifton, 1989; Nicol & Osterhout, in prep.). The results so far are inconclusive, though further refinements of these experiments could yet reveal intermediate traces. Perhaps they are difficult to demonstrate because, unlike other traces, they do not affect the meaning of the sentence. But it could be that they are not present, either because the theory that postulates them is wrong, or because the theory is right but the traces are subsequently deleted (see Lasnik & Saito, 1984).

[4]Phonological cues to the trace position are minimal. In some cases, there is a failure of phonological reduction effects, such as *wanna-contraction*. In (i), the sequence *want to* can be pronounced *wanna*, but it cannot be so pronounced in (ii) where there is an intervening trace:

i. Who$_i$ does John want to speak to *wh-trace*$_i$?
ii. Who$_i$ does John want *wh-trace*$_i$ to speak to the students?

In (iii), the sequence *John is* can be pronounced *John's*, but it cannot be so pronounced in (iv) where there is a trace following the verb:

iii. I think John is there.
iv. I wonder where$_i$ John is *wh-trace*$_i$.

However, phonological reductions only flag *non*-positions for trace; since reduction is optional, there is still an ambiguity about whether trace is present in unreduced constructions. And in any case, not all empty categories block reduction. For example, some linguists hold that there is an empty category (called *PRO*, and discussed below) as subject of *to speak* in (i).

such position in the sentence, and it is perfectly clear which it is. But in other cases, the processor may be unable to determine, at least on the basis of locally available evidence, whether a position needs an NP or not. In (3), for example, the verb *read* needs an NP object. But note that *read* does not *always* need an object; it can function as an intransitive verb, as in (9) and (10) [in (9) there is no wh-movement in the sentence; in (10) there is wh-movement, but it is from a different position, not immediately following *read*]:

9. John would never admit that he read in bed.
10. I wonder [which of the books]$_i$ John read about *wh-trace*$_i$ in the newspaper.

Thus the fact of the matter is that there must be a trace after *read* in (3), but looking at the position after *read* does not show that there must. What entails that the trace is after *read* is just that there is not any other place in this sentence for it to be. The wh-phrase must be associated with a trace *somewhere* in the sentence, and when all other positions have been excluded as impossible positions for an NP, the only possible one must be the correct one. In sentence (10), by contrast, there is another possible position for a trace after the preposition *about*. And in this case, the trace *must* be after *about* rather than after *read*, because a noun phrase object is obligatory for *about*, whereas it is merely optional for *read*.

Thus the identification of an empty category position often involves a global inference over the whole sentence. And because the sentence is not globally available, but is received word by word, the identification of empty categories often involves the processor in temporary ambiguity, with consequent "garden paths" if it guesses wrong about how to resolve the ambiguity. In (10), for example, the processor might initially guess that the trace follows *read*; then it would discover, when the sentence ends without a noun phrase after *about*, that this had been a mistake. Empty categories are by no means the only source of "garden paths" to confound a parser; there are many other examples, such as *The horse raced past the*

If there is, then it does not block *wanna-contraction*. Also, it is usually assumed that there is a wh-trace as subject of *is winning* in (v):

v. Who$_i$ do you think wh-trace$_i$ is winning?

If there is, it does not block reduction of *think is* to *think*'s (see Schachter, 1982). Some of the experiments reported below used visually presented sentences and some used auditorily presented sentences. The latter may carry a little more information about empty category positions, but not a great deal.

barn fell and *The cotton clothing is made of comes from Mississippi*. But certainly there would be far fewer garden paths if natural languages did not employ empty categories.

FINDING WH-TRACES AND ASSIGNING ANTECEDENTS

How does the human sentence processor cope with the empty category problem? In this section, I will consider what is the very best that any system could do in the circumstances, and examine the experimental evidence to see whether the human processor in fact achieves this optimum.

Antecedent Information

Unlike an empty category, an antecedent is an overt chunk of the input sentence, and therefore should be easy to recognise.[5] Berwick and Weinberg (1984) have observed that a smart parser would make use of the presence of an antecedent in deciding whether or not to hypothesise an empty category in some sentence position, when local information (e.g. about verb transitivity) does not resolve the issue. The rule is simple: Do not posit a trace at sentence position P if the sentence does not contain a suitable antecedent for a trace at P. In all the cases we will be concerned with here (though not in all natural language constructions), a legitimate antecedent would precede the trace, and therefore this rule is a usable one even for a real-time processor whose decisions must keep pace with the flow of input. Of course, it is only half a rule; it does not tell the processor what to do at P if there *is* a suitable antecedent earlier in the sentence. This is because of the global nature of the inference, discussed above. If there is

---

[5]In fact, this is not always so, at least according to GB theory (see below). An empty category may itself be the antecedent for another empty category. This is the case in example (i) of footnote 3 above, where the wh-trace after *thinks* is antecedent to the wh-trace after *Sarah*, which is antecedent to the wh-trace after *read*. Another example is shown in (i); this has wh-trace as antecedent for an NP-trace. (NP-trace is discussed on pp. 184ff. Grammatical principles do not permit it to be associated directly with the wh-phrase.)

i. I wonder [which of the books]$_i$ John thought *wh-trace*$_i$ had been read *NP-trace*$_i$ by the students.

Also, we will see (pp. 196–198) that it may sometimes be difficult to recognise an antecedent as an antecedent. But that is rarely true of a wh-antecedent, so we can ignore this problem for now.

an antecedent, a trace must be posited somewhere; but it does not follow, for any particular position P, that there must be a trace there.[6]

Thus, antecedent information is incomplete information, but it is still potentially useful. Does the human sentence processor take advantage of it? Crain and Fodor (1985) and Stowe (1986) have shown that it does, on the basis of what has been called the "filled gap effect". This occurs when the processor has found an antecedent, is looking for a trace (often called a gap, in processing parlance), and discovers that some likely gap position is in fact not empty; a "surprise" reaction by the processor at that point would indicate that it had been expecting the trace there.[7] This is illustrated in (11)–(13):

11. Who$_i$ could the little child have forced *wh-trace*$_i$ to sing those stupid French songs for Cheryl last Christmas?
12. Who$_i$ could the little child have forced us to sing those stupid French songs for *wh-trace*$_i$ last Christmas?
13. The little child could have forced us to sing those stupid French songs for Cheryl last Christmas.

Note that (11) has its trace after *forced*, whereas (12) has a lexical nounphrase (*us*) after *forced*, and the wh-trace later in the sentence. It is the position after *forced* in (12) which constitutes a "filled gap". Response

---

[6]Berwick and Weinberg (1984) also suggest that the task of finding the trace is made easier by the existence of intermediate traces in cases of "long-distance" movement, as in the example in footnote 3. But that is not so clear. The intermediate traces are *also* inaudible/invisible in the input; they too must be inferred. And in many cases, the question of whether or not an intermediate trace exists at some position depends on already having decided where the "ultimate" trace is. This is so, for example, in (i) and (ii):

i. I wonder [which boy]$_i$ Mary promised *wh-trace*$_i$ [that she would sing].
ii. I wonder [which boy]$_i$ Mary promised [*intermed-trace*$_i$ that she would sing to *wh-trace*$_i$].

In (i), there is no intermediate trace at the beginning of the lower clause, because the ultimate trace is the object of *promised* in the main clause, prior to the subordinate clause; in (ii) there *is* an intermediate trace, because the ultimate trace is down inside the subordinate clause. But the two word sequences are identical until the very end. The correct decision about an intermediate trace can be determined only when the end-of-sentence information has been used to establish the position of the ultimate trace.

[7]A standard assumption for some years has been that syntactic processing is "serial", i.e. that the processor contemplates alternative analyses for an ambiguous structure one after the other, settling for the first one it finds that is compatible with all the input. A serial model predicts that one analysis of an ambiguous string will be preferred over another. For convenience, I will presuppose a serial model in what follows. But parallel processing models are also compatible with the existence of parsing preferences or expectations, as long as it is assumed that the alternative analyses, though computed simultaneously, are ranked (see Altmann & Steedman, 1988; Gorrell, 1987; Kurtzman, 1985).

times in a self-paced, word-by-word reading task revealed that sentences like (12) are more difficult to process than sentences like (11). In particular, there is processing difficulty in (12) at the position of the "filled gap", i.e. increased reading time for the word *us*. Apparently, the processor, proceeding "from left to right" through the sentence, is aware that the object position after *forced* is a possible position for a trace, anticipates the trace there, and is surprised to find that it is not there.[8] In (13), by contrast, there is no difficulty after *forced*, even though a lexical noun phrase appears there, just as in (12). The only difference between (12) and (13) up to that point (apart from subject-auxiliary inversion) is that (12) contains a wh-antecedent and (13) does not. Therefore, the difference in the parser's responses to these two sentences is presumably due to the fact that it posits a trace only in the presence of a prior antecedent.

We conclude, therefore, that the processor notes an antecedent, and begins to form expectations about where its trace might be. Forming expectations is work. Is this work something that a sensible processor would undertake? Is it useful? Or would it be more efficient *not* to try to pre-guess the input but just to wait and see what it delivers e.g. the word *us* right after *forced* in (12)? Presumably, the work of forming expectations about traces would be more worth the effort to the extent that it is more accurate, and helps the processor to narrow in precisely on the true trace position. Therefore, what we would like to know next is whether the processor's expectations are linguistically informed. Does the processor predict traces indiscriminately, or does it distinguish between legitimate trace positions and illegitimate ones? Does it know which of the legitimate positions is most likely to be the actual trace position?

Subcategorisation Information

Let us take the second of these questions first. Its answer is a confident affirmative. The processor apparently uses its knowledge of lexical fre-

[8]There are no obvious grounds for *predicting* that the processor will anticipate a gap where there is none; it is merely convenient for us that it happens to do so, as it provides evidence bearing on the question we are interested in, about the processor's sensitivity to antecedents. Gap-anticipation of this kind falsifies Fodor's (1978) proposal that the processor, when in need of a certain constituent (say, a noun phrase), will always try the next constituent in the input to see if it is what is needed, before concluding that the constituent is missing and that an empty category must therefore be assumed. It seemed possible for a while that this strategy was correct, and that the conflicting findings were due to the relatively slow speed of presentation in the self-paced, word-by-word reading task, which could encourage an impatient processor to anticipate its input. However, an experiment by Swinney et al. (1988) reported below, shows similar anticipatory responses with sentences presented auditorily at 250–300 msec per word.

quencies to decide which post-verbal positions most likely contain traces. Fodor (1978) noted the contrast between the sentence pair in (14) and the sentence pair in (15). In both pairs, the (a) sentence has a trace right after the verb, whereas the (b) sentence has a trace later in the sentence. As in the examples above, there is temporary ambiguity about the trace position until the end of the sentence. We can tell what guesses the processor makes about trace positions by seeing which of the temporarily ambiguous sentences it finds easier to process. In (14), the (a) sentence seems to be easier; in (15), it is the (b) sentence that is easier:

14a. [Which book]$_i$ did the teacher read *wh-trace*$_i$ to the children?
b. [Which book]$_i$ did the teacher read to the children from *wh-trace*$_i$?
15a. [Which student]$_i$ did the teacher walk *wh-trace*$_i$ to the cafeteria?
b. [Which student]$_i$ did the teacher walk to the cafeteria with *wh-trace*$_i$?

This difference is explained once we note that the verb *read* occurs very frequently with a following noun phrase object, whereas the verb *walk*, though it *can* take an object, does so only rarely. The processor's best bet, therefore, on encountering *read* with no apparent object, is to assume that an object is present but is empty; but its best bet on encountering *walk* without an object is to assume that it has no object.

The estimates of relative processing difficulty for the sentences in (14) and (15) are based only on informal judgement. But the processor's sensitivity to lexical preferences has been confirmed experimentally by Clifton, Frazier, and Connine (1984) and by Tanenhaus, Stowe, and Carlson (1985; see also Tanenhaus, Boland, Garnsey, & Carlson, 1989a). I will review these studies very briefly. Clifton et al. (1984) used a timed grammaticality judgement task, and found that sentences like (16), with a verb (*stole*) that prefers to be transitive, were judged to be grammatical more often than sentences like (17), with a verb (*drove*) that prefers to be intransitive:

16. Tommy's girlfriend was impressed with what$_i$ Tommy stole *wh-trace*$_i$ at the racetrack.
17. Tommy's girlfriend was impressed with what$_i$ Tommy drove *wh-trace*$_i$ at the racetrack.

Note that both verbs can function as transitive or as intransitive, but that in these particular sentences, both verbs must be construed as transitive, with a following trace as object. This fact is not determinable, however, until the end of the sentence (by which point no other possible position for the trace has been encountered). The lower acceptance rate for sentences like

(17), shows that the processor is sensitive to transitivity preferences. It suggests that when the processor encounters *drove* with no overt object, it does not hypothesise an object trace; the end of the sentence will then appear ill-formed (for lack of any trace), and the sentence will be judged ungrammatical unless the processor can hurriedly revise its first analysis.

Tanenhaus et al. (1985) used a timed anomaly judgement task, in which subjects indicate after reading the sentence whether or not it makes sense. They compared transitive-preference and intransitive-preference verbs, in sentence contexts that required them to be transitive, with a trace as object, and in sentence contexts that required them to be intransitive, with the trace occurring later in the sentence. Just like Clifton et al.'s (1984) examples, the actual position of the trace was not determinable until the end of the sentence. For brevity's sake, I will report only a portion of the results. Example (18) shows a transitive-preference verb (*asked*) in an intransitive sentence context; (19) shows an intransitive-preference verb (*raced*) in a similar context:

18a. The district attorney found out [which witness]$_i$ the reporter asked anxiously about *wh-trace*$_i$.
b. The district attorney found out [which church]$_i$ the reporter asked anxiously about *wh-trace*$_i$.
19a. The sheriff wasn't sure [which horse]$_i$ the cowboy raced desperately past *wh-trace*$_i$.
b. The sheriff wasn't sure [which rock]$_i$ the cowboy raced desperately past *wh-trace*$_i$.

Note that in both cases there is a potential trace position which the processor might notice in object position after the subordinate verb (*asked*, *raced*), but in these sentences that is just a false alarm; the true trace position is later in the sentence. Each sentence was tested with two different wh-phrases. The wh-phrase in the (a) version above is plausible as the antecedent of a trace in the false gap position after the verb; the wh-phrase in the (b) version is implausible if associated with the false gap position. (Both wh-phrases were plausible as antecedent of the trace in the correct position later in the sentence.) Tanenhaus et al. (1985) found that for sentences like (18) the *witness* version was accepted as sensible more often and more rapidly than the *church* version. This suggests that the processor assumed there was a wh-trace after *asked*, and that when this trace had as antecedent the implausible *church*, the processor was distressed and the response was disrupted. By contrast, for sentences like (19), there was no difference in performance between the *horse* version and the *rock* version. Here the verb was a preferred-intransitive; the absence of any disruptive effect of the implausible antecedent suggests that the processor took the verb to be intransitive, and therefore did not even consider the possibility that the trace was its object.

Thus it appears that the processor's hypotheses about trace positions are sensitive to lexical preferences. The grammar and the input sentence together do not always provide enough information for the processor to be sure, until later, which of the potential trace positions in a sentence is the actual trace position; but the processor at least knows which is most *likely* to be the actual trace position. The relevant information about transitivity preference must presumably be stored in the lexical entry of the relevant verb;[9] therefore, the processor is apparently consulting the lexicon before making its decisions. If this is so, we would obviously expect to find that the processor's hypotheses also respect absolute lexical restrictions on verbs, such as *subcategorisation* restrictions which specify that some verbs can *only* be transitive, and other verbs can *only* be transitive.

There are surprisingly few experimental results that bear directly on this very basic question of whether trace identification respects subcategorisation constraints in the grammar.[10] The experiment discussed above by Clifton et al. (1984) included sentences containing pure transitive verbs (e.g. *build*) and pure intransitives (e.g. *tiptoe*). The intransitive sentences were awkwardly constructed and the results for them were inconclusive, but the results for the pure transitives were comparable to those for the preferred transitives. We cannot tell from this experiment whether the processor treats subcategorisation facts, like frequency facts, just as useful clues, or whether it treats them as true constraints to be honoured at all times.[11]

Relevant information may come from studies which test sensitivity to subcategorisation constraints in constructions that do not involve empty categories. A recent finding by Mitchell (1987; this issue) seems to indicate that there is a brief delay before the processor has access to subcategorisation information; in the meantime, it behaves as if it did not know the difference between transitive and intransitive verbs. Mitchell compared sentences like (20) and (21), presented visually in successive fragments, as

[9]Transitivity preference is not a fact about a verb that a "competence" grammar needs to record; but we may imagine that various bits of information useful for processing purposes are tagged on to the grammar's lexical entries.

[10]An interesting issue recently raised by Tanenhaus, Garnsey, and Boland (1989b), which I do not have space to discuss here, is the extent to which the processor's computations are concerned with thematic roles rather than with structural properties of constituents such as are specified by syntactic subcategorisation features.

[11]There is just a hint that the processor may take obligatory transitivity more seriously than preferred transitivity. The percentage of sentences judged grammatical was no higher for the obligatory cases, but responses were faster (though whether this response time difference was significant is not reported).

shown here by the slashes:

20. After the child had sneezed the doctor / prescribed a course of injections.
21. After the child had visited the doctor / prescribed a course of injections.

The first clause of sentence (20) has an obligatorily intransitive verb (*sneezed*), whereas the first clause of (21) has a verb (*visited*) which can be transitive or intransitive. In both cases, the sentence context requires the verb to be construed as intransitive. Mitchell found that subjects took longer to read the first chunk of (20) than to read the first chunk of (21), but they took less time to read the second chunk of (20) than the second chunk of (21). The first finding suggests that the first chunk of *both* sentences was analysed by the processor as a single clause containing a transitive verb and its object; because one cannot sneeze the doctor, this analysis would cause the processor to boggle at (20). The second finding suggests that by the time it encountered the second sentence fragment, the processor had rejected the transitive analysis of (20), on the basis of subcategorisation information about *sneeze*, so that it could then easily analyse *the doctor* as subject of the later clause. In (21), by contrast, there would be no way for the processor to know that the first fragment was not a transitive clause, and so it would be unprepared for the second chunk which is incompatible with that analysis.

The conclusion thus seems to be that subcategorisation information is accessible to the processor, but not in time to influence its initial structural hypothesis. Applying this to empty category constructions, we should conclude that subcategory information does *not* play a primary role in identifying trace positions. However, this conclusion is almost certainly stronger than is warranted. In Mitchell's (1987) experiment, the processor was strongly influenced by how the sentence was divided in the visual display. When the display was changed so that *the doctor* appeared instead at the beginning of the second chunk, both effects described above went away. Thus the processor was apparently taking it for granted that each successive sentence fragment would be a natural sentence unit, a phrase. If so, the slow reading of the first fragment of (20) is sufficiently accounted for by assuming that the processor, knowing that *sneezed* is intransitive, was puzzled by the fact that in this sentence it appears to be being used as a transitive verb.

Thus it remains unknown just how much lexical information is available for use during the early stages of syntactic processing. To find out, we must avoid biasing the processor against its own better judgement as in Mitchell's study. A good way to do so is to use examples containing empty categories (whether one's interest is in the processing of empty categories or not). If a noun phrase is fronted by wh-movement, then the processor will be free to construe it as the object of a verb or not, depending on whether it thinks the verb should have an object. Appropriate experimental materials would be as illustrated in (22):

22a. I'm not sure which of the co-op residents the new janitor we hired is notifying *wh-trace*$_i$ about . . .
b. I'm not sure which of the co-op residents the new janitor we hired is grumbling about *wh-trace*$_i$ . . .
c. I'm not sure which of the co-op residents the new janitor we hired is anxious about *wh-trace*$_i$ . . .

Note that the (a) sentence contains a purely transitive verb (*notifying*), and therefore must have a trace after it, before the preposition. The (b) sentence contains a purely intransitive verb (*grumbling*), and therefore must not have a trace after it; the trace must follow the preposition (either immediately as its object, as shown above, or in some other position later in the sentence). If the processor uses subcategory information about verbs to decide where traces are located, it should reliably identify the different trace positions in (a) and (b).

Note that the (c) sentence in (22) has the same trace position as the (b) sentence, but contains an adjective rather than an intransitive verb. It serves to establish an important baseline for the verb comparison. Suppose that the processor does not identify the traces in (a) and (b) quickly and accurately; then we would conclude that access to subcategorisation information is slow. But it would make a big difference to how we interpreted such a finding, whether access to subcategorisation information was slower than access to *other* kinds of linguistic information, or whether there is merely some general sluggishness in the system which affects all kinds of linguistic information relevant to processing. The (c) sentences with adjectives permit an estimate of this. Adjectives never take an object noun phrase. This is a general fact about the category of adjectives, not a special fact about some subcategory of adjectives that needs to be stored in their lexical entries. Therefore, the comparison between adjective and intransitive verb in (22) is a comparison between category information and subcategory information. If subcategory information is as available as category information is, the processor's performance on (b) should be as fast and accurate as on (c); if subcategory information is *less* available than category information is (which was Mitchell's hypothesis), then performance on (b) will be worse than on (c).

These sentences are currently being tested by Fodor, Swinney, & Chen, using the cross-modal lexical decision task developed by Swinney et al.

(1979) and described in detail below. This task makes it possible to determine which positions the processor contemplates as trace positions for a given antecedent. The sentences are presented auditorily; their prosodic contours are matched across versions; and they become phonetically unintelligible after the preposition, so that actual trace positions are not revealed by the sentence endings. Unfortunately, no data are yet available.

Island Constraints

We have been trying to establish whether the processor respects linguistic constraints on trace positions. So far, we have looked at subcategorisation constraints, which concern the local context of a trace. But natural languages also exhibit more global constraints on trace positions. Though a wh-phrase can be moved indefinitely far in a sentence, it cannot move freely; certain positions are off limits to it, depending on where it started out. In particular, certain kinds of sentence constituents have the property that a phrase may move only within such a constituent, and may not move out of it. Ross (1967) coined the term "island" for a sentence constituent from which a phrase cannot escape. A relative clause constitutes an island, as does a subject phrase, an embedded question, and certain other types of constituent.[12] Does the human sentence processor know about these island constraints and respect them in its search for empty categories in sentences?

Stowe (1986) examined subject islands, such as the bracketed phrase in (23). This phrase is the subject of the subordinate wh-clause which serves as the object of *asked*:

23. The teacher asked what$_i$ [the silly story about Greg's older brother] was supposed to mean *wh-trace*$_i$.

Note that in (23) nothing has been moved out of this subject phrase, and therefore the island constraint has not in fact been violated; the sentence is well-formed. The processor will encounter the antecedent *what*, and will

[12]Later work (Chomsky, 1973) unified the various island restrictions, attributing them all to a single constraint called *Subjacency*, which prevents movement across more than one NP or clause boundary (in English; in other languages the bounding categories may be different). A "long-distance" movement can now result only from a succession of shorter movements each of which respects Subjacency. Successive movement is possible only if there is a suitable pre-clause position for the moved phrase to touch down at along the way. (Where it does, it leaves an intermediate trace, as discussed in footnote 3.) Otherwise, movement is impossible and the construction constitutes an island. Note that these remarks apply to GB theory, not to the other theories outlined on pp. 177ff.

need to find a trace to associate with it. The fact that a subject phrase is an island means that there cannot be a trace inside the subject phrase in (23) associated with the antecedent *what* outside the subject phrase; the trace for *what* must occur somewhere later in the sentence.[13] Does the processor know this, or is it prepared to hypothesise traces within islands and non-islands alike? Stowe used a self-paced, word-by-word reading task, and looked for a "filled gap effect" (see above) at a tempting gap position within the subject island. In (23) the relevant position is immediately after *about*. If the processor did not know about islands, it could anticipate a trace after *about*. In that case, there should be signs of distress as the processor encounters the word *Greg's*, because this word is incompatible with the trace hypothesis. But Stowe found no such filled gap effect, suggesting that the processor does respect island constraints in the grammar as it hunts for empty categories. This is an important and interesting study, but the results were statistically rather weak. The lack of a filled gap effect inside the island is a null result, and though it contrasts with a significant effect in a non-island context that served as a control, the comparison between them was only marginally significant.

What about other kinds of islands? Frazier (1985) reports an experiment by Clifton and Frazier which examined relative clause islands, such as the bracketed clause in (24):

24. What$_i$ did John think the girl [who$_j$ *wh-trace*$_j$ always won] received *wh-trace*$_i$?

The wh-phrase *what* here has its trace at the end of the sentence, in the main clause, not in the island. [There is a second wh-phrase, *who*, inside the relative clause in (24), whose trace is the subject of *won*. This second antecedent–trace relation is not relevant to the present point.] The issue is whether the processor knows that the relative clause is an island with respect to *what* in the main clause, i.e. whether it knows that the trace associated with *what* cannot be inside the relative clause, for example as object of the verb *won*. Note that *won* can be transitive or intransitive, and therefore the processor cannot rely on local subcategorisation information to decide whether or not it is followed by a trace. Clifton and Frazier used a timed end-of-sentence grammaticality judgement task, and compared sentences like (24) with matched sentences in which the relative clause

---

[13]In fact, an antecedent may be associated with *two* (or more) empty categories: its regular trace, and also a "parasitic gap". The latter *can* appear in an island (see Engdahl, 1983). Parasitic gap constructions are often complex and are not fully acceptable to all speakers. I will not discuss them further here. On the processing of parasitic gap constructions, see Seely (1987) and Kurtzman (1989).

contained a purely intransitive verb such as *excel*, for which local information *is* sufficient to establish that it is not followed by an object trace.[14] If the *won* sentence is more difficult to process than the *excel* sentence, this would indicate that the processor is distracted by the locally acceptable trace position after *won*. And that would show that the processor is not making use of the fact that that position is inside an island and therefore off limits. The result that Clifton and Frazier obtained was a small and statistically marginal difference between the two sentences types. Therefore, there is a hint here that the processor ignores island constraints, but we cannot be sure.[15]

In general, then, this interesting set of questions about islands remains unanswered. Further experimental studies would be very welcome.

Selecting an Antecedent

Recent progress in determining whether the processor knows and uses the constraints on empty categories has come from turning the question around the other way. We have been looking at it from the point of view of the antecedent, for which the processor must find an associated trace; but now let us consider a trace, for which the processor must find the right antecedent. Given that the processor has established a trace position, does it ever ignore the grammatical constraints and contemplate an illegal antecedent for it? Given, for example, a trace inside a relative clause island, does the processor ever incorrectly associate it with a noun phrase outside the clause?

Swinney, Ford, Frauenfelder, and Bresnan (1988) have investigated this question using materials as in (25):

25. The policeman saw the boy_i $that_i$ the crowd at the party accused *wh-*$trace_i$ of the crime.

The trace here is in a relative clause, and its antecedent is the relative pronoun. [In fact, in (25) the relative pronoun has been deleted; there is merely the invariant clause introducer *that*. For convenience here, I will treat *that* as if it were the relative pronoun antecedent of the trace.] The

---

[14]Note that this investigation of the processor's sensitivity to island constraints presupposes that it is sensitive to subcategorisation constraints (see the discussion above).

[15]See Fodor (in press) for a discussion of additional complications in the Stowe experiment and the Clifton and Frazier experiment (e.g. that there could be a legitimate parasitic gap after *won* in (24); see footnote 13).

relative pronoun is co-indexed with the trace. It is also co-indexed with the immediately preceding noun, which is the head noun that the relative clause modifies. In (25), the head noun is *boy*. Thus, indirectly, via the relative pronoun, the trace is understood to refer to the boy.[16]

Swinney et al. (1988). used the cross-modal lexical decision task (and subsequently a cross-modal naming task) to detect "reactivation" of the meaning of the antecedent phrase at the position of the trace. It is assumed that the processor integrates the meaning of the antecedent into the sentence meaning when its trace is located. A sign of this reactivation of the antecedent meaning at the trace position would be that the antecedent can prime responses to stimuli presented at the trace position, just as it would if it had actually occurred there.[17] The sentences in Swinney et al.'s experiments were presented aurally. The target item for lexical decision (or naming) was presented visually, for a brief interval during the sentence presentation. The target was always a string of letters; for all the sentences of interest, it was a real word. When the task was lexical decision, the target was a semantic associate of the antecedent noun or of some other preceding noun in the sentence. There was also a control condition in which the target was a word not associated with any noun in the sentence, but was matched for length and frequency with one of the experimental targets. Faster response to an associated target than to its unassociated control is attributed to priming by the noun with which it is associated. And priming at some sentence position P, by a noun that actually appears

---

[16]Some clarification: Relative clause constructions are sometimes described in psycholinguistics as if the antecedent for the trace were the head noun, but this is only a handy approximation to the true analysis. The antecedent of the trace is the constituent that moved from the position the trace now occupies. This moved constituent is the relative pronoun (wh-word). It stands in some sort of predication relation with the head noun, which makes it coreferential with the head noun. So, for example, the actual antecedent of *wh-trace* in a sentence like *I met the boy who Betty loves wh-trace* would be *who*, and by predication this would refer to the boy. In a relative clause beginning with the invariant complementiser *that*, or with no clause introducer at all (e.g. *I met the boy Betty loves*), linguists generally assume that a relative pronoun was present, that it moved and established the predication relation, and then was deleted. These details are important to the formal characterisation of the structural conditions on coreference relationships, but they do not affect the interpretation of the wh-trace.

[17]It is not known whether "reactivation" is a matter of excitation of the relevant entry in the mental lexicon, or consists in the presence of the relevant concept in the semantic representation being constructed for the sentence (see discussion in Swinney et al., 1988). For clarity in interpreting the results of future research, it would certainly be useful to have a better understanding of the mechanism underlying the effect, but in what follows I will have to disregard this uncertainty. I will use the term "reactivation" for the priming effect in cross-modal tasks, and also for comparable effects within other experimental paradigms, particularly a probe task, discussed below, that has also been used to investigate empty categories.

earlier in the sentence, is taken to indicate reactivation of that noun at position P.[18]

In sentences like (25), Swinney et al. observed priming at the trace position (i.e. with a target presented at the boundary of *accused* and *of*), by the correct antecedent, *boy*. There was no priming at that position by other noun phrases in the sentence, i.e. *policeman* and *crowd*, which are not syntactically legitimate antecedents for the trace.[19] *Policeman* is illegitimate because it is outside the relative clause construction, and *crowd* is illegitimate because it is in an argument position, as the subject of *accused*, rather than in the pre-clausal position required of a relative pronoun. Note that *crowd* is closer to the trace than the correct antecedent is, and therefore the processor could not be relying on a simple non-linguistic criterion such as recency. These results suggest that the processor is indeed closely attuned to linguistic constraints on the relation between antecedents and traces.[20]

In another study using similar techniques, Swinney, Ford, Bresnan, Frauenfelder, and Nicol (reported in Swinney et al., 1988) tested sentences like (26), where a potential trace position after the verb *advised* does not in fact contain a trace but has an overt pronoun:

26. The boxer visited the doctor that the swimmer at the competition had advised him to see about the injury.

Notice that if there were a trace after *advised*, it would have to have as its antecedent the relative pronoun, which is associated with the head noun *doctor*. But the pronoun *him* after *advised* is subject to quite different constraints than a trace would be. It is required to be disjoint in reference from the relative pronoun, and also disjoint from the subject of its own

---

[18]A word gives rise to priming at the point at which it occurs in a sentence, and this priming declines over the course of the next couple of seconds. In these studies, a position just prior to the empty category position is tested to make sure that there is no residual priming due to the original occurrence of the antecedent; then any priming at the empty category position can be attributed to *re*activation of the antecedent.

[19]This is somewhat loose talk, because *crowd* is just the head of a larger nounphrase *the crowd at the party*. But the target for lexical decision or naming in these experiments is always a single noun associated with just the head noun of a potential antecedent phrase.

[20]It is difficult to completely rule out the possibility that the processor selects the correct antecedent, not on the basis of global island constraints, but on the basis of local properties of noun phrases which determine which can be antecedents and which cannot. For example, only a noun phrase in a pre-clause, non-argument position could be an antecedent for a wh-trace; a noun phrase followed by *who* or *that* must be an antecedent of some wh-trace. We need experimental materials designed to force the processor to use more and more precise information, if it is able to (see discussion of 26 below).

clause. This means that *him* cannot refer to either the doctor or the swimmer. So it can refer only to the boxer (or to someone not mentioned in the sentence). Swinney et al. found that the processor is responsive to these constraints on trace and pronoun interpretation. When the lexical decision target was presented immediately after *advised*, there was priming by *doctor* but not by the other noun phrases, *boxer* and *swimmer*. This suggests that the processor assumes a trace after the verb without waiting to see whether or not the verb is followed by an overt object. Note that this is another instance of the "filled gap effect" discussed above (pp. 161–162). When the target was presented immediately after *him*, there was priming by both *doctor* and *boxer* but not by *swimmer*. It is not unreasonable to suppose that the priming by *doctor* is simply a continuation of the reactivation at the preceding position. But the sudden onset of priming by *boxer* right after the pronoun suggests that the processor has rapidly consulted its linguistic knowledge and determined that the pronoun must have *boxer* as its antecedent.[21] This is a particularly important result, because it shows that the processor's good performance on sentences like (25) is not due merely to some simple-minded strategy such as: If you need an antecedent and there's a relative pronoun nearby, use that. The processor appears to be highly sensitive to facts about which sorts of dependent elements can have which sorts of antecedents, located in which positions.

The general conclusion to be drawn from these experiments is that the human sentence processing mechanism is very quick, very well informed, and very accurate. It does make mistakes, but it is noteworthy that these mistakes consist primarily of being garden-pathed in circumstances where there is temporary ambiguity, i.e. where the input so far and the grammar do not between them determine a uniquely correct analysis. Where there *is* a correct answer, the processor generally knows it. We have found only one point on which it makes errors where it need not because the input offers disambiguation. This is its tendency to anticipate empty categories in likely positions which are not, in fact, empty. Waiting for just one more word would (almost always) eliminate these temporary ambiguities. But this small fact has an interesting general implication. It suggests that the processor has capacity to spare. It does not lag behind the input, struggling to compute what is entailed about the sentence structure. Rather, it has time to access its linguistic knowledge and extract the maximal information from it, all before the next word is received.

[21]As noted, the pronoun could have been taken to refer to someone not mentioned in the sentence, but such readings are generally less common than within-sentence readings, especially when no discourse context is provided.

LINGUISTIC IMPLICATIONS

More experiments will be reviewed below. But this is a good point to pause and consider how these discoveries about sentence processing might relate to the issues that concern theoretical linguistics. What could a linguist learn from these experimental findings? To review, we have seen (a) that empty category constructions do create long-term uncertainties in processing, which in principle are as troublesome as some of the most notorious garden-path constructions; but (b) in practice the processor copes very well, making intelligent use of all the information provided by the grammar and by probabilities of occurrence. Two lines of argument of some interest to theoretical linguistics have been developed out of these observations. The early psycholinguistic work on wh-movement reflected early linguistic concerns: It sought conclusions about innateness of linguistic knowledge, and the relation between competence and performance. More recent work emphasises that a parser which is well-attuned to the competence grammar can be a source of information about the properties of the grammar. In this section, I will review these ways of exploiting psycholinguistic findings for linguistic ends, and then in the following sections we can look at the fruits of the second one in more detail.

Functional Explanation and Innateness

The innateness of many aspects of natural language structure is widely accepted today by linguists of almost all persuasions, and by a growing number of psychologists. But in the early days of generative linguistics, it was still a postulate to do battle for. One way of defending it made reference to the difficulty of processing the sorts of constructions that natural languages contain. In fact, processing difficulty bears on innateness in two ways, which look at first sight to be contradictory but turn out to be complementary.

First, a central argument for innateness of some aspect of linguistic structure is its universality; but universality is persuasive only if there is no practical explanation for it, no explanation based on the universal *function* of language for communication, under constraints of time and the physical medium (articulatory limitations, ambient noise, etc.).[22] Thus generative

---

[22]Of course, the existence of a functional explanation for a universal aspect of natural language does not mean that it is *not* innately determined; but it does preclude one kind of argument for innateness. Note also that what is at issue here is to what extent linguistic structure is innately determined by the language faculty, which houses *universal grammar*. A property of language due to practical pressures from the performance mechanisms could also indirectly be innately determined, if (as seems most likely) those mechanisms are themselves innately given.

linguistics would be expected to welcome demonstrations that some aspect of linguistic structure is *non*-functional, or better still that it is *anti*-functional, in that it actually complicates the process of using language rapidly and successfully for communication. This is why it has been fashionable in generative circles to laud the oddity of natural language facts; the odder and less explicable they are in practical terms, the more certain we can be that they must reflect innate properties of the language faculty. And this is also why it was of particular interest to note how troublesome empty categories must be for the performance routines. It suggested that this pervasive aspect of natural languge must be due to some sort of innate design pressure from the language faculty, pressure strong enough to outweigh functional influences to the contrary from the practical mechanisms for language use.[23]

But at the same time, linguistic theory has an interest in *establishing* functional explanations rather than refuting them. This is because natural languages sometimes exhibit curious phenomena that do not fit comfortably into the general theories of language structure that encompass the majority of language facts. It would be satisfactory if these recalcitrant facts could legitimately be set aside, on the grounds that they are mere "performance phenomena". That would relieve the competence theory from having to accommodate them, and would thus help linguistics to achieve its goal of drawing its descriptive net very tightly around the class of possible natural languages.[24]

In short: There can be functional explanations of language facts which serve to tidy up the range of phenomena that linguistic theory has to regard as constitutive of natural language. But also, as we saw, there can be arguments for the innateness of linguistic knowledge which are based on the *non*-functionality of natural language design. These two lines of argument are both attractive, but are they at odds with each other? In fact

[23]There may be communicative pressures other than those related to efficiency of the coding and decoding procedures. For example, a language may be more highly valued if it provides more ways of expressing messages. If so, this might be the source of the popularity of empty categories in natural language. However, Fodor (1983) argues that expressive needs do not fully explain the patterns of the distribution of empty categories, and that expressive pressures must be viewed as operating within quite narrow limits imposed by the language faculty.

[24]In recent Government Binding theory (see references on p. 177), a distinction is drawn between core facts of a language, which obey universal principles, and peripheral phenomena, which are more idiosyncratic and irregular. In these terms, it is the peripheral facts that one might hope to eliminate by appeal to performance considerations. However, in such a theory it may seem less urgent to establish functional explanations. This is because the core/periphery distinction provides an *alternative* way of making sure that the existence of some disorderliness in natural languages will not interfere with the discovery of deep general principles; the latter are expected to hold only for the core.

they are not. The optimal situation for linguistic theory would be to find that "peculiar" constraints on natural language constructions have functional sources, while the basic design of the language is shaped by innate linguistic principles rather than by practical applications. And this is just what the study of empty category processing offered to linguistic theory in the late 1970s and early 1980s.

On the one hand, some constraints were identified which serve the useful function of eliminating global ambiguities that would otherwise arise concerning the pairing up of antecedents and empty categories. One such constraint is illustrated by example (27), from Fodor (1978):

27. What_i are boxes_j easy to store $\textit{trace}_j$ in $\textit{trace}_i$?

In principle, either antecedent (*what* or *boxes*) might be associated with either trace in (27), and therefore the sentence should be ambiguous. But in fact it is unambiguous; only the antecedent–trace pairings indicated here by the subscripts are acceptable. That is, the question asks about storing boxes in something; it is not about storing something in boxes, as would be implied by the opposite antecedent–trace associations. This disambiguation of (27) is due to a constraint which requires two or more antecedent–trace relations in the same sentence to be nested if they can be, rather than intersecting.[25]

On the other hand, despite the helpfulness of constraints like this, it is clear that empty category constructions do by their very nature create headaches for a processor. We have seen several examples now of temporary ambiguity concerning empty categories, with consequent garden paths in processing. Though the human sentence processor contends with these problems remarkably competently, it is utterly implausible to suppose that the processor is what *encourages* natural languages to make such widespread use of empty categories. We may conclude, therefore, that empty categories are favoured by the principles of Universal Grammar.

---

[25]Of course, the ambiguity could have been resolved just as efficiently by a constraint requiring intersecting relations, not nested ones. The literature contains a number of attempts to explain on functional grounds why nesting is favoured. Another issue often debated was the contrast between explaining the existence of a constraint, and explaining it away. That is, a constraint such as this one might be accepted as part of the grammar of English, and the strong function motivation for it might be seen as its excuse for existing, despite the fact that it does not follow from any very central property of language. Alternatively, the constraint might be regarded as non-linguistic, as merely a matter of which analysis perceivers tend to compute in cases of ambiguity. Then a sentence that violated the constraint would not be ungrammatical, though it would strike perceivers as being so. Only in the latter case could the constraint be eliminated from linguistic theory.

Linguistic Theories and Transparency

With the innateness of language design no longer much in contention these days, there has been a shift of attention to other, more specific, kinds of conclusions about the language faculty that might be drawn from observations about processing. The experimental studies of empty categories we have examined so far have indicated that the human sentence processor is extremely efficient, and makes good use of all relevant information that the grammar provides about the language. This does not entail, but it does strongly suggest, that the human processor exhibits what Berwick and Weinberg (1984) call a "transparent" relationship with the grammar. As I will use the term here, a transparent processor is one which makes use of information about linguistic structure in the form in which the mental ("competence") grammar provides it, so that statements from the grammar do not have to be modified, translated, or "pre-compiled" before they can be applied to sentences. If the human sentence processor is indeed transparent, it follows that a linguistic theory will be more believable (all other things being equal) to the extent that the grammars it defines can be used directly, accurately, and efficiently by an on-line processor. This transparency criterion, derived from the study of empty category processing (seasoned with a dash of methodological optimism), can be put to work in evaluating the various theories of language that linguists have proposed.

Its first contribution was to rule out the Standard Theory of Chomsky (1965). The Standard Theory characterised transformational grammars which generate sentences by means of lengthy derivations. These derivations would need to be "run backward" by the perceptual routines, to recover the deep structure of an input sentence, and then determine from that the semantic representation. But reversing derivations results in indeterminancies; it is complicated and error-prone (see Fodor, 1979). A processor transparent to this kind of grammar could not be efficient; but the human processor is efficient. This argument is also now old history, of course. The inadequacy of the Standard Theory is widely accepted these days; quite apart from processing problems, linguists abandoned it long ago because of various descriptive and explanatory flaws. It has been superseded by several different theories. And the current linguistic challenge for sentence processing research is to find evidence that will help to determine which (if any) of these competing theories is correct.

The most direct descendant of the Standard Theory is Government Binding Theory (GB; see Chomsky, 1981; 1986). This is still a transformational theory, but it differs from the Standard Theory in emphasising general principles which apply to all constructions, rather than particular rules for particular constructions. It was during the course of development from the Standard Theory to GB that empty categories were first introduced (see pp. 156–157). The traces of movement in GB analyses render derivations cumulative, unlike Standard Theory derivations. The traces appear in surface structures (technically, S-structures, in GB), and they carry information about the deep positions of constituents. Thus the S-structure level now presents information that was once available only at deep structure (D-structure, in GB). This is important because it makes the D-structure less central to the derivation. In particular, it is no longer necessary to refer to D-structure for purposes of semantic interpretation; interpretation now feeds off S-structure, via a new level called Logical Form (LF), which represents structural aspects of meaning such as quantifier scope.

Other theories of language have developed out of the Standard Theory by rejecting its transformational rules. These include Lexical Functional Grammar (LFG; see Kaplan & Bresnan, 1982), Generalised Phrase Structure Grammar (GPSG; see Gazdar, Klein, Pullum, & Sag, 1985), Head-driven Phrase Structure Grammar (HPSG; see Pollard & Sag, 1987; Sag & Pollard, 1987), Relational Grammar (RG; see Perlmutter, 1983; Perlmutter & Rosen, 1984), and various forms of categorial grammar (see, for example, Steedman, 1989).[26] To group all these theories together fails to do them justice, but to discuss them separately is beyond the bounds of this paper. In what follows, I will refer generically and very loosely to "non-transformational grammars". Though they differ considerably in their details, they have in common that they generate surface sentences directly, rather than deriving them from some deeper syntactic structure,[27] and that even the surface structures that they assign are less abstract, more closely related to the actual word sequence, than are the S-structures of GB. GB S-structures are more abstract in that they contain more empty categories than other theories admit (discussed at length below), and in that GB assumes a component of "stylistic rules" which can rearrange structure and constituent order after the S-structure level, so that word order in the input string need not match word order in the S-structure assigned to it. In what

[26]For an introductory exposition of GB, GPSG, and LFG, see Sells (1985). It is not really clear whether RG ought to be classified as a non-transformational theory (see footnote 27), but it does have strong affinities with them, especially with LFG.

[27]LFG differs from the other non-transformational theories in assigning to a sentence not only a surface syntactic structure but also another syntactic representation called a "functional structure", which does a considerable amount of work in eliminating ungrammatical sentences. Relational Grammar recognises many levels (called "strata") of syntactic representation, as in a transformational derivation, but recent work in this and related frameworks does not present these levels as derived one from another by movement, etc., but instead characterises the well-formedness of a simultaneous representation of all levels (a "relational network").

follows, I will use GPSG analyses to illustrate the non-transformational approach.

Non-transformational theories do not assume that constituents move from one sentence position to another. They characterise the same kinds of language facts as movement transformations do, but by various other formal means. Let us consider first the potentially "long-distance" movements such as wh-movement. In a non-transformational framework, both the antecedent and the trace must be generated directly in their surface positions.[28] Some kind of relationship needs to be established between them because they are dependent on each other, but the relationship must be a static one. Non-transformational theories differ from each other with respect to how this is formally represented. The GPSG analysis is shown in

28.

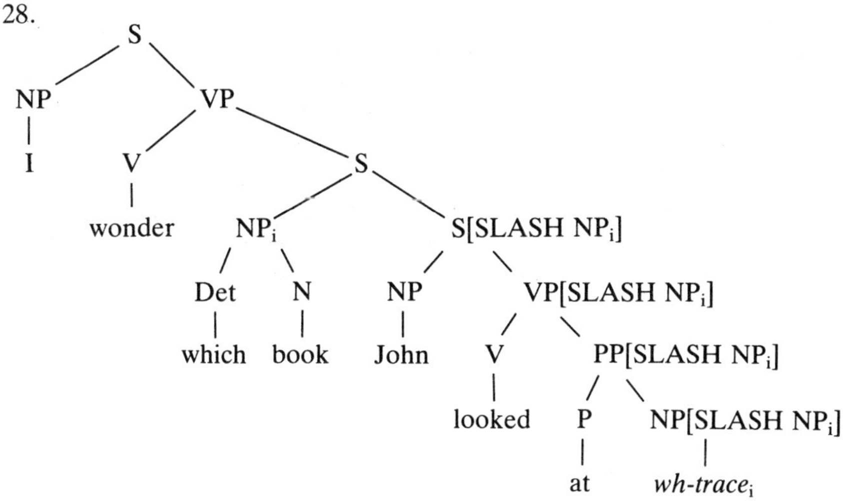

The [SLASH NP$_i$] markings on the nodes in (28) are what is special to GPSG. These "slash features" form a path between the antecedent (*which book*) and the trace, and represent the fact that there is a binding relationship between them. (The slash features actually run from the node that is sister to the antecedent, to the node that is mother to the trace.) The tree in (28) is generated by context-free phrase structure rules, which arc shown in (29). The slash features are introduced into the tree by these rules in just the same way as more familiar features such as [+PAST] or [−

---

[28] A trace is not essential. As noted, the Standard Theory had no traces, though GB does. Familiar formulations of LFG assume an empty category in wh-constructions, but it is dispensed with in recent work (Kaplan & Zaenen, 1989). Categorial grammar does not assume a wh-trace, though it does distinguish wh-constructions from local dependencies by treating them in the syntactic component.

PLURAL].[29] In fact, every category name in these rules would be spelled out as a collection of features, though I have not shown them all here. (Feature values are often predictable on the basis of universal principles; then they can be omitted from the rules, simplifying the grammar.)

29. S → NP , VP
VP → V , S
S → NP_i , S[SLASH NP_i]
S[SLASH NP_i] → NP , VP[SLASH NP_i]
VP[SLASH NP_i] → V , PP[SLASH NP_i]
PP[SLASH NP_i] → P , NP[SLASH NP_i]

A [SLASH NP] feature can be read as saying that the constituent to which it is attached must contain, somewhere within it, an empty NP. The rule that introduces the antecedent also introduces the slash feature; and a slash feature must be passed down by the rules until it results in an empty category at the level of terminal symbols. Together, these conditions ensure that no sentence will contain an antecedent without also containing an empty category to serve as its trace (e.g. **I wonder which book John looked at the magazine*), or vice versa (e.g. **I wonder John looked at*). If a prepositional phrase were the antecedent, the slash feature would be [SLASH PP], to indicate that an empty PP is needed somewhere in the sentence (as in *I wonder [with whom]$_i$ John was reading the book PP-trace$_i$)*. Thus the dependencies which a transformational theory explains in terms of movement can also be captured without movement, by means of slash features (or comparable devices in other non-transformational theories).

Other constructions derived by movement in a transformational framework (e.g. passive) exhibit purely local dependencies, and these are typically handled quite differently by a non-transformational theory. A local dependency can be regarded as a purely lexical relationship, between a word (e.g. a verb) and the constituents which can co-occur as its sisters.

[29]The term "slash" has no special significance; it derives from an earlier notion for GPSG which employed a *sui generis* annotation /NP. The move to feature notation is intended to bring out the fact that this is indeed just another syntactic feature, subject to all the usual universal constraints on syntactic features. This is a point of some importance to the descriptive and explanatory power of the theory. Another point of theoretical importance is that, because phrase structure rules are strictly local (i.e. each rule characterises just one mother node and its daughters), long-distance syntactic relationships can be captured only if they are analysable into a series of strictly local dependencies. (But note that this inherent locality constraint does not eliminate all problems of processing long-distance dependencies, because a trace and its antecedent can still be indefinitely far apart in the surface string, and the trail of slash features which must connect them is not evident in the input.)

These will be specified by the subcategorisation features(s) in the verb's lexical entry. There need be no movement in the syntactic component, and nothing that even simulates movement, as the chain of slash features does for wh-constructions. For example, a passive construction can be generated directly, with all argument phrases in their surface positions and the passive verb entered from the lexicon. The fact that there is a systematic relationship between the active and the passive constructions is captured by a lexical rule. The rule derives the morphological, subcategorisational, and semantic properties of the passive item from those of the active one. Passive is discussed further below.

It obviously matters a great deal to linguistics to decide which of these theories is right. Lingusitic methods may be sufficient to settle the matter (see below). But the transparency criterion suggests that it may also be possible to decide by considering the sorts of parsing procedures that each linguistic theory implies. Processing is efficient, and therefore the transparency criterion favours grammars that support efficient processing; all we need do, then, is see which account of wh-movement and passive, etc., is best from the point of view of the processor. However, though this is sufficient to disqualify the Standard Theory, it does not do a good job of discriminating between current theories. This is because they *all*, in their own somewhat different ways, seem to allow fairly efficient processing. (There are many variants of each approach, and many ways of implementing them. So what follows is necessarily very broadly sketched.)

It is generally agreed that a parser making the most direct use of a GB grammar would be one that treats the grammatical principles as axioms, and deduces what properties an S-structure that fits the input string must have. From the S-structure, the processor can derive the logical form of the sentence, which together with the meanings of lexical items will give the semantic interpretation. Because the S-structures of GB incorporate D-structure information (see above), D-structures are no longer essential to semantic interpretation, and so there is no longer any need to engage in the problematic "backward" transformational derivations of deep structures from surface structures as in Standard Theory processing (for specific GB processing models, see Abney & Cole, 1986; Abney, 1987; Berwick & Weinberg, 1984; Correa, 1987; Johnson, 1989; Stabler, forthcoming).

Parsing with a GPSG or LFG grammar also requires finding an analysis which satisfies the input and all grammatical principles. Processing with a non-transformational grammar lends itself to a method of "unification", by which information from various locations in a tree structure can be integrated and propagated. Consider, for example, the sentence *You men are wise*. The first word carries the feature [PERSON 2], the second word carries the feature [+PLURAL], and both features will percolate up to the level of the dominating NP and establish it as second person plural; then these features can be passed to the verb phrase so that it agrees with the subject NP, and from the verb phrase down to the verb it dominates, so that it must be *are* rather than *is*. In this way, the feature specifications for a whole phrase marker can be established, by starting with the lexical features from the input and projecting them up to non-terminal nodes in accord with the grammar rules and universal principles (for more details, see Shieber, 1986, and references therein).

Interesting work is being done to develop these and other parsing procedures, and establish their capabilities. Computational efficiency or inefficiency can be established and compared across models. Possibly, computational methods will one day establish which (if any) of these approaches to processing is optimal for natural language, or, more importantly, which (if any) has exactly the same characteristic strengths and weaknesses as the human processing routines. (For example, the human processor does not characteristically lag further and further behind the input as processing proceeds; it does sometimes overlook well-formed analyses. Parsing models of interest for psycholinguistic purposes would do the same, regardless of whether there are others that perform better.) If we can find a model that matches the human processor, then to the extent that that processor presupposes a certain theory of grammars, it would be reasonable (other things being equal) to favour that theory as the theory of natural language grammars. At present, though, it is not clear that one approach to processing is distinctly superior to the others. As noted, a variety of current processors seem to be reasonably effective. It is true that there have been formal demonstrations of intractability (i.e. demonstrations that sentence processing can carry exponential costs in computation time or memory space; see Barton, Berwick, & Ristad, 1987). But these proofs focus on "worst case" situations (unlikely horrors, such as each word in a sentence introducing a new, multiple ambiguity; or sentences which contain more empty categories than lexical items), and they thus give bleaker estimates than one would expect from considering the success of these processors on realistic inputs. But in any case, the estimates are fairly uniformly bleak. Different processors, presupposing different kinds of grammar, do have their different strengths and weaknesses. But as Barton et al. (1987) observe, computational intractability often arises from the facts of language themselves, and then it does not select between models but equally afflicts all models that address the facts. At least at present, then, it is not a simple matter to identify the true theory of language on the basis of any gross argument about the possibility of efficient parsing.

An alternative way of exploiting the transparency criterion is to conduct psycholinguistic experiments which hunt for the grammatical constructs (rules and representations) of a linguistic theory, at work in the course of sentence processing. If transparency is correct, we are entitled to take discoveries about the means by which the *processor* characterises sentences, as evidence of the means by which the *grammar* characterises sentences. For example, one might try to determine experimentally whether the processor does or does not compute a deep structure for a sentence. If it does not, no clear conclusion would follow; but if it does, only a transformational theory would be tenable (for some experiments on this topic, see Crain & Fodor, 1987; Forster & Stevenson, 1987; Freedman & Forster, 1985). Or one might try to establish whether the information about the language that is available to the processor is organised into packages which correspond to the components (modules) of the grammar as defined by one linguistic theory or another (for experiments bearing on this, see Clifton & Frazier, 1986; Crain & Fodor, 1985; Fodor, 1988; Frazier, Clifton, & Randall, 1983). Of more relevance for present purposes, and especially because experimental psycholinguistics seems to be rather good at studying empty categories, we might try to establish whether the processor constructs empty categories of all the kinds, and at all the positions, predicted by some linguistic theory.

So far, we have looked only at experiments on wh-trace. By the very strictest criteria (see pp. 198ff), none of the experiments cited above may provide an indisputable demonstration of the existence of wh-trace in syntactic structures, but these experiments do at least show a variety of effects that it makes sense to attribute to wh-trace, and at precisely the sentence positions in which linguistic theories assert that wh-trace is present. This is encouraging, and for the moment we may set aside any quibbles and declare wh-trace to be "psychologically real". But then we must note that this does not discriminate between competing linguistic theories, because they all recognise wh-trace or something comparable to it,[30] even though we have seen that they generate the structures containing it by very different means.[31] However, linguistic theories do differ sharply with respect to other empty categories.

GB posits four kinds of empty category. These are listed in (33), together with some of their distinguishing properties; not all of these

---

[30]This is much too sweeping. But at least GPSG, HPSG, and traditional LFG posit an empty category in the same position as the "ultimate" wh-trace in a GB representation (see footnote 28). LFG also had a device not unlike the "intermediate" wh-traces in the GB treatment of long-distance movement. CG does not have wh-trace, but does represent when a phase is "missing" a constituent of some kind. RG has not addressed wh-constructions.

[31]See Frazier (1989) for an interesting recent attempt to evaluate experimentally the differences in the derivations proposed by different theories, as reflected in the number of nodes in the tree that are implicated in the antecedent–trace relation (e.g. the number of nodes on the path of slash features in a GPSG representation, compared with the number of nodes that a moved phrase makes contact with in a GB derivation).

properties are relevant to the discussion below, but they serve to illustrate the fact that these empty categories are different from each other, even though they are all inaudible/invisible.[32]

30.

	Created by Movement	*Anaphoric*	*Pronominal*	*Has Case*	*Has Theta Role*	*Lexical Antecedent has Case*	*Lexical Antecedent has Theta Role*
wh-trace	+	−	−	+	+	−	−
NP-trace	+	+	−	−	+	+	−
PRO	−	+	+	−	+	+	+
pro	−	−	+	+	+	+	+

An NP-trace is an empty category created when an NP moves locally, from one argument position to another,[33] as in passive and "raising" constructions, illustrated in (31):

31. Passive: [The cake]$_i$ was eaten *NP-trace*$_i$ by the boy.
    Raising: [The cake]$_i$ seems *NP-trace*$_i$ to please the boy.

A PRO, shown in (32), does not result from movement; it is base-generated. It is the empty subject of an infinitival complement clause, in constructions of the kind that used to be derived by an "Equi-NP deletion" transformation. The antecedent may be the subject or the object of the next highest clause, depending on the verb of that clause. Sentences with PRO are often called "control constructions", because the antecedent of PRO is called its controller. But there are also examples of PRO without any controller; it then receives an "arbitrary" or generic interpretation.

32. Subject control [The boy]$_i$ tried PRO$_i$ to eat the cake.
    [The boy]$_i$ promised [his sister]$_j$ PRO$_i$ to eat the cake.
    Object control [The boy]$_i$ persuaded [his sister]$_j$ PRO$_j$ to eat the cake.
    No control It was unclear what PRO to do.

---

[32]The linguistics here, as elsewhere, is too intricate to summarise in a simple table. The specifications in (30) would need to be more complicated to cover antecedents that are themselves empty categories, or the traces of expletive phrases (e.g. "dummy" *it* and *there* in English), and so forth.

[33]An argument position is roughly the position of a subject, direct object, or oblique object of a predicate, as contrasted with the positions of adjuncts (modifying phrases), and with the pre-clausal position of a moved wh-phrase or topic phrase.

A *pro* (sometimes referred to as "little pro") is a base-generated empty pronoun which, like an overt pronoun, can refer to someone or something identified in the discourse. It appears as the subject of a tensed clause in a number of languages, such as Italian (33), though not in English. It may also appear in the object position in some languages. I will not discuss *pro* any further in this paper, because it has not been addressed in psycholinguistic experiments.

33. Italian: Ecco Gianni. *pro* Sta mangiando.
Ecco Gianni. Lui sta mangiando. (emphatic)
English: Here is John. **pro* Is eating.
Here is John. He is eating.

By contrast, non-transformational theories such as LFG and GPSG do not assume the existence of NP-trace or PRO.[34] "Raising" and "Equi" constructions, as in (31) and (32), are directly generated as they stand, without any subject at all (even an empty one) in the subordinate clause. In fact, an expression like *to eat the cake* in (32) is *not* a clause; it is just an infinitival verb phrase standing by itself as the complement of *tried* or *persuaded*. (In GB, by contrast, every verb phrase has to have a subject, if not lexical then empty.) As we noted earlier, according to LFG and GPSG, a passive sentence is not derived by syntactic movement, or even by some non-movement analogue to syntactic movement. Its only relation to an active construction is in the lexicon. English has an active verb *eat*, specified as taking a subject (e.g. *John*) and an optional direct object (e.g. *the cake*). English also has a passive participle *eaten*, specified as taking a subject (e.g. *the cake*), no direct object, and an optional agent phrase (e.g. *by John*). These two items are obviously not independent of each other;

[34]For sheer lack of space, I have been saying what the various theories postulate without saying what their arguments are for doing so. The arguments fill volumes and I cannot even summarise them intelligibly here. But, *very* roughly: GB values the systematicity that results from admitting several empty categories, each one of which parallels a lexical category (e.g. NP-trace exhibits formal properties very like those of lexical reflexive anaphors such as *himself*). Non-transformational theories wish for explanatory reasons to eschew descriptive devices which are not essential for natural languages, and they point out that empty categories other than wh-trace (for some theories, even including wh-trace) behave very much as if they were not there (e.g. there is *wanna-contraction* across PRO; see footnote 4).

Incidentally, it should be noted that once the transformational framework adopted empty categories, much (conceivably, all) of the descriptive work that had been done by constraints on movement could be done instead by constraints on structural representations containing traces of movement (see footnote 2); and traces of movement, despite their name, might even be base-generated. Thus the acceptance or rejection of explicit movement operations becomes a less significant differentiator between theories, and their different inventories of empty categories is correspondingly more important.

their phonological and syntactic specifications overlap significantly, as do those of many other active/passive verb pairs in the language. As noted above, a non-transformational theory uses a lexical rule to capture this systematic overlap; and lexical rules do not create traces.

Thus GB has a richer inventory of empty categories than other current theories have. A variety of linguistic arguments have been given in a attempt to establish which account of empty categories is correct (for a partial survey and some references, see Newmeyer, 1986). These arguments are clever and interesting, and yet it is surprisingly difficult to get them to deliver a decisive verdict. The reason is that each theory has an interlocking network of assumptions which permit it to account for the observed facts. A difference in the treatment of one construction requires, for consistency, a difference in the treatment of some other phenomenon, which in turn calls for another difference somewhere else in the theory. But all the theories are (or hope one day to be) responsive to essentially the same array of facts, albeit in their quite different ways. They do not (or do not intend to) make different empirical predictions about which sentences are well-formed. If they did, the one that made the wrong prediction would rapidly repair itself by modifying one of its assumptions. Therefore, it is not easy to come up with a fact which definitively supports one theory and falsifies the others. As elsewhere in linguistics (perhaps in all heavily theoretical disciplines), a theory is rarely disproved outright but simply declines in attractiveness, relative to other theories, as it is shown to be forced into more and more complications to handle the data. But this can be a slow business. The empty category issue in linguistics cannot be resolved without taking up the many other issues it connects with, and weighing them all. And that is why linguists still do not all agree about the proper taxonomy of empty categories.

So, maybe psycholinguistics can help. In psycholinguistics too, one question all too often leads to another. But at least in principle, the psycholinguistic approach to empty categories is a direct one: We find out what mental representations people assign to sentences when they comprehend them, and then we look to see what empty categories the representations contain.

Terminological note: We are going to need a theory-neutral way to refer to the positions in which GB posits empty categories and other theories do not, but nothing satisfactory suggests itself. Therefore, in what follows I will use the GB terminology (i.e. I will refer to NP-trace positions and PRO positions as well as wh-trace positions) but without meaning thereby to beg the question of which theory is right. So, for example, I shall feel free to raise the question, without inconsistency, of whether there really is an NP-trace in an NP-trace position.

WHICH EMPTY CATEGORIES?

Previous Experiments

To review briefly, what would support GB is evidence that all wh-trace, NP-trace, and PRO are present in syntactic structures. What would support a theory like GPSG is evidence that wh-trace is the only empty category present in syntactic structures. Note that the predictions of the two models converge at the level of semantics. The "who did what to whom" of passive, raising, and "Equi" constructions will be established, in the case of GB, by semantic interpretation of the relevant empty syntactic categories. LFG and GPSG will assign these same constructions the very same interpretations (or near enough to be indistinguishable in our experiments). It is just that in these latter frameworks, the semantic rules will do *all* the work of identifying the patient of a passive construction, or the agent of an infinitival verb phrase; there is no indexed syntactic entity for semantic interpretation to work from. This point is important, because it seems quite possible that the experimental paradigms available in this area (e.g. priming and probing paradigms which look for reactivation of a potential antecedent at an empty category position) arc tapping the semantic representations assigned by the processor, rather than the syntactic representations. We will return to this issue on pp. 198–206. In the meantime, it is easier to get a sense of how the experiments address the empty category question, if we temporarily suspend this methodological worry and just assume that the data do reveal syntactic structure.

What we are looking for in these experiments is signs that PRO positions and NP-trace positions elicit activities from the processor similar to those it engages in at wh-trace positions.[35] The processes need not be identical, even on GB predictions, because as (30) shows, NP-trace and PRO differ in some of their properties from wh-trace, and their antecedents differ in some of their properties from the antecedent of wh-trace. Thus to support GB, what would be needed is some similarity in processing at the three types of empty category position, of a kind that is indicative of the presence of a syntactic entity standing in a coreference relation with an antecedent.

[35] Caplan and Hildebrant (1988) have looked at patterns of loss and preservation in aphasia as evidence for the proper array of empty categories. A dissociation between two empty category constructions, such that one is preserved while the other is lost, can be taken to indicate that they involve distinct grammatical mechanisms. Caplan and Hildebrandt's experimental data show a high degree of dissociation. This favours a theory which maximally differentiates the constructions in question. Caplan and Hildebrandt argue that it supports GB and disconfirms LFG.

Spelling out what we mean by "indicative" here is the hardest part of the whole project. But at least we may begin by taking as benchmark the relationship between an overt lexical pronominal and its antecedent. The question, then, is: Does anything happen at a putative empty category position that is comparable to what happens when the processor encounters a *she* or a *him* or an *it* and establishes who or what it refers to?[36]

For wh-trace, the similarities are fairly convincing. Swinney et al.'s experiments indicate rapid recognition of the trace position, and grammatically correct selection of its antecedent. This is comparable to results for pronouns in the same experimental paradigm. Nicol (1988; see Nicol & Swinney, 1989) tested sentences such as (34):

34a. The boxer told the skier that the doctor for the team would blame him for the recent injury.
b. The boxer told the skier that the doctor for the team would blame himself for the recent injury.

Using the cross-modal lexical decision priming paradigm described above (see p. 171), Nicol tested the position immediately following the pronoun or the reflexive anaphor (*him* or *himself*). She found evidence of reactivation of all and only the appropriate antecedent(s). That is, for *him*, there was reactivation of *boxer* and of *skier*, either of which is grammatically legitimate as the antecedent, but no reactivation of *doctor*, which is not a legitimate antecedent; for *himself*, there was reactivation of *doctor*, which is the only legitimate antecedent, and no reactivation of the other nouns.

Another similarity between wh-trace and overt pronouns in processing is that neither shows an immediate influence of semantic or pragmatic factors on the choice of antecedent. For overt pronouns, Corbett and Chang (1983) demonstrated this using a post-sentence probe task with sentences

[36]This comparison is arguably too crude. Because different GB empty categories resemble different lexical entities (see footnote 34), the proper benchmark may differ from one empty category to another. For wh-trace, the optimal control might be an overt pronoun whose antecedent is a quantified noun phrase, as in *[Every fool]*$_i$ *thinks he*$_i$ *is clever*, rather than a name or other referring expression (e.g. *[This fool]*$_i$ *thinks he*$_i$ *is clever*). Chomsky (1981) and others have observed that the relation between a wh-phrase and its trace is a true binding relation, similar to that between a quantified expression and the variable it binds. With a referential antecedent, by contrast, one need suppose only that each noun phrase is independently assigned a referent, and in some cases it happens that both are assigned the same one. No experiment has yet explored antecedent assignment in quantified sentences. For NP-trace, on the other hand, the closest overt counterpart is arguably not a pronoun (e.g. *him*) but a lexical anaphor such as a reflexive (e.g. *himself*). Overt anaphors have been studied by Nicol (see below).

such as in (35):

35a. Ellen aimed a pistol at Harriet, but she did not pull the trigger.
b. Ellen aimed a pistol at Harriet, but Ellen did not pull the trigger.

Note that the pronoun *she* in the (a) sentence has two syntactically legitimate potential antecedents, one that is pragmatically plausible (*Ellen*) and one that is pragmatically less plausible (*Harriet*). The control sentence (b) has no pronoun, but an explicit reference to the pragmatically plausible individual. When the probe word was *Ellen*, response times did not differ significantly between the two versions of the sentence, which is as expected if the pronoun *she* reactivates the plausible antecedent. When the probe word was *Harriet*, responses were faster following the (a) sentence than following the (b) sentence, which suggests that the pronoun *also* reactivated *Harriet*, the pragmatically implausible antecedent.

For wh-trace, Swinney (reported in Swinney & Osterhout, in press) investigated sentences like (36) with the cross-modal priming paradigm. He found reactivation, at the trace position, of the syntactically appropriate antecedent (*boxer*), and no significant reactivation of the syntactically inappropriate antecedent (*boy*), even though pragmatics would dictate exactly the opposite assignment.

36. Everyone watched [the enormous heavyweight boxer]$_i$ that$_i$ [the small 12-year-old boy on the corner]$_j$ had beaten *wh-trace*$_i$ so brutally.

Garnsey, Tanenhaus, and Chapman (1989) investigated sentences like (37) using an anomaly detection task, and monitored evoked brain potentials. Of particular interest was the so-called "N400" component, which has been shown to occur in response to perceived anomalies.

37a. The businessman knew [which customer]$_i$ the secretary called *wh-trace*$_i$ at home.
b. The businessman knew [which article]$_i$ the secretary called *wh-trace*$_i$ at home.

They observed an N400 response at the trace position (after *called*), when the antecedent was implausible as its object (*article*) but not when it was plausible as its object (*customer*). This is just what would be expected if the antecedent was being assigned on-line to the trace. This result is particularly interesting because, as Nicol (1988) notes, it shows that the pragmatic anomaly of a potential antecedent of wh-trace trace is readily detectable, even though the anomaly evidently does not block assignment (at least momentary assignment) of the antecedent to the trace.[37]

For PRO and NP-trace, by contrast, the experiments that have been conducted so far suggest that antecedent reactivation is much more sluggish and less precisely tuned to syntactic constraints. For PRO, Osterhout and Nicol (reported in Nicol & Swinney, 1989) tested the sentences in (38) for reactivation effects, at several points following the PRO position:

38a. [The actress]$_i$ invited [the dentist from the new medical centre]$_j$ PRO$_j$ to go to the party at the mayor's house.
b. [The actress]$_i$ was invited *NP-trace*$_i$ by [the dentist from the new medical centre]$_j$ PRO$_i$ to go to the party at the mayor's house.

The shift from an active main clause in (38a) to a passive main clause in (38b) has the effect of changing the antecedent of PRO: In (38a) it is *dentist* and in (38b) it is *actress*.[38] Osterhout and Nicol found no reactivation of either noun when the target word for lexical decision immediately followed the infinitival marker *to*, which reveals the presence of PRO, or when it was presented 500 msec later. Test points 1000, 1200, and 1500 msec after the *to* did show an effect, but the noun that was reactivated was not invariably correct. It appeared that for *both* sentences, *both* nouns in the

---

[37]Another comparison that could be made between wh-trace and lexical pronouns concerns the sensitivity of antecedent selection to syntactic features, such as agreement features. It has been shown by Nicol (1988; see also Ehrlich, 1980) that for lexical pronouns the processor selects only antecedents that are appropriate in number and gender, as well as in syntactic position. This has not been tested for wh-trace. In fact, only number agreement can be tested in English, and only for traces in the subject position, where the inflectional ending on the associated verb shows number agreement with the subject. Thus (i) is acceptable, and (ii) is not:

i. [Which ointment]$_i$ does the famous Austrian physician believe *wh-trace*$_i$ soothes all known forms of skin disease?
ii. *[Which ointment]$_i$ does the famous Austrian physician believe *wh-trace*$_i$ soothe all known forms of skin disease?

Fodor, Smith, and Swinney are currently conducting a cross-modal priming experiment with materials like these, testing immediately after the trace at the verb *soothe(s)*. Evidence that the processor is sensitive to the feature mismatch in (ii) (but not to pragmatic anomaly; e.g. if the antecedent were *doorstep*) would indicate a further parallel between pronouns and wh-traces.

[38]In (38b) there is also an NP-trace due to passivisation of the main clause, and it may be argued that the interpretation of the PRO is mediated by this NP-trace, i.e. that the actual antecedent of the PRO is the NP-trace, whose antecedent is *actress*. I am following Osterhout and Nicol here in assuming that it is safe to ignore this mediating role of the NP-trace, especially as the trace precedes the PRO by a good margin in all the experimental sentences (see the discussion on pp. 203–205).

main clause were reactivated, one after the other, first the more recent one and then the more distant one. Nicol (1988) argues that the antecedent of PRO is not uniquely determined by the syntax [or at least that the processor cannot establish it on the basis of syntax alone, because it requires discriminating between complement constructions as in (32) above, purpose clauses, rationale clauses, etc.]. She observes that reactivation of all potential antecedents in the sentence should therefore be expected, because this is what occurs in the case of a lexical pronoun whose antecedent is not unique (see 34). I will return to this point on p. 203.

For NP-trace, the cross-modal priming results are similar to those for PRO. Osterhout and Swinney (in prep.) report a study using sentences such as (39), with an NP-trace created by passivisation:

39. [The baker who had just moved into the neighbourhood]$_i$ was asked *NP-trace*$_i$ by the woman PRO$_i$ to help out at the party.

Details aside, this sentence is similar to (38b) used to investigate PRO, but Osterhout and Swinney looked for reactivation following the NP-trace instead. They found no significant reactivation when the target word was presented simultaneously with the *by* which immediately follows the NP-trace, or when it was presented 500 msec later, but they did observe significant reactivation of the correct antecedent (*baker*) when the target occurred 1000 msec after the NP-trace position.[39] It is not feasible to test for accuracy of antecedent assignment with these materials, because *baker* is the only reasonable candidate which precedes the NP-trace. But at least with respect to latency, this result for NP-trace is reminiscent of the finding for PRO, and quite unlike the prompt effect for wh-trace.

Significant reactivation effects have also been found for all three types of empty category with a different experimental task. Bever and McElree (1988) and McElree and Bever (1989) used a probe task, in which subjects indicated whether a word presented following a sentence did or did not occur within the sentence.[40] They tested sentences like those illustrated in (40):

40a. The stern judge / who met with the defence / adamantly refused PRO to / argue about the appeal.

---

[39]The effect was quite weak even at the 1000-msec delay; though significant, it did not differ significantly from the non-significant results at the earlier test positions.

[40]The probe word was also presented right after the empty category, before the sentence was complete, but no significant effects were obtained with this early probe position in any of Bever and McElree's experiments.

b. The stern judge / who met with the defence / is sure *NP-trace* to / argue about the appeal.
c. The stern judge / was difficult for the defence / to argue with *WH-trace* about / the pending appeal.
d. The stern judge / who met with the defence / thought he should / argue about the appeal.
e. The stern judge / who met with the defence / flatly rejected the / arguments for an appeal.

The first three examples contain different kinds of (potential) empty categories;[41] the (d) sentence contains a lexical pronoun; the (e) sentence establishes a baseline, as it contains no coreference relation at all. All presentation was visual, with the sentence presented in successive chunks as indicated by the slashes in (40). The probe word for the experimental sentences was always the adjective appearing within the NP which was the correct antecedent for the empty category or lexical pronoun; therefore, for the sentences in (40), the probe word was *stern*. If the response to the probe word was faster after one of the (a)–(d) sentences than after the (e) sentence, it was concluded that the empty category or pronoun in the (a)–(d) sentences had reactivated its antecedent.

The lexical pronoun and all three types of empty category showed reactivation effects, though the size of the effects differed. The reactivation of the antecedent was greatest for wh-trace, intermediate for NP-trace, and smallest for PRO. The difference between wh-trace and NP-trace was not significant. The difference between NP-trace and PRO was significant (though only for error rate; for response time it was marginal). McElree and Bever take these results to show that all three empty categories are real, and that the two movement traces form a natural class, because they are more like each other than either is like the base-generated PRO. We certainly do not see here, as we seemed to in the cross-modal priming

[41]The NP-trace in (40b) results from *raising*; passive NP-trace has not so far been compared with other kinds of empty category (see below). I have glossed the empty category in the so-called "tough-movement" construction in (40c) as a wh-trace, following Chomsky (1977). Chomsky (1982a) argues that the antecedent of this empty category is an empty operator that is located at the beginning of the subordinate clause and is co-indexed with the subject of the main clause. But the status of this empty category is not completely settled, and McElree and Bever are more cautious; they refer to it merely as a trace of movement. (Though, as it happens, even that has been disputed among linguists; see Lasnik & Fiengo , 1974.) For the cross-theoretical comparisons that we are attempting to make here, what matters most is whether all theories agree that this empty category exists. GPSG does assume a trace in tough constructions, and uses slash features to position it just as for wh-trace. LFG also assumed an empty category for tough constructions, as long as it assumed one for wh-constructions (see Kaplan & Bresnan, 1982).

experiments, a sharp difference between the response to wh-trace, on the one hand, and the response to NP-trace and PRO, on the other.

A reactivation effect for NP-trace in passives with an end-of-sentence probe task has also been reported by MacDonald (1989) (though her study did not compare NP-trace with the other empty categories).[42] Verbal passive constructions containing NP-trace (according to GB) were compared with adjectival passive constructions which contain no trace (even in GB), because they are assumed to be lexically rather than syntactically derived. Simple adjective constructions were also tested, which also contain no trace on any theory. These are illustrated by (41a–c), respectively. The probe word was the head noun of the surface subject NP, in this case *mayor*.

41a. [The new mayor]$_i$ at the centre podium was shot NP-trace$_i$.
b. The new mayor at the centre podium was surprised.
c. The new mayor at the centre podium was furious.

Responses to the probe were significantly faster following the verbal passive construction than following the adjective and adjectival passive constructions.[43] Other aspects of MacDonald's experiment are discussed below.

Current Experiments

To review, one set of experiments, involving on-line cross-modal priming of lexical decision or naming, seems to show an immediate and accurate effect for wh-trace contrasted with a delayed and not entirely accurate response to PRO and NP-trace. Another set of experiments, involving an end-of-sentence probe task, also shows a strong effect for wh-trace and a weaker effect for PRO, but the onset of reactivation does not vary across the empty categories, and in terms of the strength of reactivation, NP-trace is more similar to wh-trace than it is to PRO. This difference in outcomes for the two sets of experiments is greatly frustrating because the uncertainty sits at the heart of our project of cross-theory comparison. The priming results suggest that wh-trace might be the only genuine empty

[42]McElree and Bever (1989) also tested NP-trace in passive constructions, in their experiments 3, 4, and 5. The passives were compared with active verb and adjectival constructions, and showed a significant reactivation effect.

[43]Unlike McElree and Bever (1989), MacDonald found significant reactivation when the probe was presented immediately after the empty category. But in MacDonald's materials, the NP-trace always occurred at the end of the sentence, and therefore the probe task did not interrupt the sentence.

category, whereas the probe results suggest the full panoply of GB empty categories.[44]

Is it possible to reconcile these apparently contradictory findings? Of course, it might be argued that any such attempt would be premature, because they are early results in a very new line of research, and caution is needed in interpreting them. But still it is worth mapping out the terrain a little, so that we can see where the conflicts actually lie, and what sorts of experiments need to be done next to try to resolve them. One obvious point is that the different empty categories have not been tested in perfectly matched environments. Because it is part of their linguistic essence that they must occur in distinct environments, there cannot be a "perfectly controlled" psycholinguistic comparison. But it is possible to approach the ideal a little more closely.

The test environments for NP-trace and PRO can be well matched; they need to differ only in the choice of predicate in the main clause. McElree and Bever (1989, experiment 2) compared . . . *was eager PRO to* . . . with . . . *was sure NP-trace to* . . .; this is a tidier version of the (40a)/(40b) comparison, as both predicates are adjectives, and the number of words is matched without need for an extra adverb as in (40a).[45] What has been less well controlled is the theoretically crucial comparison between these empty categories (PRO and NP-trace) and wh-trace. In the probe studies, this is particularly important, because responses are compared *across* the different sentence types. The estimates of how energetically each empty category reactivates its antecedent are therefore critically dependent on how well matched the sentence types are with each other and with the pronoun and no-coreference sentences that serve as standards. In the cross-modal priming paradigm, by contrast, the target words can be chosen more freely, since they do not have to be drawn from the sentence as probe words do. Therefore, instead of comparing responses to the same target word across different syntactic constructions, one can compare responses to different target words for the same sentence. And the latter comparison is easier to control: Each target word of interest (i.e. associated with a potential antecedent) can be compared with a control target word (i.e. not associated with a potential antecedent) that is matched to it in length and

---

[44]In what follows I will have frequent occasion to compare these two tasks. I will refer to them as the *priming task* and the *probe task* but these terms are just a convenient shorthand, as the probe task could also be said to involve priming.

[45]In this experiment, the PRO sentence did not show a significant reactivation effect, and the reaction time difference between the NP-trace sentence and the PRO sentence was significant. This suggests that materials may make some difference, but it does not greatly change the theoretical interpretation of the probe results, particularly as there was no comparison with wh-trace in this experiment.

frequency.[46] Even this cannot absolutely guarantee that different results across sentence types could be due only to differences between their empty categories, but it does ensure that the task is picking up reactivation effects rather than irrelevant effects of local structural complexity, sentence plausibility, familiarity of lexical items, etc. In this respect, at least, the priming studies are more trustworthy than the probe studies.

Consider, for example, (40b), where the third fragment is *is sure to*, compared with (40c) where the third fragment is the strange sequence *to argue with about*, and the non-coreference baseline sentence (40e) which has *flatly rejected the*, another non-constituent but of a different kind. If probe responses following the wh-trace sentence were slower than following the NP-trace sentence, one might well suspect the greater processing difficulty of its third fragment, rather than any effect of the empty category *per se*. In fact, responses were slightly (non-significantly) *faster* for the wh-trace sentence, and one can only speculate as to how much faster still they might have been if the processor had not had to contend with the irrelevant processing difficulty. Notice that this alone would be sufficient to resolve the discrepancy between the probe task findings and the cross-modal priming findings, because the major difference is whether or not the wh-trace effect is very much livelier than the NP-trace and PRO effects.

The crucial comparisons with wh-trace could be controlled more tightly with examples constructed along the lines of (42) and (43):[47]

---

[46]MacDonald tested two probe words at the empty category position, one drawn from the antecedent noun phrase, and one drawn from a noun phrase in a prior sentence. (The correct answer to a probe was "yes" if it had appeared anywhere in the two-sentence sequence.) A non-antecedent probe could offer a baseline that is not confounded with differences in sentence materials and hence is less vulnerable than Bever and McElree's (40e). However, the two probes in MacDonald's study were not matched in other respects (length, frequency, position in discourse relative to test site), and therefore they could not be directly compared. Therefore, the comparison was again across sentence types, though these were well-matched (see examples in 41 above). Unlike the antecedent probes, the non-antecedent probes showed no significant differences across sentence types (see further discussion on pp. 199–201).

[47]These examples pit wh-trace against other empty categories. Wh-trace could also be compared with a lexical pronoun (e.g. *they/them*) or full lexical NP (e.g. *the twins*) in quite closely matched contexts, as in (i) and (ii):

ia. These are the children who$_i$ we suspect John believes *wh-trace*$_i$ are the best readers.
b. These are the children who$_i$ *wh-trace*$_i$ suspect John believes they$_i$ are the best readers.
c. These are the children who$_i$ *wh-trace*$_i$ suspect John believes the twins$_i$ are the best readers.
iia. These are the children who$_i$ we are all convinced that John punished *wh-trace*$_i$.
b. These are the children who$_i$ *wh-trace*$_i$ are all convinced that John punished them$_i$.
c. These are the children who$_i$ *wh-trace*$_i$ are all convinced that John punished the twins$_i$.

42a. These are the children who$_i$ we all fervently believed *wh-trace*$_i$ to be the best readers.

b. These are the children who$_i$ *wh-trace*$_i$ were all fervently believed *NP-trace*$_i$ to be the best readers.

c. These are the children who$_i$ *wh-trace*$_i$ were all fervently trying PRO$_i$ to be the best readers.

43a. These are the children who$_i$ we only very rarely observed *wh-trace*$_i$ in the classroom.

b. These are the children who$_i$ *wh-trace*$_i$ were only very rarely observed *NP-trace*$_i$ in the classroom.

In (42), the three empty categories appear as the subject of an infinitival clause. In (43), the empty categories are in direct object position (where PRO cannot appear). Note that the (a) sentences contain a clear instance of wh-trace, rather than the less well-understood empty category of a "tough" construction (see footnote 41). In the (b,c) sentences, the empty category of interest is NP-trace or PRO, but these sentences also contain a wh-trace which serves to keep the overall structure similar to that of the (a) sentence. I assume that this wh-trace will not interfere with the interpretation of the results; it is adjacent to its antecedent (*who*), and should have been processed well before the NP-trace or PRO is encountered.[48] Fodor and Swinney are currently conducting a cross-modal priming study with materials such as these.

However, even these precautions cannot exclude all potentially confounding effects. Nicol (1988) has pointed to a difference between the three kinds of empty category which cannot be eliminated just by matching the sentence structures in this way. She notes that the speedy wh-trace effects and the slow PRO and NP-trace effects with cross-modal priming might be due to how much warning the processor has that an empty category is going to occur. The antecedent for a wh-trace often occurs well before the trace, and in the typical case it is immediately and unambiguously recognisable as the antecedent of a wh-trace, not just because it is a wh-phrase, but also because it is in a pre-clause, non-argument position. Therefore, the processor can often know, well in advance, that a wh-trace is forthcoming, even if it does not know exactly where. Indeed, the processor often *anticipates* a wh-trace (see pp. 161–162). On the other

[48]The movement in the (b) and (c) sentences is from subject position to pre-clause position, with no change in surface word sequence. Even some theories which assume movement do not assume that movement occurs in this case; it is possible instead to assume that *who* stays in the subject position and there is no wh-trace (see Chomsky, 1986; Gazdar et al., 1985). This makes a difference to whether the antecedent of NP-trace or PRO is the *who* or the wh-trace, but there is no reason to think that this should have a significant effect on the outcome of the experiment.

hand, the antecedents of NP-trace and PRO are typically normal argument NPs which cannot, when they are encountered, be recognised *as* antecedents. When the processor encounters the predicate (e.g. *invited*, *refused*, *is sure*, etc.) it can tell that an empty category *may* be forthcoming, but even then it is not certain. Nicol (1988, p. 108ff.) notes that a passive verb is often confusable with an adjective, and a passive *by-phrase* may be confusable with a temporal or locative phrase. Similarly, a raising verb may be homonymous with a non-raising verb (as in *John appeared NP-trace to dislike the cake / John appeared to Susan in a dream*); and a sentence containing PRO may be temporarily indistinguishable from a non-PRO construction (e.g. *John intended PRO to leave / John intended no harm*). Thus an NP-trace or PRO may sneak up on the processor with little or no warning, and the processor would need extra time to recognise the empty category and then go back and look for its antecedent.

This difference in the "expectability" of different empty categories is a serious obstacle to extracting linguistically interesting conclusions from the reactivation experiments. No really satisfactory way round it is known at present (though see p. 203 for an idea). The differential predictabilities of the various empty categories could be evened up either by making wh-trace less predictable or by making NP-trace and PRO more predictable. To make wh-trace less predictable, we might try testing "*too/enough* constructions" like those in (44):

44a. [That old wall]$_i$ is too dilapidated for the children to play on *wh-trace*$_i$.
b. [That old wall]$_i$ is too dilapidated for the children to play on it.
c. [That old wall]$_i$ is too dilapidated for the children to play on the top.

These are similar to the "tough-movement" constructions tested by Bever and McElree (see 40c), except that the empty category is optional rather than obligatory. It is not entirely clear whether this empty category is a wh-trace, as I have glossed it here (see discussion in footnote 41). If it is, sentences like (44a) could be compared with matched wh-questions or relative clause constructions where a wh-trace is obligatory. Because of the existence of sentences like (44b,c) without any empty category, the processor could not securely anticipate the wh-trace in (44a), as it can in a wh-question or relative clause. An even closer comparison would be between a *too/enough* construction and a similar tough-movement construction, as in (45), where the existence of an empty category somewhere in the subordinate clause is predictable in (b) though not in (a):

45a. [That old wall]$_i$ is too dangerous for the children to play on *wh-trace*$_i$.

b. [That old wall]$_i$ is very dangerous for the children to play on *wh-trace*$_i$.

As for making NP-trace and PRO more predictable, we could of course look for unambiguous passive, raising, and control verbs, and could make sure that they precede their respective empty categories by a good margin, by inserting extra material such as adverbs in between. This may be more feasible in languages other than English. For instance, in Chinese, the preposition *bei* unambiguously signals a passive construction, and it precedes the verb which is followed by the NP-trace. The processor can be given time to compute the implications of *bei* before it encounters the trace, because the agent NP between the two can be made as long as one likes.

46.

[Na	ben	shu]$_i$	bei	[nage	ganggang	zhai	tushuguan	kanshu
that	(quantifier)	book	by	that	just now	(particle)	library	reading

de	nianqing	nuhai]$_j$	dai	NP-trace$_i$	dao	jiali	quie.
(relative particle)	young	girl	take		toward	home	to

(That book was taken home by the young girl who was reading in the library.)

However, even with examples like these, we can never be sure that we have *exactly* equated the processing-expectation factor across different kinds of empty category constructions, and therefore we may never quite be able to subtract that factor out of the linguistic comparisons we are interested in.

Possible Interpretations

For the sake of the mental exercise, let us now imagine that the results obtained so far are confirmed and strengthened by future experiments with cleverly tailored materials and control conditions that do exclude the possibility of artefact. However improbable this is, it will at least allow us to think through how such results could or should be interpreted. In particular, this forces us now to address the question we postponed on p. 187, of whether these tasks tap syntactic or semantic processing. This is crucial, because all three types of empty category construction might reasonably be expected to show a reactivation effect during *semantic* processing, even on a theory which denies their *syntactic* existence. Therefore, if the experiments are only picking up semantic effects, they cannot after all differentiate between linguistic theories.

To set about deciding this issue, we might try to establish the characteristics of these priming and probe tasks on sentences which have nothing to do with empty categories, but which are designed to pit syntactic and semantic factors against each other so that their effects can be clearly distinguished.[49] For instance, we might look for reactivation effects in the case of what are called "implicit" or "understood" arguments, which are not regarded as syntactically present by any linguistic theory. If such effects are observed, it would strongly suggest that the tasks are responsive to semantic representations and are therefore not suited to establishing the syntactic existence of empty categories. For example, one might see whether the cross-modal priming task shows any sensitivity to implicit arguments such as the direct object of a verb like *eat*, *shave*, or *notice*, when it appears with no following noun phrase. In (47), for example, the verb *eating* is likely to be understood as having *pizza* as its implicit object, in contrast with the verb *snoozing*, which is semantically as well as syntactically intransitive. (*Drinking* has an implicit object but it is not *pizza*; for *notice*, the implicit object is the whole situation described by the prior sentence.)

47. A pizza was on a tray in the middle of the kitchen table.
    John was eating.
    John was drinking.
    John was snoozing.
    John didn't notice.

Interestingly, MacDonald (1989) has already conducted just such a test of implicit arguments (though not under that description) in her probe study of NP-trace in passives. Her materials actually consisted of two-sentence discourses, as in (48):

48. The terrorists wanted to disrupt the ceremonies.
    [The new mayor at the centre podium]$_i$ was shot NP-trace$_i$.

At the NP-trace position at the end of the second sentence, MacDonald probed with its antecedent (*mayor*), as noted above. But she also probed with *terrorists* from the preceding sentence (as a control to check for possible discourse topic shifts). Now *terrorists* happens to be the (probable)

[49]For example, Cloitre and Bever (1988) have looked for effects on probe response times to lexical pronouns and noun anaphors, of the semantic (or conceptual) factor of abstractness. A finding that probe words with concrete meanings give faster responses than probe words with abstract meanings is taken as an indicator of conceptual, rather than purely syntactic, processing. Also, Cloitre and Bever argue that facilitation of a lexical decision task is a mark of surface processing, whereas facilitation of a category decision task is a mark of conceptual processing. Applied to their data, these criteria indicated that "pronouns provide direct access to a conceptual representation of the antecedent, whereas repeated noun anaphors do so indirectly, priming a surface (lexical) level of representation as a preliminary to accessing the conceptual representation" (p. 293).

understood agent of the passive sentence. So here we have an interesting difference between (a) the understood patient, which is phonologically empty but syntactically present following the verb (according to GB) in the form of an NP-trace, and (b) the understood agent, which is neither phonologically nor syntactically present but is established only by semantic interpretation.[50] MacDonald's results indicate that sentence processing respects this subtle distinction between an invisible/inaudible constituent and a non-existent constituent. She found reactivation of the patient following the verb, but no reactivation of the implicit agent.

A natural conclusion to draw from this is that the probe task is not sensitive to all elements in the semantic representation of a sentence, but is only sensitive to elements which are also present at a syntactic level.[51] If this were correct, we should further conclude that NP-trace and PRO are genuine syntactic elements. Because of its importance, this link in the reasoning needs to be explored thoroughly. Other possible explanations for MacDonald's null finding for implicit agents must be eliminated. For example, it might be just that the implicit agent occurred too far back in the discourse to be retrieved after the passive verb in time to affect responses there; positional effects should be controlled for. Or, possibly, the subject of the prior sentence was not always interpreted by perceivers as the agent of the passive sentence.[52] The likelihood of that interpretation can be manipulated. The presumption that it was the terrorists who shot

[50]Older transformational theories assumed that the agent NP was in subject position in the deep structure and was moved into a clause-final *by*-phrase by the passive transformation, which was then optionally deleted if the agent was non-specific (*someone, something*). In GB, the subject position of a passive sentence is empty at D-structure. Syntactic realisation of the agent is optional; when it is present it is base-generated in place of the *by*-phrase following the verb. Thus a "short passive" without a surface *by*-phrase does not contain an agent phrase at any level of derivation. (As discussed above, in GPSG and other non-transformational theories, neither the agent nor the patient is syntactically present after the verb in a short passive.)

[51]This may be an oversimplification. Fodor and Fodor (1980) argued that implicit arguments are not represented at any linguistic level, but are established by inference. So perhaps there are three levels of potential existence to be considered for any unrealised argument: syntactic, semantic, and inferential.

[52]Alternatively, it is conceivable that the subject of the prior sentence *was* always interpreted as the implicit agent of the verbal passive, but that it was *also* interpreted as an implicit argument (not necessarily agent) in the adjective and adjectival passive constructions (see 41). For example, *The new mayor at the podium was furious* might be construed as implying that he was furious *at* the terrorists. Because these other sentences establish the baseline against which the verbal passive is compared, this would create an appearance of no effect for the implicit agent of the verbal passive. Thus to pursue the contrast between empty *vs* implicit arguments, would necessitate designing new control sentences free of all possible implicit arguments.

the mayor is only moderately strong in (48); it is closer to obligatory in (49):

49. The terrorists were firing at the city officials on the platform. The new mayor at the centre podium was shot.

It is conceivable that with such materials a reactivation effect for the implicit agent might be obtained. However, if the null finding for implicit arguments persists under such manipulations, in contrast with the significant reactivation effect for the NP-trace, it would strongly suggest that the GB characterisation of empty categories is correct.

On the other hand, if the contrast between NP-trace and merely implicit arguments dwindles in further studies, it would be natural to infer that the probe task taps semantic representations. Then it would be possible to reconcile the currently conflicting patterns of results across tasks, if it were assumed that the cross-modal priming task is responsive primarily to syntactic representations. On that assumption, all the experimental findings so far (tentative and incomplete though we know them to be) would be accounted for by a non-transformational model which admits only wh-trace. In the priming task, wh-trace behaves *unlike* the other putative empty categories, and behaves *like* lexical pronouns. Because lexical pronouns are present in syntactic representations, a plausible explanation would be that wh-trace is also present in syntactic representations, but that all the other putative empty category effects are a matter of semantic interpretation.[53]

Is there any independent reason to suppose that the tasks split across

[53]Three notes here. First, the fact that the wh-trace effect in the probe task does not contrast in immediacy of onset with the NP-trace and PRO effects, as it does in the priming task, is quite possibly due to artefact, as suggested in connection with example (40c). If so, the data could be accounted for without appeal to the sort of difference I am about to sketch with regard to how the two tasks are performed. But, secondly, in McElree and Bever's study, even the lexical pronoun showed no reactivation effect when tested immediately, but only when the probe was sentence-final [and comparison of (40d) above with (40c) suggests that in the case of the lexical pronoun this was not artefactual). This contrasts with the immediate effect for lexical pronouns as well as wh-trace with cross-modal priming. Thus in each task, lexical pronouns and wh-trace pattern like each other. This suggests that, whatever else is going on, there really is a linguistically relevant difference between the tasks. Thirdly, Cloitre and Bever's conclusion (see footnote 49) that a lexical pronoun directly accesses a non-syntactic conceptual representation of its antecedent, might suggest by parity that wh-trace does also; but because their data came from a probe task, this does not conflict with my current proposal. On the other hand, my proposal cannot be correct unless there is some other explanation for the data which led Cloitre and Bever to conclude in the case of noun anaphors that the probe task shows a reactivation effect at a stage at which the absence of a concrete/abstract difference indicates that processing is still syntactic, not yet semantic.

linguistic levels in this way? We know painfully little about how the processor performs these tasks, or about the exact dovetailing of events (lexical, syntactic, semantic) within any brief time-slice of sentence processing. Therefore, we have only the sketchiest of clues to guide speculation here. However, we do know that the cross-modal lexical decision task is performed more rapidly than the probe task; response times are of the order of 600–700 msec, which (though not exactly speedy) is 250–300 msec faster on average than responses in the probe task. We also know that the cross-modal priming is occurring during processing of the sentence, whereas the probe task is insensitive until after the whole sentence has been received. As noted above, McElree and Bever report that no reactivation effects were obtained for any type of empty category when the probe was presented immediately after the empty category, but only when it was presented at the end of the sentence (approximately 900 msec later). MacDonald did observe reactivation with the probe at the empty category position, but in all of her materials the empty category coincided with the end of the sentence. Thus it is at least imaginable that the cross-modal priming task catches the processor in the course of constructing a representation for the sentence, while the probe task interrogates a finished representation. If we view syntax as the means by which the processor achieves its end of computing the meaning of the input, then it is not unreasonable to suppose that syntactic factors have a sharper effect on a task performed *in medias res* than on one performed when procesing is complete.

If there is any truth to this tale, then the striking difference between wh-trace and the other putative empty categories in the priming task would reflect the fact that only wh-trace is a syntactic entity, and/or that only wh-trace is associated with lexical/syntactic material as its antecedent.[54] Note that there is no reason, on these assumptions, why the priming task should not *also* be sensitive to semantic entities such as PRO and NP-trace and other implicit arguments, because these are also presumably being processed as the sentence proceeds. But to tidy up the loose ends, we do need to add some account of why sensitivity to semantic entities is delayed. (For simplicity, I will refer just to PRO in what follows, but the discussion applies equally to NP-trace.)

The simplest explanation would be that semantic interpretation lags behind syntactic analysis. Thus the reason why PRO exhibits a reactivation

[54]Though I have been presenting this whole discussion in terms of syntactically real *vs* semantically real *entities*, nothing that has been said so far and nothing that follows discriminates clearly between entities and *processes*. So as Mark Steedman reminds me, my account of the experimental data is just as compatible with Categorial Grammar as with GPSG; the former treats wh-dependencies in the syntax, unlike the other constructions that have empty categories in GB, even though it does not posit a syntactic empty category wh-trace.

effect only for the 1000-msec-delayed lexical decision target would be that PRO is only just being semantically interpreted 1000 msec after its occurrence in the sentence. This may indeed be so. But one second is a long time for semantic processing; many processing studies in the last few years have emphasised how rapidly semantics follows upon syntax.[55] A more interesting possibility is that PRO gives a delayed effect in the priming task even though it is interpreted quickly, perhaps just as quickly as wh-trace. If we could show that this is so, it would eliminate explanations of the slow response to PRO that are based on its unexpectedness in the sentence, or on ambiguity with respect to its antecedent (see p. 191, p. 196); all such explanations presuppose that antecedent assignment is slow for PRO. This is an important point, for with these other accounts ruled out, the only obvious explanation remaining would be that cross-modal priming of lexical decision is (for whatever reason) triggered primarily by lexical/syntactic entities. In other words, this would provide some support for the speculation that immediacy of cross-modal priming constitutes a diagnostic for syntactic existence.

How might it be shown that PRO is rapidly interpreted though it does not give rise to rapid priming? One way would be to show that it can transmit its interpretation to a nearby item in the sentence which does show rapid priming. Consider the sentences in (50) and (51):

50a. [The electrician]$_i$ convinced [the architect who owned the small company]$_j$ PRO$_j$ to give him$_i$ a raise in pay.
b. [The electrician]$_i$ convinced [the architect who owned the small company]$_j$ PRO$_j$ to give himself$_j$ a raise in pay.
51a. [The electrician]$_i$ was convinced *NP-trace*$_i$ by [the architect who owned the small company]$_j$ PRO$_i$ to give him$_j$ a raise in pay.
b. [The electrician]$_i$ was convinced *NP-trace*$_i$ by [the architect who owned the small company]$_j$ PRO$_i$ to give himself$_i$ a raise in pay.

In these sentences, a PRO mediates the coreference relationship between the pronoun or anaphor (*him* or *himself*) and its antecedent in the main clause.[56] It is impossible to establish the referent of the pronoun or

---

[55]Bever et al. (in press) propose a model in which semantic processing precedes most syntactic processing.

[56]In (51), unfortunately, there is an NP-trace which also arguably mediates this relationship (see also 38b). This would not be so for a sentence with an active main clause such as *[The electrician]$_i$ promised [the architect who . . .]$_j$ PRO$_i$* to give *him/himself* a raise in pay, but English contains far too few verbs like *promise* to test in an experiment. So passive verbs, with their NP-traces, must be resorted to, even though, if the NP-trace did a poor job of transmitting its interpretation to the PRO, it could create a misleading impression that PRO is not rapidly interpreted. However, the intervening material in (51) ought to allow the NP-trace to be interpreted in good time before the PRO occurs.

anaphor unless the referent of PRO has already been established. For example, in (50a), the pronoun *him* can only refer to the electrician (or to someone not mentioned in the sentence); it cannot refer to the architect. The reason is that *convinced* is an object control verb, so PRO refers to the architect; then, given that PRO and *him* are in the same clause and are therefore required to be disjoint in reference, it follows that *him* cannot refer to the architect. In (51a), by contrast, the pronoun *him* must refer to the architect (or to someone not mentioned in the sentence), not to the electrician, because PRO refers to the electrician, and PRO and *him* must be disjoint in reference. Comparable reasoning shows that the interpretation of *himself* in the (b) sentences also depends on prior interpretation of the PRO. From Nicol's work we know that lexical pronouns and anaphors show rapid reactivation of their antecedents in contexts where there is a direct, unmediated relation between them, as in (34). If reactivation at the pronoun/anaphor position is *equally* rapid in examples like (50) and (51), it can be concluded that the PRO has been assigned its antecedent by the time the pronoun/anaphor is processed. The final step would be to show that all this occurs *before* the point at which the PRO itself shows a reactivation effect.[57] The only natural explanation then would seem to be that the priming task cannot "see" PRO (or can see it only dimly, or only after long exposure to it, etc.), though it can see lexical pronouns and it can see wh-trace. And though there might be other explanations for that, the likeliest is surely that there is a level of representation which contains lexical pronouns and wh-trace but not PRO.

Fodor, McKinnon, and Swinney are currently conducting an experiment with this design. Only very preliminary data are available as yet, but they do point in the direction anticipated above. That is, *him* and *himself* in constructions like (50) and (51) do show immediate and accurate reactivation of their antecedents. We also plan to conduct a similar study with NP-trace in place of PRO, as in (53):

53a. [The architect]$_i$ seemed to [the electrician who worked at the site]$_j$ *NP-trace*$_i$ to pay him$_j$ too little.
b. [The architect]$_i$ seemed to [the electrician who worked at the site]$_j$ *NP-trace*$_i$ to pay himself$_i$ too little.

Comparable results for NP-trace would draw the argument one notch tighter. In GB theory, though PRO exists as a constituent at the level of S-structure, it is often assumed that PRO is assigned its antecedent only at

[57]This can be tested cleanly only in the (a) sentences in (50) and (51), where the PRO differs in reference from the lexical pronoun.

the level of Logical Form (LF). Though it is emphasised that LF is a syntactic level, it is considerably more abstract than S-structure; it represents semantically relevant information that may not be explicit at S-structure. Possibly, then, a sluggish response on the priming task, even after antecedent assignment, is characteristic of elements that are not assigned their antecedents at S-structure, regardless of whether they *exist* at S-structure. If so, the PRO experiment would not distinguish one linguistic theory from another. But this loophole is absent in the case of NP-trace, because in GB theory NP-trace not only exists at S-structure but also has an antecedent at S-structure, associated with it by a syntactic movement operation, just as in the case of wh-trace.[58]

CONCLUSION

I will not attempt to draw this discussion together into one tidy final conclusion. That would be silly at this time when new experiments on empty categories and new interpretations of their findings are blooming all about us. We are in the thick of things, and will be there for a while. I will merely summarise the story of how we got there.

The study of empty categories is (in part) the study of long-distance syntactic dependencies. The more extended a dependency is, the more opportunities for error there are for a processor which lacks precise knowledge of what relationships are legitimate. Therefore, long-distance binding of traces should provide many pitfalls for a rough-and-ready processor which relies on informal strategies rather than consulting the information provided by the grammar (except perhaps as an emergency back-up). The hypothesis that the human sentence processing mechanism is such a device (see Fodor, Bever, & Garrett, 1974; Bever et al., in press) becomes quite implausible in the face of the speed and accuracy with which the human sentence processor interprets traces. We can conclude, instead, that the human processor is very closely attuned to the grammar of the language.

If that is so, then differences in how the processor responds to different (putative) empty categories can be taken seriously as evidence of how they are treated by the grammar. The excitement of the last two or three years has been the discovery that the processor does respond to empty categories, in ways that we can measure and replicate. To get the most out of that discovery, we then have to probe the internal mechanics of the system to try to find out exactly what it is responding to. Because we cannot actually

---

[58]Though in both cases, the antecedent–trace relation has to meet additional conditions at LF.

observe its computations, that means devising further experiments that will allow the original findings to be parcelled out into task effects and linguistic effects, and will allow linguistic effects to be pinned down to a particular linguistic level. In this paper, I have tried to make a case for one way of integrating the results that have been obtained so far, a way which sets long-distance dependencies involving wh-trace apart from more local relationships.

REFERENCES

Abney, S. (1987). Licensing and parsing. In J. McDonough & B. Plunkett (Eds), *Proceedings of the North Eastern Linguistics Society*, *17*, 1–15.

Abney, S. & Cole, J. (1986). A government-bindig parser. *Proceedings of the North Eastern Linguistics Society*, *16*.

Altmann, G. T. M. & Steedman, M. (1988). Interaction with context during human sentence processing. *Cognition*, *30*, 191–238.

Barton, G. E., Berwick, R. C., & Ristad, E. S. (1987). *Computational complexity and natural language*. Cambridge, Mass.: Bradford Books.

Berwick, R. C. & Weinberg, A. S. (1984). *The grammatical basis of linguistic performance: Language use and acquisition*. Cambridge, Mass.: MIT Press.

Bever, T. G. & McElree, B. (1988). Empty categories access their antecedents during comprehension. *Linguistic Inquiry*, *19*, 35–43.

Bever, T. G., Straub, K., Juliano, C., Shenkman, K., Kim, J., Carrithers, C., McElree, B., & Zamparelli, R. (in press). The integrated study of a selectional model of comprehension. In D. Swinney & J. D. Fodor (Eds), special volume of the *Journal of Psycholinguistic Research*.

Caplan, D. & Hildebrandt, N. (1988). *Disorders of syntactic comprehension*. Cambridge, Mass.: Bradford Books/MIT Press.

Chomsky, N. (1965). *Aspects of the theory of syntax*. Cambridge, Mass.: MIT Press.

Chomsky, N. (1973). Conditions on transformations. In S. Anderson & P. Kiparsky (Eds), *A festschrift for Morris Halle*. New York: Holt, Rinehart and Winston. Reprinted in N. Chomsky, *Essays on form and interpretation*. New York: North-Holland.

Chomsky, N. (1976). Conditions on rules of grammar. *Linguistic Analysis*, *2*, 303–351. Reprinted in N. Chomsky, *Essays on form and interpretation*. New York: North-Holland.

Chomsky, N. (1977). On wh-movement. In P. Culicover, T. Wasow, & A. Akmajian (Eds), *Formal syntax*. London: Academic Press.

Chomsky, N. (1981). *Lectures on government and binding*. Dordrecht: Foris.

Chomsky, N. (1982). *Some concepts and consequences of the theory of government and binding*. Cambridge, Mass.: MIT Press.

Chomsky, N. (1986). *Barriers*. Cambridge, Mass.: MIT Press.

Clifton, C. & Frazier, L. (1986). The use of syntactic information in filling gaps. *Journal of Psycholinguistic Research*, *15*, 209–224.

Clifton, C., Frazier, L., & Connine, C. (1984). Lexical expectations in sentence comprehension. *Journal of Verbal Learning and Verbal Behavior*, *23*, 696–708.

Cloitre, M. & Bever, T. G. (1988). Linguistic anaphors, levels of representation, and discourse. *Language and Cognitive Processes*, *3*, 293–322.

Corbett, A. T. & Chang, F. R. (1983). Pronoun disambiguation: Accessing potential antecedents. *Memory and Cognition*, *11*, 283–294.

Correa, N. (1987). An attribute grammar implementation for Government-binding Theory.

Proceedings of the Twenty-fifth Annual Meeting of the Association for Computational Linguistics, Stanford University, Stanford, Calif.

Crain, S. & Fodor, J. D. (1985). How can grammars help parsers? In D. Dowty, L. Karttunen, & A. Zwicky (Eds), *Natural language parsing: Psychological, computational, and theoretical perspectives*. Cambridge: Cambridge University Press.

Crain, S. & Fodor, J. D. (1987). Sentence matching and overgeneration. *Cognition*, *26*, 123–169.

Ehrlich, K. (1980). Comprehension of pronouns. *Quarterly Journal of Experimental Psychology*, *32*, 247–255.

Engdahl, E. (1983). Parasitic gaps. *Linguistics and Philosophy*, *6*, 5–34.

Fiengo, R. W. (1977). On trace theory. *Linguistic Inquiry*, *8*, 35–61.

Fodor, J. A., Bever, T. G., & Garrett, M. F. (1974). *The psychology of language: An introduction to psycholinguistics and generative grammar*. New York: McGraw-Hill Book Company.

Fodor, J. A. & Fodor, J. D. (1980). Functional structure, quantifiers and meaning postulates. *Linguistic Inquiry*, *11*, 759–770.

Fodor, J. D. (1978). Parsing strategies and constraints on transformations. *Linguistic Inquiry*, *9*, 427–473.

Fodor, J. D. (1979). Superstrategy. In W. E. Cooper & E. C. T. Walker (Eds), *Sentence processing: Psycholinguistic studies presented to Merrill Garrett*. Hillsdale, N.J.: Lawrence Erlbaum Associates Inc.

Fodor, J. D. (1983). Constraints on gaps: Is the parser a significant influence? *Linguistics*, *21*, 9–34.

Fodor, J. D. (1988). On modularity in sentence processing. *Journal of Psycholinguistic Research*, *17*, 125–168.

Fodor, J. D. (in press). Sentence processing and the mental grammar. In T. Wasow, P. Sells, & S. Shieber (Eds), *Foundational issues in natural language processing*. Cambridge, Mass.: MIT Press.

Forster, K. I. & Stevenson, B. J. (1987). Sentence matching and well-formedness. *Cognition*, *26*, 171–186.

Frazier, L. (1985). Modularity and the representational hypothesis. In *Proceedings of the North Eastern Linguistic Society*, *15*, 131–145.

Frazier, L. (1989). Parsing with chains. Paper delivered at the Second Annual CUNY Conference on Human Sentence Processing March 1989.

Frazier, L. & Clifton, C. (1989). Successive cyclicity in the grammar and the parser. *Language and Cognitive Process, 4*, 73–157.

Frazier, L., Clifton, C., & Randall, J. (1983). Filling gaps: Decision principles and structure in sentence comprehension. *Cognition*, *13*, 187–222.

Freedman, S. A. & Forster, K. I. (1985). The psychological status of overgenerated sentences. *Cognition*, *19*, 101–131.

Garnsey, S. M., Tanenhaus, M. K., & Chapman, R. M. (1989). Evoked potentials and the study of sentence comprehension. *Journal of Psycholinguistic Research*, *18*, 51–60.

Gazdar, G., Klein, E., Pullum, G. K., & Sag, I. A. (1985). *Generalized phrase structure grammar*. Cambridge, Mass.: Harvard University Press.

Gorrell, P. (1987). Studies of human syntactic processing: Ranked parallel versus serial models. Ph.D. dissertation, University of Connecticut.

Johnson, M. (1989). Parsing as deduction: The use of knowledge of language. *Journal of Psycholinguistic Research*, *18*, 105–128.

Kaplan, R. & Bresnan, J. (1982). Lexical-functional grammar: A formal system for grammatical representation. In J. Bresnan (Ed.), *The mental representation of grammatical relations*. Cambridge, Mass.: MIT Press.

Kaplan, R. M. & Zaenen, A. (1989). Long-distance dependencies, constituent structure, and functional uncertainty. In M. Baltin & A. Kroch (Eds), *Alternative conceptions of phrase structure*. Chicago: Chicago University Press.

Kurtzman, H. S. (1985). Studies in syntactic ambiguity resolution. Ph.D. dissertation, MIT. Distributed by Indiana University Linguistics Club.

Kurtzman, H. S. (1989). Human processing of parasitic gaps. Paper presented at the 27th Annual Meeting of the Association for Computational Linguistics.

Lasnik, H. & Fiengo, R. W. (1974). Complement object deletion. *Linguistic Inquiry*, *5*, 535–571.

Lasnik, H. & Saito, M. (1984). On the nature of proper government. *Linguistic Inquiry*, *15*, 235–289.

MacDonald, M. C. (1989). Priming effects from gaps to antecedents. *Language and Cognitive Processes, 4*, 1–72.

McElree, B. & Bever, T. G. (1989). The psychological reality of linguistically defined gaps. *Journal of Psycholinguistic Research*, *18*, 21–35.

Mitchell, D. C. (1987). Lexical guidance in human parsing: Locus and processing characteristics. In M. Coltheart (Ed.), *Attention and performance XII: The psychology of reading*. Hillsdale, N.J.: Lawrence Erlbaum Associates Inc.

Newmeyer, F. J. (1986). *Linguistic theory in America*, 2nd edn. London: Academic Press.

Nicol, J. (1988). Coreference processing during sentence comprehension. Ph.D. dissertation, MIT.

Nicol, J. & Osterhout, L. (in prep.). Reactivating antecedents of empty categories during sentence processing. Unpublished.

Nicol, J. & Swinney, D. (1989). The role of structure of coreference assignment during sentence comprehension. *Journal of Psycholinguistic Research*, *18*, 5–19.

Osterhout, L. & Swinney, D. (in prep.). Activation of antecedents to NP-trace.

Perlmutter, D. M. (Ed.) (1983). *Studies in relational grammar 1*. Chicago: University of Chicago Press.

Perlmutter, D. M. & Rosen, C. (Eds) (1984). *Studies in relational grammar 2*. Chicago: University of Chicago Press.

Pollard, C. & Sag, I. A. (1987). *Information-based syntax and semantics*, Vol. I. *Fundamentals*. CSLI Lecture Notes Series No. 13. Stanford, Calif.: CSLI.

Riemsdijk, H. C. van & Williams, E. S. (1986). *Introduction to the theory of grammar*. Cambridge, Mass.: MIT Press.

Ross, J. R. (1967). *Constraints on variables in syntax*. Ph.D. dissertation, MIT. Distributed by Indiana University Linguistics Club.

Sag, I. & Pollard, C. (1987). Head-driven phrase structure grammar: An informal synopsis. CSLI Report No. CSLI-87-79, Stanford University, Calif.

Schachter, P. (1984). Auxiliary reduction: An argument for GPSG. *Linguistic Inquiry, 15*, 514–523.

Seely, T. D. (1987). The dependence hypothesis: Toward a theory of the processing of parasitic gaps. *Proceedings of the West Coast Conference on Formal Linguistics*.

Sells, P. (1985). *Lectures on contemporary syntactic theories: An Introduction to Government-Binding Theory, Generalized Phrase Structure Grammar, and Lexical-Functional Grammar*. Stanford, Calif.: CSLI.

Shieber, S. M. (1986). *An introduction to unification-based approaches to grammar*. CSLI Lecture Notes 4. Stanford, Calif.: CSLI.

Stabler, E. P. (forthcoming). Implementing Government-binding Theory. To appear in R. Levine (Ed.), *Formal grammar: Theory and implementation*. University of British Columbia Press.

Steedman, M. (1989). Grammar, interpretation, and processing from the lexicon. In W. Marslen-Wilson (Ed.), *Lexical representation and process*. Cambridge, Mass.: MIT Press.

Stowe, L. A. (1986). Evidence for on-line gap location. *Language and Cognitive Processes*, *1*, 227–245.

Swinney, D. & Osterhout, L. (in press). Inference generation during auditory language comprehension. In A. Graesser & G. H. Bower (Eds), *The psychology of learning and motivation*. London: Academic Press.

Swinney, D. A., Onifer, W., Prather, P., & Hirshkowitz, M. (1979). Semantic facilitation across sentence modalities in the processing of individual words and sentences. *Memory and Cognition*, *7*, 159–165.

Swinney, D., Ford, M., Bresnan, J., & Frauenfelder, U. (1988). Coreference assignment during sentence processing. In M. Macken (Ed.), *Language structure and processing*. Stanford, Calif.: CSLI.

Tanenhaus, M. K., Garnsey, S. M., & Boland, J. (1989b). Combinatory lexical information and language comprehension. In G. Altmann (Ed.), *Computational and experimental approaches to speech and language*. Cambridge, Mass.: MIT Press.

Tanenhaus, M. K., Stowe, L. A., & Carlson, G. (1985). The interactions of lexical expectation and pragmatics in parsing filler-gap constructions. In *Proceedings of the Seventh Annual Cognitive Science Society Meeting*, pp. 361–365. London: Lawrence Erlbaum Associates Ltd.

Tanenhaus, M. K., Boland, J., Garnsey, S. M., & Carlson, G. (1989). Lexical structure in parsing long-distance dependencies. *Journal of Psycholinguistic Research*, *18*, 37–50.

LANGUAGE AND COGNITIVE PROCESSES, 1989, *4*, (3/4) SI 211–234

The Role of Thematic Structures in Interpretation and Parsing

Michael K. Tanenhaus, Greg Carlson, and John C. Trueswell
Department of Psychology, University of Rochester, Rochester, N.Y. 14627

This paper explores how thematic role information associated with verbs is used in language processing. We suggest that thematic roles are useful for co-ordinating different types of information in language processing because they represent aspects of conceptual/semantic representation that map directly on to syntactic form. We review some recent studies investigating the use of thematic information in syntactic ambiguity resolution and present some new evidence that thematic information can be used to eliminate completely the garden path typically associated with reduced-relative clauses. We then review some of our recent work investigating lexical structure in the processing of sentences with long-distance dependencies, and conclude that thematic structure guides the initial interpretation of these sentences. We conclude with a discussion about how thematic information might enable the processing system to make early semantic commitments that take into account relevant aspects of discourse context.

INTRODUCTION

Language comprehension is clearly an integrative process in which different types of linguistic and non-linguistic knowledge are rapidly combined to develop a mental representation of the input (Swinney, 1982). Many of the most basic questions about language processing focus on how different aspects of representation are co-ordinated during comprehension. In recent work that builds upon earlier proposals by Frazier and colleagues (e.g. Frazier, 1987; Rayner, Carlson, & Frazier, 1983), we have argued that, given certain assumptions, lexical representations can provide much

Requests for reprints should be addressed to Michael K. Tanenhaus, Department of Psychology, University of Rochester, Rochester, N.Y. 14627.
This research was partially supported by NSF Grant BNS-8617738 and NIH Grant HD-22271. We would like to thank Gerry Altmann, Chuck Clifton, and Don Mitchell for their helpful comments on an earlier draft of this paper.

of the machinery necessary to integrate rapidly different types of knowledge during comprehension (Carlson & Tanenhaus, 1988; Tanenhaus & Carlson, 1989; Tanenhaus, Garnsey, & Boland, in press). In particular, we have suggested that verb-based *thematic roles* help guide parsing decisions and mediate between discourse information, general knowledge, and parsing. In addition, we have suggested that the use of thematic structures allows the comprehension system to make early commitments in the face of indeterminate structure, yet recover rapidly from mistakes. This is particularly important given the persuasive evidence that listeners and readers make immediate commitments to a single interpretation of locally ambiguous segments, rather than maintaining parallel interpretations or delaying commitment until subsequent structural information disambiguates the input (Frazier, 1978; Marslen-Wilson & Tyler, 1987).

The general phenomenon of thematic roles goes under a number of different terms in the linguistics literature, including "case roles", "thematic relations", "semantic case", and others. Thematic roles are the possible semantic roles that may be played by the subcategorised complements (or arguments) of a verb.[1] So, for example, the verb "put" subcategorises for three syntactic complements, a subject nounphrase, an object nounphrase, and a locative prepositional phrase, e.g. *The man* (subject) put *the car* (object) *in the garage* (PP). In standard accounts of thematic roles, each of these complements is assigned a different thematic role by the verb, where the role characterises the semantic role or "mode of participation" for (the denotation of) that argument in the event denoted by the verb. In this case, the subject of "put" is an *agent*, the object is the *theme* (the thing in motion), and the prepositional phrase designates the *location* or *goal*. It is important to keep in mind that the theoretical status of thematic roles within the linguistics literature remains unresolved. Not only is there considerable question about whether thematic roles are syntactic, semantic, or conceptual in nature, but also whether they should be regarded as grammatically significant entities at all (see Dowty, 1988; Ladusaw & Dowty, 1988). In this paper, we assume that thematic roles are part of the semantic or conceptual phenomena that are closely associated with the syntactic/lexical structure of a sentence. We need not claim that these roles are primitives: All that is important for our claim, is that there are certain types of semantic/conceptual information that play a distinguished role in defining verb–argument relations implicit in the labels "agent", "instrument", "theme", etc. We are also assuming, for the sake of simplicity, that

[1]We will speak of a verb assigning a thematic role to an argument (or a complement), but we intend throughout that the thematic role actually constitutes a relation between denotations of the expressions and are only derivatively a syntactic relation holding between linguistic expressions themselves (see, e.g. Carlson, 1984; Parsons, 1980).

a verb has associated with it a set of thematic roles, or a thematic grid, with each argument of the verb being assigned a single thematic role that differs from the roles assigned to the other arguments of that verb.

Thematic roles are of particular interest in the study of sentence processing because they cut across aspects of representation that are typically considered distinct from one another. On the one hand, thematic roles are aspects of conceptual representation. Events and modes of participating in events are arguably conceptual notions. It is also commonplace to assume that events and their participants are elements of a discourse structure. More locally, thematic roles are closely tied to the syntactic structure of a sentence, as only those modes of participation that are realised as syntactic complements of a verb are associated with thematic roles. Thematic roles, then, provide a form of representation with access to concepts and meaning and elements of discourse structure that map directly on to syntactic form. This property of thematic roles suggests that they should be useful to the comprehension system in co-ordinating different types of information. In addition, the way that the comprehension system exploits the information supplied by thematic roles may provide interesting insights into its architecture.

In order for thematic information to be used in sentence processing, we assume that the recognition of a verb makes available the following information:

1. The semantic representation or "sense" of the verb.
2. The thematic roles associated with the verb.
3. The types of constituents that can serve as complements of the verb.
4. How roles and syntactic constituents are connected to one another.

Let us take the verb "donate" as an example. Its sense, we assume, is a certain type of event with typical causes, effects, time-courses, etc. It is also an event in which one finds an entity participating as an agent, another as a theme, and another as a recipient; thus, there are three roles associated with the event. The verb itself always requires a subject, as do all English verbs, and most typically takes an object NP and a dative PP afterwards (i.e. "John donated *fifty dollars to his favourite charity*"). The verb may also appear less often without an object NP ("John donated to few charities"), or without the PP ("John donated fifty dollars"). In each case, the subject NP plays the role of the agent, the object NP is the theme, and the PP is the recipient. Even in cases where one of these last two constituents is missing, the existence of an entity playing that role is implied by the lexical entry (e.g. "John donated \$50" still requires that the money be donated to *somebody* or *something* that remains unspecified).

Now, suppose that the comprehension system makes use of all this information whenever the verb "donate" is encountered in an ongoing discourse. Not only can it project an expectation about what kinds of linguistic elements occur after the verb, but it can also assign a provisional meaning for the whole sentence by leaving the particular identities of the elements playing the theme and recipient roles temporarily unspecified, awaiting the denotation of the post-verbal phrases. Or, as we will suggest later, if a likely entity has already been introduced in the discourse or even the same sentence, it may be provisionally assumed to be playing one of those roles until further evidence shows otherwise.

This paper will explore ways in which thematic roles contribute to language comprehension. Our focus will be on when thematic roles associated with verbs are accessed, when thematic assignments are made, and the role that thematic representations play as an interface between discourse-level and sentence-level processing. We will address these questions by examining the recent literature in two domains. The first domain is attachment ambiguity, where a number of recent studies have explored the question of whether or not thematic information can influence syntactic decisions. The second domain is long-distance dependencies. We have been using long-distance dependency constructions to explore both the use of lexical representations in language processing, and the hypothesis that the interpretation of certain empty categories makes direct use of thematic representations.

EXPERIMENTAL EVIDENCE

In this section we briefly review some recent studies examining the interaction between thematic assignment and syntactic ambiguity resolution. A central assumption that is common to all recent proposals about how thematic information is used in sentence processing (with the possible exception of Pritchett, 1988), is that the process of thematic role assignment provides information that is used in resolving syntactic ambiguity. It seems likely that thematic assignments in processing are made on the basis of the meaning of an argument, the core meaning of the verb, and also general world knowledge. Therefore, "pack the suitcases" prefers "suitcases" as the location, whereas "pack the clothes" prefers "clothes" as the theme, because of the nature of suitcases and clothes but not because of the grammatical properties of words used to refer to them. It also seems likely that thematic assignments can be guided by discourse context, as suggested by Frazier (1987). Therefore, "his sister" would be assigned the theme role in the context "John didn't know who he could trust with the errand. He finally decided to send *his sister* . . .", whereas it would be assigned the recipient or goal role in the context, "John didn't know which present to mail to his sister for her birthday. He finally decided to send *his sister* . . .". Two questions then arise about thematic assignments and how they influence parsing. First, when are thematic assignments made and, secondly, what is the timing of thematic assignments *vis-à-vis* parsing decisions? To the extent that thematic assignments can mediate initial parsing decisions, they provide a mechanism whereby grammatically relevant world knowledge and discourse context enter into one of the most basic parsing processes the determination of grammatical relations.

There is now a small but rapidly growing experimental literature on the interaction of thematic and syntactic processing. Recent studies have focused on three locally ambiguous syntactic structures where thematic information can provide disambiguating information: (1) prepositional phrase attachment ambiguity; (2) clause boundary ambiguity with optionally transitive verbs; (3) past-tense–past-participle ambiguity with reduced relative clauses.

Prepositional Phrase Attachment Ambiguity

The ambiguity in sentences containing prepositional phrase attachments lies in the attachment of the prepositional phrase to either the verb or the object nounphrase (as in sentences 1a and 1b). According to Frazier and colleagues, attachment to the object NP requires the building of a more complex syntactic structure than the attachment to the verb, and therefore would be the unpreferred structure.

In one study, Rayner et al. (1983) monitored eye movements while subjects read sentences containing prepositional phrase attachment ambiguities like the ones in (1):

1a. The spy saw the cop with the binoculars, but the cop didn't see him.
b. The spy saw the cop with the revolver, but the cop didn't see him.

Sentence (1a) contains a prepositional phrase that is semantically biased towards verb attachment, because the noun "binoculars" contains semantic information supporting its use as an instrument of the verb "see". Sentence (1b) is semantically biased towards object attachment because the noun "revolver" is a poor instrument for the verb "see". Rayner et al. (1983) found that people frequently re-read the prepositional phrase in (1b) but not in (1a), suggesting that the prepositional phrase was initially attached to the verb and then the anomaly was detected afterwards. Rayner et al. (1983) proposed the existence of two separate processors in the sentence comprehension system: the syntactic processor and the thematic processor. The thematic processor receives and analyses the output of the syntactic processor through the use of semantic and pragmatic knowledge concerning the constituents. If the output of the syntactic processor does not match the output of the thematic processor, then the conflict is resolved in favour of the thematic processor.

Taraban and McClelland (1988) argued against Rayner et al.'s (1983) interpretation on the grounds that Rayner et al.'s results were due to the semantic content biasing the verbphrase attachment in their materials. They developed a set of sentences that have a semantic bias towards the nounphrase attachment. Using these materials and Rayner et al.'s materials, Taraban and McClelland demonstrated in a self-paced reading study that reading times were equally fast for both semantically biased attachments. They further suggested that the attachment preferences were due to an expectation about the thematic role of the phrase following the verb that was based upon the preceding semantic context.

Clause Boundary Ambiguity

Stowe (1988) used causative/ergative verbs such as "stopped". When used transitively (e.g. "The police stopped the car"), the subject is the agent and the object is the theme; when used intransitively (e.g. "The car stopped"), the subject is the theme. These verbs were placed in sentences where a subordinate clause preceded the main clause, as in "Even before the police stopped the driver was getting nervous." Frazier (1978) and Frazier and Rayner (1982) have shown that in the absence of punctuation, readers have difficulty beginning at "was", indicating that the NP following the verb "stopped" is taken to be its object, rather than the subject of the next clause.

Stowe (1988) manipulated the animacy of the first noun in the subordinate clause, and whether there was a prepositional phrase following the verb, comparing sentences like those in (2):

2a. Even before the police stopped the driver was getting nervous.
 b. Even before the truck stopped the driver was getting nervous.
 c. Even before the police stopped at the light the driver was getting nervous.
 d. Even before the truck stopped at the light the driver was getting nervous.

In general, animate nouns will be readily interpreted as likely agents, whereas inanimate nouns will not be. (However, as Taraban and McClelland (1988) point out, one can create contexts in which an inanimate noun has agent-like properties.) Stowe hypothesised that if thematic assignment takes place at the verb and provides immediate feedback to the parser, then readers should not experience a garden path at the verb in sentences like (2b). The reason is that an inanimate subject will force the intransitive "ergative" analysis in which there is no argument position for an NP following the verb. As a result, processing the NP ("the driver") should signal the beginning of a new clause.

Subjects read sentences one word at a time, pressing a button if and when the sentence became ungrammatical. Reading times and judgements of ungrammaticality were recorded. As expected, reading times were longer at the verbphrase in the main clause for the sentences with animate subjects (2a) than in the control condition (2c), where the NP ("the driver") unambiguously signals the beginning of the main clause, indicating that subjects had initially pursued the transitive analysis of the verb "stopped". However, there was no evidence of a reading time difference between the two inanimate conditions (2b and 2d).

These results would seem to show that the thematic assignment of the subject NP in the subordinate clause (e.g. "police" or "truck") determined the structural analysis pursued by the parser for the subsequent verb. When the NP was animate and thus a good agent, the verb was processed as a causative, whereas when the NP was inanimate and thus a poor agent but a good theme, then the verb was processed as an ergative.

Stowe's (1988) study suggests that thematic assignments are made rapidly and that they have immediate parsing consequences. The study, though, is far from definitive. For one thing, it does not show that only a restricted range of semantic dimensions come into play, as predicted by the thematic analysis. Also, the reading times are quite long—more than 700 msec per word. A likely explanation for the long reading times has to do with the task. Stowe provided subjects with feedback following the grammaticality judgements. A subject who judged a sentence to be ungrammatical when garden-pathed (e.g. at "was" in the sentence, "Even before the police stopped the driver was getting nervous"), would be told that he or she had made a mistake. This kind of feedback may well have made subjects think carefully before responding. More recently, however, Stowe has replicated her results using a self-paced, word-by-word reading task without requiring subjects to make grammaticality judgements (Stowe & Cupples, 1989). Stowe's results, then, provide at least preliminary evidence that thematic assignment can influence syntactic closure.

Reduced Relative Clauses

The ambiguity associated with reduced relative clauses such as sentence (3), a variation on Bever's (1970) famous "The horse raced past the barn fell" example, provides another testing ground for thematic feedback:

3. The lawyer sent the memo arrived late.

The ambiguity arises because the past-tense and the past-participle *forms* of the verb "sent" are identical. If "sent" is taken to be a past tense, it is the matrix verb of a main clause with the preceding nounphrase as its subject. If it is taken to be a past-participle, then "sent" is part of a reduced relative clause which itself is part of a nounphrase that is the subject of a later verb. In the main clause analysis, the nounphrase preceding the verb plays the role of agent, whereas in a relative clause analysis the nounphrase plays the role of theme. There is, of course, a strong main clause bias when the subject is animate, accounting for the typical garden path associated with the reduced relative form.

Ferreira and Clifton (1986, experiment 1) manipulated the animacy of the first nounphrase within the relative clause in order to determine whether thematic information could be used by the processing system to eliminate the usual garden path for reduced relative clauses, compared to controls with unreduced relatives. Their reasoning was that inanimate nounphrases cannot be plausible agents (or are unlikely to be agents) and thus could, in principle, provide thematic feedback to the parser that would block a past-tense/main clause analysis. Sample materials from their study are presented in (4):

4a. The defendant examined by the lawyer turned out to be unreliable.
b. The defendant that was examined by the lawyer turned out to be unreliable.
c. The evidence examined by the lawyer turned out to be unreliable.
d. The evidence that was examined by the lawyer turned out to be unreliable.

Using an eye-tracker to monitor fixation durations, Ferreira and Clifton (1986) found striking evidence against the immediate use of thematic information. In the animate conditions, the usual garden-path effects for reduced relatives obtained—namely, longer fixation durations at the disambiguating prepositional phrase for the reduced relative clauses compared to the unreduced controls, and also more regressive ("second-pass") eye movements. In the inanimate conditions, reading times were still longer at the prepositional phrase ("by the lawyer") in the reduced condition compared to the unreduced condition. However, fixation durations at the ambiguous verb ("examined") were also longer in the reduced condition, indicating that readers had found the inanimate nounphrase to be implausible as the agent of the verb. Thus Ferreira and Clifton (1986) concluded that readers pursued the main clause analysis despite the availability of biasing thematic information.

However, there are two problems with Ferreira and Clifton's materials that weaken their conclusions. First, and most seriously, at least half of the materials used by Ferreira and Clifton used inanimate nounphrases that could be completed sensibly using the past-tense form of the verb, e.g. "The car towed . . ." could be plausibly continued as "The car towed the trailer." The problem arises because inanimate nounphrases can occur in the subject position as instruments of many verbs. Thus Ferreira and Clifton did not provide the most stringent test of the thematic feedback hypothesis. Secondly, unreduced relative clauses may not provide the most appropriate baseline control for reduced relatives. Crain and Steedman (1985) have argued that relative clauses require special discourse conditions to be felicitous. Basically, relative clauses are used to pick out a unique antecedent; therefore, one would not say "The car towed yesterday was badly damaged" unless there was at least one other car and the reduced relative allowed the listener to identify which car was being referred to (see also Altmann & Steedman, 1988). If Crain and Steedman (1985) are correct, then more processing would be required for readers to construct an appropriate discourse representation for a relative clause in isolation than for a main clause. For reduced relatives, this processing would be distributed over fewer words than for unreduced relatives. Fortunately, the discourse effects can be controlled for by using reduced relatives with morphologically unambiguous verbs (e.g. "The evidence *stolen*").

Trueswell, Tanenhaus, and Garnsey (submitted) conducted an eye-tracking experiment using the same methodology as Ferreira and Clifton (1986), but with slightly different materials. First, care was taken to make sure that the inanimate nounphrases did not allow plausible past-tense completions. Secondly, reduced and unreduced relative clauses with inanimate nounphrases were included for a set of morphologically unambiguous verbs. A sample of the materials is presented in (5):

Ambiguous verb

5a. The man recognized by the spy took off down the street.
  b. The man that was recognized by the spy took off down the street.
  c. The van recognized by the spy took off down the street.
  d. The van that was recognized by the spy took off down the street.

Unambiguous verb

5e. The money taken by the student was finally returned.
  f. The money that was taken by the student was finally returned.

The results for first- and second-pass fixation durations are presented in Table 1.

For reduced relative clauses with animate nounphrases, the usual garden-path effects occurred, similar to those obtained by Ferreira and Clifton (1986). Reading times were significantly longer at the "by-phrase" for the reduced relatives compared to the unreduced relatives in the first-pass reading times (i.e. 5a was more difficult to read than 5b). In addition, the

TABLE 1
Mean First-pass and Second-pass Reading Times (msec per character)

	First Pass (sentence region)			*Second Pass (sentence region)*		
Condition[a]	*V1*	*by-phrase*	*V2*	*V1*	*by-phrase*	*V2*
	recognised	*by the spy*	*took off*	*recognised*	*by the spy*	*took off*
AR: *The man . . .*	37.1	39.4	43.9	29.2	14.9	15.5
AU: *The man that was . . .*	36.8	34.6	39.6	12.1	9.6	15.1
IR: *The van . . .*	37.7	36.8	41.5	19.9	5.8	9.0
IU: *The van that was . . .*	38.1	36.9	43.6	10.9	8.0	12.8
	taken	*by the student*	*was finally*	*taken*	*by the student*	*was finally*
UR: *The money . . .*	52.8	33.1	46.4	13.2	4.9	10.3
UU: *The money that was . . .*	49.7	33.3	46.9	7.3	6.1	6.6

[a]AR, animate reduced; AU, animate unreduced; IR, inanimate reduced; IU, inanimate unreduced; UR, unambiguous reduced; UU, unambiguous unreduced.

second-pass reading times showed longer fixation durations at the by-phrase and at the ambiguous verb.

The results were markedly different for the sentences with inanimate nounphrases. Neither the first-pass reading times nor the second-pass reading times showed any reliable differences between the reduced and the unreduced relatives at the by-phrase (the by-phrase of 5c was as easy as the by-phrase in 5d; the crucial interactions between reduction and animacy were significant in both the first- and second-pass reading times). Second-pass reading times at the ambiguous verb were longer for the reduced relatives; however, a similar effect obtained for the reduced relatives with *unambiguous* verbs (5e and 5f), suggesting that the effect is not due to garden-pathing, but is likely to be an inferencing effect. The pattern of results obtained in the experiment, then, provide strong support for the hypothesis that thematic information can determine parsing decisions.

Note that this does not mean that thematic information actually supersedes syntactic analysis. In fact, the model argued for in Trueswell et al. (submitted) is one in which thematic information selects among two competing analyses. The basic idea is that ambiguous morphological forms are accessed in the same manner as other lexical ambiguities with parallel access of competing morphological forms (Seidenberg, Tanenhaus, Leiman, & Bienkowski, 1982; Swinney, 1979; Tanenhaus, Leiman, & Seidenberg, 1979). In addition, each verb-form makes available its associated thematic structures (Cottrell, 1988; McClelland & Kawamoto, 1986), as well as information about how the thematic roles are to be assigned to syntactic complements. Thematic role assignment then can provide disambiguating information. Thus the thematic information helps to select from among potential morphological possibilities.[2] Note that a similar model will account for Stowe's ergative–causative results. However, it is debatable whether one should treat the causative–ergative ambiguity as a lexical ambiguity or as a case of the same core meaning of a verb having associated with it two incompatible thematic grids (see Carlson & Tanenhaus, 1988 and Tanenhaus & Carlson, 1989, for a discussion). The parallelism in a model like this comes not from pursuing several complete parses in parallel, but rather from the parallel access of morpho-

[2]It is important to note, though, that thematic role assignment is not the only factor relevant to selecting between the past-tense and past-participle forms of a verb. The relative frequency of the past-tense and past-participle forms is likely to be important (Burgess & Hollbach, 1988). Clearly, there is also a strong general bias in favour of the past-tense form when the subject nounphrase could be either an agent or theme. Described by Bever (1970) as the NVN strategy, this bias is likely to be determined by a range of factors (see Trueswell et al., submitted). It seems unlikely, though, that a syntactically based simplicity metric such as Minimal Attachment underlies the past-tense/main clause bias.

logical forms and more generally from the immediate access and use of lexical information.

The studies cited above lead to the conclusion that thematic roles provide a mechanism for general knowledge and context to interact with syntactic processing in syntactic ambiguity resolution. In the final section of this article, we will briefly review some of our recent work on verb argument structure, which suggests that thematic structure provides a mechanism for early semantic interpretation and interaction with discourse. The evidence comes from studies investigating sentences with filler–gap dependencies. We will be suggesting that at least the initial association of fillers with empty category or gap positions takes place using thematic rather than syntactic categories, a hypothesis first explored—and rejected—by Fodor (1979).

Long-distance Dependencies

In a recent series of studies, we have been developing the hypothesis that thematic representations are used in interpreting sentences with long-distance dependencies (Boland, Tanenhaus, Carlson, & Garnsey, in press; Carlson & Tanenhaus, 1988; Tanenhaus & Carlson, 1989; Tanenhaus et al., in press). In a sentence with a long-distance dependency, a questioned or relativised phrase (or "filler") must be associated with an empty category (or "gap") that occurs later in the sentence. For example, in the sentence illustrated in (6) (a wh-question), the questioned phrase "which customer" must be semantically interpreted as the direct object of "call":

6. *Which customer*$_i$ did the secretary call $\_\__i$ about the article?

In the Government and Binding grammatical framework (Chomsky, 1981), an empty category or trace follows the verb "call". The trace is assigned the thematic role normally associated with the object of "call". "Which customer" then inherits the thematic role from the trace through the process of co-indexing.

We have been studying the processing of wh-questions in order to explore the time-course with which information about verb–argument structure is accessed and used in sentence processing. Wh-questions provide a useful domain for exploring these questions because the wh-phrase (e.g. "which customer") is a nounphrase filler that needs to be assigned a role, and the argument positions associated with verbs define possible roles for the filler. The paradigm that we have been using is a variant of an oddity detection task that we have referred to as the *embedded anomaly* approach. We contrast fillers that are either semantically plausible or implausible with respect to a particular gap position using an on-line judgement task combined with self-paced, word-by-word (or, in some cases, phrase-by-phrase) presentation. The place in the sentence where plausibility effects are "noticed" by the subject, reflected in overt "does not make sense" judgements or in slowed reading times, indicates when the filler has been associated with the gap. Contrast the sentences in (7):

7a. *Which book*$_i$ did the boy read $\_\__i$ in class?
b. *Which food*$_i$ did the boy read $\_\__i$ in class?

Which book is a plausible direct object of *read*, because one typically reads books, whereas *which food* is not, because one cannot plausibly read food (setting aside metaphoric interpretations). Thus sentence (7b) becomes implausible when the reader or listener interprets *which food* as the direct object of *read*.

The position of the gap in a filler–gap construction is often locally ambiguous. To see this, consider the sentences in (8) in which the filler phrase is now the object of a preposition that comes after the verb. Sentence (8b) is now plausible:

8a. *Which book*$_i$ did the boy read about $\_\__i$?
b. *Which food*$_i$ did the boy read about $\_\__i$?

On a syntactic account of gap filling, a thematic role is assigned to a filler once it has been indexed with an empty category that has been identified by the parser (see Clifton & Frazier, 1989, Frazier & Clifton, 1989, and Fodor, this volume, for a discussion of the distinction between gap-driven and filler-driven syntactic accounts of gap-filling). In contrast, a thematically based account assumes that a filler can be associated directly with a thematic role that is made available when a verb is recognised, which can be before an empty category has been encountered.

In studies in collaboration with Susan Garnsey and Julie Boland using the embedded anomaly logic, we have obtained a constellation of results that, taken together, make what we feel is a persuasive case that fillers are initially associated with thematic rather than syntactic representations (see Boland et al., in press; Garnsey, Tanenhaus, & Chapman, 1989; Tanenhaus et al., in press; Tanenhaus, Boland, Garnsey, & Carlson, forthcoming). We will discuss a few of these results here.

For verbs that are typically used transitively, such as *read*, we find an anomaly effect at the verb (and before the empty category has been encountered) for fillers that would be implausible as the object of the verb, using both behavioural response measures and event-related brain potentials (ERPs). In the studies using ERPs, an implausibility effect is indexed by an N400—a brain potential sensitive to the plausibility of a word in context (Garnsey, Tanenhaus, & Chapman, 1989). In the behavioural studies, subjects read sentences one word at a time and respond "no" if the sentence stops making sense. "No" responses to sentences with implausible fillers begin at the verb (Tanenhaus, Boland, Garnsey, & Carlson, 1989).

In subsequent research, we have shown that the place in the sentence where anomaly effects occur depends upon the argument structure of the verb. In particular, we do not find anomaly effects at the verb when the filler would be implausible as the object of the verb, but the argument structure of the verb makes available another argument position in which the filler could be plausible. Thus far, we have looked at two types of verbs in addition to simple transitive verbs. The first type is dative verbs like "grant". We have examined these verbs in sentences in which the filler would be implausible as the direct object, but plausible as the indirect object, such as (9):

9. *Which secretary*$_i$ did the boss grant the maternity leave to $\_\__i$?

The second type is verbs like "remind", verbs that are typically used transitively and with an infinitive complement, such as (10):

10. The man reminded *the woman to call home*.

We have examined these verbs in sentences in which the filler would be implausible as the direct object of the verb but plausible somewhere within the infinitive complement, such as (11):

11. *Which movie*$_i$ did your brother remind us to watch $\_\__i$?

In order to illustrate the differences that we observe among verb types, we will briefly present the results from a recent study conducted in collaboration with Julie Boland and Susan Garnsey (Boland et al., in press; Tanenhaus et al., forthcoming). This experiment used three types of verbs, all of which are typically used transitively: simple transitive verbs such as "watch", transitive verbs that frequently occur with infinitive complements, such as "remind", and "dative" verbs that can be used with a direct and an indirect object, such as "read". Note that we included some dative verbs like "read" in earlier studies, but always with fillers that would have been implausible as either the direct or indirect object. In this experiment, the plausible fillers were plausible direct objects of the verb and the implausible fillers were implausible direct objects. Sample materials are presented in (12) and in Table 2:

12a. Which star / stone did the assistant watch all through the night.
  b. Which poem / baby did the babysitter read in a funny voice.
  c. Which girl / movie did the woman remind to watch the show.

For all three verb types, the word immediately after the matrix verb provides unambiguous syntactic evidence that the filler was in fact the direct object of the verb, therefore making the sentence implausible when

TABLE 2

Condition[b]		Critical Word Positions[a]					
		N	*V*	*V + 1*	*V + 2*	*V + 3*	*V + 4*
Tran-plaus Tran-implaus	*Which star did the* *Which stone did the*	assistant	watch	all	through	the	night
Dat-plaus Dat-implaus	*Which poem did the* *Which baby did the*	babysitter	read	in	a	funny	voice
Icomp-plaus Icomp-implaus	*Which girl did the* *Which movie did the*	woman	remind	to	watch	the	show

[a]The final four words in a sentence formed either an adverbial phrase (for the first two verb types) or an infinitive complement (for the Icomp verb type).

[b]Tran, transitive; Dat, dative; Icomp, infinitive complement; plaus, plausible; implaus, implausible.

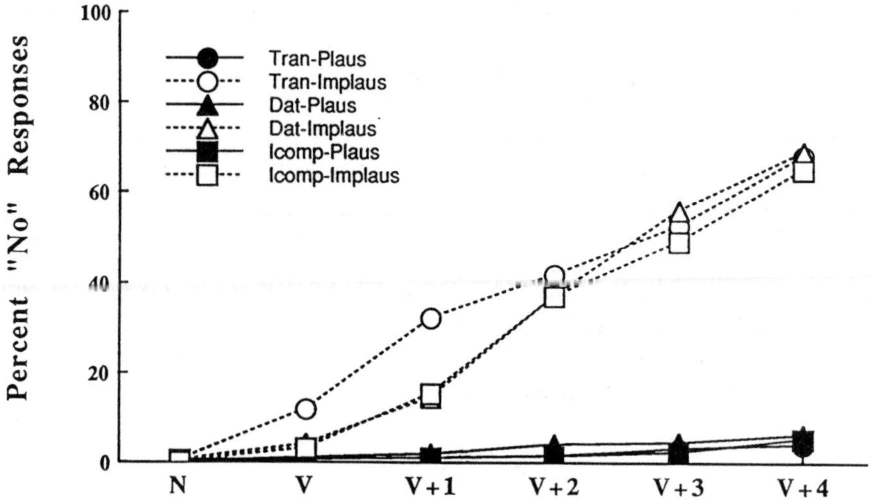

FIG. 1 Cumulative percentages of sentences judged to make sense up through each word for wh-sentences with plausible and implausible fillers. Data for three verb types are shown: transitive, dative, and infinitive complement verbs.

the filler is an implausible direct object. The results that we typically obtain are illustrated in Fig. 1 (from Boland et al., in press).

The cumulative percentage of trials on which subjects judged sentences to stop making sense at the word positions indicated on the graph, are plotted for the simple transitive, dative, and infinitive complement-taking verbs. Note that the implausibility is first detected at the verb itself for the simple transitive verbs, but not until the next word for the dative and infinitive complement verbs. Note also that at the end of the sentence, the cumulative percentage of sentences judged to make sense are nearly identical for the plausible and implausible conditions across verb types. This is important given Mitchell's suggestion (this volume) that verb differences might be due to baseline plausibility differences.[3]

The interpretation that we have offered for these results is that recognition of the verb makes available the set of thematic roles associated with the verb, which define the possible gap sites. Thus for a dative verb, both

[3]Mitchell has also suggested that plausibility detection is a weak response measure because many implausible sentences are judged to be plausible. Subjects are instructed that most of the sentences in the experiment will be plausible; therefore, subjects have a relatively high threshold for making a "no" judgement. This also accounts for the relatively low "false alarm" rate to plausible sentences. More importantly for Mitchell's argument, we find plausibility effects when we analyse reading times for only those trials on which subjects respond that the sentence made sense.

the direct object and indirect object roles are available immediately at the verb. A filler which is an implausible direct object, but plausible indirect object, is immediately assigned the indirect object role. For an infinitive complement verb, the direct object role and the role associated with the infinitive complement would be available immediately. A filler that is implausible in the direct object role is assigned to the role associated with the infinitive complement.

Several additional studies provide results that support the hypothesis that the thematic structure of the verb is being used to associate fillers with roles (see Boland et al., in press; Tanenhaus et al., forthcoming). In a recent study we examined "dative-like" verbs such as "donate" that take a direct and an indirect object and in addition allow only the direct object to follow the verb. Thus sentence (13a) is acceptable, but (13b) is not:

13a. John donated some cheap liquor to the campus party.
b. *John donated the campus party some cheap liquor.

We used two types of fillers that were plausible indirect objects of the verb, such as "public library" and "campus party", with a direct object that was only plausible with one of the fillers, as in (14):

14. Which campus party / public library did John donate some cheap liquor to?

Thus an implausibility effect at "liquor" when "which public library" was the filler, would indicate that the filler had been interpreted as the indirect object. Plausibility effects obtained at the direct object. This result clearly demonstrates that the filler is being interpreted as the indirect object prior to the syntactic location of the gap.

We have also ruled out the possibility that readers are simply delaying filler–gap assignment for infinitive complement verbs. Tanenhaus et al. (forthcoming) found that readers do interpret a filler as belonging to a direct object gap at the verb, when it would be a plausible direct object, as in (15):

15. *Which friend*$_i$ did your brother remind us to visit $\__i$?

The result supporting this interpretation is that reading times at "us" are longer in wh-questions like (15) than in control sentences where there is no possible gap following the verb (e.g. "Your brother reminded us to visit his friend"). This "filled gap effect", first observed by Crain and Fodor (1985) and Stowe (1986), indicates that the filler has been incorrectly assigned to the direct object role, so that when the true direct object "us" is encountered, readers are confused. Crucially, no filled gap effect occurs when the filler would be implausible as the direct object of the verb. Recall that the results with the simple transitive verbs suggested that the absence of a gap position associated with the verb *where the filler could be plausible* results in an implausibility effect. That result in combination with the result that there is no implausibility effect at the verb for infinitive complement-taking verbs, converge on the interpretation that subjects "know" that there will be an infinitive complement which could contain the real gap. Clearly, one cannot know that an optional complement will be there in the linguistic input before it is actually encountered. But the thematic structure of the verb, coupled with the meaning of the verb, does provide the processing system with sufficient information to construct a semantic representation that would allow the filler to be interpreted. To see this, consider the verb "invite", which typically is used transitively and with an infinitive complement (e.g. Mary invited *Bill to go along to the party*). In an "invite" event, somebody is inviting someone to do something. Thus at the verb in a sentence beginning "Which movie did Bill invite . . .", the listener or reader could interpret "movie" as a constituent of the embedded event. Note that even when a verb like "invite" is used without an infinitive complement, then the embedded event is strongly implied, as is illustrated by the sentence "Bill invited Tom." In the example, Tom is clearly being invited to go or come somewhere.

The claim advanced by Frazier, Clifton, and Randall (1983), that access to verb-based "control" information is delayed, would seem to argue against the hypothesis that this type of event structure information can be used rapidly in sentence processing. However, we have recently demonstrated that people can, in fact, use control information rapidly. Boland, Tanenhaus, and Garnsey (1989) examined sentences like those in (16) in an anomaly detection task:

16a. Which horse/outlaw did the cowboy refuse to surrender to the sheriff?
b. Which horse/outlaw did the cowboy force to surrender to the sheriff?

"Refuse" is a "subject" control verb, meaning that the subject of the verb "the cowboy" is understood as, or controls, the subject of the following infinitive complement. In contrast, "force" is an object control verb. In sentence (16b), the wh-phrase is the object of force and this phrase is the understood subject of the infinitive. Implausibility effects obtained at "surrender", when the filler was "which horse" (horses cannot surrender) for the object control verbs but not for the subject control verbs, indicating that readers used the control information correctly.

What our filler–gap studies demonstrate, then, is that the meaning and thematic structure of the verb allow the reader or listener to construct rapidly a schematic representation that includes the central components of the "situation" described by the verb. Thus this type of representation may well play an important role in allowing the comprehension system to develop interpretations as rapidly as it does.

DISCOURSE, SYNTAX, AND THEMATIC ROLES

One interesting observation that supports our conjectures about the use of thematic structure in parsing and that complements our results with dative verbs and infinitive complement verbs, is that argument roles made available at the verb seem to function as anaphors when not associated with an actual constituent in the sentence. Consider the short discourses in (17):

17a. Bill almost forgot to go to the bank.
Fortunately, Tom reminded him.

b. The library had its budget slashed.
So, Bill donated some books.

Note that "remind" in (17a) has an infinitive phrase following it, and that "donate" has no "to"-phrase designating a recipient. Still, each is somehow implied in the sentences. The example in (17a) illustrates null complement anaphora (Hankamer & Sag, 1976). In (17a), the empty infinitive complement, or alternatively its thematic representation, functions as an anaphor, taking as its antecedent "to go to the bank" from the context sentence before it. Likewise, in (17b), the otherwise unspecified recipient role seems to function as an anaphor leading to the inference that it was the library that Bill donated books to. Note that in isolation the sentences with the missing complements seem less complete than versions that include the complements, whereas in a context that supplies an antecedent for the complement, the truncated versions are more natural and the "full" versions (18a and 18b) seem somewhat awkward because they feel redundant:

18.a. Bill almost forgot to go to the bank.
Fortunately, Tom reminded him to go to the bank.

b. The library had its budget slashed.
So, Bill donated some books to the library.

We should note that our claims that thematic structures allow early interpretation do not in any way mean that syntactic analysis is bypassed. On the contrary, the success of early interpretation requires the successful linkage of thematic structures and syntactic forms. If a thematically based interpretation is incorrect, then the syntactic analysis will provide clear evidence to that effect, as well as clear information about how it is to be revised.

Of course, early interpretation will sometimes be incorrect. However, in many cases, mistaken interpretations preserve the basic thematic or situational structure of the correct analysis. For example, listeners will initially assume that John is reading the book in "Which book did John read about?" However, when it turns out that he is reading *about* the book, the situation remains basically the same. He is still reading something. But an early interpretation presents problems when the thematic structure assumed by the comprehender is incompatible with the actual input. This presents an alternative interpretation for Pritchett's (1988) interesting claim that garden paths can be defined thematically.

Pritchett (1988) proposes that the difficulties associated with various garden-path sentences can be accounted for with a sentence processing system that makes immediate thematic assignments. Pritchett assumes that upon encountering a verb, the maximal thematic grid for that verb, which is the grid containing the largest number of thematic roles, is initially accessed. For example, for the verb "warned", a maximal grid of (agent, goal, proposition) is first accessed. Pritchett proposes two principles that describe the comprehension process:

1. *Theta-attachment*: The parser attempts to assign a theta role to a potential argument at every point in processing.
2. The *theta-reanalysis constraint*: if a syntactic reanalysis involves a syntactic constituent that has already been assigned a thematic role, then the new syntactic constituent (which syntactically dominates the structure of the old constituent) should be assigned the same thematic role that was assigned the constituent it now dominates, or else the reanalysis will be "costly".

Pritchett's second principle, theta-reanalysis, makes the prediction that once a structure has been assigned a thematic role, any reanalysis that results in a change in thematic assignment to that structure or any structure that syntactically dominates it, will result in a garden path. Pritchett's lead example is the garden-path sentence "Mary warned her mother hated her." On his account, "her" is initially assigned the goal role. Then, when "mother" is encountered, a reanalysis must be done, in which "her mother" is assigned the goal role. This does not violate the theta-reanalysis principle because "her" is still part of the goal, and thus the reanalysis is not costly. However, when the verb "hated" is encountered, "her" becomes the goal again, and "mother hated . . ." becomes an incomplete proposition. This reanalysis violates the theta-reanalysis constraint because the noun "mother", which was previously in a structure assigned the goal role, is now in a structure assigned the proposition role, and thus processing becomes difficult.

However, difficulties arise with Pritchett's thematic account of garden-path sentences. Pritchett's proposal cannot account for the results found in

Taraban and McClelland (1988) and Trueswell et al. (submitted), because he requires that only one grid—"the maximal grid"—is initially accessed, and, more crucially, because his thematic assignments are based only on *syntactic* information associated with the grid. In other words, Pritchett proposes early assignment of thematic roles, but not early semantic interpretation. Semantically inappropriate thematic assignments can thus be made without the immediate detection of an anomaly. As a result, Pritchett's proposal predicts that both sentences (19a) and (19b) would be equally difficult to process:

19a. The doctor warned the patient would be contagious.
b. The doctor warned the virus would be contagious.

In both sentences, "the patient" and "the virus" would initially be assigned a goal role. The verb "would" causes a reanalysis that violates the theta-reanalysis principle, because the new role of proposition dominates a noun that was initially assigned the goal. However, intuition suggests that the garden path associated with (19a) is substantially reduced or perhaps even avoided in (19b), where semantic information indicates that "virus" is an unlikely goal for "warned". Intuition also suggests that the garden path associated with (19a) can be avoided in a context that supplies a likely *goal*, as is illustrated in (20):

20. The nurses started to come into the room but they stopped when the doctor warned the patient was contagious.

Clearly, experimental data investigating these issues is required. However, the data based on intuitions that we have presented suggests that thematic assignment makes use of both semantic and discourse-model information.

CONCLUSION

The evidence that we have reviewed, especially the studies of sentences with long-distance dependencies, provide clear evidence that thematic information is rapidly accessed once a verb is recognised, and that it is used to structure the interpretation of a sentence. In addition, we have reviewed evidence which indicates that thematic information can eliminate garden paths that are frequently attributed to syntactic attachment strategies. This evidence demonstrates that thematic information is rapidly accessed and used in parsing. On the assumption that thematic and syntactic information are distinct types of information, it is natural to ask how they are coordinated. Clearly, thematic processing depends at least partially on the output of syntactic processing, in so far as evaluating the fit of a constituent to a particular role depends upon having correctly parsed the constituent.

Also, thematic processing and syntactic processing clearly interact, in that syntactic information can be used to revise an incorrect thematic assignment, and vice versa. Our reading of the current literature is that there is evidence that thematic information can be used to select among competing syntactic analyses, on the assumption that there is a certain degree of (perhaps lexically based) parallelism in the system. We find little or no evidence suggesting that thematic analysis allows the processing system to bypass syntactic analysis. Likewise, there is no conclusive evidence that syntactic structures are actually proposed on the basis of earlier thematic commitments, although we would not want to rule out this latter possibility.

REFERENCES

Altmann, G. & Steedman, M. (1988). Interaction with context during human sentence processing. *Cognition*, *30*, 191–238.

Bever, T. G. (1970). The cognitive basis for linguistic structures. In J. R. Hayes (Ed.), *Cognition and the development of language*. New York: John Wiley.

Boland, J., Tanenhaus, M. K., Carlson, G., & Garnsey, S. M. (in press). Lexical projection and the interaction of syntax and semantics in parsing. *Journal of Psycholinguistic Research*.

Boland, J., Tanenhaus, M. K., & Garnsey, S. M. (forthcoming). Evidence for the immediate use of verb control information in sentence processing.

Carlson, G. N. (1984). Thematic roles and their role in semantic interpretation. *Linguistics*, *22*, 259–279.

Carlson, G. N. & Tanenhaus, M. K. (1988). Thematic roles and language comprehension. In W. Wilkins (Ed.), *Syntax and semantics*, Vol. 21: *Thematic relations*. London: Academic Press.

Chomsky, N. (1981). *Lectures on Government and Binding*. Dordrecht: Foris.

Clifton, C. & Frazier, L. (1989). Comprehending sentences with long-distance dependencies. In G. Carlson & M. Tanenhaus (Eds), *Linguistic structure in language processing*. Dordrecht: Reidel.

Cottrell, G. (1988). A model of lexical access of ambiguous words. In S. Small, G. Cottrell, & M. Tanenhaus (Eds), *Lexical ambiguity resolution*, pp. 195–228. San Mateo, Calif.: Morgan Kaufmann.

Crain, S. & Fodor, J. A. (1985). How can grammars help parsers? In D. Dowty, L. Kartunnen, & A. Zwicky (Eds), *Natural language parsing: Psychological, computational and theoretical perspectives*. Cambridge: Cambridge University Press.

Crain, S. & Steedman, M. (1985). On not being led up the garden path: The use of context by the psychological parser. In D. Dowty, L. Kartunnen, & A. Zwicky (Eds), *Natural language parsing: Psychological, computational and theoretical perspectives*. Cambridge: Cambridge University Press.

Dowty, D. (1988). Thematic proto roles, subject selection and lexical defaults. Unpublished manuscript.

Ferreira, F. & Clifton, C. (1986). The independence of syntactic processing. *The Journal of Memory and Language*, *25*, 348–368.

Fodor, J. A. (1979). Superstrategy. In W. E. Cooper & E. C. T. Walker (Eds), *Studies in sentence processing: Papers presented to Merrill Garrett*. Hillsdale, N.J.: Lawrence Erlbaum Associates Inc.

Frazier, L. (1978). On comprehending sentences: Syntactic parsing strategies. Ph.D. Thesis, University of Connecticut. Indiana University Linguistics Club.

Frazier, L. (1987). Theories of sentence processing. In J. Garfield (Ed.), *Modularity in knowledge representation and natural language processing*. Cambridge, Mass.: MIT Press.

Frazier, L. (in press). Exploring the architecture of the language processing system. In G. Altmann (Ed.), *Cognitive models of speech processing: Psycholinguistic and computational perspectives*. Cambridge, Mass.: MIT Press.

Frazier, L. & Clifton, C. (1989). Successive cyclicity in the grammar and the parser. *Language and Cognitive Processes*, *4*, 93–126.

Frazier, L. & Rayner, K. (1982). Making and correcting errors during sentence comprehension: Eye movements in the analysis of structurally ambiguous sentences. *Cognitive Psychology*, *14*, 178–210.

Garnsey, S. M., Tanenhaus, M. K., & Chapman (1989). Evoked potentials and the study of sentence comprehension. *Journal of Psycholinguistic Research*, *18*, 51–60.

Hankamer, J. & Sag, I. A. (1976). Deep and surface anaphora. *Linguistic Inquiry*, *7*, 391–426.

Ladusaw, W. A. & Dowty, D. (1988). Toward a non-grammatical account of thematic roles. In W. Wilkins (Ed.), *Syntax and semantics*, Vol. 21: *Thematic relations*. London: Academic Press.

Marslen-Wilson, W. (1975). Sentence perception as an interactive parallel process. *Science*, *189*, 226–228.

Marslen-Wilson, W. & Tyler, L. (1987). Against modularity. In J. Garfield (Ed.), *Modularity in knowledge representation and natural language processing*. Cambridge, Mass.: MIT Press.

McClelland, J. L. & Kawamoto, A. (1986). Mechanisms of sentence processing: Assigning roles to constituents of sentences. In J. McClelland & D. Rumelhart (Eds), *Parallel distributed processing, Part 2: Psychological and biological models*. Cambridge, Mass.: MIT Press.

McElree, B. & Bever, T. G. (1989). The psychological reality of linguistically defined gaps. *Journal of Psycholinguistic Research*, *18*, 21–35.

Parsons, T. (1980). Modifiers and quantifiers in natural language. *Canadian Journal of Philosophy*, *VI* (Suppl.), 29–60.

Pritchett, B. L. (1988). Garden path phenomena and the grammatical basis of language processing. *Language*, *64*(3), 539–576.

Rayner, K., Carlson, M., & Frazier, L. (1983). The interaction of syntax and semantics during sentence processing. *Journal of Verbal Learning and Verbal Behavior*, *22*, 358–374.

Seidenberg, M. S., Tanenhaus, M. K., Leiman, J. M., & Bienkowski, M. (1982). Automatic access of the meanings of ambiguous words in context: Some limitations of knowledge-based processing. *Cognitive Psychology*, *14*, 489–537.

Stowe, L. A. (1986). Parsing wh-constructions: Evidence for on-line gap location. *Language and Cognitive Processes*, *2*, 227–246.

Stowe, L. A. (1988). Thematic structures and sentence comprehension. In G. Carlson & M. Tanenhaus (Eds), *Linguistic structure and language processing*, pp. 319–356. Dordrecht: Reidel.

Stowe, L. A. & Cupples, L. (1989). Animacy and reduced relative clauses. Poster at the Conference on Sentence Processing, City University of New York.

Swinney, D. A. (1979). Lexical access during sentence comprehension: (Re)consideration of context effects. *Journal of Verbal Learning and Verbal Behavior*, *18*, 645–659.

Swinney, D. A. (1982). The structure and time-course of information interaction during speech comprehension: Lexical, segmentation, access, and interpretation. In J. Mehler,

E. C. T. Walker, & M. Garrett (Eds). *Perspectives on mental representation*. Hillsdale, N.J.: Lawrence Erlbaum Associates Inc.

Tanenhaus, M. K. & Carlson, G. N. (1989). In W. D. Marslen-Wilson (Ed.), *Lexical representation and processing*. Cambridge, Mass.: MIT Press.

Tanenhaus, M. K., Leiman, J. M., & Seidenberg, M. S. (1979). Evidence for multiple stages in the processing of ambiguous words in syntactic contexts. *Journal of Verbal Learning and Verbal Behavior*, *18*, 645–659.

Tanenhaus, M. K., Garnsey, S. M., & Boland, J. (in press). Combinatory lexical information and language comprehension. In G. Altmann (Ed.), *Cognitive models of speech processing: Psycholinguistic and computational perspectives*. Cambridge, Mass.: MIT Press.

Tanenhaus, M. K., Boland, J., Garnsey, S. M., & Carlson, G. (forthcoming). Argument structure and the comprehension of long-distance dependencies.

Taraban, R. & McClelland, J. (1988). Constituent attachment and thematic role assignment in sentence processing: Influences of content-based expectations. *The Journal of Memory and Language*, *27*, 1–36.

Trueswell, J. C., Tanenhaus, M. K., & Garnsey, S. M. (submitted). Semantic influences on parsing: Use of thematic role information in syntactic disambiguation.

LANGUAGE AND COGNITIVE PROCESSES, 1989, *4*, (3/4) SI 235–262

What, When, and How?: Questions of Immediacy in Anaphoric Reference Resolution

A. J. Sanford and S. C. Garrod

Department of Psychology, University of Glasgow, and ESRC Interdisciplinary Research Centre in Human Communication, Universities of Edinburgh and Glasgow, U.K.

This paper considers the question of the immediacy of interpretation of anaphors. Two aspects of immediacy are considered: (1) immediacy in terms of the initiation of processes that might be considered as *supporting* resolution, and (2) immediacy in terms of achieving resolution as an *outcome*. The functional justification, and the logic of these aspects are considered. The bulk of the paper is a review of pertinent experimental evidence. On the basis of studies both on speech and reading comprehension, we argue that the evidence favours immediate initiation. However, it is argued that immediacy of outcome must take into account the variety of different forms of definite anaphora: proper names, full definite descriptions, and pronouns. Whereas there is good evidence for early resolution in the case of the first two, it does not hold for all cases of pronominal anaphora. Furthermore, evidence from a variety of stylistic phenomena indicate the need to disentangle carefully the semantic constraints introduced by all forms of description. We conclude that immediacy must be understood in the context of the component processes making up reference resolution in relation to interpreting the sentence as a whole.

INTRODUCTION

The purpose of this paper is to discuss the question of the immediacy of anaphor interpretation, and to evaluate some of the pertinent empirical evidence. This is part of the broader question of the extent to which processes of language understanding in general are immediate, and to what

---

Requests for reprints should be addressed to A. J. Sanford, Department of Psychology, University of Glasgow, Glasgow, U.K.

Preparation of this paper was supported by Grant R000231492 from the ESRC to A. J. Sanford.

extent some processes might be deferred. There is a view known as the immediacy hypothesis that amounts to the proposal that each word of a discourse is interpreted as deeply as possible and as quickly as possible, i.e. as soon as it is encountered (Just & Carpenter, 1980). We shall use this position as a baseline for discussion. Let us begin by setting out some of the reasons why the question of immediacy has arisen at all.

THE FUNCTIONAL JUSTIFICATION FOR IMMEDIACY

At its broadest, the immediacy hypothesis concerns the interpretation of more than just anaphors. Indeed, Just and Carpenter (1980) hypothesise that each and every content word is interpreted to the "deepest possible level" as soon as it is encountered, even at the expense of making guesses that sometimes turn out to be wrong. In a similar vein, Marslen-Wilson and Tyler (1981) argue that for speech the on-line goal of the processor is to achieve a message-level interpretation of the signal as rapidly and as early as possible. The general debate about immediacy, therefore, concerns two basic issues: (1) how soon any process is initiated and carried out, and (2) the extent to which immediacy applies at all levels of processing.

The functional argument for immediate initiation and rapid completion of any linguistic process is at least twofold. In the first place, holding off interpretation until more information has been sampled will impose a concurrent memory load on the system as the signal is held over for subsequent consideration, and this should be avoided. Secondly, it will mean that any contextual benefit that might accrue from interpreting the earlier expression will not be available to help in interpreting the subsequent expressions in the sentence. It should be noted, that for this to be a strong argument, it must be assumed that in general context constrains in a forward direction rather than backward. Other, more subtle, functional arguments can be made in favour of immediacy in speech comprehension. In speech, the signal itself is transient and not under the listener's control. Therefore, deferring a decision until more information has accrued imposes a processing debt to be redeemed at a later date when the signal may still be coming in and competing for attention. Ideally, the decision rate should be geared to that of the signal if the processor is to avoid the risk of falling behind the speaker, so to speak. In reading, this is not such a major consideration, as the reader can always choose to pause at any point. Thus, there would seem to be good *a priori* grounds for immediacy in language processing in general, which come from a requirement to synchronise the processing with the sampling.

The second part of the immediacy hypothesis concerns the question of doing the immediate processing as deeply as possible. The basic justification here is that the main goal of the processing system should be to determine the significance of what is being said or written, and it would seem efficient to do this at the earliest possible time. However, justifying immediacy at the message level is more controversial. It may be more efficient overall to pull in a lot of evidence before being committed, thus saving time-consuming and confusing backtracking. So the functional argument can go either way. It really hinges on the question of whether at any level of processing forward contextual constraints tend to outweigh backward constraints in securing a final interpretation. In fact, even in the case of lexical identification in continuous speech, there is some evidence for the operation of subsequent context in the process, leading to delayed decisions at this level (Bard, Shillcock, & Altmann, 1988). This would suggest that the immediacy question in relation to anaphors is very much an empirical one, even if one takes for granted the assumption that the processing system as a whole has evolved to operate with optimal real-time efficiency.

Important though these general arguments might be, it is therefore at a more detailed level that the discussion proliferates and the opportunities for experimental examination lie. The present paper is concerned rather more specifically with immediacy in the context of anaphoric reference resolution. Such resolution is arguably a necessary part of building up a coherent mental representation of a discourse. Until anaphoric relations are fixed, other aspects of coherence establishment may be delayed; at the very least, anaphora is a good *a priori* candidate for immediacy. Yet nowhere is it clearer that the plausibility of immediacy is a function of the linguistic input. In this paper we concentrate on personal pronoun anaphors (he, she), it, and fuller nounphrases. To illustrate some of the issues, let us first consider personal pronouns. In (1), it is clear that we cannot understand the sentence fully until we recognise that it is John who crossed the road, and such a resolution could take place as soon as the pronoun is encountered, at point a:

1. John saw Mary, and he_a crossed the $road_b$.

Of course, in many cases, anaphor resolution is apparently not possible until information after a pronoun has been utilised, as in (2):

2. Mary gave Sue some money because she_a was hard up_b.

In the first case, the fact that there is only one matching antecedent allows a decision to be made regarding the antecedent at point a in sentence (1), whereas in sentence (2), the decision has to be deferred to point b. The advantage of an early decision, triggered at point a in sentence (1), is that the information that follows could be related to the correct individual as soon as it is encountered, whereas the delay necessitated by the ambiguity of antecedent in (2) means that the information after a has to be used to determine the referent of *she*, and then related to that referent. If there are many more unambiguous cases than ambiguous ones in language use, then an early assignment (immediacy) processing configuration may be preferable over deferral. It is of course true that the referent at point a in example (2) cannot be logically determined, but certain default biases may be used to force a decision. For instance, there is evidence that in at least some situations, naturally occurring examples of ambiguity can be settled on the basis of such things as sentence topic. An example is the observation made by Broadbent (1973) with the following, taken from a manual:

3. The feedpipe lubricates the chain, and it should be adjusted to leave a gap half an inch between itself and the sprocket.

In this study, it was established that most people took the intended referent of *it* to be *the feedpipe*, and not *the chain*, although the subjects were quite ignorant of what any of these things were.

Immediacy is interesting because it is related to what the understander takes to be sufficient evidence to resolve anaphoric reference. The examples discussed above are just a few of many, but illustrate some of the boundaries of the problem. Even with logically ambiguous reference, heuristic principles may be used to produce an early interpretation, but there will always be a risk of error. The importance of the error in terms of the overall efficiency of the system will depend upon how often the heuristic principle runs foul of a real example. If producers on the whole do not produce utterances that require delay, then the system does not need to delay. Of course, our example concerns the personal pronouns *he* and *she*. With the pronoun "it", the opportunities for multiple interpretations are even greater, as shown in (4):

4. Mary went to the Market with John. It . . .

Here, *It* could refer to the event, the market, or even be non-referential (*It was a lovely day for an outing*). So when we turn our attention to this pronoun, deferred processing seems a lot more sensible. In contrast, fuller nounphrases are seldom ambiguous at the point of encountering them:

5. Mrs Thatcher discussed the modification of Britain's Universities with Mrs Currie. The prime minister . . .

With fuller nounphrases, immediacy of anaphor resolution seems sensible. Therefore, if the system is optimally tuned to the constraints of real-time efficiency, the answer to the immediacy question may well depend upon the type of phrase or word in question.

THEORIES OF PROCESSING, AND IMMEDIACY

In the discussion so far, we have taken the distinction between immediate *vs* deferred interpretation as straightforward, but as Bierwisch (1983) reminds us, giving a precise characterisation of immediacy is problematical. It is a truism that all processes take time, and so it is necessary to discriminate between the onset of processes and the point of their completion. This is complicating for any discussion of immediacy, because one must be careful to distinguish between experimental evidence favouring an immediate onset of processes supporting reference resolution, and evidence showing when resolution is completed. The idea of immediate initiation seems relatively simple: One can imagine some sort of ballistic process initiated as soon as the right trigger conditions are met. In the case of anaphora, we might hold that simple definite nounphrases should be such a trigger condition. Therefore, as soon as the processor determines that such a nounphrase is present, procedures to discover reference should be initiated. Hence, any definite description should be enough to trigger the process on the strictest version of the immediacy hypothesis. With complex descriptions containing restrictive relative clauses, for instance, the first possible nounphrase should result in some aspect of the resolution process being initiated, even if the rest of the clause is required to provide the necessary individuating information. With definite pronouns, processes should be initiated as soon as the system detects the presence of the pronoun. Operationally, therefore, immediacy of anaphoric resolution depends upon activity starting as soon as a definite nounphrase or pronoun is detected.

To make a claim about immediate completion of reference resolution is much more complex, both conceptually and experimentally. For resolution to have occurred, an anaphoric (semantic) relationship must have been computed, and this will take processing time. A demonstration of immediacy at this level would therefore depend upon demonstrating both rapid completion of the process, and that no other significant operations had taken place on subsequent input in the meantime. A strong version of this is the claim by Just and Carpenter (1980) that eye fixations are maintained until the item has been processed to the deepest possible level. A weaker, and equally interesting view, would be that completion takes place rapidly, even when there are arguable opportunities for deferral. This version underlies accounts of processing that assume temporary assignment with the possibility of later revision.

Theories of completion are inevitably more complex than accounts of initiation, and are discussed more thoroughly later in this paper. Our first concern is with evidence for immediate initiation of process, and with the time course of various processes once initiated. For each technique discussed, we shall examine just what kind of processes are being detected.

EVIDENCE FOR IMMEDIATE PROCESSES IN REFERENCE RESOLUTION

A wide variety of methods have been used to probe the time course of processes associated with reference resolution. Often, these have been treated as though they answered questions about specific versions of the immediacy hypothesis, when in fact they are not sufficient to do so. However, there is a great deal of evidence supporting early (immediate) triggering of processes that are arguably pertinent to reference resolution. We begin with evidence from processing speech.

Speech

As we shall see, there are many experiments that bear on the immediacy hypothesis in reading. In speech comprehension the evidence is sparser, but what evidence there is does tend to give general support for immediacy in all the main forms of definite anaphor.

The speech experiments that we consider have all employed some variant of the cross-modal priming paradigm (Swinney, 1979), where a written word is presented for lexical decision (or naming) at some critical point in the speech stream. The first was reported by Shillcock (1982), using materials like (6):

6. The teacher$_a$ did not board the train for the$_b$ simple reason that it/he$_c$ was not going to the south of England.

In this study, the written target word related to a potential antecedent for a pronoun in the speech. Consider the potential target contrast *school vs street*. Either probe could be presented before the pronoun had been encountered (at b) or immediately after (at c). So in this case, the test of immediacy comes from a comparison of the pre- to post-presentation priming effect for the lexical decision, where the priming effect is measured in terms of the difference in lexical decision time between *school* and *street*. Any priming difference in favour of the appropriate antecedent should then indirectly reflect resolution of the pronoun at that point.

Shillcock's (1982) results did give partial support for this in that he was able to report a pre- to post-presentation priming difference, but only to the extent that the pronoun which did *not* identify the probed antecedent resulted in a *reduced* effect over the pre-presentation priming level. Presumably, in this case, the probed antecedent was sufficiently in focus at point b (prior to encountering the pronoun) to produce a priming effect, but then was defocused by the presence of a pronoun identifying a different antecedent. Therefore, although it would have been more satisfactory if the antecedent had not already been primed before encountering the pronoun and a positive advantage could have been detected, this result is certainly consistent with early resolution. However, as we shall stress repeatedly, priming results of this kind do not necessarily evidence *completion* of referential resolution. They simply indicate that the pronoun has in some way immediately activated the antecedent or in this case deactivated a non-antecedent. (A similar observation was made by Gernsbacher, 1989, using word-by-word visual presentation.) What type of semantic relationship has been computed to hold between anaphor and antecedent (if any) is not in any way addressed with this procedure, let alone *when* such a relationship is established. The remaining speech comprehension experiments are somewhat clearer on this point.

Tyler and Marslen-Wilson (1982) reported a more extensive study using a slightly different form of cross-modal priming as an index of resolution. Their experiment is best discussed in relation to an example of the materials and procedure. The subject was required to name the visually presented probe *him* or *her* following one of the auditorily presented fragments (a, b, or c) shown below:

As Philip was walking back from the shop, he saw an old woman trip and fall flat on her face. She seemed to be unable to get up again.

a. Philip ran towards . . .
b. He ran towards . . .
c. Running towards . . .

The probes were chosen so that one (e.g. *her*) was consistent with the contextual interpretation of the fragment, and the other (e.g. *him*) inconsistent. They reasoned that any advantage in terms of naming latency for contextually appropriate probes could only arise if the subject of the clause had been established at that point and hence the anaphor resolved. In fact, the results indicated that in all conditions such an advantage occurred, even though the distinction was somewhat sharper for both the proper name and pronoun anaphors than the zero anaphor with the verb phrase alone. Therefore, this result gives strong support for the resolution of both the anaphoric pronoun and proper name by the time the verb has been encountered. Even more striking is the numerically smaller result they found in favour of immediate resolution of the zero anaphors (condition c).

This experiment is more informative than Shillcock's (1982) in a number of ways. It demonstrates a broad similarity of effect for all forms of anaphora studied and it uses a technique that addresses more clearly the nature of the anaphoric relation which is having the effect. In order to impose such a constraint on the continuations (e.g. *him* or *her*), the subject of the clause must have been established to some degree (i.e. at least to the extent that it accounts for all antecedents of that gender in the context and this requires computing a semantic relation between anaphor and antecedent). However, it is worth noting that the probe is downstream of the critical anaphor in coming after the main verb, and it may well be that the verb is the functionally critical point for triggering assignment of subject pronouns. Therefore, does this study clearly favour some version of immediate completion over the weaker immediacy of activation?

A more recent follow-up by Marslen-Wilson, Tyler, and Koster (reported in Marslen-Wilson & Tyler, 1988) throws some doubt on an immediate completion explanation of the result. They used the same basic procedure but within a factorial design including a number of additional manipulations. The targeted antecedent could either be a thematic subject of the discourse or not (see below for a fuller discussion of the importance of this variable in the context of the reading experiments). The pronoun could either match the antecedent in gender or not, and finally the verb could be congruent, incongruent, or neutral with respect to the context and the targeted antecedent. Examples of materials in all conditions are shown below:

1. *Thematic subject antecedent with congruent verb:*
After the surgeon had examined the 12-year-old girl with the badly broken leg, he decided he would have to take immediate action. He'd had a lot of experience with serious injuries. He knew what he had to do next.

a. He quickly injected . . .
b. She quickly injected . . .
c. Quickly injecting . . .

2. *Thematic subject antecedent with neutral verb:*
As Bill was buying popcorn at the movies, he saw an old girlfriend get in line for a ticket. He had arrived at the movies especially early. He wanted to be sure of getting a good seat.

a. He waved at . . .
b. She waved at . . .
c. Waving at . . .

3. *Thematic subject with opposing verb bias:*
Mary lost hope of winning the race to the ocean when she heard Andrew's footsteps approaching her from behind. The deep sand was slowing her down. She had trouble keeping her balance.

a. She overtook . . .
b. He overtook . . .
c. Overtaking . . .

The factorial design allowed the experimenters to establish both the role of the different factors in determining the assignment after encountering the verb, as well as the interactions between them. In the first place, the results indicated that each of the factors alone was sufficient to determine resolution at this point. Therefore, for instance, in condition 2b there was a naming effect in favour of the antecedent matching the gender of the pronoun, going against the thematic subject bias but in the absence of a constraining verb. In condition 2c, the effect favoured assignment of the subject to the antecedent which was the thematic subject of the discourse, so confirming the importance of this factor when not in competition with either gender (because there is no pronoun here) or verb congruency (because the verb is neutral). Similarly, they found strong effects of verb congruency in all conditions when it did not go against pronoun gender. But the most interesting results come from looking at what happens when these various factors are pitted against each other. In particular, pitting verb congruency against gender seems to produce a dramatic effect. Hence, in the cases where the verb goes against the gender of the pronoun (conditions 1b and 3a), the average effect in favour of the gender matched assignment is only 15 msec, compared to an average effect of 60 msec when the two factors converge (e.g. conditions 1a and 3b).

Altogether, these results seem to be more consistent with a model of immediacy in which, as relevant information is encountered, it has an immediate and cumulative effect on interpretation, rather than one in which the earliest evidence results in a full categorical assignment. Clearly, in the absence of contrary evidence, the system prefers to go along with the first piece of evidence available, in this case thematic subjecthood or gender, but is nevertheless immediately capable of taking into account subsequent evidence as soon as it is encountered, as in the case of a contextually biasing verb. Thus at any point in the process, the system can operate with some weighted balance of accumulated evidence in favour of one assignment or another. Although not conclusive, this would seem to favour the immediate accumulation of evidence version of the process as opposed to a model of serial revision of categorical assignments.

Written Discourse

The presentation of written discourse is harder to tie to time than is speech, and so correspondingly more indirect and off-line measures have been used. A notable exception is the use of eye-tracking techniques, which represent the closest physical coupling of the reader to the text.

Self-paced Reading Time. With this method, materials are presented either a sentence, a clause, a phrase, or even a word at a time, in response to the subject pressing a button to see the "next piece of text". With the whole-sentence version, such a task has the advantage of being easy for the subject to do and requires little practice. But it has the disadvantage of being a rather crude instrument, in that the locus of an effect can only be inferred. While it has been used to make claims about factors influencing the ease of anaphor resolution, in the main these claims are being inferred from the ease (speed) with which sentences containing anaphors are read following sentences in which antecedents are manipulated.

Among the results pertinent to the immediacy question are those related to focus and thematic subject. It is widely argued that only a subset of conceptualisations resulting from discourse is available in attentional *focus*, a kind of working memory containing representations of currently important discourse entities. Focus can be understood in terms of the ease of accessibility of potential antecedents and control of inference patterns (see, for example, Grosz, 1977; Hudson, Tannenhaus, & Dell, 1986; Sanford & Garrod, 1981). Thus it will be easier to access representations which are in focus than those which are in longer-term memory, and this has implications for ease of reference resolution. Pronoun reference is demonstrably sensitive to focus. Thus Anderson, Garrod, & Sanford (1983) showed that pronominal references to characters which depend upon being situated in a scene are more difficult to process when that scene is cued as completed. (An example of dependence is that *a waiter* is dependent on a restaurant scene.) However, main characters, not dependent upon a particular scene, can easily be referred to by a pronoun after a change from the scene in which they have just appeared.

Hudson et al. (1986) manipulated reference to either the agent or patient of active sentences, and showed a processing preference for pronouns to be associated with agents (the "centred" target, in their terminology; cf. Grosz & Sidner, 1985). One contrast was between (7′) and (7″) as continuations of (7):

7. Jack apologised profusely to Josh.
7′. He had been rude to Josh yesterday. (Centred target)
7″. He had been offended by Jack's comment. (Non-centred target)

They observed that reading times for centred targets were faster than those for non-centred targets, and suggested that "He" is immediately interpreted as Jack in both cases, so that in the non-centred case, reassignment would have to occur. Of course, these results do not demand an assumption of a completed categorical process; they are equally consistent with continuous evidence evaluation at a sub-threshold level. But they strongly suggest an immediate "attachment" of the pronoun to the agent. In a further experiment, similar materials were presented for self-paced reading on a clause-by-clause basis, with the second clause of the second sentence being the locus of disambiguation of the pronominal reference.

Reading times for the second clause were longest when this indicated that the pronoun in the first clause referred to a non-centred antecedent.

The different roles that antecedents play in the discourse also influence reading times. For example, in simple narratives, with pronouns as anaphors, reading times to sentences containing references to the main character are faster than those for sentences containing references to secondary characters (Anderson et al., 1983). Sanford, Moar, and Garrod (1988) found that sentences containing pronominal references to characters introduced through proper names (e.g. *Bill*) were read faster than those referring to characters introduced through role descriptions (e.g. *the waitress*). This at least suggests that main characters—signalled through agency, dominant role, or proper name—may influence the speed with which assignments are made, and probably the bias in any initial pattern of activity leading to eventual resolution. This is consistent with the findings of Marslen-Wilson et al. (1982) on the importance of thematic subjecthood in the speech studies. We shall return to this point shortly.

Reading time experiments have also been useful in highlighting processing differences between nounphrase and pronominal anaphors. Studies of production in naturalistic settings suggest that nounphrases are used to reintroduce individuals which have slipped from focus, whereas pronouns are used to maintain reference to focused individuals (e.g. Marslen-Wilson, Levy, & Tyler, 1982). Hudson et al. (1986) substituted proper names for pronouns in examples like (7), and found no effect of centring. Sanford et al. (1988) substituted repeat nounphrases or proper names in their experiment, and found that there was no longer a differential effect of name/role antecedent. Taken together, the pattern of observations shows pronominal reference to be sensitive to theme and focus effects, which are top-down system states. Fuller nounphrases are not so sensitive, and appear to override top-down guidance in the resolution process. This will be elaborated further. But the emerging picture is one in which immediacy and type of process is likely to be dependent jointly on focus state and incoming description type, a conclusion that is also consistent with the findings from the speech experiments cited above.

Priming Studies. Priming has been used as an index of the immediacy of resolution by a number of researchers. In general, the technique relies upon the subject judging whether or not a word has been presented in a text, carrying out a lexical decision task on a word, or reading a word out loud. If a facilitation can be obtained for a word either related to or the same as an "antecedent" when an anaphor has been presented, then this constitutes evidence for an active process, as discussed in the section on speech. McKoon and Ratcliff (1980; in press) have used recognition memory for single words in relation to nounphrase anaphors, as shown below:

A burglar surveyed the garage set back from the street.
Several bottles of milk were piled at the curb.
The banker and her husband were on vacation.
The criminal slipped away from the streetlamp.

The criminal and *A burglar* are coreferential, and the argument is that if this relationship is established during reading the final sentence, then recognition of the test word *burglar*, presented at the end of the sentence, should be facilitated relative to a suitable control, such as replacing *the criminal* with *a cat*. They found that recognition of *burglar* was facilitated by the reference to *the criminal* rather than *a cat*. There was no difference for the control word *bottles* when presented in each condition. The suggestion is, therefore, that the anaphor activates some representation of the antecedent *a burglar*. The activation also seems to spread through a representation of the original action in which *a burglar* was involved (surveying the garage), because additional tests showed that *garage* was also primed by the reference to *the criminal*. Therefore, there is evidence for integration supporting anaphoric resolution with full nounphrase anaphors, at least by the end of the sentence in which the anaphors appear.

Although McKoon and Ratcliff's (1980) study did not pinpoint the time course of the priming effect, a subsequent study by Dell, McKoon, and Ratcliff (1983) did. Using a modification of the procedure described above, the test word was displayed in positions after every word of the final sentences of the materials. The words were presented at a rate of one per 250 msec, at a fixed rate. Priming for the referent of the noun of the anaphor reached its maximum (asymptotic) value only 250 msec after the appearance of the anaphor, indicating a fast activation process. The companion words from the same proposition reached a peak on a similar time-scale, indicating an early spread of activation over the representation of the action in which the protagonist was involved.

There are several problems with this study, one of which is that at best the results only show that a word conceptually related to the referent serves to activate the referent. If *the criminal* activated the antecedent *burglar*, we might suppose that it is because the expression is an anaphor that the priming pattern obtained, but it might be because the word "criminal", rather than the anaphor *the criminal*, is facilitating. This issue can be addressed by comparing non-anaphoric nounphrases containing the critical word as a control. This was done by O'Brien, Duffy, and Myers (1986), who compared *the stalled vehicle* as an anaphor of *the bus (which had come to a halt)* with *a police vehicle*, which is non-anaphoric, but semantically related in that it contains the term *vehicle*. They observed that even the non-anaphoric expression resulted in priming, though not quite to the same extent as the anaphoric case.

Whereas this indicates that some priming might be due to pre-existing lexical associations, it does not explain why other elements of the proposition containing the antecedent are also primed. Indeed, this data suggests that it is the entire antecedent conceptualisation that is being facilitated as soon as the anaphor is encountered. Such a finding indicates that the resolution process is well advanced immediately after encountering the nounphrase anaphor and before encountering any other information.

Another problem is highlighted by O'Brien et al. (1986): Fast recognition times could reflect either semantic priming or backward integration effects. Backward integration results from a probe being compatible with antecedent material and is known to influence priming effects with lexical decision tasks (e.g. Seidenberg, Waters, Sanders, & Langer, 1984). O'Brien et al. attempted to control for this possibility by using a task in which subjects had to name probes rather than perform a recognition check, on the assumption that naming is not sensitive to backward integration (Seidenberg et al., 1984). When this was done, the non-anaphoric condition did not show any evidence of a priming effect, whereas the anaphoric condition did. On the strength of this, it could be argued that naming is better than lexical decision as an index of an inferential process (Keenan et al., in press). Regardless of this, Dell et al.'s (1983) data on whole conceptualisation priming indicates an increased sensitivity, consistent with resolution processes.

Stevenson (1986) studied pronoun anaphora by using phrase-by-phrase presentation, coupled with recognition of whether or not a test word had been previously presented. An example of the material is as follows:

John apologised to Anne
at the end of the class {*early*}
because he regretted {*late*}
having caused so much trouble.

On a probe trial, the word *John* or *Anne* was presented instead of one of the phrases. In the early condition, it followed the second phrase, whereas in the late condition it followed the third phrase. Subjects had to decide whether the probe words had been presented in the text (made possible by various filler conditions). Stevenson (1986) found that recognition times to test words that were antecedents were shorter than times for non-antecedents, when compared with the early control. This result was taken by Stevenson as indicating that "selection of a unique antecedent" has taken place by the time one word after the pronoun has been read. When gender cues are eliminated by making the two protagonists the same sex, there is no reliable difference between recognition times for antecedent and non-antecedent. This pattern would be anticipated, because resolution is not possible until the second clause has been read. These results imply that the pronoun immediately activates a representation of its antecedent if that antecedent is unique and of the same gender. It does not, however, mean that reference is "resolved" at that point, although this interpretation is given by Stevenson.

Taken together, data from priming studies of both nounphrase and pronominal anaphora suggest that some processes, which may support the establishment of anaphoric relations, are initiated early, as discussed in relation to the speech data. However, precisely what kind of processing is being revealed is at present somewhat contentious, and there is little to support or deny the claim that reference resolution goes through to completion on the basis of minimal disambiguating evidence. There is clearer evidence in the case of full nounphrases, but no strong evidence either way for pronouns in this respect. A recent study by Gernsbacher (1989) using word-by-word presentation in conjunction with recognition probe latency reinforces this position.

Explicit Assignment. In the case of pronouns where there is more than one possible antecedent, an explicit assignment task can be used in which the subject is required to press a particular button to indicate which assignment has been made. Because the subject's task depends upon making a choice of referent, there would appear to be no question of whether or not an assignment is actually made, although we shall be at pains to point out that the picture may not be so ideal as this would seem to suggest. This widely used task enables one to assess the utilisation of cues from a number of sources.

There is evidence from a variety of such experiments that the more cues there are supporting an interpretation, the faster the assignment can be made. For instance, a gender cue can be used to disambiguate a potential antecedent, so that in (8), the processor could determine the referent of the pronoun unambiguously by point a:

8. Steven blamed Jane because she_a spilled the coffee.

In contrast, the following case requires an analysis of the event before an unambiguous interpretation could be given:

9. Steven blamed Frank because he spilled the coffee.

Ehrlich (1980) showed that assignment times were shorter for examples like (8) than for (9), although when pragmatic information is consistent with a gender-driven resolution, the time to make that resolution is still reduced somewhat. Her pincipal conclusion was that gender cues, when available, are used to resolve reference (immediate resolution of some sort), extra information playing a major role only if necessary. Therefore, in the absence of a gender cue, the assignment is inevitably slowed down. Similar observations and arguments have been made by Springston (1976).

One problem with the study is the length of the response times, which are longer even than reading times for complete sentences under self-paced conditions. This makes it difficult to use such data to evaluate whether any process supporting anaphor resolution is initiated as soon as the pronoun is encountered. However, it does suggest that evidence *after* the pronoun may enter into the final resolution process, even when the gender cues are sufficient to disambiguate the referent on the basis of the pronoun alone. This seems to suggest an ongoing evidence collection process, which takes into account available evidence as it appears.

There is other evidence to suggest that subsequent information will influence overt assignment times, even when such information is not strictly necessary. Thus Caramazza, Grober, Garvey, and Yates (1977) found an effect of subsequent pragmatic information even when gender cues were available to cue a unique assignment. Hirst and Brill (1980) and Stevenson and Vitkovitch (1986) obtained similar findings. For example, Stevenson and Vitkovitch compared assignment times for the four cases shown below:

Jane stood watching.
Henry jumped across a ravine
and (he) fell into the river.

Jane stood watching.
Henry jumped across a ravine
and (he) picked up some money.

The parentheses denote the option of ellipsis or pronoun. In the upper example, the second clause of the second sentence is a highly plausible continuation of the first clause. In the lower example, it is implausible. Stevenson and Vitkovitch (1986) showed that the time to decide that "he" refers to Henry was longer in the second than in the first case, although the pronoun is completely unambiguous on gender grounds. The investigators claimed that this showed the duration of the resolution process to be dependent upon the pragmatic information that followed the pronoun. Certainly, it is possible to make an assignment as soon as the pronoun is encountered, and this does not seem to have happened.

As with assignment studies in general, the latencies were very long, averaging 3.7 sec. Perhaps under other conditions, there would be less opportunity for pragmatics to intervene when gender cues suffice. In explicit judgement tasks, there may be time for pragmatic information to speed up a response that is based on an outcome already established, a possibility that makes it difficult to relate the results to theory. So the evidence from direct assignment tells us little about immediacy, and gives little definitive information about late processes in resolution. Even worse, perhaps, the task itself forces explicit decisions to be made, while in more normal reading situations, it is even possible that anaphor resolution does not always take place anyway.

When we turn to the studies using eye-tracking techniques, the relationship between findings from overall reading time, explicit assignment studies, and measurements of fixation durations in the vicinity of a pronoun, do turn out to be complicated in just the way one might expect.

Eye-tracking Experiments. On the face of it, recording eye movements during reading should prove to be the most secure way of establishing the timing of anaphoric processing under conditions of normal reading. On the one hand, it is possible to tell precisely which bits of text are being fixated at a given moment and, on the other, the technique is not intrusive. If one can demonstrate that fixation durations on the critical anaphoric word or phrase are both a function of the difficulty of the resolution process *and* that any increase in duration does not spill over to subsequent fixations, then this should evidence on-line activity. Of course, any claim concerning resolution would depend upon an independent demonstration.

In reviewing the eye-tracking studies, the situation does not seem to be quite so straightforward. For one thing, the critical words to be fixated are often exceptionally short, as in the case of personal pronouns, and such words only attract direct fixations on relatively few occasions (roughly 60%). This makes it difficult to predict where the increased fixation duration should be occurring (for instance, is it on the pronoun itself or in part on the word preceding it, or even the word following?). The second problem, which may well arise from this lack of resolution, is that different experimenters have reported different results from apparently similar studies. Therefore, whereas some experimenters (e.g. Ehrlich & Rayner, 1983) have been able to detect reliable effects in the vicinity of pronouns, others have not (e.g. Carroll & Slowiaczek, 1987). Bearing these limitations in mind, we shall briefly mention some of the relevant studies.

The main eye-tracking experiments that have some bearing on the immediacy question have been directed at the resolution of pronouns, the first of which was by Ehrlich and Rayner (1983). In this experiment, they manipulated the textual distance between an unambiguous pronoun and its antecedent and recorded fixation durations in the vicinity of the pronoun. This revealed increased overall durations around the pronoun with increasing text distance. But as the antecedent became less accessible (i.e. with ever-increasing distance), so the fixation effects tended to migrate to words downstream of the pronoun itself. Therefore, Ehrlich and Rayner concluded that the data only supported a weak version of immediacy, because the reader did not hold fixation on the pronoun until it had been fully resolved.

A further study by Vonk (1984; see also Vonk, 1985) highlights the complicated relationship between the different measurement methods. Vonk used materials similar to those of Ehrlich's (1980) explicit resolution study (see sentences 8 and 9). But she compared the results in terms of (1) assignment (choice) latency for the antecedents of pronouns with or without a gender cue, (2) overall reading time for the critical second clause, and (3) fixation durations on the pronoun itself under the various conditions. The pattern was most enlightening. First, she replicated Ehrlich's earlier result and found increased assignment latency for the antecedent when no gender cue was present, but she also demonstrated that there was *no* overall increase in reading time for the second clause when the subjects were simply required to read the sentence. Finally, she was able to show a clear eye-fixation effect on the pronoun. If the gender disambiguated the pronoun, subjects were more likely to fixate it (83 *vs* 60%), and when they did so they spent 50 msec longer on the pronoun than in the case where there was no gender cue. Therefore, this study both highlights the difficulty of interpreting the off-line assignment studies in terms of immediacy, and the way various cues such as gender can lead to immediate processing effects when informative.

Spelling Error Detection. A task suited to nounphrases as well as pronouns goes some way towards overcoming the problem that resolution is perhaps being forced in an unnatural way through the demand for explicit assignment, yet still requires something like assignment to have taken place. This technique is in some ways parallel to the task of Marslen-Wilson et al. (1982). Garrod and Sanford (1985) used materials like those shown in Table 1, which depict interactions between two characters—a main character and a secondary character. In the last line, either the main character (Elizabeth) or the secondary character (the lifeguard) is introduced. The verb that follows (jumped or sank) is predictable for one character, given his or her state or role, and is not predictable for the other (although it is logically possible). Therefore, the verb *sank* is predictable for Elizabeth, whereas *jumped* is not. Now if this predictability were detectable through the ease of processing the verb, at the time the verb was encountered, then it must mean that on encountering Elizabeth, the processor activates the data structure corresponding to what is known about Elizabeth, and this results in a bias on processing the verb. The same argument applies to the lifeguard.

Garrod and Sanford (1985) investigated any on-line effect of verb predictability by changing the crucial verbs to misspelled versions (e.g.

TABLE 1
A Dangerous Incident at the Pool (after Garrod & Sanford, 1985)

Elizabeth was a very inexperienced swimmer and wouldn't have gone into the pool if *the lifeguard* hadn't been nearby. But as soon as she was out of her depth she started to panic and wave her hands about in a frenzy.

a. Within seconds Elizabeth b. Within seconds the lifeguard	*jumped** into the pool
c. Within seconds Elizabeth d. Within seconds the lifeguard	*sank** beneath the surface

*Misspellings: j*i*mped, s*e*nk.

jumped was changed to *jimped*; *sank* to *senk*). The subjects' task was to read each passage a line at a time, and press a button as soon as a spelling error was detected. Error detection latencies were shorter for predictable verbs for both character types. By using fillers in which errors appeared at various positions in the sentence, it was possible to carry out control regression analyses of detection latency against position in the sentence. Such analyses indicated that the errors were being detected as soon as the word was read.

One interpretation of these results is that when the anaphor is encountered, the result is to bias lexical analysis in favour of verbs that are compatible with the state of the character to which the anaphor refers. This is a complex pattern of activation, equivalent to "resolving" an anaphor. Therefore, for proper names, and for nounphrases denoting characters, we would claim that there is early initiation of processes of activation, and that these processes are consistent with the establishment of reference-based significance.

A second study suggested that nounphrases may bring about fuller interpretation (or richer activation) than pronouns seem to. In this experiment, Garrod and Sanford (1985) used the error technique on the same materials but with he/she pronouns substituted for the repeat names or role descriptions. The pattern of results was the same for main characters: Predictable verbs were processed faster than unpredictable verbs. However, for secondary characters, this was not true. Indeed, there was marginal evidence for a bias in the opposite direction, with the unpredicted verbs being processed faster. These complex results can be interpreted as showing that when a pronoun is encountered, an immediate "bonding" occurs between the main character (thematic subject) and the pronoun, a strong top-down influence of theme. If the fit is good (in terms of gender), the system will be as though resolution has taken place, although an explicit relation has not necessarily been computed. The verb predictability pattern, which goes with the main character under these circumstances, is appropriate. But if the fit is poor, this is discovered relatively late, and so there is still a verb bias towards the main character, albeit a smaller and presumably diminishing one. Indeed, Garrod and Sanford (1985) noted that some of the subjects worried that the pronouns might be "wrong" (e.g. *he* should be *she*, etc.). Thus the bottom-up impact of a pronoun is very weak with respect to thematic subject, whereas the bottom-up impact of a nounphrase or a proper name is strong, consistent with our earlier observations.

Of course, this study is not without problems. Reading rates for subjects were about twice as long as normal, at 2 words per sec, and the error detection requirement is of course intrusive. Nevertheless, the results show that immediate events can and do occur, and the pattern fits the observations which come from reading time measures.

SUMMARY AND CONCLUSIONS FROM THE DIRECT MEASURE STUDIES

As we have seen, there is now quite a body of experimental research on immediacy of processing for both pronoun and nounphrase anaphors. All of the evidence, with the possible exception of Ehrlich and Rayner's (1983) eye-tracking study, is consistent with the immediate triggering of anaphoric processes for both pronouns and fuller descriptions. In the case of the fuller nounphrases, evidence is also strong for a rapid completion of the process, whose results feed into the interpretation of subsequent material in the sentence. In other words, there is no evidence to suggest that a full nounphrase ever receives delayed interpretation, or that any immediate interpretation can be overridden by subsequent context.

The situation with pronouns looks much more complicated. The problem is that pronoun resolution is apparently subject to a number of constraints apart from gender and number matching. Evidence both from speech and reading indicates the prior influence of antecedent focus, and the subsequent influences of verb congruency. Therefore, while all these factors, including number and gender, seem to have an immediate processing influence, the resolution may be open to revision, or even not fixed at all, until well downstream of the pronoun itself. This raises the question of whether a pronoun receives an immediate categorical interpretation at the earliest point, which may be subject to revision, *or* that the final categorical interpretation is only made after a lag to see whether more disambiguating evidence is going to become available (such as after a main verb, or by the end of a sentence). No direct evidence is available to test these hypotheses, but some indirect evidence from investigations of stylistic phenomena may have some bearing on the matter.

STYLISTIC PHENOMENA AND IMMEDIACY OF PROCESSING

Apart from attempts at relatively direct measurement (as discussed above), there is a variety of related anaphoric phenomena that need to be understood in terms of the immediacy of processes, and their completeness. These phenomena are manifest when discourse structures are used, which are commonly avoided by any writer with average sensitivity for the reader. As such, they constitute situations in which component processes are being inappropriately or inadequately combined for the task at hand. In other domains, garden-path and related phenomena are well-known parallels. The present examples all use stylistic rather than grammatical unacceptability as a measurable aspect of processing strain. They can be viewed as phenomena that should be explained within the context developed above, or as tools for further exploring immediacy effects.

Sanford, Garrod, Lucas, and Henderson (1984) studied a phenomenon which they termed "false bonding", and which they relate to the issue of immediacy. The subjective impression (termed a *sounds-like effect*) emerges clearly in examples where a pronoun is used to refer to an intended referent that is merely implied, and where there is another entity in the antecedent sentence that matches the pronoun in number and gender:

10. Harry was sailing to Ireland. It sank without trace.

Such materials produce a strong false-bonding, in which there is an impression that "Ireland sank". Although the reader will know that this was not the intended anaphoric relation, and that it is effectively ruled out as a final interpretation by the condition *sank without trace*, there is still a strong impression of false bonding. The effect is also reflected in reading times for falsely bonding target sentences: Times are much longer than for controls in which there is no suitable false antecedent, as in (11):

11. Harry was sailing the seas. It sank without trace.

The phenomenon is not restricted to examples where the intended referent is merely implied, as the following indicates:

12. If the books are too difficult, don't get your knicker's in a twist. Leave them in the library and go for a walk.

These examples can be interpreted in the following way (Sanford et al., 1984): When a pronoun is encountered, it immediately triggers a process which is effectively seeking a match in terms of number and gender, where the major candidate is that which is in focus. Although other processes may be recruited to solve the resolution problem, the matching process will predominate. Indeed, it could be argued that the phenomena are strong evidence for an immediate resolution process which becomes the subject of reassignment when more evidence appears—a kind of garden-pathing.

Further work casts severe doubt on this account. Sanford (1985a,b) showed that if a sentence initial pronoun turns out to be non-coreferential, as in (13), then there is no trace of the sounds-like effect associated with false-bonding:

13. Harry sailed to Ireland. It_a was a beautiful day.

There is no trace of a subjective problem, and no trace of a reading time problem either. It might be argued that this case is different from the earlier ones because the pronoun is not referential. But if on the original argument, bonding began at point a, then why did it not begin at point a with the present example? The processor would have no way of knowing whether (10) or (13) was the material at hand. An account which preserves the undeniable existence of false bonding, and yet allows the lack of an effect in examples like (13), might be based on a two-part resolution theory. On encountering a pronoun, a match is sought between its primitive characteristics (number, gender) and possible antecedents, with the most likely candidate match being determined by foregrounding and focus. If a match is found, then a site has been discovered for the development of a semantic relationship (like anaphora). However, in the present cases, the relationship is not instantiated until evidence coming in later demands it. Therefore, in the usual case, later evidence will suggest a referential interpretation, and if this is tested at the site (established link), then all will fit together. In the case of the false bonding examples, instantiation of the required referential relationship will result (ultimately) in the discovery that the site is not the right one, hence the disturbing effect. Finally, in the non-referential cases, a referential relation will never be tested, and therefore there will never be a false bonding effect.

Although this argument is speculative, the evidence does seem to support the early initiation of a matching process, distinct from a process of reference resolution (such a process might be being detected by some of the priming task results). Because the task is indirect, there is no real way of knowing that thc matching process was initiated as soon as the pronoun was encountered, even though it is only the information accessible from the pronoun which is involved. An alternative might be to suppose that the pattern match is just a dominant process (encapsulated) that happens after some (unspecified) delay following encountering the pronoun, and impervious to evidence running against an alternative assignment. While it may indeed be a dominant process (the impression of false bonding does not go away in the face of new evidence), it would be extraordinary if its onset were purposely deferred until after the arrival of information which the process was going to ignore! In summary, there is indirect evidence for immediate initiation of a process linking pronouns with potential antecedents, but not necessarily leading to an instantiated semantic relationship.

There is also a little evidence suggesting bonding effects with nounphrases as well as with pronouns. Sanford (1988; in prep.) discusses cases in which there is a weak parallel to false pronoun bonding:

14. The car came tearing around the bend. It almost hit a car.

In a series of studies on the acceptability of materials, (14) obtained low ratings. The reasons given were that the second occurrence of car leaves the impression that it is not clearly enough signalled as different from the first car (see Garrod & Sanford, 1977, for reading time data showing that the two nounphrases are being compared). Despite the fact that the pronoun is in the sentence-initial position and the action rules out coreference of the object, some automatic process seems to bring the two together. Of course, such a process is far from nonsensical. It has to take place to recognise the following close relative as an instance of identity of sense rather than identity of reference:

15. The car came tearing around the bend. It almost hit another car.

This case demonstrates how some sort of sensible relation can hold between the two instances of car. The underlying mechanism which spuriously links the instances in (14), and sensibly links them in (15), may depend upon a simple pattern match, simpler even than that which we speculate underlies the pronoun bonding effect. But what kind of object is the link? Unlike the pronoun example, in the absence of a coreferential environment there is some impression of referential confusion. This suggests that, whereas in the case of pronouns the bond formed is relatively unspecified, with nounphrases the link is restricted to a class of relations including identity of sense and identity of reference (but with which undecided). Unless the cues strongly support one or the other, the utterance will be unsatisfactory.

DISCUSSION

The evidence from the priming and spelling error detection tasks in reading suggests that with full nounphrases, there is an early or immediate initiation of reference resolution processes. With the former, the strongest support must come from the presence of priming of action terms from the same proposition as the antecedent before anything after the anaphor is presented. With the second task, errors are detected on verbs immediately following anaphoric nounphrases, and therefore information regarding the role being played by the character denoted by the anaphor must have been immediately available. Tyler and Marslen-Wilson's (1982) evidence from speech is in line with this, but it may include a contribution from the verb.

Pronouns present a more complex picture. There is good evidence from a number of sources for the immediate instigation of some processes which might be considered components of reference resolution. One complication is that top-down influences strongly affect the pattern of processing. There is consistent evidence that with character-based narratives, the resting bias is towards main rather than secondary characters. Therefore, the use of a proper name rather than a role description seems to facilitate pronominal (but not repeat-name) anaphora. Clause-by-clause reading times showed a strong bias towards agents (Hudson et al., 1986). But perhaps the most compelling illustration of the influence of main characters comes from the spelling error study by Garrod and Sanford (1983). This provides fairly direct evidence for immediate resolution, but only providing the pronoun refers to the main character—otherwise, resolution seems to be delayed. Our interpretation of this is that pronouns, when encountered, trigger an immediate mapping on to the main character, and if subsequent data rules this out, then a bottom-up assignment is made. Subsequent data may be gender information from the pronoun, and pragmatic information from the verb.

The immediacy question is further complicated for pronouns by evidence that although processes supporting resolution may be initiated on encountering a pronoun, full resolution may depend upon later evidence. Indeed, there is some indication that even when unambiguous resolution is possible, later evidence may be taken into account in making a final assignment. Regrettably, this evidence comes from overt assignment tasks, which are arguably very artificial. However, studies of speech by Marslen-Wilson and his colleagues show in a very detailed way how successive cues alter the apparent commitment of the system to particular biases in interpretation. A third strand of evidence, perhaps a little more indirect, comes from the studies of the bonding effect summarised in Sanford (1985b). Although there appears to be an immediate (pronoun-initiated) bonding effect, perhaps along the lines needed to explain the thematic subjecthood effect in the spelling error task, this does not appear to amount to the establishment of a full-blown identity of reference relationship.

The evidence thus supports a version of the immediacy hypothesis: Some processes, apparently relevant to reference resolution, are initiated by the appearance of a definite expression (pronoun or nounphrase). In the case of nounphrases or proper names, a process equivalent to resolution appears to be detectable, in that the process produces a pipeline through to information about the actions and the state of the character denoted by the referent. In the case of pronouns, the early process seems more akin to specifying a locus which is interpretable semantically either on the basis of default system-states (top-down influences), or in terms of later input. There is no evidence against this weak version of immediacy, and such evidence would require the demonstration of deferral of any relevant processing until some critical point (such as a clause boundary or a sentence boundary). To go further in our analysis of immediacy, we need to consider the more general implications of these findings for anaphor resolution in a broader context.

The structural analysis of discourse has identified a number of devices which appear to be necessary for producing a coherent representation of that discourse. One of these is anaphora: Correctly identifying the relations among sets and individuals seems to be vital for both internal coherence and external correspondence. Correct identification is a major component of understanding. This has naturally led to the idea of anaphor resolution as a separately identifiable process in its own right.

It is this assumption which really motivates the functional argument for immediacy in relation to anaphora. Clearly, if anaphor resolution is seen as a major goal, a process in its own right, then it makes sense to suppose that in so far as it is possible, resolution will go on to completion as soon as the appropriate trigger conditions are met. If the resolution turns out to be wrong, then reassignment will have to take place. But such a theory depends upon anaphor resolution being the key to other aspects of interpretation, rather than other processes being the key to anaphor resolution. However, it can be readily argued that there are other candidates for key processes, such as the establishment of causal and temporal links, and the assignment of entities to case- or theta-roles, so the very serious question arises as to which key process takes precedence over any other. This, of course, is the multiple constraint satisfaction problem currently enjoying exploration in connectionism.

The problem can be sensibly approached by looking at immediacy in terms of its functional significance at the *message* level. That is, the processor should try to establish significance at the message level as early as possible, regardless of how this is achieved. Precisely what this means is an interesting question in its own right. But for present purposes, it means that we should be careful about the assumption that early reference resolution is a major goal (let alone *the* major goal). None of this means that resolution processes should be deferred, and it certainly does not mean that processes supporting resolution should not be initiated immediately. Indeed, the processing load arguments for immediacy hold at all levels of processing. One would expect each bit of the input to have an immediate impact, depending upon the current state of the system (e.g. focus and main characterhood in the present context).

These arguments about functionality are important for the immediacy question, because they suggest an account where immediacy of initiation is going to be the rule for all meaningful input triggers, but where what happens next will vary a great deal, depending upon the current system-state, and the impact of any new input. This fits very nicely with the nounphrase/pronoun differences unearthed throughout this paper, and also reflects some existing proposals from Marslen-Wilson et al. (1982) about pronoun resolution. They argue that in a

> distributed processing framework, the lexical information carried by pronouns no longer functions in an all-or-none fashion to preselect candidate antecedents. Rather, the pronoun contributes just one of several inputs to a distributed utterance resolution procedure, whose outcome depends on decision criteria that cannot be satisfied just by information carried by the pronoun alone.

There is an additional problem for the view that reference resolution can be treated as an isolated process, because its outcome may be very different under different circumstances. What precisely is the relation calculated for the following pair, for example?:

John bought the new Hoover vacuum cleaner.

He saw it in the electrical store window.

Was the one which John bought in the window? Who knows. Although we might argue for a default (and argue *about* a default), we could accept a number of possible relations between or among the relata. This is a problem for a theory holding that some processor has a specific goal to resolve references by specifying a semantic relationship between anaphor and antecedent. Such a theory is tantamount to the claim that there is an evidence-accumulating machine (a "specialist") aimed at evaluating the fit of possible relationships over possible antecedent–anaphor pairs, and this requires the specification of the relationship. Rather than postulate a specialist which has to produce a categorical outcome, we might argue for a restriction on possibilities; the linguistic evidence rules out possible relationships, rather than specifying one in particular.

It is possible to describe the various types of anaphoric expressions within this framework. For zero anaphors, the constraints forcing the post-gap material on to the surface subject eliminate the need for any explicit signal. The locus is fixed, and the relation, by default, is restricted to identity of reference. With personal pronouns (at least in sentence initial position), the default locus for testing relations is the thematic subject, but the presence of a pronoun allows a switch to be tested for. The range of possible relations is large, but in most instances amounts to identity of reference, simply because of the kind of potential computable relations that normally hold between antecedent states and what is being added (for some exceptions, note the bonding discussion above). Full nounphrases restrict relations even further, effectively to identity of sense or reference.

Much of this could be accomplished by a pattern-matching mechanism forging initial conceptual links between anaphoric expressions and potential antecedents, serving as loci around which more specific semantic analysis might take place. The attraction of this alternative is that it dispenses with the need for an anaphor-resolving specialist, which itself would require an arbitrary and complex relationship-tester as a component. The pattern-matcher itself could be regarded as real-time, hence "immediate", and could be realised within a connectionist framework. The significance of this formulation is that anaphor resolution becomes just a way of describing part of a more general process of sentence resolution (Marslen-Wilson et al., 1982) which relies upon constraints in the world and in the utterances of the producer to solve the problem of reference to the required degree of accuracy. Oakhill, Garnham, and Vonk (this volume) present arguments which further illustrate the constraint approach, albeit from a different perspective, and Sanford (in press) discusses a similar approach to inference in general.

REFERENCES

Anderson, A., Garrod, S. C., & Sanford, A. J. (1983). The accessibility of pronominal antecedents as a function of episode shifts in a narrative text. *Quarterly Journal of Experimental Psychology*, *35a*, 427–440.

Bard, E. G., Shillcock, R. C., & Altmann, G. T. M. (1988). The recognition of words after their acoustic offsets in spontaneous speech. *Perception and Psychophysics*, *44*, 395–408.

Bierwisch, M. (1983). How on-line is Language Processing? In G. B. Flores d'Arcais & R. J. Jarvella (Eds), *The process of language understanding*. Chichester: John Wiley & Sons.

Broadbent, D. E. (1973). *In defence of empirical psychology*. London: Methuen.

Carroll, P. J. & Slowiaczek, M. L. (1987). Modes and modules: Multiple paths to the language processor. In J. L. Garfield (Ed.), *Modularity in knowledge representation and natural language understanding*. Cambridge, Mass.: MIT Press.

Caramazza, A., Grober, E. H., Garvey, C., & Yates, J. B. (1977). Comprehension of anaphoric pronouns. *Journal of Verbal Learning and Verbal Behavior*, *16*, 601–609.

Dell, G. S., McKoon, G., & Ratcliffe, R. (1983). The activation of antecedent information during the processing of anaphoric reference in reading. *Journal of Verbal Learning and Verbal Behavior*, *22*, 121–132.

Ehrlich, K. (1980). Comprehension of pronouns. *Quarterly Journal of Experimental Psychology*, *32*, 247–255.

Ehrlich, K. & Rayner, K. (1983). Pronoun assignment and semantic integration during reading: Eye movements and immediacy of processing. *Journal of Verbal Learning and Verbal Behavior*, *22*, 75–87.

Garrod, S. C. & Sanford, A. J. (1977). Interpreting anaphoric relations: The integration of semantic information while reading. *Journal of Verbal Learning and Verbal Behavior*, *16*, 77–90.

Garrod, S. C. & Sanford, A. J. (1985). On the real-time character of interpretation during reading. *Language and Cognitive Processes*, *1*, 43–61.
Garrod, S. C. & Sanford, A. J. (1989). Referential processes during reading: Focussing on roles and individuals. In D. A. Balota, G. B. Flores d'Arcais, & K. Rayner (Eds), *Comprehension processes in reading*. Hillsdale, N.J.: Lawrence Erlbaum Associates Inc.
Gernsbacher, M. A. (1989). Mechanisms that improve referential access. *Cognition*, *32*, 99–156.
Grosz, B. (1977). The representation and use of focus in dialog understanding. Technical note 15, SRI International Artificial Intelligence Center.
Grosz, B. & Sidner, C. (1985). Discourse structure and the proper treatment of interruptions. *International Journal of the Conference of Artificial Intelligence*, August, 832–838.
Hirst, W. & Brill, G. A. (1980). Contextual aspects of pronoun assignment. *Journal of Verbal Learning and Verbal Behavior*, *19*, 168–175.
Hudson, S. B., Tannenhaus, M. K., & Dell, G. S. (1986). *Proceedings of the Eighth Annual Conference of the Cognitive Science Society*. Hillsdale, N.J.: Lawrence Erlbaum Associates Inc.
Just, M. A. & Carpenter, P. A. (1980). A theory of reading: From eye fixations to comprehension. *Psychological Review*, *87*, 329–354.
Keenan, J. M., Potts, G. R., Golding, J., & Jennings, T. (in press). Which elaborative inferences are drawn during reading?: A question of methodologies. In D. A. Balota, G. B. Flores d'Arcais, & K. Rayner (Eds), *Comprehension processes in reading*. Hillsdale, N.J.: Lawrence Erlbaum Associates Inc.
Marslen-Wilson, W. D. & Tyler, W. K. (1981). Central processes in speech understanding. In H. C. Longuet-Higgins, J. Lyons, & D. E. Broadbent (Eds), *The psychological mechanisms of language*. London: Royal Society and British Academy.
Marslen-Wilson, W. D. & Tyler, L. K. (1987). Against modularity. In J. L. Garfield (Ed.), *Modularity in knowledge representation and natural language understanding*. Cambridge, Mass.: MIT Press.
Marslen-Wilson, W. D., Levy, E., & Tyler, L. K. (1982). Producing interpretable discourse: The establishment and maintenance of reference. In R. J. Jarvella & W. Klein (Eds), *Speech, place, and action*. Chichester: John Wiley.
McKoon, G. & Ratcliff, R. (1980). The comprehension processes and memory structures involved in anaphoric reference. *Journal of Verbal Learning and Verbal Behavior*, *20*, 204–215.
McKoon, G. & Ratcliff, R. (in press). Textual inferences: Models and measures. In D. A. Balota, G. B. Flores d'Arcais, & K. Rayner (Eds), *Comprehension processes in reading*. Hillsdale, N.J.: Lawrence Erlbaum Associates Inc.
O'Brien, E. J., Duffy, S. A., & Myers, J. L. (1986). Anaphoric inference during reading. *Journal of Experimental Psychology: Learning, Memory and Cognition*, *12*, 346–352.
Sanford, A. J. (1985a). Aspects of pronoun interpretation: Evaluation of search formulations of inference. In G. Rickheit & H. Strohner (Eds), *Inferences in text processing*. Amsterdam: North-Holland.
Sanford, A. J. (1985b). Pronoun reference resolution and the bonding-effect. In G. Hoppenbrouwers, P. Seuren, & A. Weijters (Eds), *Meaning and the lexicon*. Dordrecht: Foris.
Sanford, A. J. (1988). Automatic and incomplete processes in the establishment of local cohesion. Paper presented at the International Workshop on Discourse Processing and the Representation of Coherence, University of Brabant, Tilburg, The Netherlands.
Sanford, A. J. (in press). On the nature of text-driven inference. In D. Balota, G. Flores d'Arcais, & K. Rayner (Eds), *Comprehension processes in reading*. Hillsdale, N.J.: Lawrence Erlbaum Associates Inc.
Sanford, A. J. (in prep.). Local cohesion problems revealed by stylistic phenomena.
Sanford, A. J. & Garrod, S. C. (1981). *Understanding written language*. Chichester: John Wiley.

Sanford, A. J., Garrod, S. C., Lucas, A., & Henderson, R. (1984). Pronouns without antecedents? *Journal of Semantics*, *2*, 303–318.

Sanford, A. J., Moar, K., & Garrod, S. C. (1988). Proper names as controllers of discourse focus. *Language and Speech*, *31*, 43–56.

Seidenberg, M. S., Waters, G. S., Sanders, M., & Langer, P. (1984). Pre- and postlexical loci of contextual effects on word recognition. *Memory and Cognition*, *12*, 315–328.

Shillcock, R. (1982). The on-line resolution of pronominal anaphora. *Language and Speech*, *24*, 4.

Springston, F. (1976). Verb-derived constraints in the comprehension of anaphoric pronouns. Paper presented at the Eastern Psychological Society Association (USA).

Stevenson, R. J. (1986). The time course of pronoun comprehension. *Proceedings of the Eighth Annual Conference of the Cognitive Science Society*. Hillsdale, N.J.: Lawrence Erlbaum Associates Inc.

Stevenson, R. J. & Viktovitch, M. (1986). The comprehension of anaphoric relations. *Language and Speech*, *29*, 335–360.

Swinney, D. A. (1979). Lexical access during sentence comprehension: (Re)consideration of context effects. *Journal of Verbal Learning and Verbal Behavior*, *18*, 545–567.

Tyler, L. K. & Marslen-Wilson, W. D. (1982). Processing utterances in discourse contexts: On-line resolution of anaphors. *Journal of Semantics*, *1*, 297–315.

Vonk, W. (1984). Pronoun comprehension. In A. G. Gale & F. Johnson (Eds), *Theoretical and applied aspects of eye-movement research*. Amsterdam: North-Holland.

Vonk, W. (1985). The immediacy of inferences in the understanding of pronouns. In G. Rickheit & H. Strohner (Eds), *Inferences in text processing*. Amsterdam: North-Holland.

LANGUAGE AND COGNITIVE PROCESSES, 1989, *4*, (3/4) SI 263–286

The On-line Construction of Discourse Models

Jane Oakhill and Alan Garnham
Laboratory of Experimental Psychology, University of Sussex, Brighton, U.K.

Wietske Vonk
Max Planck Institute for Psycholinguistics, and Department of Dutch, University of Nijmegen, Nijmegen, The Netherlands

This paper discusses the on-line interpretation of texts within the framework of the mental models theory of discourse comprehension. In the first part, we discuss some general issues: the nature of the representations constructed, the time course of interpretation within a sentence, and the incremental construction of discourse models. In the second part, we discuss the specific problem of anaphor interpretation. After setting this issue in the general context provided by the first part of the paper, we introduce the notion of an *incomplete* interpretation of a text, which we make explicit in terms of mappings between the roles that people and things play in different sentences of a text, and between roles and names. We use the idea of an incomplete interpretation to explain some discrepancies between experimental findings that we have obtained separately.

INTRODUCTION

Experience suggests that we understand discourse and text as we hear or read it—that interpretation is to a large degree an *on-line* process. This observation raises two crucial questions: What is the nature of the mental representations of the content of text that are constructed and what processes construct them? In this paper, we discuss these questions within

Requests for reprints should be addressed to Jane Oakhill, Laboratory of Experimental Psychology, University of Sussex, Brighton BN1 9QG, U.K.

This research was supported in part by Grant C00232439 to Alan Garnham and Jane Oakhill. Some of our ideas about anaphoric processing were first developed when A.G. and J.O. were visiting fellows at the Max Planck Institute for Psycholinguistics in Nijmegen, in September and October 1986. We would like to thank Gerry Altmann and two anonymous reviewers for their comments on an earlier draft of this paper.

the framework of the mental models theory of text comprehension (see, e.g. Garnham, 1981; 1982a; Johnson-Laird, 1980; 1983). By sketching answers to them we attempt to clarify what is meant by saying that people understand texts as they read them.

The paper is in two parts. In the first we outline the mental models theory and discuss some general issues about text interpretation. We begin by considering the nature of text representations. We then address two questions about on-line interpretation processes. The first concerns the time course of interpretation within a single clause and, in particular, the extent to which interpretation proceeds on a word-by-word basis. In answering this question, we attempt to clarify what is meant by the rather loose claim that interpretation is an on-line process. The second question is how and when are mental models incremented? In the second section of the paper, we focus on the specific question of anaphor interpretation, and we relate the conclusions of the first section to this particular problem of text interpretation. We also introduce the idea of an "incomplete" interpretation of a text—one in which not all of the information in the text is encoded—and show how it explains some conflicting experimental results on anaphor resolution.

THE MENTAL MODELS THEORY: A BRIEF OUTLINE

The mental models theory of text comprehension rests on three crucial assumptions. First, mental models are representations of part of the real or an imaginary world, and not representations of the linguistic structure of texts. Secondly, mental models are dynamic representations that are constructed incrementally, with the model constructed so far providing part of the context for interpreting the current clause. The information in the current clause is used to update the model and, hence, to change the context (Isard, 1975). Thirdly, the model corresponding to a particular text contains tokens standing for a limited set of entities and, therefore, severely restricts the set of possible referents for expressions in the current clause.

The mental models theory is a psycholinguistic theory, which attempts to characterise the mental representations and processes that contribute to text comprehension. However, although the theory's primary motivation is psychological, its central tenets are closely related to those in theories of discourse representation from formal semantics (e.g. Kamp, 1981; Seuren, 1985) and artificial intelligence (e.g. Webber, 1979). The mental models theory also bears similarities to other psychological theories of text comprehension (e.g. van Dijk & Kintsch, 1983). These diverse lines of research have converged on the idea that the mental representation of the content of a text is best thought of as a model of the part of the real or imaginary world that the text is about. Such a representation goes beyond a semantic representation of the text in the narrow Montagovian sense of "semantics", which is now widely accepted within formal linguistics. It is for this reason that representations of the content of texts are referred to as mental models, and not as semantic representations.

ASPECTS OF TEXT REPRESENTATIONS

Mental models are only one part of the mental representation of texts. As a large number of psycholinguistic studies have shown, text representations have (at least) two aspects. The first encodes details of the surface form of a text and, as Jarvella (see Jarvella, 1979, for a summary) and others have shown, this aspect of the representation is short-lived under normal circumstances. The second—the mental model—is a more permanent representation of the content of the text (see, e.g. Garnham, 1987a; Johnson-Laird, 1983). The importance of distinguishing between these two aspects of a text's representation is demonstrated, for example, in the work of Johnson-Laird and his collaborators (see, e.g. Mani & Johnson-Laird, 1982, which is discussed in more detail later).

The nature of the two aspects of text representations remains controversial. Two important questions about the first aspect remain unresolved. First, how superficial is the representation? We do remember some physical attributes of both spoken and written texts, but some authors (e.g. Johnson-Laird, 1983) describe the representation of surface details as "propositional". It may be that there is more than one "superficial" aspect of text representation. Van Dijk and Kintsch (1983), for example, postulate both a representation of surface form and a propositional representation called a *textbase*, in addition to the representation of content, which they call a *situation model*. However, the exact form of the superficial representation will not be discussed in this paper, as it is not crucial to any of our arguments. For present purposes, we simply need to distinguish between a superficial representation of a text and a representation of the content, which we will refer to as a mental model. The second unresolved question is under what circumstances the life of a superficial representation can be extended. Deliberate memorisation is possible, but difficult, as thespians will attest, but memory for exact wording is longer-lived if it affects the message conveyed, as in some jokes (e.g. Keenan, MacWhinney, & Mayhew, 1978). However, this latter effect may be reconstructive, because the crucial details of surface form can be reconstructed from the meaning of the joke.

The model-like nature of text representations is most straightforwardly demonstrated in memory for descriptions of linear arrays. For example,

Barclay (1973) asked subjects either to remember a series of sentences that described an array of five objects, or to use the sentences to figure out the array. In a subsequent recognition memory test, those subjects who had to figure out the array were able to distinguish between sentences that were true or false of the array, but they could not decide which of the true sentences had been presented to them. These results suggest that the subjects had derived an integrated representation of the array that did not retain information about the exact way it was described. The other subjects were reasonably successful at recalling the exact wording of the sentences—people can learn things by heart if they try. Barclay's conclusions were further supported by the work of Potts (e.g. 1972), who measured how long it took people to retrieve information from mental representations of arrays. The further apart the objects were in the array, the quicker judgements were made of whether a test sentence was true or false of the array, even when the linguistic description had only mentioned pairs of objects that were adjacent in the array.

More recent experiments on the encoding of spatial arrays provide further evidence for a difference between superficial representations and mental models of text. These experiments indicate that subjects use the two types of representation for spatial descriptions of different kinds. Some descriptions, such as those used by Barclay (1973), are *determinate*, in that they describe a single spatial layout. However, other descriptions, which may be linguistically very similar, are *indeterminate* (i.e. compatible with more than one spatial layout). For example, given the description:

The bookshelf is to the right of the chair.
The chair is in front of the table.
The bed is behind the chair.

the bed could be either in front of or behind the table. Mani and Johnson-Laird (1982) compared subjects' recognition memory for determinate and indeterminate descriptions. They found that people were better at remembering the content of determinate descriptions, but better at remembering the exact wording of indeterminate ones. These results suggest that indeterminate descriptions are represented in a superficial form, but that determinate ones are encoded in the form of a mental model that does not retain information about the verbatim form of the original sentences.

Johnson-Laird (1983) assumes that these two forms of representation correspond to two stages in the comprehension process. First, a propositional representation of the text is derived—a relatively superficial representation that encodes, among other things, the order in which things were mentioned, and which is used to resolve some types of anaphora. In the second, optional, stage, a model is constructed in which propositional representations of individual sentences or clauses are integrated into a representation that enables the reader or listener to grasp what Johnson-Laird (1977) termed the *significance* of the text, and to make inferences from it. Sometimes, for example with indeterminate descriptions, it may be unhelpful or even misleading to construct a single model. Instead, it may be better to wait and see if information later in the text resolves the indeterminacy.

In this section, we have argued that there are at least two distinct types of text representation—a superficial representation in which surface features of the text are encoded, and a representation of the meaning, or a mental model. In the remainder of this paper, we will focus on mental models and how they are constructed and what is represented in them.

THE TIME COURSE OF SENTENCE INTERPRETATION

As has already been stated, people have the subjective impression that they understand texts as they read them. However, the import of this feeling is unclear, because introspection is an unreliable indicator of cognitive processing. For example, the feeling that people have of understanding sentences as they read them might be explained by the fact that they recognise, and access the meanings of, the words in them. This alone could be the basis of the feeling that sentences are understood in a cumulative manner. The real semantic work might be done at the end of each clause.

Indeed, a *clausal processing* hypothesis, which claims that a substantial amount of interpretive processing is delayed to clause boundaries, has been proposed, in stronger or weaker forms, by a number of psycholinguists. Proponents of this hypothesis, if they are not merely to dismiss the introspective evidence, must explain it in terms of comparatively low-level processing. An early and influential version of the clausal processing hypothesis was developed by Fodor, Bever, and Garrett (1974). Fodor et al. argued, primarily from the results of click location experiments, that clauses function as perceptual units. Their further assumption that the unit of analysis is the deep structure clause (or sentoid) in the sense of Chomsky (1965) led them to claim that a substantial amount of syntactic and semantic processing is delayed to clause boundaries. Because the surface structure of a sentence is not an accurate guide to its underlying structure, and because meaning is derived directly from underlying structure, at least in the "standard theory" of transformational grammar (Chomsky, 1965), most semantic processing must be delayed until underlying clauses can be reconstructed. As Fodor et al. (1974) point out, this idea is compatible with findings from immediate memory experiments, such as those of Jarvella,

phrase introduce into discourse models is given by Webber (1979). However, there are also various types of retrospective indirect introduction, which can be shown to involve extra processing. For example, parts of already mentioned items may be introduced by bridging inferences (Haviland & Clark, 1974), and items related to mentioned activities may also be introduced (Garnham & Oakhill, 1988; 1989). Garnham and Oakhill suggest that such retrospective construction processes may be more common in the interpretation of real texts than has been previously assumed. For example, they argue that in a passage such as:

At the factory Robbie cans soup.
They come to him along a conveyor belt.

the cans, as opposed to the activity of canning, are only introduced into the mental model when the second sentence is read.

The incremental construction of mental models is also affected by other, more general, factors. Garnham, Oakhill, and Johnson-Laird (1982) suggest two main influences on this construction process—referential continuity and plausibility. A text is referentially continuous to the extent that each of its sentences refers back to things mentioned in the sentence that immediately precedes it. It is plausible to the extent that it describes a sequence of events that its readers can readily make sense of using their knowledge of the world, in the widest sense of that term. These two factors correspond, roughly, to local and global influences on the construction of mental models.

Garnham et al. (1982) criticised an account of the global factors that make texts easy or difficult to understand, one based on the notion of a story grammar. The less controversial part of their argument was that findings cited in support of the "story grammar" theory could partly be explained in terms of the local cohesion of text, to which referential continuity makes an important contribution. The more controversial part was that the global structure that story grammarians discovered in simple stories reflects the structure of what the stories are about, and has nothing to do with the fact that the incidents are related in a text. Garnham (unpublished) generalises this argument to a much wider range of texts. In particular, he argues that providing a taxonomy of *coherence relations* only makes sense if those relations are seen not primarily as holding between parts of a text, but rather as a reflex of the temporal, spatial, causal, intentional, or argumentational structure of what the text is about. We will have little further to say about global aspects of text interpretation in this paper, because it remains unclear, except in very general terms, how knowledge about the world is used in the on-line interpretation of texts. The local aspects of interpretation are, on the other hand, more experimentally tractable, and it is to these that we will now turn.

It is worth emphasising that referential continuity, unlike some other factors that contribute to the local cohesion of texts (see Halliday & Hasan, 1976), has its effect on the construction of mental models and not on the production of a more superficial representation. In the early version of their theory of text processing, Kintsch and van Dijk (1978) argued that referential continuity had its effect at the propositional level. They postulated that selected propositions from the text so far were held in a limited-capacity buffer. When the next chunk of text was processed, the propositions derived from it were compared with those in the buffer. This comparison led to a cohesive link being established if an argument (in the formal logical sense) was shared between two propositions in the buffer. However, Garnham et al. (1982) argued that a theory of this kind can produce incorrect reference assignments and, in the revised version of their model, van Dijk and Kintsch (1983) concede that relations other than argument overlap are important, and that referential links are made at the level of the "situation model".

The effect of referential continuity on the interpretation of texts has been investigated in a series of experiments by Johnson-Laird and his colleagues. Ehrlich and Johnson-Laird (1982) presented descriptions of two-dimensional spatial arrays. To manipulate referential continuity, they varied the order of three sentences that described an array of four objects. In referentially continuous descriptions, each sentence after the first referred to an item mentioned in the previous one. For example:

The knife is in front of the pot.
The pot is to the left of the glass.
The glass is behind the dish.

In a discontinuous description, by contrast, the first and second sentences had no referent in common, and the connection was only established by the third sentence. For example:

The knife is in front of the pot.
The glass is behind the dish.
The pot is to the left of the glass.

Ehrlich and Johnson-Laird found that continuous descriptions were easier to remember than discontinuous ones—subjects more often drew the correct layout in a memory test. They argued that continuous descriptions were easier because the information in each sentence could be immediately incorporated into an integrated model, and the first two sentences did not need to be stored as (separate) partial models or in propositional form. Ehrlich and Johnson-Laird also presented *semi-continuous* descriptions, in which the first and second sentences had a referent in common, but the third sentence had no item in common with the second, though it did refer back to something in the first. Performance on such descriptions was similar to that on continuous descriptions. This finding can be explained by the fact that the third sentence, although discontinuous with the second, refers to an object that is present in the model constructed so far. The information in the third sentence can, therefore, be immediately integrated into the model.

Ehrlich and Johnson-Laird also measured reading times for individual sentences in the descriptions. They found, in particular, that reading times for the last sentences of discontinuous descriptions were very long. This finding is consistent with their interpretation of the results of the memory experiments. When the third sentence of a discontinuous description is read, the information from the first two sentences, which has previously been unconnected, has to be integrated using the information provided in the last, and this integration results in a heavy processing load. Similar effects have been shown by Stenning (1986). He found that, in indeterminate texts, there are large increases in processing time at the point where the indeterminacy is resolved and previously unconnected information can be integrated into a single model.

The effect of referential continuity on the understanding of *narrative* texts has also been investigated. Garnham et al. (1982) presented three types of text: simple stories, and two types of scrambled stories constructed by randomising the order of the sentences in the simple stories. No further changes were made to the simple random versions, but in the "revised random" versions, continuity of reference was restored by, for example, replacing pronouns with full nounphrases, or vice versa, where appropriate. The original narratives were better recalled, and rated as more comprehensible, than the scrambled versions, neither of which described a plausible sequence of events. However, of the two types of random story, the revised ones, which were referentially continuous, were easier. A second experiment tested 7- to 8-year-olds' ability to recall stories of the same three types. Both good and poor comprehenders were better able to recall the original than the randomised stories, but only the good comprehenders benefited from the restoration of referential continuity.

However, as we have already pointed out, the referentially discontinuous texts in the above experiment described a less *plausible* sequence of events than the continuous ones. Black, Freeman, and Johnson-Laird (1986) devised a method of manipulating the plausibility of a text independently of its referential continuity. Using a variant of George Miller's technique for generating approximations to English, they provided a referential skeleton for a text and asked people to complete sentences around that skeleton, allowing them to see a variable number of preceding (completed) sentences. Using these specially constructed passages, Black et al. found that the more plausible a text, the better it was recalled.

However, the differences between the revised and unrevised random versions in the earlier study of Garnham et al. (1982), cannot be explained in terms of plausibility: both relate the *same* sequence of events. The unrevised texts lacked cohesion and often appeared to refer to a greater number of entities than their revised counterparts. Furthermore, the information in the unrevised texts typically was difficult to integrate into a single representation.

In this section, we have considered some of the characteristics of a text that affect how readily a model of it can be constructed, and have argued that a major factor is how easily the referential links in a text can be established.

MENTAL MODELS AND THE INTERPRETATION OF PRONOUNS

We have shown that referential continuity affects the construction of mental models, but have said little about how two expressions are determined to have the same referent. However, it is the complexity of this problem that underlies Garnham et al.'s (1982) argument against an account of referential continuity being established at a superficial level. Anaphoric expressions, such as definite pronouns, refer to something in the mental model of the text so far, yet in *form* they may be very different from the expression that introduced the referent into the model. Furthermore, without the context of the mental model, the referent of a pronoun would be indeterminate. For example, the definite pronoun *it*, could potentially refer indefinitely to many things. But its reference should be restricted to a unique item, given the current model as context. In the rest of this paper, we will focus on the question of how definite pronouns are interpreted on-line.

One important issue that has been only briefly alluded to in the literature on mental models, is whether such models contain a complete encoding of (at least) the information that is explicit in a text. Many psycholinguists, perhaps focusing their attention on the short texts typically used in experiments, assume that all of the explicit information and some of the implicit information in a text typically gets encoded into its mental model. However, our everyday experience and the fact that reading is usually goal-directed suggest otherwise. There are various ways in which a text representation might be, in some sense, "incomplete". For example, Garnham (1982b), in his omission theory of inference making, suggests that even case fillers that are explicit in the text can be left out of its representation if they are highly probable and can readily be inferred from an incomplete representation. Furthermore, research by Vonk and Noordman (in press) suggests that, under some circumstances, inferences that are necessary for a fully coherent representation of a text are not always made.

They gave their subjects passages about topics that were unfamiliar to them. The kind of inference that was investigated can be illustrated by the following example (from a passage about spray cans and the environment). From the sentence *Chlorine compounds are frequently used as propellants, because they do not react with other substances*, one can draw the inference *Propellants must not react with other substances*. The information that had to be inferred was either explicit in the text, preceding the *because* sentence (explicit condition), or was not included at all (implicit condition). Vonk and Noordman reasoned that, if subjects make the necessary inference while reading the text, then they should take longer to read the *because* clauses in the implicit than in the explicit condition. In fact, there was no difference in reading times between the two conditions. However, a difference did appear when the subjects were subsequently asked to verify the inference statements: These verification times were significantly shorter in the explicit than in the implicit condition. This result can be taken as evidence that the inference is not made on-line, but is only made if it is subsequently needed for the verification task.

In the last section of this paper, we will discuss another way in which a person's interpretation of a text may be *incomplete*—the pronouns in it may be only partially interpreted. We will introduce the idea that there are (at least) two aspects of pronoun interpretation: mapping them on to the *name* of, and other previously mentioned facts associated with, the antecedent, and mapping them on to the *role*(*s*) that the character they refer to has in events previously mentioned in the text. Before discussing this idea in more detail, we will consider some more general factors that influence the interpretation of anaphoric expressions.

The On-line Interpretation of Pronouns

Although pronoun interpretation is only one component process of on-line interpretation, it is a central example of the kind of local process whose study is at present relatively tractable. In this section, we will provide a brief outline of the factors that are known to affect the interpretation of pronouns. We will start with a discussion of some more general factors, and will then focus on two aspects (gender cue and "verb bias") that will be crucial to our discussion of "incompleteness" in the next section.

Some definite pronouns in spoken language are interpreted with the aid of deictic gestures, and refer to an element of the (non-linguistic) context. Others—the ones we will be primarily concerned with—are interpreted with reference to the preceding text. These pronouns usually have explicit antecedents with which they agree in number and gender.

There are some syntactic *constraints* on the interpretation of definite pronouns. In particular, a pronoun cannot command its antecedent (Reinhart, 1981), so "he" and "John" cannot be coreferential in:

He hoped that John would win the race.

A number of other factors also influence the interpretation of pronouns, but unlike the syntactic constraints, they specify preferences rather than actually ruling out coreference possibilities, and these preferences can be overridden. However, sentences that conform to these preferences are easier to interpret than ones that do not.

One such factor is the distance between the pronoun and its antecedent—close antecedents are preferred to distant ones. This fact is prima facie puzzling, given that definite pronouns are what Sag and Hankamer (1984) call *model-interpretive* anaphors—they can, at least in principle, take their meaning directly from an element in a mental model without reference to a representation of the expression in the text that introduced the element into the model. There is no reason why mental models should contain information about the order in which possible antecedents occurred in a text. Nevertheless, several experiments suggest that pronouns with distant antecedents are more difficult to understand (e.g. Clark & Sengul, 1979; Daneman & Carpenter, 1980; Ehrlich & Rayner, 1983). Indeed, the effect of the distance between an anaphoric NP and its antecedent can sometimes cause problems in interpreting data from experiments addressed to quite different problems (see the exchange between Clifton & Ferreira and Altmann & Steedman in this volume).

In most of the studies on pronoun interpretation, the distance in words, clauses, or whatever, is not the crucial variable. The nature of the material between anaphor and antecedent is more important (see Garnham, 1987b). In particular, if the intervening material keeps the antecedent in *focus*, a subsequent reference to it is easier to understand because information about the antecedent is likely to have remained in immediate memory (see Garrod & Sanford 1982, for a discussion of the importance of focus in the processing of anaphora). As Kintsch and van Dijk (1978) argue, some items should be held in working memory longer than others, because cues in the intervening sentences indicate that they may be referred to again. Indeed, in Kintsch and van Dijk's model, it is tempting to equate focused items with those in the buffer.

Lesgold, Roth, and Curtis (1979) showed experimentally that distance *per se* did not affect anaphor resolution time. They compared reading times for passages with either zero, two, or four sentences intervening between a full definite nounphrase anaphor and its (topical) antecedent. They found that the interpretation of the anaphor was slowed by intervening material *only* when that material changed the topic (see also Clifton & Ferreira,

1987). Similarly, Whitehead (1982) showed that up to eight sentences between a definite pronoun and its antecedent did not slow resolution time as long as the intervening material maintained the antecedent in focus. By contrast, when there were two or more sentences that shifted the antecedent out of focus, the pronoun was more difficult to understand. Other distance effects can also be explained in terms of backgrounding (e.g. Ehrlich & Rayner, 1983).

There is as yet no fully satisfactory account of how items in a text are maintained in focus, or of how they go in and out of focus (but see, e.g. Bosch, 1988, Grosz, 1981, and Sidner, 1983, for some interesting suggestions). However, a number of factors that affect focusing have been identified. For example, Anderson, Garrod, and Sanford (1984) showed that episode-bound characters, such as waiters in restaurant scenes, go out of focus at episode boundaries, though main characters do not.

Another factor that influences pronoun interpretation is the grammatical position of the antecedent. Antecedents in the subject position in the preceding clause are preferred to direct or indirect objects. For example, Grober, Beardsley, and Caramazza (1978) asked subjects to complete sentence fragments, such as:

John apologised to Bill but he . . .

and found that in the majority of cases, the sentence was completed so that the pronoun referred back to the subject of the first clause (see also Caramazza & Gupta, 1979; Frederiksen, 1981).

There is evidence from a variety of experiments that subjects use cues such as gender and number to identify a pronoun's antecedent. Such cues have been shown to affect antecedent naming and verification times, and times to answer questions and read pronoun-containing clauses (Caramazza, Grober, Garvey, & Yates, 1977; Ehrlich, 1980; Garnham & Oakhill, 1985; Vonk, 1984). Garnham and Oakhill (1985) showed that, in a sentence such as:

Pam lent a pen to Bill, because he wanted to write a letter.

subjects make use of the gender cue, and spend less time reading the "because" clause than in corresponding sentences without a gender cue (Fred lent a pen to Bill . . .). It is not possible to tell from the above experiments, in which the sentences were about people, whether gender has its effect at the level of a superficial representation or at the level of a model-based one. However, we are planning to investigate this question using pronominal references to inanimate objects in languages with non-semantic gender, such as French, German, and Spanish.

Caramazza and his colleagues (e.g. Garvey & Caramazza, 1974; Garvey, Caramazza, & Yates, 1975; Grober et al., 1978) identified a further factor that affects pronoun assignment in sentences that do not contain such syntactic cues. When subjects were asked to complete sentence fragments ending in pronouns with more than one possible antecedent, the choice of antecedent depended on the verb in the preceding clause. In particular, in sentences of the form:

NP1 V-ed . . . NP2, because PRONOUN . . .

whether the pronoun was taken as referring to NP1 or NP2 depended on the verb in the main clause. Verbs such as *sell* and *question* favoured antecedents in the subject position (hereafter called *NP1 verbs*), whereas others (e.g. *punish*, *envy*) favoured antecedents in the object position (*NP2 verbs*). Similarly, in antecedent naming experiments (Caramazza et al., 1977), antecedents that conform to the "bias" of a particular verb are named faster than those that do not. Caramazza explains these results in terms of the *implicit causality* signalled by a verb. For example, if A punishes B, the cause of the action is probably something B has done, rather than something about A, so a following *because* clause will typically refer to B (who will, in a simple active sentence, have been mentioned in the NP2 position). However, a model-based interpretation of this finding is possible and, perhaps, preferable. In giving a reason (in a *because* clause) for an act of punishment, attention is likely to focus on the person who did wrong, usually mentioned in the object position in the main clause. Conversely, the asking of a question is usually explained in terms of the questioner's motives.

Caramazza's findings have implications for the on-line interpretation of pronouns. If subjects access information about the "implicit causality" of a verb as they read a sentence or, in model-based terms, if they make use of their knowledge of the type of situation that the sentence describes, they may use this information to predict which NP will be pronominalised in any second clause. Vonk (1985b) has shown that they do. However, it is unlikely that the verb is the sole determinant of which NP is likely to be the antecedent of a subsequent pronoun, Indeed, some of Oakhill and Garnham's unpublished data shows that, with verbs of transfer such as *sell* and *give*, the nature of the object transferred also influences the choice of antecedent in a sentence completion task. This finding favours a model-based interpretation of verb bias, rather than one that focuses on the verb alone.

What Information gets into the Model? "Incomplete Interpretations"

So far, we have considered a number of factors that affect the interpretation of pronouns, without worrying about whether pronouns are always interpreted, at least by the end of their clause. However, as we mentioned earlier, a theory of on-line interpretation must take seriously the question of the conditions under which explicit or implicit information in a text is encoded into its mental representation. In the final section of this paper, we will consider the possibility that pronouns are often only partially interpreted.

We have all had the experience of reading texts that have so many protagonists that it becomes very difficult to keep track of their names, and their relationships to one another (certain Russian novels, and some newspaper articles, for example). Indeed, even in quite a simple text, we may forget the name of one or more of the main characters. However, as we read through such a text, we feel that we know what is happening. We would not say that we fail to understand the text in any important respect. One reason why we lose track of names is that characters are not referred to by name each time they engage in some action. Many anaphoric references use nounphrases, pronouns, or null elements. However, if these anaphors were resolved and linked to characters' names, these names should be readily available. How can we "understand" a text without performing this mapping?

In one sense we can understand a text, locally at least, in terms of the protagonists' roles and the interactions of these roles. A concrete example illustrates this point. In the sentence:

Tom confessed to Sam because he wanted a reduced sentence.

the verb *confess* carries with it two roles: confessor and confessee. Likewise, the verb *want* has two roles, the desirer and the thing desired. The sentence therefore describes one action of confessing and one state of wanting with four NPs denoting role fillers *Tom*, *Sam*, *he*, and *a reduced sentence*. One part of understanding this sentence is to decide that the person who takes the role of confessor is the same person who wants the reduced sentence. Another part is deciding that the name of that person is Tom. (In a corresponding sentence with a gender cue, these two decisions could be made independently of one another.) The first decision is, in many circumstances, the more important one. When the sentence is presented out of context, for example, the names *Tom* and *Sam* are more or less meaningless labels for two unknown people. To grasp the import of the sentence, it is more important to realise that someone was confessing to try to get his sentence reduced than to realise that that person was called Tom or that he was confessing to someone called Sam. There are separate questions about how these two types of mapping affect the on-line processing, and the representation, of the text. But here, we will focus on the issue of representation.

Someone reading this sentence out of context might construct a mental representation of two people, called Tom and Sam, and the fact that one of those people confessed to the other, with the one wanting a reduced sentence being the confessor. However, the representation may not encode any connection between the roles that the people played and the names. Another possibility, though a less plausible one, is a representation of someone called Tom confessing to someone called Sam with one of the two wanting a reduced sentence, but with no indication of whether the confessor or the confessee wanted a reduced sentence. We will term such representations "incomplete" models of the text, though we will be particularly concerned with representations in which roles are linked but in which the role fillers are not linked to names or other descriptions of the persons or objects who fill those roles. Because characters always have roles in the events in which they participate, these roles should always be available, and it should always be possible to construct representations in which at least the roles are linked. Furthermore, in many circumstances, such representations are sufficient for understanding. When a character or an object is subsequently mentioned, whether by name or anaphorically, context will usually allow the identification of that person or thing in its current role with something that filled other roles earlier in the text. Hobbs (e.g. 1978) argues that coreference is often established as a by-product of establishing cohesion. What we are claiming is that coreferentiality is often not encoded at all.

One could, of course, understand texts more completely by making sure that the new information that each referring expression—and the clause containing it—provided about the expression's referent, was linked with all the previously established facts about that referent. However, this strategy might produce very heavy processing loads in the understanding of complex narratives. We do not need to encode everything we are told about a character or to remember the name of every minor character. Only sometimes does comprehension demand that such encoding takes place. This idea that comprehension *requires* a particular type of processing is more readily applicable to psycholinguistic experiments, with their relatively clear task demands, than to reading for pleasure, but we hope, in further work, to establish links between experimental tasks and "tasks" that people set themselves in ordinary reading.

The distinction between complete and incomplete representations helps to explain several of our experimental findings on the on-line interpretation of anaphors, and why superficially similar experiments (Garnham & Oakhill, 1985; Vonk, 1984; 1985a,b) produced different results. We will first sketch these findings, and then show how the distinction helps to explain them.

As we mentioned above, Garnham and Oakhill (1985) showed that subjects make use of gender cue information to speed up their reading of the *because* clause, when processing sentences such as:

Pam lent a pen to Bill, because he wanted to write a letter.

However, another manipulation in the same experiment, congruity of the actual referent of the pronoun with the verb's bias (in the sense of Caramazza), did not have a *general* effect on reading times: A completion that made the pronoun consistent with the bias only reduced reading times when there was also a gender cue to the pronoun's antecedent. In this experiment, the effects of verb bias and congruity were examined only in a *post hoc* analysis: The materials were not specifically constructed to test hypotheses about verb bias.

In two further experiments, Garnham and Oakhill used materials that were balanced for bias and congruity. For each sentence in which the interpretation of the pronoun was consistent with the bias of the verb, there was a closely matched sentence in which it was inconsistent. For example:

Max confessed to Bill because he wanted a reduced sentence.
Max confessed to Bill because he offered a reduced sentence.

Polly punished Pam because she was very annoying.
Polly punished Pam because she was very annoyed.

There were two versions of each sentence, one in which the two NPs referred to people of the same sex and one in which they referred to people of different sexes. The sentences were presented in two parts, with a break after the word *because*. The sentences were broken there so that subjects knew that a subordinate clause would follow. Such knowledge should encourage "predictive" computation of which NP is likely to be pronominalised. In one experiment, the subjects answered a yes/no question that required them to resolve the pronoun, and in the other experiment the subjects had to indicate which of the two people fitted the description in the second clause of the sentence. This name selection task also required pronoun resolution. Both experiments used the self-paced reading technique. The results were remarkably clear-cut for both of the tasks. There were effects of gender cue on the second-clause reading times, and on the question-answering/name selection times. These effects were highly significant both by subjects and by materials. However, there was little evidence that processing was facilitated when the position of the antecedent was congruent with the bias of the verb. The only effect of congruity was on second-clause reading times when the task was question-answering, but it was significant only by subjects.

These results are puzzling because in a series of experiments using similar materials, Vonk (1984; 1985a,b) has shown effects of congruity but not of gender cue on reading times, and effects of both congruity and gender cue on verification and naming latencies. How can we reconcile these results?

We believe that the links subjects make between names and roles depend on how they perceive their task. When sentences are presented out of context, the names of the people mentioned in them appear arbitrary and uninteresting. It is more important to realise that someone confessed because they (and not the person they were confessing to) wanted a reduced sentence, than to remember that the person's name was Max. Mappings between roles in different clauses are more important than mappings between roles and names.

Vonk's experiments usually contained a large number of filler items. These fillers were difficult, and were intended to distract attention from the passages containing pronouns. An example of such a filler is:

Mary had finished the soup before Anna came to the table.
(Statement for verification: Anna was eating first.)

Vonk's subjects probably did not "see" their task as working out the names of the people that the pronouns referred to, so that they could answer the appropriate "who did what" question. In these circumstances, in which subjects are not "preparing" answers to questions about pronouns' antecedents, they may perform role-to-role mapping, but not role-to-name mapping. Congruity with verb bias should aid role mapping, because a verb's bias generates predictions about which role in the main clause should map on to the role filled by the pronoun in the subordinate clause. For example, with *confess to*, an NP1 verb, a *because* clause will probably give more information about the confessor. If this expectation is not fulfilled, subjects will be slowed in their interpretation of the subordinate clause. Thus, bias works by "suggesting" which of two *roles* will subsequently be pronominalised.

In Garnham and Oakhill's experiments, where there were strong effects of gender cue on reading times, but only unreliable effects of congruity, the need to resolve the pronouns was made apparent to the subjects: either there were no filler passages, or the fillers also required pronoun resolution. Thus, role mapping alone would not have enabled the subjects to answer the questions efficiently, because they were asked if a predicate applied to a named person. The task required role-to-name mapping, and gender cue is an obvious and very reliable cue to such mapping when it is available. So it is not surprising that subjects picked up on it.

The difference in findings with respect to the congruity effect between Garnham and Oakhill's and Vonk's experiments may also be attributable to the sometimes obscure relation between the events described in Garnham and Oakhill's main clauses and the reasons given for them in the *because* clauses. For example:

Julie blamed Trudy because she had discovered some relevant evidence;

is much less straightforward than:

Harry won the money from Albert because he played skillfully (Vonk, 1985a).

The extra "inferencing" that is needed to check that a pronoun assignment leads to a plausible interpretation, at least in some of Garnham and Oakhill's materials, may have obscured any effects of congruity.

Further support for our account comes from the fact that effects of gender cue are invariably found on question-answering and verification times and on referent naming times (e.g. Caramazza et al., 1977; Ehrlich, 1980; Garnham & Oakhill, 1985; Vonk, 1985b), where role-to-name mapping is needed to perform the task. When there is also an effect of gender cue on reading time, it may be that role-to-name mapping is only partly completed during reading. When there is no effect of gender cue on reading times, but only on question-answering times, role-to-name mapping may only be occurring when the question is presented. However, there are other reasons why gender cue might affect question-answering times, even if role-to-name mapping has already occurred. Information such as gender may make the representation of two people more distinct and, therefore, affect how readily information can be accessed. In addition, when subjects have to answer a question they may recheck their initial assignment, a process that may be facilitated by a gender cue (see Garnham & Oakhill, 1985).

FINAL REMARKS

In this paper, we have considered several aspects of text interpretation, and discussed the sense in which they are carried out on-line. In the last part of the paper we have focused, in particular, on aspects of processing that one might expect to be carried out on-line but which often are not, such as the linking of the referents of pronouns with their previously mentioned names. Garnham and Oakhill (1989) have argued that there are other aspects of processing that one might *not* expect to be carried out on-line, but which are. One obvious example is that there are types of reading (e.g. study reading) in which people make more inferences than are strictly necessary for understanding a text. However, Garnham and Oakhill focused on a different type of example—processes that might be predicted on *a priori* grounds not to be part of ordinary text comprehension, but which clearly are, such as the interpreting of a pronominal anaphor when its antecedent has been introduced only implicitly, for example by the use of a verb, as in:

> I drink very little and I give it up completely during Lent every year (from "A Life in the Day" of Kenneth Baker, *Sunday Times Magazine*, 1 November 1987).

Intuitions about how people understand text, which are often informed—too strongly it seems—by linguistic and psycholinguistic theories, lead psycholinguists astray. If they are to obtain a clearer picture of the facts, and thus develop more adequate theoretical descriptions of language processing, they will need to carry out more detailed empirical investigations of how language is really processed.

REFERENCES

Altmann, G. T. M. & Steedman, M. (1988). Interaction with context during human sentence processing. *Cognition*, *30*, 191–238.

Anderson, A., Garrod, S. C., & Sanford, A. J. (1984). The accessibility of pronominal antecedents as a function of episode shifts in narrative text. *Quarterly Journal of Experimental Psychology*, *35A*, 427–440.

Barclay, J. R. (1973). The role of comprehension in remembering sentences. *Cognitive Psychology*, *4*, 229–254.

Black, A., Freeman, P., & Johnson-Laird, P. N. (1986). Plausibility and the comprehension of text. *British Journal of Psychology*, *77*, 51–62.

Bosch, P. (1988). Representing and accessing focused referents. *Language and Cognitive Processes*, *3*, 207–231.

Caramazza, A. & Gupta, S. (1979). The role of topicalisation, parallel function, and verb semantics in the interpretation of pronouns. *Linguistics*, *17*, 497–518.

Caramazza, A., Grober, E. H., Garvey, C., & Yates, J. (1977). Comprehension of anaphoric pronouns. *Journal of Verbal Learning and Verbal Behavior*, *16*, 601–609.

Chomsky, N. (1965). *Aspects of the theory of syntax*. Cambridge, Mass.: MIT Press.

Clark, H. H. & Sengul, C. J. (1979). In search of referents for noun phrases and pronouns. *Memory and Cognition*, *7*, 35–41.

Clifton, C. & Ferreira, F. (1987). Discourse structure and anaphora: Some experimental results. In M. Coltheart (Ed.), *Attention and performance XII: The psychology of reading*. London: Lawrence Erlbaum Associates Ltd.

Daneman, M. & Carpenter, P. A. (1980). Individual differences in working memory and reading. *Journal of Verbal Learning and Verbal Behavior*, *19*, 450–466.

Dell, G. S., McKoon, G., & Ratcliff, R. (1983). The activation of antecedent information during the processing of anaphoric reference in reading. *Journal of Verbal Learning and Verbal Behavior*, *22*, 121–132.

van Dijk, T. A. & Kintsch, W. (1983). *Strategies of discourse comprehension*. London: Academic Press.

Ehrlich, K. (1980). Comprehension of pronouns. *Quarterly Journal of Experimental Psychology*, *32*, 247–255.

Ehrlich, K. & Johnson-Laird, P. N. (1982). Spatial descriptions and referential continuity. *Journal of Verbal Learning and Verbal Behavior, 21*, 296–306.

Ehrlich, K. & Rayner, K. (1983). Pronoun assignment and semantic integration during reading: Eye movements and immediacy of processing. In K. Rayner (Ed.), *Eye movements in reading: Perceptual and language processes*. London: Academic Press.

Fodor, J. A., Bever, T. G., & Garrett, M. F. (1974). *The psychology of language*. New York: McGraw-Hill.

Frederiksen, J. R. (1981). Understanding anaphora: Rules used by readers in assigning pronominal referents. *Discourse Processes, 4*, 323–347.

Garnham, A. (1981). Mental models as representation of text. *Memory and Cognition, 9*, 560–565.

Garnham, A. (1982a). *On-line construction of representations of the content of texts*. Bloomington, Ind.: Indiana University Linguistics Club.

Garnham, A. (1982b). Testing psychological theories about inference making. *Memory and Cognition, 10*, 341–349.

Garnham, A. (1987a). *Mental models as representations of discourse and text*. Chichester: Ellis Horwood.

Garnham, A. (1987b). Understanding anaphora. In A. W. Ellis (Ed.), *Progress in the psychology of language*, Vol. 3. London: Lawrence Erlbaum Associates Ltd.

Garnham, A. (unpublished). What the mental models theory might say about text coherence. Laboratory of Experimental Psychology, University of Sussex.

Garnham, A. & Oakhill, J. V. (1985). On-line resolution of anaphoric pronouns: Effects of inference making and verb semantics. *British Journal of Psychology, 76*, 385–393.

Garnham, A. & Oakhill, J. V. (1988). "Anaphoric Islands" revisited. *Quarterly Journal of Experimental Psychology, 40A*, 719–735.

Garnham, A. & Oakhill, J. V. (1989). The everyday use of anaphoric expressions: Implications for the "mental models" theory of text comprehension. In N. E. Sharkey (Ed.), *Modelling cognition: An annual review of cognitive science*, Vol. 1. Norwood, N.J.: Ablex.

Garnham, A., Oakhill, J. V., & Johnson-Laird, P. N. (1982). Referential continuity and the coherence of discourse. *Cognition, 11*, 29–46.

Garrod, S. C. & Sanford, A. J. (1982). The mental representation of discourse in a focussed memory system: Implications for the interpretation of anaphoric noun phrases. *Journal of Semantics, 1*, 21–41.

Garvey, C. & Caramazza, A. (1974). Implicit causality in verbs. *Linguistic Inquiry, 4*, 459–464.

Garvey, C., Caramazza, A., & Yates, J. (1975). Factors influencing assignment of pronoun antecedents. *Cognition, 6*, 117–133.

Green, D. W., Mitchell, D. C., & Hammond, E. J. (1981). The scheduling of text integration processes in reading. *Quarterly Journal of Experimental Psychology, 33A*, 455–464.

Grober, E. H., Beardsley, W., & Caramazza, A. (1978). Parallel function in pronoun assignment. *Cognition, 6*, 117–133.

Grosz, B. (1981). Focusing and description in natural language dialogues. In A. K. Joshi, B. L. Webber, & I. A. Sag (Eds), *Elements of discourse understanding*. Cambridge: Cambridge University Press.

Halliday, M. A. K. & Hasan, R. Q. (1976). *Cohesion in English*. London: Longman.

Haviland, S. E. & Clark, H. H. (1974). What's new? Acquiring new information as a process in comprehension. *Journal of Verbal Learning and Verbal Behavior, 13*, 512–521.

Hobbs, J. R. (1978). Coherence and coreference. *Cognitive Science, 3*, 67–90.

Isard, S. D. (1975). Changing the context. In E. L. Keenan (Ed.), *Formal semantics of natural language*. Cambridge: Cambridge University Press.

Jarvella, R. J. (1979). Immediate memory and discourse processing. In G. H. Bower (Ed.), *The psychology of learning and motivation*, Vol. 13. London: Academic Press.

Johnson-Laird, P. N. (1977). Psycholinguistics without linguistics. In N. S. Sutherland (Ed.), *Tutorial essays in psychology*, Vol. 1. Hillsdale, N.J.: Lawrence Erlbaum Associates Inc.

Johnson-Laird, P. N. (1980). Mental models in cognitive science. *Cognitive Science*, *4*, 71–115.

Johnson-Laird, P. N. (1983). *Mental models*. Cambridge: Cambridge University Press.

Kamp, H. (1981). A theory of truth and semantic representation. In J. Groenendijk, T. Janssen, & M. Stokhof (Eds), *Formal methods in the study of language*. Amsterdam: Mathematical Centre Tracts.

Keenan, J. N., MacWhinney, B., & Mayhew, D. (1978). Pragmatics in memory: A study of natural conversation. *Journal of Verbal Learning and Verbal Behavior*, *16*, 549–560.

Kintsch, W. & van Dijk, T. A. (1978). Toward a model of text comprehension and production. *Psychological Review*, *85*, 363–394.

Lesgold, A., Roth, S., & Curtis, M. (1979). Foregrounding effects in discourse comprehension. *Journal of Verbal Learning and Verbal Behavior*, *18*, 291–308.

Mani, K. & Johnson-Laird, P. N. (1982). The mental representation of spatial descriptions. *Memory and Cognition*, *10*, 181–187.

Marslen-Wilson, W. D. (1973). Linguistic structure and speech shadowing at very short latencies. *Nature*, *224*, 522–523.

Marslen-Wilson, W. D. (1975). Sentence perception as an interactive parallel process. *Science*, *189*, 226–228.

Mitchell, D. C. & Green, D. W. (1978). The effects of context and content on immediate processing in reading. *Quarterly Journal of Experimental Psychology*, *28*, 325–337.

Potts, G. R. (1972). Information processing strategies used in the encoding of linear orderings. *Journal of Verbal Learning and Verbal Behavior*, *11*, 727–740.

Reinhart, T. (1981). *Anaphora and semantic interpretation*. London: Croom Helm.

Sag, I. A. & Hankamer, J. (1984). Toward a theory of anaphoric processing. *Linguistics and Philosophy*, *7*, 325–345.

Seuren, P. A. M. (1985). *Discourse semantics*. Oxford: Basil Blackwell.

Sidner, C. L. (1983). Focusing in the comprehension of definite anaphora. In M. Brady & R. C. Berwick (Eds), *Computational models of discourse*. Cambridge, Mass.: MIT Press.

Steedman, M. (1987). Combinatory grammars and human sentence processing. In J. Garfield (Ed.), *Modularity in knowledge representation and natural language processing*. Cambridge, Mass.: MIT Press.

Stenning, K. (1986). On making models: A study of constructive memory. In T. Myers, K. Brown, & B. McGonigle (Eds), *Reasoning and discourse processes*. London: Academic Press.

Stevenson, R. (1986). The time course of pronoun comprehension. In C. Clifton (Ed.), *Proceedings of the Eighth Annual Conference of the Cognitive Science Society*. Hillsdale, N.J.: Lawrence Erlbaum Associates Inc.

Tanenhaus, M. K., Carlson, G. N., & Seidenberg, M. S. (1985). Do listeners compute linguistic representations? In D. R. Dowty, L. Karttunen, & A. M. Zwicky (Eds), *Natural language parsing*. Cambridge: Cambridge University Press.

Tyler, L. K. & Marslen-Wilson, W. (1982). The resolution of discourse anaphors: Some on-line studies. *Text*, *2*, 263–291.

Vonk, W. (1984). Eye movements during the comprehension of pronouns. In A. G. Gale & F. Johnson (Eds), *Theoretical and applied aspects of eye movement research*. Amsterdam: North-Holland.

Vonk, W. (1985a). The immediacy of inferences in the understanding of pronouns. In G. Rickheit & H. Strohner (Eds), *Inferences in text processing*. Amsterdam: North-Holland.

Vonk, W. (1985b). On the purpose of reading and the immediacy of processing pronouns. In R. Groner, G. W. McConkie, & C. Menz (Eds), *Eye movements and human information processing*. Amsterdam: North-Holland.

Vonk, W. & Noordman, L. G. M. (in press). On the control of inference processes in text understanding. In D. A. Balota, G. B. Flores d'Arcais, & K. Rayner (Eds), *Comprehension processes in reading*. Hillsdale, N.J.: Lawrence Erlbaum Associates Inc.

Webber, B. L. (1979). *A formal approach to discourse anaphora*. New York: Garland.

Whitehead, E. L. (1982). Distance and foregrounding effects on pronoun interpretation. Paper presented to the Experimental Psychology Society, Cambridge, 25–26 March.

LANGUAGE AND COGNITIVE PROCESSES, 1989, *4*, (3/4) SI 287–335

Sentence Comprehension: A Parallel Distributed Processing Approach

J. L. McClelland, Mark St. John, and Roman Taraban
Department of Psychology, Carnegie Mellon University, Pittsburgh, U.S.A.

In this paper, we review basic aspects of conventional approaches to sentence comprehension and point out some of the difficulties faced by models that take these approaches. We then describe an alternative approach, based on the principles of parallel distributed processing, and show how it offers different answers to basic questions about the nature of the language processing mechanism. We describe an illustrative simulation model that captures the key characteristics of the approach, and illustrate how it can cope with the difficulties faced by conventional models. We describe alternative ways of conceptualising basic aspects of language processing within the framework of this approach, consider how it can address several arguments that might be brought to bear against it, and suggest avenues for future development.

INTRODUCTION

What is constructed mentally when we comprehend a sentence? How does this constructive process occur? What role do words play in the construction process? How is the ability to construct such a representation acquired? These are some of the central questions that face any attempt to build a model of language processing.

In this paper, we present a view that differs from most existing notions about the general form of the answers to these questions. We briefly outline what we take to be a generic version of existing notions. Then, we point out some difficulties with these notions. After this, we present a sketch of an alternative that seems to us to have promise to address these problems. We illustrate the alternative by describing a preliminary model,

---

Requests for reprints should be addressed to J. L. McClelland, Department of Psychology, Carnegie Mellon University, Pittsburgh, PA 15213, U.S.A.

The work reported here was supported by NSF Grants BNS 86–09729 and BNS 88–12048, ONR Contracts N00014–86–G–0146 and N00014–86–K–0349, and an NIMH Career Development Award MH00385 to J. L. McClelland.

and consider how it gives different answers to some of the questions raised above, and note how it addresses the problems faced by models that give conventional answers to these questions. We examine some of the arguments, both theoretical and empirical, that have been taken as counting against this sort of alternative, and show that they can in fact be countered. Finally, we describe future directions for the further development of this approach.

CONVENTIONAL APPROACHES TO SENTENCE COMPREHENSION

The comprehension of sentences has been studied extensively, and there are many disparate views about the nature of this process. We do not mean to assert that all previous researchers have adhered to the views we describe in this section. However, quite a bit of work has been done which we believe either tacitly or explicitly adopts the views we describe here. We tend to cite the paper by Fodor and Pylyshyn (1988), because it articulates these views clearly. Where relevant, we will site works that apply these ideas and general texts where they are used or assumed.

What is Constructed when We Comprehend a Sentence?

It is typical to assume that what is constructed is an interconnected set of propositions (e.g. Clark & Clark, 1977), or *propositional representation*. The exact nature of these propositions varies from implementation to implementation, but in general they are taken to be symbolic expressions which have a combinatorial syntax and semantics (Fodor & Pylyshyn, 1988). According to Fodor and Pylyshyn, combinatorial representations are those which exhibit the following properties:

- They may be atomic or molecular expressions.
- If they are molecular, they have constituents which may be either atomic or molecular.
- The semantic content of a molecular expression is a function of the semantic content of each of the parts of the expression and of the organisation of the constituents.

What Role do Words Play in the Comprehension Process?

Implicit in many theories of comprehension is the notion that words have meanings, and that these meanings are the constituents of the meanings of the propositions that are constructed from sentences that contain these words. This view appears to underlie Fodor and Pylyshyn's (1988) principle of *compositionality:* According to this principle, "a word makes approximately the same semantic contribution to the meaning of every sentence in which it occurs." Let us use their example:

1. John loves the girl.
2. The girl loves John.

Fodor and Pylyshyn use these sentences to illustrate what they mean by compositionality. They ask us to consider the meaning of the word "loves" that appears in both of these sentences. They state that the relationship that John is said to bear to the girl in the first sentence is the same relationship that the girl is said to bear to John in the second sentence. This common relationship can be taken to be the meaning of the word "loves", and it occurs in the representation of the meaning of both of these sentences.

How does the Process of Constructing a Representation of the Propositions Underlying a Sentence Occur?

Often, this process is taken to be one of building a structural description using a system of *structure-sensitive* rules. Following Fodor and Pylyshyn, we take *structure-sensitive* to mean that the operations that apply to representations are sensitive to their form and not their content (Fodor & Pylyshyn, 1988). This means, for example, that they care only if some constituent is an item of the right very general type (N, V, NP, VP, etc.).

How is the Ability to Construct a Representation Acquired?

To the extent that we assume that the process of constructing representations of sentences proceeds by the use of structure-sensitive rules to structure the constituent expressions corresponding to words, it seems natural to assume that acquisition amounts to a process of determining what the rules are and what the constituent expressions are that words are used to designate. Researchers interested in acquisition of comprehension skill do not of course assume that the rules that are actually used in comprehension are the same rules that characterise the abstract linguistic competence of the speaker-hearer, but they are rules none the less.

Summary

In brief, the comprehension of sentences is generally taken to be the process whereby a listener uses a set of structure-sensitive rules to construct a propositional representation that constitutes the "meaning" of the sentence. The constituents of this representation include the meanings of the words in the sentence. Following Fodor and Pylyshyn's terminology, we call this view the *classical* view. These authors intend it to be taken as applying more broadly than to just the interpretation of sentences, but they make clear that language is a "paradigm of systematic cognition". We will not have anything to say about its broader applicability; instead, we will focus on the reasons why we feel that it may be worth seeking an alternative framework for addressing the problem of language comprehension.

PROBLEMS FOR THE CLASSICAL VIEW OF SENTENCE COMPREHENSION

Conceptual Guidance and Rule Conflicts

A central problem for the conventional view is the fact that sentence interpretations cannot in general be recovered correctly from structure-sensitive rules alone. Even those who try to go the farthest using structure-sensitive rules (Frazier, 1986; Marcus, 1980) are accurately aware of this problem. The problem is not just a curiosity; it comes up almost every time a prepositional phrase is encountered. Consider, for example:

3. The spy saw the policeman with binoculars.
4. The spy saw the policeman with a revolver.

In (3), most readers interpret the binoculars as the instrument used by the spy in seeing the policeman. In (4), most readers interpret the revolver as a possession of the policeman. This simple example illustrates clearly that it is necessary at a minimum to consider whether the object of the prepositional phrase is a plausible candidate for use as an instrument of the verb. In general, as the next example makes clear, it is also necessary to consider whether in fact the subject of the sentence might be the kind of actor that can use the instrument:

5. The bird saw the birdwatcher with binoculars.

Indeed, Oden (1978) has shown that every constituent of sentences like (3)–(5) can potentially influence the interpretation of the role of the prepositional phrase.

It is widely accepted that the *ultimate* interpretation that a sentence receives is affected by content. Many researchers accept this, but resist the idea that the initial processing of attachment ambiguities is influenced by non-syntactic content. Thus, for example, Frazier (1986) has proposed that initial parsing decisions are based on a purely syntactic mechanism that proposes its preferred alternative for consideration by semantic processes. Later in the paper, we review empirical evidence relevant to this claim. For the moment, we point out a more conceptual problem with it. The difficulty is that the decision as to which interpretation of an ambiguous sentence will win out in the end does not seem in general to be based on a simple yes–no decision about the acceptability of the supposedly syntactically preferred interpretation (Crain & Steedman, 1985). Thus in (5), it is not really plausible to argue that the interpretation in which the bird is using the binoculars as instrument is strictly blocked. For example, we have less difficulty accepting such an interpretation in "The bird saw its prey with binoculars", even if we find it somewhat odd for a bird to be using an instrument. Rather, it appears that the alternative interpretation is simply more plausible in the case of (5). It thus appears that more than one alternative interpretation must be evaluated for plausibility, thereby robbing the parser of any special role in providing a single alternative for consideration.

It is also important to note that it is not simply the case that decisions can either be made by syntactic rule or need to be left for semantic determination. As Marcus (1980) points out, language comprehenders have preferences for syntactic interpretation which must be seen as matters of degree, and therefore they sometimes win and sometimes loose when placed in conflict with other considerations. Very clear examples of this arise in sentences like (6) and (7):

6. We ate some food with some friends that we like.
7. We found a painting in the attic that was covered with cobwebs.

A structure-sensitive rule would allow us to parse (6) correctly, based on the idea that relative clauses should be taken to attach to the immediately preceding nounphrase rather than an earlier one, especially when, as in this case, attachment to the earlier nounphrase would violate the so-called "no-crossover" constraint. However, it is exactly this constraint that is violated in (7), where it is the painting, rather than the attic, which native speakers take to have been covered with cobwebs. Violating this constraint may make the sentence seem a bit awkward, but it does not prevent the cobwebs from attaching to the painting.

Contextual Shading as well as Selection of Word Meaning

The problem of word-meaning indeterminacy also poses a problem for conventional approaches. It is, of course, typical to assume that an individual word can have more than one meaning. The problem of sentence interpretation, then, is seen as one of selecting the right meaning from a set of possible meanings that are stored in a "mental lexicon". One problem with this is the potential combinatorial explosion that can result, as discussed below. Here we focus on a different problem: The problem is that it seems rather limiting to suppose that the range of meanings that a word can have is restricted in advance to the set of known usages of the word. Let us consider some examples:

8. The hostess threw the ball for charity.
9. The slugger hit the ball over the fence.
10. The baby rolled the ball to her daddy.

The distinctions between the meanings of ball as it appears in (8) and (9) seem well enough captured by the idea that the specification of a meaning for this word involves a selection of one of two alternatives, one that means something like "fancy dance" and one that means something like "spherical object". But in (10), it seems that the specification of the ball is somewhat different from the specification that we get from (9). It is possible to assert that here again we are selecting between two alternative meanings—one, let us say, in which the spherical object is smallish, hard and white, and the other in which it is larger, squishier, and probably multicoloured. But taken to its extreme, this view seems to lead to a vast explosion of lexical entries, one for each of the possible balls that we can envisage being implicitly described in a sentence. Is there to be a separate lexical entry for every shade of meaning that can be comprehended, for every word in the language?

A Similar Problem with Roles

A similar problem arises when we attempt to specify the set of thematic roles that are available to be filled by word meanings in the structural description that represents a sentence. In early work on roles (Fillmore, 1968), attempts were made to enumerate the set of roles that constituents could fill. However, this effort quickly ran into the problem that there are a large number of slight distinctions among roles, all of which have interpretive significance. The problem is so bad that many workers have taken the tack of assuming that for each verb there is an idiosyncratic set of roles. This is, of course, not terribly satisfactory either, because this simply obscures the broad commonality that does exist among, for example, the constituents which we would tend to call agents if we did not look too closely.

Implied Constituents

The notion that the representation of a sentence consists of an assemblage of representations of constituents of a sentence fails to provide any direct way of understanding why it is that many sentences convey implied constituents which native speakers do not need to hear mentioned. Thus in 11 and 12,

11. The boy spread the jelly on the bread.
12. The man stirred his coffee.

we can infer a knife and a spoon, respectively. That such inferred constituents are expected to be parts of the representations we form in listening to sentences, is indicated by the fact that we can refer to them as though they have been mentioned. Thus we can say, for example,

13. The boy spread the jelly on the bread.
    The knife was covered with poison.

and we can expect the reader to know that someone is in danger of being poisoned if they eat the sandwich.

Now, typically, it would be conventional to assume either that implied constituents are parts built into the representations of the lexical items (e.g. the knife is built into the representation of the verb *spread*) or that they are inferred by post-processes. However, it is by no means an easy task to decide when something should be built in; nor is it easy to decide when something should be inferred. We do not *always* stir coffee with a spoon, and we do not even *necessarily* spread jelly with a knife; therefore, drawing an inference in an all-or-nothing way can lead to over-commitment. We might draw inferences and assign them strengths, but there is no end to the inferences that we might draw. Should we draw all of them? Where should the line be drawn? These problems have plagued inference-based comprehension programs for years (Schank, 1981).

Combinatorial Explosion or Premature Commitment?

The multiplicity of alternative meanings of words and of possible roles, and the wide range of possible inferences which might follow from each possible combination of roles and meanings, becomes an extremely serious problem when we consider the implications for processing. Famous examples like

14. Time flies like an arrow.

remind us of the potential combinatorial explosion associated with the multiplicity of possible word-meaning and structural possibilities that arise in processing virtually every sentence. Models built in the classical tradition are forced to take one of two approaches to this problem: Either they can create a potentially exponential number of possible interpretations, or they can make an early commitment to pursue only a limited range of alternatives. In the extreme form, a single track is chosen, subject to backtracking if that track turns out to fail.

The Difficulty of Acquisition

As a final note, we remind the reader of the problem of acquisition. Several serious problems face anyone who attempts to build a model of acquisition of the rules and word meanings posited by the classical view:

- The rules are often overridden, as we saw above.
- The correct choice of rules is drastically underdetermined by the evidence available to the child.
- The feedback children receive on the correctness of their constructions is notoriously impoverished.
- A given sentence may have more than one perfectly acceptable interpretation. This makes it hard to know when to reject a rule as wrong or simply not always right.
- Correct performance requires not only the knowledge of the constraints but how much weight each one should be given.
- The child faces a very serious boot-strapping problem in learning to map sentences on to their meanings. This problem is reviewed by Gleitman and Wanner (1982).

These and other problems have led many psycholinguists committed to the view that acquisition involves learning rules to the view that acquisition is impossible. Instead, it has often been proposed that the rules of all languages are innate and that acquisition simply amounts to setting parameters where there are degrees of freedom. It has even been proposed (e.g. Chomsky, 1988) that it is not implausible to imagine that all concepts are innate.

Summary

We do not wish to make light of classical models. Such models do have considerable appeal, and they seem to us to capture approximately some of the general characteristics of natural languages. Indeed, there are regularities in the way we structure sentences which give clues to the ideas we wish these sentences to convey; and there are regularities in the ways in which we use words. These two facts seem consistent with the idea that words have meanings that are parts of the meanings of the sentences that they occur in and that the meanings of the wholes are constructed from these parts by structure-sensitive rules. Fodor and Pylyshyn (1988) are, of course, correct when they point to the productivity and systematicity of language, and it is no mean accomplishment of the classical view that it captures these essential characteristics of natural language.

But it is our view that the classical approach is destined to remain strapped with many, if not all, of the problems listed above. Of course, others have taken a different view, and many proposals have been made for augmenting or tuning classically based models of sentence processing. Thus, for example, we find that many current researchers working within the classical tradition allow lexical information associated with the heads of constituents to be referred to in parsing. Similarly, techniques such as beam search can be used to find a reasonable compromise between the combinatorial explosion that results from computing all possible parses and the premature commitment that arises from computing only one; essentially, one simply computes the best few and hopes that what turns out to be the correct interpretation happens to be among them.

It is, of course, possible that an accumulation of incremental fixes of this kind will ultimately provide an adequate framework for modelling the sentence comprehension process. But our bet is that it will not. Using lexical information associated with heads of constituents does not solve the whole problem of content sensitivity of parsing for reasons we have already tried to make clear, and beam search is just a way of eliminating some, but not all, cases of premature commitment without paying too high a cost in terms of maintaining multiple parses.

Our point is simply this: Models formulated in the classical framework face many serious problems—problems which authors like Fodor and Pylyshyn do not acknowledge when touting the virtues of the classical approach. While we acknowledge the achievements of the classical approach, we simply believe that it makes sense to explore the possibility of an alternative which deals directly with the difficulties that it faces, on the view that such an approach may turn out ultimately to lead to a superior overall account. The rest of this paper is an attempt to give the reader a sense of what this alternative may be like.

A PDP ALTERNATIVE

Denied Presuppositions

The PDP alternative which we will propose denies the point of departure, implicit in classical approaches, is necessary to require information to be displayed in structured form in the representation itself (van Gelder, in press). Rather, we ask only that the representations provide a sufficient basis for performing the task or tasks that are required of them. Thus, representations of sentences are not required to exhibit a specificially propositional format *so long as they can be used to perform the tasks we require*. Similarly, representations of knowledge about how to form representations are not required to take the form of rules *as long as this knowledge allows us to act in lawful ways as the environment demands*, and representations of word-specific knowledge are not required to have any visible internal structure representing the meaning of the word. Indeed, the knowledge of rules and of word-specific information may well be encoded in a densely compiled form, as long as this information can be used effectively to meet the imposed demands.

Nature of the Task

Our first step, then, must be to develop some conception of the nature of the imposed demands. At a general level, we think it is reasonable to think of the sentence comprehension task in the following terms. A sequence of words is presented, and the comprehender must form a representation which allows him to respond correctly when probed in various ways. In general, the probes can take a wide range of different forms, requiring actions, verbal responses, etc. Among the things we would expect is that we would be able to answer various questions using this representation. For example, on apprehending "The man stirred the coffee", we would expect a device that has understood this sentence to be able to give correct answers to many questions: Who did the stirring?, What did he stir?, What did he stir with?, and so on.

Of course, there are other aspects to language processing; for example, in processing language we have expectations for what the next word will be, and we can think of part of the task of language processing as the anticipation of the next word. Recently, Elman (1989) has applied an approach similar to the one we take here to this sequential anticipation task. In this task, listeners learn to construct representations that reflect the purely sequential structure of language. Here we focus on learning to construct representations that reflect the constraints sentences impose on the representations we form, in order to be able to answer simple questions about the events these sentences describe.

Given this conception of comprehension, we will need a model which can actually apprehend sentences and then respond correctly to a set of probes. Because we do not stipulate exactly what form the representations must take, we must rely on the adequacy of the performance of the model to determine if in fact its representations are adequate.

For the purposes of what follows, we will distinguish between the process of comprehension itself—the formation of a representation from a sentence—and the use of this representation to respond appropriately to probes. Our main interest is in the former, but for the reasons just given, the latter must be considered as well, or we have no measure of successful performance.

Constraint Satisfaction Processing

We think of the process of comprehension as a constraint satisfaction process (Rumelhart, Smolensky, McClelland, & Hinton, 1986b). In the comprehension of isolated sentences, there are two sorts of constraints: those imposed by the sequence of words, and those imposed by knowledge about how such sequences are to be interpreted. Both types of constraints are taken to be *graded*. They are assumed to act as forces shaping the formation of a representation, and to have magnitudes which determine their degree of influence. For our purposes, the sequence of words in the sentence can be instantiated as a sequence of patterns of activation over a set of processing units. As each new word comes in, we assume that it is used to update the sentence representation, which is also taken to be a pattern of activation over a set of processing units. In fact, if we consider the process at each time-step, it is useful to view it as a constraint satisfaction process in which there are two inputs: the sentence representation from the previous time-step and the new input. These two inputs are used to produce an updated sentence representation for the next time-step. The knowledge of how this updating is to be performed is stored in the connections that allow these inputs to update the sentence representation.

It may be worth noting that graded constraints can vary in magnitude from those that are so weak that they are very easily overridden to those that are so strong that they are nearly impossible to override even by a conspiracy of other quite strong constraints. Thus the existence of cases in which constraints are not overridden does not argue against the idea that they are graded; it just indicates that sometimes they can be very strong.

After each update of the sentence representation, it can be used to respond to one or more probes. Responding to these probes is also viewed as a constraint satisfaction process, where the goal is to produce externally

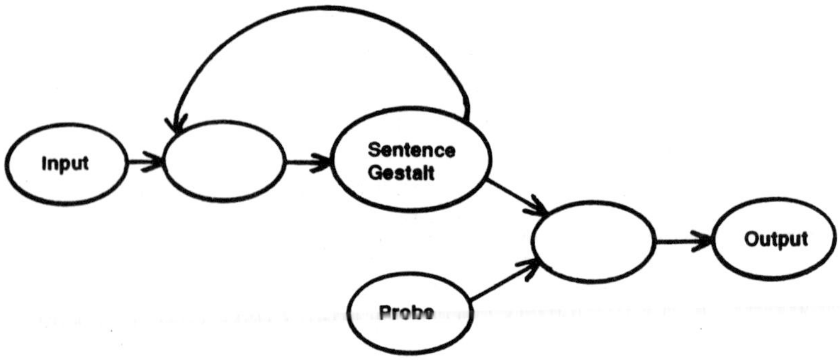

FIG. 1 A sketch of the present conception of the sentence comprehension mechanism. The ovals represent groups of units, and the arrows represent modifiable connections.

specified outputs in response to externally provided probes. There are now three sources of constraint: the sentence representation, the probe, and knowledge about what outputs should be produced for particular sentence/probe combinations. Both the sentence representation and the probe can be instantiated as patterns of activation over processing units, as can the desired outputs; and the knowledge of how to produce these outputs from the corresponding inputs can be encoded in the connections among the processing units.

So far we have outlined a general framework for sentence comprehension and for using the results of comprehension to respond to probes. A sketch of the network that instantiates this framework is shown in Fig. 1. In the figure, the ovals correspond to pools of units and the arrows correspond to connections. There is a pool of units for representing the successive words; a pool of units for representing the evolving sentence representation, or *Sentence Gestalt*; a pool for representing probes; and a pool for representing responses to the probes. The arrows represent connections, from each unit in the pool at the sending end of the arrow to each unit in the pool at the receiving end. The units in the unlabelled pools, which will simply be called "hidden units", serve to allow *combinations* of aspects of the patterns on the input side of these pools to constrain the patterns of activation on the output side.

Learning by Connection Adjustment

Three crucial questions remain. First, what determines the form of the sentence representation itself? Secondly, how is the form of this representation communicated to the inner part of the network? Thirdly, how is the knowledge acquired that governs the construction of the sentence representation from the sequence of words, and the production of appropriate outputs to sentence/probe combinations? The answer to all of these questions is the same: connection strength adjustment through error-correcting learning.

We assume that the output pattern actually generated by the network in response to each probe is compared to the correct output that is provided as part of the environment. The mismatch between the network's actual output and the correct answer is then used as the basis for connection strength adjustment, following the back-propagation learning procedure. This connection adjustment process occurs for connections in both the comprehension network and for connections in the readout network, gradually leading the network to learn both how to represent the information in each sentence and how to use it to respond to each probe.

Note that this connection strength adjustment process cannot actually result in perfect performance, because many of the sentences that the network sees are in fact ambiguous. Furthermore, early on during processing of a particular sentence, before the whole sentence has been presented, the network can only make its best guess as to the answers to certain questions, without any possibility that it can always be right. It turns out that it can be shown that the learning procedure is adjusting the strengths of the connections among the units in the network in the direction of minimising the discrepancy between the activation of each unit and the probability that it should be active, given the input that has been presented up to this point. And, indeed, the activations come gradually to reflect these probabilities reasonably well. In our simulations they tend to gradually approach an equilibrium, in which they jitter about the true probabilities based on the vicissitudes of the most recent set of training examples.

A MODEL ILLUSTRATING THE APPROACH

The model we describe here exemplifies the approach described above. It is in many ways highly simplified. It will not convince the reader that we have already succeeded in providing a complete alternative to conventional approaches. Rather, it provides a concretisation of the general approach as well as an illustration of some of the reasons for its appeal, which we hope will suggest that the further exploration of this new framework is worthwhile. The model is called the Sentence Gestalt or SG model. It is described briefly here (a fuller description is available in St. John & McClelland, in press).

The Environment

The model consists of a network placed in an environment consisting of sentence/event description pairs. The sentences are of but one clause, and they consist of a sequence of stripped-down constituents. Each constituent consists of a single contentive (noun, verb, or adverb) together with a single preposition or the verbal auxiliary element "was". For example, the English sentence "The school girl was kissed by the boy" is reduced to three constituents—"schoolgirl", "was kissed", "by boy". The most complex sentences involved dative passives like "The teacher was given a rose by the bus driver", with additional locative, manner, and/or instrumental prepositional phrases possible, depending on the verb.

The event descriptions are simple too; they consist only of a list of role-filler pairs. For "The schoolgirl was kissed by the boy", the list is: {agent: boy; action: kiss; patient: schoolgirl}. The roles are agent, action, object, recipient, location, manner, instrument, and what might best be called "accompanist" (as in "the bus driver ate the ice-cream with the schoolgirl").

While the sentences and the events they describe are both quite simple, the relationships which hold between them are not. For one thing, words used in a sentence may be ambiguous or vague, as in (15) and (16):

15. The pitcher hit the ball with the bat.
16. The adult ate something.

In both cases, the model is asked to do its best to recover the correct event description. In the latter case, the event description involves a specific adult and a specific something eaten, which may not be uniquely predictable (in the small world of the model, the adult might be a teacher or a bus driver; the something might be soup or a steak). The model must do its best based on the information given.

Constituents may also be left out of sentences, as in (17):

17. The bus driver stirred the coffee.

Here the network is expected to understand that the event being described involved an instrument, which in the case of stirring is always a spoon.

Role assignment is made difficult in two ways. First, both active and passive constructions are used. Though there are semantic constraints that often make a correct interpretation of passives possible, this is not always the case, as in sentences like (18):

18. The teacher was given the rose by the bus driver.

In this and other kinds of cases, the corpus was structured so that the two human participants were equally likely to serve as agent or as recipient, thereby forcing the model to rely on the syntactic cues in the sentence. (Note that the difficulty here is further increased by the fact that the model does not distinguish "gave" from "given". We simply use a single form for each verb throughout, because for most verbs the past and past participle are the same in English.)

The other source of role assignment difficulty arises from the ambiguity of surface role cues. Prepositions and word-order information provide some cues, but these cues are often quite ambiguous as to the roles that they signify. Thus in (19) and (20),

19. The bus driver ate the steak with the teacher.
20. The bus driver ate the steak with the knife.

the semantics of the role-filler must be considered in determining whether the object of the with-phrase is an instrument or an accompanist.

The actual set of sentence–event pairs that the model sees is generated as follows. First, an action is selected at random from a set of possible actions. Then, an agent is selected from a set of possible agents who might perform the action. Following this, an object, an instrument, or indirect object if applicable, and other roles are filled. An illustration is given for the action "eat" in Fig. 2. Note that the selection process is inherently probabilistic, and that there are complex dependencies. Given, for exam-

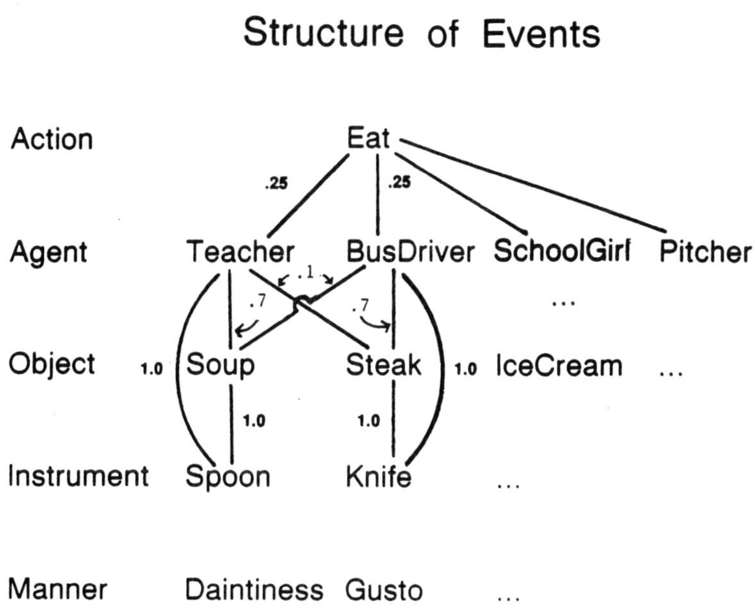

FIG. 2 Structure of the event generator for the action *eat* used in training the SG model.

ple, that the action is eat and the agent is bus driver, the object is probably steak ($P = 0.7$) but may be soup ($P = 0.1$); the instrument depends on the object eaten, the manner on the agent of eating.

This procedure produces an ensemble of event descriptions which are strongly constrained. These constraints can be absolute or *hard*, so that, for example, animal bats do not show up at all as the instruments of hitting; or they may be *soft*, so that, for example, steak is the preferred but not the unique object of eating for the bus driver. Note that the constraints are fairly complex, in that they depend on particular conjunctions of verbs and role fillers. Steak is the preferred food only of the bus driver, the knife is the instrument of eating when the food is steak but not soup, etc.

The assignment of words to events is also probabilistic. Thus, the bus driver in the eating example might be described with the words *bus driver* or with the word *adult*; the steak might be described as *steak* or as *food*; the instrument as *knife* or as *utensil*. Thus, the actual specific participants in the events can only be inferred by using information from context. Sometimes, the sentence contains sufficient information to remove all uncertainty with respect to a particular participant (as in "the bus driver ate the food with the knife"; the food can only be steak), but other times not (as in "the bus driver ate the food"). Even here some answers may be more likely than others, though in some cases there may be at least two equally likely alternatives (in "the adult ate the food", soup and steak are equally likely).

Sometimes, whole constituents are simply left out of sentences describing events in which their referents appear. Thus, the knife can be left out of the sentence on the bus driver eating steak. The model adheres to the conventions that subject and verb are always mentioned (however vaguely), but other constituents may go unmentioned, depending on the specific actions.

The Task and the Interface to the Environment

The model's task is to process the sequence of constituents that represents a particular sentence and, as each constituent comes in, to update a representation which is intended to allow it to respond to probes querying its comprehension of the event described by the sentence. To assess the model's performance, we can actually probe it after each constituent has been processed.

Each input constituent consists of a content word and possibly a preposition or "was". Each such word is represented by a single unit. Thus there is a unit for "bat" (regardless of meaning), a unit for "gave", a unit for "adult", a unit for "was", "with", "by", etc. Altogether, there were units for 58 words.

A similar localist representation scheme was also used for probes and responses. Responding to a probe can be thought of as completion: filling in a member of a role–filler pair, when probed with either the role or the filler. Note that the fillers are now concepts rather than words, and that fillers in particular events are always specific concepts, rather than superordinate categories. There were a total of 45 concept units, covering actions, manners, and noun-concepts, including persons, places, and things.

Given this scheme, we often find sentence–event pairs where a word is used (say "bat") that corresponds to two distinct concepts (baseball bat/flying bat). As in real languages, it is not the word itself which tells us which of the concepts is intended; the correct answer must be derived by making use of cues provided by the context in which the word occurs.

In some simulations using the model, St. John and McClelland included a few units representing superordinate concepts in addition to the units for specific concepts. In this case, a concept is represented not by a single unit, but by a set of units representing the specific concept and its superordinate features. Thus, for example, there are units for person, for male and female, for adult and child. The bus driver is an adult male and the teacher is an adult female, etc.

In considering the task of the network, it is worth noting that there is not always a single right answer. Indeed, early on in a sentence, just after the presentation of the first constituent, there is a great deal of indeterminacy; the initial nounphrase need not even describe the agent of the sentence. Nevertheless, it is possible to view each constituent, as it is presented, as imposing constraints on the possible event-descriptions that might be correct. In this context, we can characterise the task of the network as being one of indicating, in response to each probe, what the range of possibilities might be, and of giving an indication, by the activations that it assigns to the completions of the various probes, of its estimate of the probability associated with each.

Network Architecture and Processing

The architecture of the network, as shown in Fig. 1, can be treated as consisting of two basic parts. One part is the actual comprehension mechanism itself, the part that reads in the constituents sequentially and updates the sentence representation; the other part is the output mechanism, that performs the probe completion task. The sentence gestalt units are in both parts, and form the interface between the two.

Processing occurs as follows. At the beginning of a sentence, the pattern of activation on the sentence gestalt units is set to all 0's, and the unit or units representing the first input constituent in the input pool are turned on. Activation feeds from the SG units (via the feedback loop) and the input units to the hidden units in the comprehension part of the system, and from these it feeds on again to the SG units, where the initial SG representation of all 0's is replaced by a new pattern of activation reflecting the influence of the first constituent of the sentence. This representation is now part of the input at the next time-step, when the next constituent is input in place of the first. This process continues to the end of the sentence.

Each of the units inside the network is a simple logistic processing unit; that is, the activation that a unit takes on is equal to the logistic function of its net input, where the net input is simply the sum over all connections coming to the unit of the input on each connection. The input on each connection is just the product of the activation of the sending unit at the end of the connection × the weight on the connection. Activations range from 0 to 1; weights are floating-point numbers initialised in a range between +/− 0.3, and adjusted according to the learning procedure described below.

Processing in the output network is also quite simple, and can occur at any point during or after the presentation of a sentence. The two inputs to the output network are the pattern on the SG units and the pattern on the probe units. This pattern consists of a single unit on, representing either a queried role or the queried filler. Activation feeds forward from the SG units and the probe input units to a set of hidden units and then from these to the probe output units, where the pattern is taken to represent the network's response to the probe.

Learning

Learning in the network occurs via the back-propagation learning procedure. When a probe is presented, the response to the probe can be compared to the response that would be correct for the current sentence–event pair, and a measure of error called cross-entropy can be computed. Back-propagation is used to adjust the connection strengths so as to minimise this measure (see St. John & McClelland, in press, for details).

It is important to note that the minima in this measure occur at those points where the activations of units in particular situations represent the probabilities that the units should be on in these situations. We think of the activations of the output units as representing the probability that the unit should be on. The training procedure can be seen as trying to find an ensemble of connection weight values that allow the network to get these probabilities correct.

In training the network, we followed the procedure of presenting a complete set of probes after the presentation of each constituent of each of a large number of training sentences. The complete set of probes consisted of a role probe and a filler probe for each role–filler pair in the event description for the sentence–event pair currently being processed.

This training procedure was intended to approximate the situation in which a language learner has just witnessed an event, so that he already has a description of it; and hears a sentence spoken about that event. We imagine that as the learner processes the sentence, he is continually (implicitly) asking himself, "how well does the machinery that I have for language comprehension allow me to describe correctly the event I have just witnessed". The question is posed in the form of the set of probes, and the answer is the set of responses to the probes. The mismatch between the responses to the probes and the correct responses dictated by the description then serves as the basis for learning.

This procedure has two interesting characteristics. First, it does not provide the learner with any specific alignment between the constituents of the sentence and the corresponding constituents of the event description. Thus it forces the network to discover the solution to the bootstrapping problem mentioned earlier for itself. Secondly, the procedure requires the network to do its best at each time-step to predict all of the constituents of the event from what is has seen so far. If learning reaches the global minimum in the error measure described above, then the activations will always reflect the best achievable estimates of the probabilities that the units should be on at each point in the processing of every sentence.

Several different runs of the model have been undertaken. The one from which we report results here involved 630,000 training trials, each involving the presentation of an independently generated sentence–event pair. Some sentence–event pairs occur often, whereas others occur extremely rarely. The low-frequency items also involve relatively atypical role–fillers, and it is the process of learning from rare errors to overcome the tendency to give the most typical answer that makes learning take such a very long time. A fuller discussion of the time-course of acquisition is provided by St. John and McClelland (in press).

Results

After training, the model was first tested on a set of 55 randomly generated sentences that are unambiguous given the hard constraints built into the corpus. That is, although each of these sentences actually contained at least one ambiguous word or unspecified filler, the hard constraints built into the corpus were enough to allow it to respond correctly to all probes. For example, "The teacher ate the soup with the utensil" is unambiguous because the only utensil that could be used for eating soup is a spoon. After the presentation of each sentence, we tested the full set of probes for the role–filler pairs in the event described by the sentence. The network activated all of the correct output units more strongly than any output units it should not have activated on more than 99% of the probes.

The network was also tested specifically on several sets of sentences designed to assess its ability to handle different aspects of the comprehension task. The tasks are broken down into two broad categories, having to do with role assignment on the one hand and specification of the identity of role fillers on the other. With regard to role assignment, St. John and McClelland probed with fillers from the events described by test sentences and examined the roles assigned to these fillers. The use of both syntactic and semantic constraints was examined. Thus, for a sentence like "The schoolgirl stirred the kool-aid with the spoon", semantic constraints must be used to determine that the spoon is an instrument, and not, for example, an accompanist of the schoolgirl (cf. "The schoolgirl stirred the kool-aid with the teacher"). In other sentences, syntactic constraints were examined. Thus, for the sentence "The bus driver was given the rose by the teacher", the order of the constituents, together with the presence of the passive marker and the preposition "by", are necessary to determine the correct role assignments of "bus driver" and "teacher", because either could play the role of agent or recipient. In tests involving five sentences of each of four types (active, passive, crossed with a need to rely on semantic or syntactic constraints), all of the fillers were assigned to the correct roles. The top part of Fig. 3 illustrates a passive syntactic role assignment case. Examples illustrating the other kinds of cases may be found in St. John and McClelland (in press).

For the specification fillers, three distinct variants were considered: The first is the straightforward resolution of word ambiguity, in which the network is asked simply to choose between two alternative and quite distinct interpretations of the fillers of one or more roles. For example, in "The pitcher hit the bat with the bat", the subject, object, and prepositional phrase object are all ambiguous words in the corpus, but each is sufficiently constrained by the context, given the training experience of the model, to yield a unique interpretation. The middle portion of Fig. 3 illustrates what happens in this case. When we probe for the agent, the model activates the concept unit corresponding to the baseball-playing pitcher; when we probe for the patient, it activates the concept unit corresponding to the flying bat; and when we probe for the instrument, it activates the baseball bat. This occurs because, in training, people but not pitchers occur as agents of hitting, flying bats but not baseball bats occur as patients of hitting, and baseball bats but not flying bats occur as instruments of hitting.

The second variant is concept instantiation. The sentence "The teacher kissed someone" illustrates a particularly interesting case, because the someone cannot be resolved uniquely given the context but can be resolved

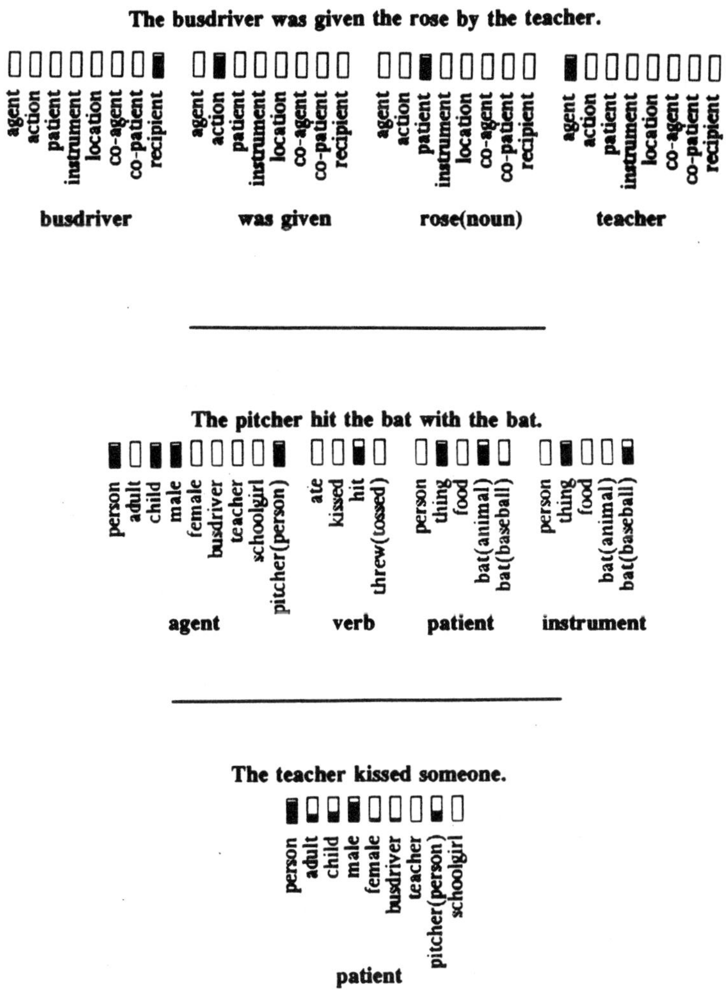

FIG. 3 Activations of relevant output units in response to the indicated probes after presentation of the sentences shown.

partially. In the experience of the network, the teacher is a female, and the event generator is constrained so that kissing is always a heterosexual activity; but the teacher is just as likely to kiss the pitcher (a child) or the bus driver (an adult). Thus we would expect the model to be able to identify the someone as a male but not to determine his age or whether specifically it was the pitcher or the bus driver. In the bottom panel of Fig. 3, the output produced in response to a probe for the patient in "the teacher kissed someone" is shown, where the context partially specifies the filler. Here we can see that the sex, but not the age, is clearly specified. (There appears to be a slight preference for the pitcher over the bus driver. These preferences often reflect the effects of specific training trials that occurred just prior to testing.)

The third type involves what might be called "inference of implicit arguments", because in this case the sentences contained no overt indication even that there was a filler of a particular role. For example, in "The teacher ate the soup", there is no instrument mentioned; but during training, the eating of soup always occurred with the use of a spoon, and so the spoon is inferrable in this context. In this case (not shown) the model learns to fill in spoon when probed for the instrument.

The model was tested with five different example sentences for each of these three types of filler specification cases. In all cases it performed correctly (see St. John and McClelland, in press, for further details and examples).

HOW DOES THE MODEL WORK?

In this section, we begin by following the time-course of processing one example sentence, to give the reader a feeling for the step-by-step processing activity that occurs in the model. We then return to the questions raised at the beginning of this paper, to see how the model gives very different answers to each of these questions.

The sentence we shall study is "The adult ate the steak with daintiness". The sentence is interesting, in that there are three different sources of information as to the identity of the subject. One of these is the word *adult* itself. The second is the fact that the adult is eating *steak*. And the third is the adverb (with *daintiness*); in the model's experience it is only the teacher (a female) who ever eats with daintiness. As we shall see, the example illustrates the model's ability to make use of a variety of cues of varying strength, spread throughout the sentence, to identify a particular constituent.

After the presentation of each constituent (adult, ate, steak, with daintiness), we can examine the response of the network to probes assessing the fillers of the agent, action, instrument, and patient roles (see Fig. 4). Later, we will return to consider the pattern of actication over the SG units, which provides the representation of the whole sentence.

We consider first the response to "agent", because it is here that we see the effects of several constituents operating most clearly. After the presentation of "adult", the model takes the agent to be an adult person; there is some activation of both male and female, and of both bus driver and teacher, the only two adults in the set. There is a slight bias favouring male. Child is included to illustrate that it is not active at any point. There is little

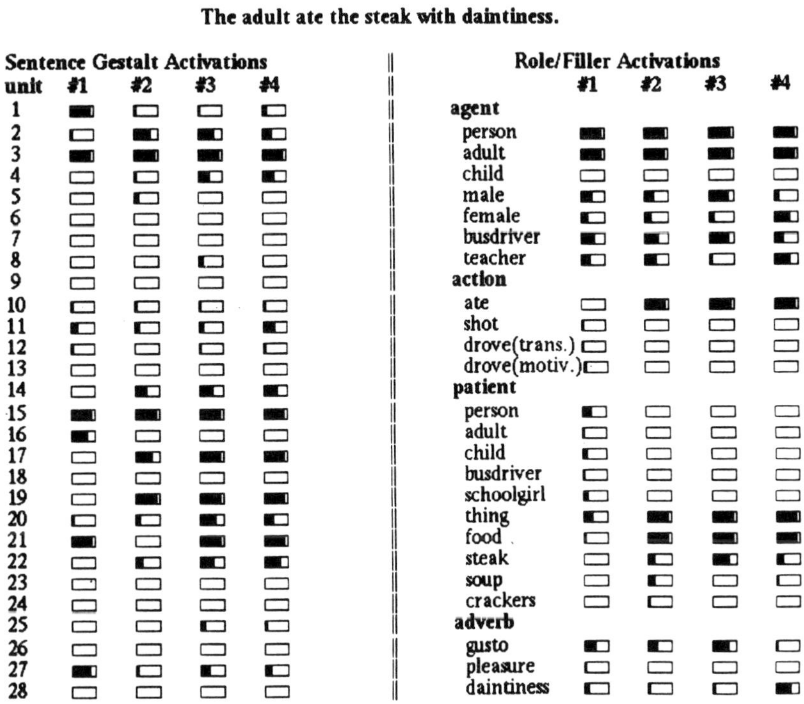

FIG. 4 Activation of a subset of the sentence gestalt units (on the left) and of relevant output units in response to the indicated probes (on the right) after presentation of each constituent of the sentence "The adult ate the steak with daintiness". The columns labelled #1, #2, etc., refer to the state after each of the successive constituents (#1 = adult, etc.).

change after the presentation of the verb, because this does not really provide any constraints on the identity of the adult (the teacher and the bus driver appear equally often in sentences involving eating). The presentation of "steak", however, produces a shift in the direction of male and bus driver. This shift is reversed (though not completely) when the final constitutent, "with daintiness", is presented.

For the other roles, the reader will note that the model performs in a generally sensible way. The one slight problem appears in the case of the patient. We see the activation of "steak", which was quite strong just after the presentation of the steak constituent, weaken considerably when "daintiness" is presented. We will return to a consideration of this specific aspect of the model's performance later.

Given the overall success of the model, let us now ask what kinds of answers do we get to the questions raised at the begining of this paper when we use a model of this sort?

What is Constructed when We Comprehend a Sentence?

In this case, the answer is not "a structural description". What is constructed is a pattern of activation which permits the performance of a specific task or tasks. In this case, the task is to provide a basis for completing role–filler pairs; but one can imagine a wide variety of other uses as well. Whatever the tasks were that we were called upon to use the results of comprehension to perform, a model with the general structure of the one used here could be used to learn to perform that task.

Given this, it becomes a matter of empiricial research to ascertain just how a network will choose to use its units in learning to perform the tasks that it is given to perform. We know from other connectionist research that the answers to these questions are dependent both on the specific tasks the network is asked to perform, and on the details of network architecture (Hinton, 1986; McClelland, in press). In this instance, just perusing the pattern of activation in the sentence gestalt at each successive presentation of a new input constituent, we can see two things. First, many of the units take on graded activations, and several of these seem only partially correlated with particular role–filler activations. This suggests that the activations of particular output units in response to particular probes are generally determined by the joint influence of a number of hidden units; thus they provide a distributed, coarse-coded representation of the role–filler information conveyed by the sentence (cf. Hinton, McClelland, & Rumelhart, 1986).

What Role do Words Play in the Comprehension Process?

In the present model, as each word is presented, it changes the pattern of activation in the sentence gestalt. In this case, we see each word as exerting constraints on the representation. It will be noted that these constraints can in general influence the responses to all of the probes we might present after presentation of a word. Thus the presentation of "ate" affects not only responses to probes for the action but also probes for the patient; and the presentation of steak and daintiness each influence responses to probes for the agent, the patient, and the manner. Thus a word is a clue that constrains the interpretation of the event as a whole.

The influence that a particular word will have on the comprehension process depends on what has already been presented. But, there is a systematic contribution that each word makes. This systematic contribution is represented by the set of connection strengths from the input unit that represents a particular word to the set of hidden units inside the comprehension part of the network.

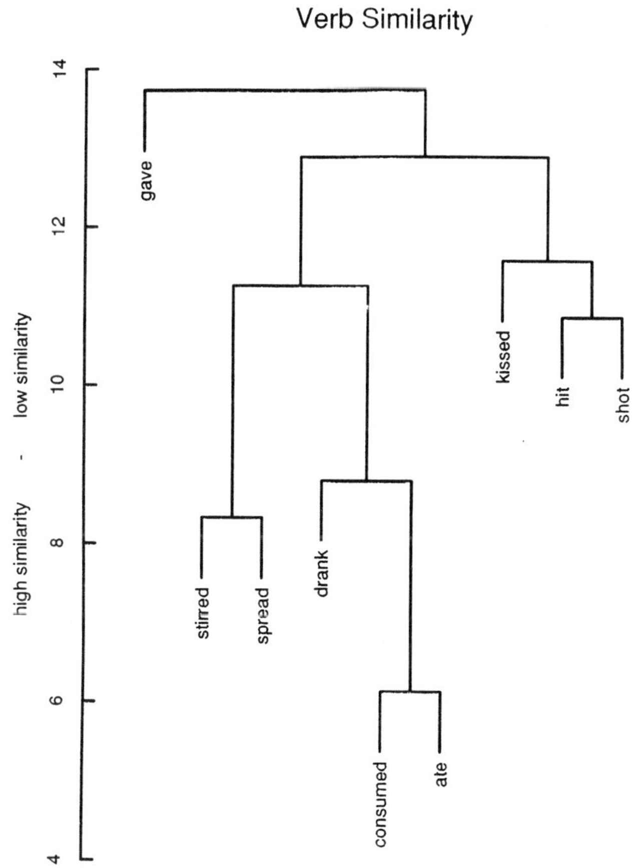

FIG. 5 Cluster analysis of the weight vectors emanating from each word input unit to the hidden units in the comprehension part of the SG model, for the units representing the 11 unambiguous verbs shown. The vertical position of the horizontal bar joining two branches indicates the similarity of the leaves or branches joined.

To examine these contributions, St. John and McClelland extracted the vector of connection weights emanating from each word input unit to this first layer of hidden units. These feature vectors were then entered into a hierarchical cluster analysis (separate analyses were performed for the nouns and verbs). The analysis for the verbs (Fig. 5) displays clearly that the model has captured the similarity structure among the "frames" represented by these verbs as used in our training corpus. The verb "give" is the only dative verb in the corpus, and is clustered separately from all the others. The verbs "ate", "drank", and "consumed" all take animate things as subjects and inanimate things (food) as their objects; the verbs "stirred" and "spread" each take a human subject, food as an object, and a spoon or

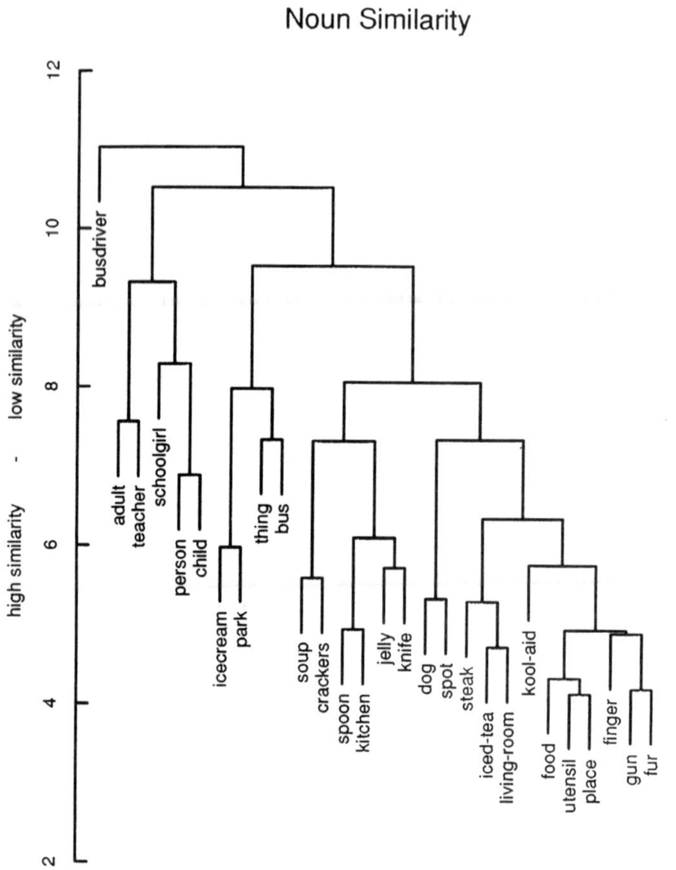

FIG. 6 Cluster analysis of the weight vectors emanating from each word input unit to the hidden units in the comprehension part of the SG model, for the units representing the unambiguous nouns shown. The vertical position of the horizontal bar joining two branches indicates the similarity of the leaves or branches joined.

a knife as the instrument; and "hit", "kicked", and "kissed" are all passivisible in the corpus (unlike the food-related verbs), and all involve a patient that may be animate.

The analysis for the nouns (Fig. 6) is less clear; it appears that there are two organisational principles that are both at work. Sometimes, nouns cluster by meaning. Thus all the human nouns cluster separately from the rest of the nouns. However, at a finer grain, the nouns sometimes appear to cluster by co-occurrence in the same events. Thus ice-cream clusters with park because in our corpus ice-cream is eaten in the park, and that is the only thing that ever happens in the park. Once again, the model appears to be picking up what might be called the frames that the nouns enter into, rather than their individual meanings *per se*. Of course, the dctails of this depend on the particular training corpus; in ordinary life, much happens in parks besides the eating of ice-cream. In general, it seems likely that noun-frames are much weaker than verb-frames; but to the extent that such frames do exist, they can be captured by models such as this.

How does the Process of Constructing a Representation of a Sentence Occur?

In the connectionist model, there is no separation of the structure-sensitive rules and the lexical content of words. The process is inherently susceptible to guidance by content as well as structural information.

In some sense, the model represents the strongest possible alternative to a modular approach. Not only are all different sources of constraint taken into account simultaneously, the knowledge underlying each source of constraint is inextricably interwoven in the connections.

There are limits on the kinds of processing ambiguities which our model actually deals with, and on the kinds of information that it brings to bcar in dealing with them. The first of these limits is due primarily to the simplicity of the task we have asked the network to perform; we can study role ambiguities, because we can probe for the fillers of particular roles, but we cannot study attachment ambiguities, because the role–filler completion task is too limited. If the language of the probe completion task were enriched, however, it should be possible for the network to learn to deal with more interesting structural ambiguities as well. To make this concrete, suppose we had trained the network to complete head–role–filler triples, rather than simply role–filler pairs. For example, consider again sentences like (3) and (4):

3. The spy saw the policeman with the revolver.
4. The spy saw the policeman with the binoculars.

Suppose that the probes specified a head noun or verb, and a role, and the task was to fill in the filler. In the case of Y, we would want the network to fill in the concept corresponding to revolver when probed for the modifier of *policeman*, but not when probed for the instrument of *saw*. In the case of (4), we would want the network to fill in *binoculars* when probed for the instrument of saw, but not when probed for the modifier of *policeman*. In principle, we see no reason why some version of this approach should not be able to extend to multiclause sentences, though clearly this is a matter for further research.

A complete model would, of course, also provide some representation of context prior to the beginning of the current sentence. As the work of Crain and Steedman (1985) and Altmann and Steedman (1988) makes clear, constraints arising from the tendency for multisentence texts to maintain referential coherence can influence attachment ambiguity resolution. We would expect that a model that somehow kept a record of prior context could learn to exploit it for the resolution of attachment ambiguities.

Of course, what we have just described are hoped-for extensions, not real results at this point. Some relevant research, indicating an ability to use context to resolve ambiguities of reference in multisentence texts, has been carried out (see, e.g. Allen, 1987; 1988; Miikkulainen & Dyer, 1989), but to our knowledge nothing relevant has yet been done with regard to the resolution of structural ambiguity.

How does Acquisition Work?

Acquisition works by a process of gradual connection strength adjustment. This is quite different from the formulation of a system of explicit rules. Certain problems are avoided right from the start, such as the question of when to form a rule, and when to simply list exceptions. However, it would certainly not be accurate to suggest that the model we have presented here is a *tabula rasa*, acquiring knowledge of language without any prior structure. Indeed, the input is parsed for the model into constituents and words; and the role–filler representation of the event descriptions and the set of concepts used in the output network are predetermined as well. Finally, the structure of the network is preordained, and tailored to the task. These features of the model were not adopted out of any belief that their adoption was necessary but simply out of a desire to establish a simple illustrative model. Just how much prior structure has to be built in, and in what way it is built in, remain basic and central issues for connectionist models in this and a number of other domains.

CAN THE PDP APPROACH SOLVE THE PROBLEMS WITH CONVENTIONAL MODELS?

Earlier we enumerated a set of problems with conventional models. Here we consider how they are or could be solved in models of the kind we have considered here.

Conceptual Guidance and Rule Conflicts

The problem of conceptual guidance is naturally solved by the integrated handling of both syntactic and content-based constraints on processing. The problem of rule conflicts is dealt with by the connection adjustment process. That process assigns strengths to the features so that the correct interpretations are achieved across the entire corpus.

Contextual Shading as well as Selection of Word Meaning

This characteristic of PDP models is not illustrated so clearly by the present model because of its use of local representations for concepts. We can see this kind of thing to a limited degree in such examples as "The adult ate the steak with daintiness". Though "teacher" and "female" are ultimately more active than "bus driver" and "male", the fact that it is a steak that is eaten definitely shades the activations in the network with maleness; the model seems only too natural in its ability to capture stereotypes like the one immortalised in the phrase, "real men don't eat quiche", and to use innuendo in shading its representations.

The use of local representations for concepts makes it possible to see contextual shading only in the relative degree of activation of the few superordinate feature units that were included in the model. However, this use of local representations is not inherent in the connectionist approach and we adopted this usage here only for ease of testing and to avoid building undue amounts of knowledge into the concept representations. However, an earlier model that did use distributed representations does illustrate shading effects on a grander scale (McClelland & Kawamoto, 1986). In that model, concepts were represented by fully distributed patterns. The model was trained to interpret a variety of sentences involving breaking one object with another, and all but one of the objects that could occur as the instrument shared a feature indicating that the object was hard. The one exception, the ball, was encoded as soft, and the model correctly treated it as such when it occurred in most contexts. However, when it was used to break other objects, the model shaded the representation, giving it the feature hard instead of soft; this happened just because things that break other things were typically hard, and the model became sensitive to this fact. It is worth noting that the resulting pattern was not one of the existing patterns on which the model had been trained but an extension by the model of the ensemble of possible concepts.

The Similar Problem with Roles

The shading of concept representations that is captured in McClelland and Kawamoto's model has been applied to roles by Touretzky and Geva (1987). The idea is simply that the set of possible roles is not some fixed set of *N* alternatives but an extensible set with a rich similarity structure, such as is naturally captured by distributed representations.

Implied Constituents

The handling of implied constituents is not a problem in the model. It is quite natural for the model to learn that events involving eating steak always involve a knife as the instrument. There is no special "inference step" required to fill in the knife. This is in part a direct result of the fact that there is no prior stipulation that a particular part of the representation of the sentence corresponds to the internal reflex of each particular constituent of the sentence. It's just that events described by sentences with "ate" as the verb and "steak" as the object always involve knives as instruments. The probabilistic nature of many implied constituents is not a problem either, because of the inherently graded nature of the activation process, coupled with the fact that intermediate activation values directly reflect probabilities intermediate between 0 and 1.

Combinatorial Explosion or Premature Commitment

The model avoids combinatorial explosion by keeping multiple alternatives implicit in the single pattern of activity over the sentence gestalt. It avoids the catastrophic side-effects of premature commitment because its graded activations can be adjusted as each new constraint is introduced. In a sense, it does make commitments as each new constituent is encountered, but these are not all-or-none choices, but simply continuous shifts in the pattern of activation. Thus commitments made can be reversed without any backtracking. It is true that some constituents cause a more marked adjustment of the SG representation than others. These marked adjustments can be related to experimental data on reading times if we make the simple assumption that larger adjustments take longer to make. This assumption holds in systems that adjust their activations continuously (McClelland, 1979) rather than in a single time-step. We view these continuous systems as more realistic that the discrete time-step system used here; as with the use of localist representation, the use of discrete time in the illustrative example model is simply a matter of greater tractability.

The notion that larger changes in the SG are associated with longer reading times provides a natural way of accounting for a lot of reading time data in which a slowdown in processing is observed in one condition relative to another. In these cases, it seems unnecessary to invoke the notion of reprocessing, which is often associated with theoretical discussions of these effects in the experimental literature coloured by the classical framework. But, it does sometimes happen that language readers and listeners experience a true garden path. By a true garden path, we mean the strong feeling that something has gone awry—that the sentence no longer makes any sense at all. This occurs when one reaches the word "fell" in a sentence like this one of Bever's (1970):

21. The horse raced past the barn fell.

The question is, why is it, on the story that we are telling, that subjects are not at this point able to recover, based on the constraints on the interpretation imposed by the final word?

The answer is that the word "fell" by itself may not exert a strong enough influence to reorganise the SG representation all on its own. This argument implies that if the sentence continues in a way that imposes additional input favouring the correct interpretation, the garden-path effect might actually be overcome. Thus we expect that the garden-path effect can be ameliorated if the reader just continues to read and the sentence goes on and provides additional relevant constraints:

22. The horse raced past the barn fell into the ditch.

Obviously, this is a topic for careful research, rather than the jaded intuitions of theoretically biased psycholinguists; but we feel the example supports our sense that even in such dramatic cases as (21), we may not really be forced to reprocess, as long as there is subsequent information that allows us to overcome the effects of what has come earlier in the sentence.

The Problem of Acquisition

The use of gradual connection adjustments in the model helps it overcome some of the problems conventional approaches face in learning to interpret sentences. First, the strengths of constraints imposed by various words on the interpretation process are naturally graded and are brought gradually into balance by the connection adjustment process. Secondly, the solution to the bootstrapping problem emerges naturally through the exposure of the model to the statistical properties of an ensemble of sentence–event pairs. It is true that the sentence "the boy kissed the girl" could map on to the event of a boy kissing a girl in two different ways; but these alternatives are further constrained by other sentences. Thus in every sentence where the subject of the verb "kiss" is girl, there is a girl in the event and she is the agent.

We do not wish to suggest at all that the problems of acquisition are fully solved by the present model; the sentences and events are highly simplified, and the pre-parsing of sentences into words and constituents, together with the pre-structuring of events into role–filler pairs certainly makes things easier for the model.

Our only claim is that the connectionist learning procedure we have used does have some signficant advantages over rule-learning approaches. As noted above, it remains for further research to establish how much support these procedures require from pre-existing structure and how much they can induce from the environment.

Comparison with Other Connectionist Models

As many readers will doubtlessly be aware, a number of researchers have noted the appeal of the PDP or connectionist modelling framework for capturing aspects of language processing, and have chosen to build models within this framework. Our approach certainly falls well within this tradition, but differs from most of the previous work in one important way. Earlier models have tended to incorporate, in one way or another, specific characteristics of conventional models of language directly into the internal representations used. Our earlier work is no exception to this rule. For example, the interactive activation model of visual word recognition (McClelland & Rumelhart, 1981; Rumelhart & McClelland, 1982) incorporated units that represent letters and words; the TRACE model of speech perception (Elman & McClelland, 1986; McClelland & Elman, 1986) incorporates phonemes and words. McClelland and Kawamoto (1986) use semantic features such as "animate", "inanimate", etc., and gave over slots within the model to each of several possible representational roles. By taking these steps—reifying some aspects of conventional representations inside connectionist networks—these and other models have in fact fallen prey to some of the difficulties that are faced by conventional models. The most serious problem is the problem of combinatorial explosion. Unlike conventional models, in which the problem of combinatorial explosion is only faced during processing, these connectionist models have to face it in advance, and construct networks of units and connections that will allow all possible inputs to be processed.

Two approaches have been taken to avoid this problem. The first is to exploit the idea of coarse coding, in which units do not correspond to specific representational entities, but to conjunctions of pre-specified features of possible representational entities. It is well established that this can limit the problem in some domains, and some models have been successful using this approach (c.f. Touretzky & Hinton, 1988), but we have found it unworkable for sentence processing (St. John & McClelland, 1987). The problem is that the number of features that need to be pre-specified is unbounded, as is the number of these that may need to be conjoined to represent any particular specific proposition. Again the combinatorics can be devastating.

The other approach—the one that is taken here—is to let connectionist learning procedures do the work of determining what the internal representation should be like. Of course, the approach has only become possible since the advent of learning rules that allow internal representations to be formed in response to task demands (Rumelhart, Hinton, & Williams, 1986a). This approach has one serious disadvantage—learning can be very slow. But it does have some very important advantages. It allows the network to learn to form representations that make efficient use of the available representational resources, given the task as specified by the inputs that are presented and the outputs that the network is expected to generate in response to these inputs. A number of researchers have been exploring this approach. Elman (1989), for example, has developed a simple network that learns to anticipate the next element of a sequence of words. In so doing, it learns to form an internal representation of each word that reflects the sequential constraints in the sequences. If the words form sentences, and the sentences reflect co-occurrence constraints—such as the fact that a certain verb requires an animate subject and an inanimate object—the representations come to reflect the relevant semantic distinctions.

Just how far this kind of approach can be taken remains to be seen. Some (e.g. Touretzky, 1988) have suggested that more structure needs to be built into the network, and the facts of learning speed do suggest that something must be done before the approach can be successfully extended to large corpuses of complex sentences (see also Miikkulainen & Dyer, 1989). At present, it is too early to tell just what will be the most effective way to provide for an extension of the approach.

ARGUMENTS AGAINST THE PDP APPROACH

Several different types of arguments might be given in favour of conventional approaches and against the approach that we have taken. Here we consider three that seem particularly central. In all three cases, we believe that the arguments are less compelling than the proponents of alternatives have alleged.

Systematicity and Productivity

In their critique of connectionist models, Fodor and Pylyshyn (1988) point out that an inherent feature of the conventional approach is the fact that it accounts for the systematicity and productivity of language. These characteristics follow directly, they point out, if we assume that our cognitive apparatus makes use of a combinatorial syntax and semantics; they also claim that these characteristics do not follow from the PDP approach. Let us examine these characteristics.

Systematicity refers to the fact that if a speaker can understand a sentence like "John loves the girl" and (let us say) "Bill dislikes the teacher", then he can also understand other sentences, such as "John loves the teacher", "Bill dislikes John", etc. In other words, sentences are not just isolated, unanalysed wholes but are composed of parts which can be recombined to produce other sentences that the speaker will understand.

To test the capability of a model such as ours to exhibit systematicity, we generated a new corpus, containing 10 persons and 10 actions. Each of the actions could be done by any person to any person so that there were a total of 1000 possible events. Each could be expressed in an active or passive sentence for a total of 2000 possible sentences.

We trained the same network described above with all but a randomly chosen 250 of the possible sentences; then, after training, we tested it on the remaining 250 sentences. A stringent accuracy criterion was adopted: A sentence was scored correct only if the unit representing the correct person or action was more active than any other unit in response to probes for the actor, action, and patient. The model got 97% of these novel sentences correct.

Now obviously this is but the first step in demonstrating that connectionist networks can exhibit systematicity. The corpus is finite, and 87.5% of it was used during training. Nevertheless, there is considerable systematicity in the model's performance.

Now, it might be noted that systematicity is not in fact an inherent attribute of the model that we have proposed. In fact, it is probably true that the model could learn to treat sentences as unanalysed wholes, if in fact the constituent structure of sentences had no relation to their actual meanings. Thus, we could train the model to produce arbitrary answers to probes given in conjunction with each member of a list of sentences. Learning would be slower than if the sentences had a systematic structure, and it would require more units and connections, but in principle this could be done.

The question arises, then, as to why it is that languages turn out to be systematic. One possibility is that it is an inherent characteristic of human cognition to be systematic in just this way, and this is the crux of Fodor and Pylyshyn's argument. On this view, human languages are systematic because our minds force them to be that way, due to their use of a combinatorial syntax and semantics. Indeed, Fodor and Pylyshyn argue that connectionist models cannot explain the systematicity of language, because connectionist models do not inherently impose a combinatorial syntax and semantics.

Our response to this argument has two parts. First, we question the implicit assumption that the explanation for the systematicity of language must lie with inherent characteristics of the mechanisms of thought.

Indeed, we would look to the tasks that humans must perform with linguistic stimuli, and the experiences from which they learn, for at least some part of the explanation. If the task is to form representations of events which themselves have a combinatorial structure, then a computational mechanism that becomes systematic may be simply discovering the systematicity in the environment.

Systematicity in the environment is probabily only part of the story. It has been the force of much work in linguistics and elsewhere to argue that the systematicity in the environment is much less than the systematicity that is imposed by the human observer. Indeed, we suspect that there is some truth to this claim.

This leads us to our second point, which is that in fact connectionist models *do* tend to impose systematicity, even though they do not have a combinatorial syntax and semantics. Networks do not, as a matter of fact, simply memorise individual input–output pairs and treat each one as an isolated individual case; the generalisation experiment just described is just one of a very large number of relevant demonstrations that in fact they do exhibit a tendency to behave systematically. A tendency towards behaving systematically is in fact a characteristic that our model shares with mechanisms which simply stipulate a combinatorial syntax and semantics.

From here on, the argument simply gets tendentious. One side can claim that connectionist models do not in their present form exhibit *enough* systematicity; and while this may be true, it places any in-principle argument against systematicity in connectionist models in considerable doubt. Or it might be claimed that a tendency to behave systematically has been snuck into the model by some slight of hand. It is in fact true that particular choices of details of network architecture do influence the degree of systematicity; and indeed it is quite important to get a clearer picture of what aspects of network architecture are conducive to good generalisation. We do not doubt that evolution may have shaped our cognitive structures so as to make them more likely to be able to act systematically; but we see no reason to suppose that it has done so by endowing them in advance with an explicitly combinatorial syntax and semantics.

What about productivity? Productivity is of course intimately linked to systematicity; it refers to the fact that we can understand many sentences that we have not actually heard before. The experiment just described addressed this point, though again, in a fairly limited way. It is generally assumed that humans can comprehend an infinite number of sentences, while in our experiment the corpus was indeed only a bit larger than the training set.

Other research on the productivity of connectionist networks is currently underway. Servan-Schreiber, Cleeremans, and McClelland (1988) have shown that a simple network architecture first introduced by Elman (1988) can learn to accept all and only the grammatical tokens of a simple finite state language. Because in the case of this finite state language the corpus is infinite, we have the first clear indication that a network can learn from finite experience to process an infinite corpus. The handling of long-distance dependencies is currently under rather active exploration (Servan-Schreiber et al., 1988; Elman, 1989). Extension to comprehension, rather than mere acceptance of grammatical tokens, awaits as the next challenge.

There is an aspect of the productivity of language that appears to be better explained by our connectionist approach than by conventional approaches. This is the use of context to shade meanings of concepts as they are instantiated in particular events which may be contextually appropriate. The example of the ball from McClelland and Kawamoto illustrates this. In another case, they presented their model with the sentence "The doll moved". This sentence was novel to the model. Among the features that the model had learned were associated with "doll" was inanimacy. However, in interpreting this sentence the model "animated" the doll. This is because, in all of the sentences that the model had been trained on, the subject of the sentences of the form "X moved" were always animate. It seems to us that this interpretive liberty on the part of the model is entirely correct and appropriate, and illustrates a productivity that extends far beyond the capabilities of conventional models.

Beyond Compositionality

We have discussed two out of the three characteristics Fodor and Pylyshyn (1988) claim language has that are captured by conventional approaches. The third characteristic is compositionality: The idea that a word contributes the same thing to the meaning of all of the sentences in which it occurs. In the introduction, we criticised the notion of compositionality, indicating that in fact it represents an impoverished view of the comprehension process. In our illustrative model, a word does always exert the same influence on the net input to the first set of hidden units in the comprehension part of the model. But, due to the non-linearities in the hidden units at that layer in the network, and due to the concurrent influence of inputs from context, the actual impact of the word can differ greatly from context to context. The word exerts the same *force* on the representation at each occurrence, but this force is combined with those applied by context, thereby allowing for context sensitivity.

It might be argued that the model is too sensitive to context, in that in fact it allows context sometimes to override the correct interpretation of a word. This happens, for example, with the steak in the example presented above: After the presentation of *with daintiness*, the activation of *steak* on probing for the patient is weakened. In fact, at earlier points in learning, the model actually activates soup more strongly than steak after *with daintiness* is presented.

This behaviour must be taken as an error, but it is an error of the kind that people often make. For example, Erickson and Mattson (1981) asked subjects to answer the question:

How many animals of each kind did Moses take on the ark?

Most subjects said two, and noticed nothing amiss, even though they had been warned to look out for trick sentences. Indeed, many subjects could not pinpoint the problem with this sentence even after being told that there was something wrong. Apparently, the constraints imposed by the word *Moses* itself are not sufficiently strong to override those imposed by the context.

Some may view errors of the Moses type as abberations, though the effect is easy to produce with other examples. To us it is a reflection of the fact that the doctrine of compositionality misrepresents the contributions of words to an understanding of the meanings of sentences.

In sum, we do not see any reason to suppose that the observed degree of systematicity, productivity, and compositionality of human language need be attributed to inherent structural characteristics of the kind that Fodor and Pylyshyn have advocated. In part, the systematicity of the world may be to blame; beyond this it is clear that networks do tend to impose systematicity; productivity does not appear to be beyond the power of PDP models like the one we have considered here; and there are aspects of the expressive capability of human language that go beyond what can be captured in a combinatorial syntax and semantics which seem naturally to follow from a PDP account.

Lexical and Syntactic Autonomy

We turn now to a set of considerations that arise from psychological experiments, where it is claimed that at least during some initial stage of processing, both lexical access (i.e. activation of the possible meanings associated with words) and syntactic processing (i.e. assigning attachment relations between sentence constituents) are autonomus processes. These claims run directly counter to the basic tenets of the approach that we have taken here, because the approach assumes that these processes are inextricably intertwined with each other and with the exploitation of contextual influences. Clear evidence for autonomy would therefore undercut our approach completely. So let us see, what is the evidence?

Lexical Access. In well-known experiments (Swinney, 1979; Tanenhaus, Leiman, & Seidenberg, 1979), subjects had to listen to a spoken text containing an ambiguous word (such as BUGS) and were probed for a lexical decision immediately after the offset of the word with another word related to either meaning of the ambiguity. Thc oft-cited result of such experiments is the finding that decisions to words related to either meaning of the ambiguity are faster than decisions to unrelated words, indicating that both meanings are initially accessed; only later is the ambiguity resolved to fit the context, so that the contextually appropriate reading is the only one that remains active.

There are two points to be made. The first is that a recent meta-analysis (St. John, 1988) of a total of 19 studies, using both lexical decision and word naming methods, reveals that in fact there is a reliable advantage for the contextually appropriate reading, even at an immediate test. The pattern exhibited in Fig. 7 from the seminal experiment of Swinney (1979) is exemplary of the general pattern of the results.

The second point is that this pattern is very close to what is found in a simulation of the processes of settling on an interpretation of an ambiguous word in a PDP model of the disambiguation process (Kawamoto, 1985; 1988; see Fig. 7). Kawamoto's model differs from the illustrative model described here in three crucial ways. First, it uses a continuous, gradual activation process, so that units gradually settle into their final state, rather than being thrust into a state in a single step. Secondly, it makes use of full recurrence in the connections among the units, so that units within the same part of the system feed back on each other. Thirdly, it does not actually simulate the full process of sentence interpretation, but only considers the process of settling on an interpretation of an individual word as a joint function of contextual and phonological input. We view Kawamoto's model as an attempt to characterise the fine-grain temporal processes involved in lexical access that are more coarsely approximated in the SG model.

Now, Kawamoto's model most clearly does not assume that the process of accessing meaning is autonomous; as in the SG model, both contextual and input-based constraints influence the process from the start. However, what happens in the model is that at first both of the possible meanings consistent with the input word are activated. It is only as the activation process continues, that one interpretation is gradually pushed out and the other comes to dominate completely. Thus it appears that the empirical evidence is quite similar to what should be expected on the PDP account.

Autonomous Syntax? A number of studies have been reported indicating that syntactic preferences initially determine the outcome of on-line parsing processes, so that sentences in which the context eventually requires an alternative interpretation are processed more slowly than those in which the content is consistent with the syntactic bias. A variety of

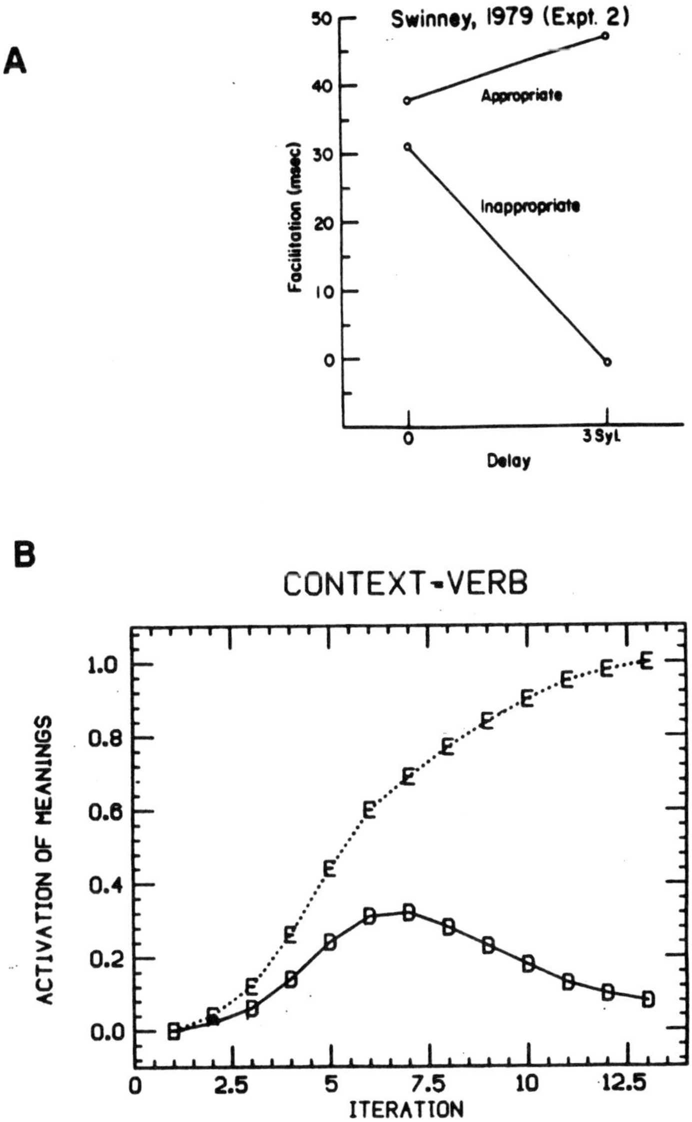

FIG. 7 (a) Data from Swinney (1979); (b) activations of contextually appropriate and inappropriate meanings of the ambiguous word *wind* (from Kawamoto's distributed model of ambiguity resolution). The context specifies that a *verb* is expected, and the two curves represent activations of patterns corresponding to the contextually appropriate meaning (E for encircle) and the contextually inappropriate meaning (D for draft). (a) is reprinted from McClelland (1987) and (b) from Kawamoto (1985).

constructions have been examined in studies of this type. One of these is the reduced relative construction, in sentences like (23) and (24):

23. The actress sent the flowers was very pleased.
24. The florist sent the flowers was very pleased.

Another is the N-V-N-PP construction, as in (25) and (26):

25. The spy saw the policeman with the binoculars, but . . .
26. The spy saw the policeman with the revolver, but . . .

Using the first kind of construction, Rayner, Carlson, and Frazier (1983) found that subjects have difficulty processing the reduced relative clause in both cases, even though in one of the examples (the actress sent the flowers) semantic constraints are said to favour the idea that the actress would be the recipient rather than the sender of the flowers as is required in the reduced relative interpretation.

Such a finding is, in our view, not particularly telling in indicating whether there is some *initial* syntactic process that favours one interpretation over the other, or whether, alternatively, there is simply a strong *weight* associated with the syntactic preference to treat a N-V-N sequence as actor–action–object. It certainly is the case that the initial part of the sentence

The actress sent the flowers . . .

is unambiguously interpreted by native speakers as indicating that the actress is the sender not the recipient of the flowers; plausible continuations might involve a recipient (herself, perhaps?) or another clause. Thus it appears that the syntactic cues are simply overriding in this case. Similar arguments apply to many of the materials used in the subsequent study by Ferreira and Clifton (1986).

In the second kind of construction, it was found (Rayner et al., 1983) that there was an advantage for sentences of the form of (25), in which the prepositional phrase is ultimately attached to the verbphrase, compared to sentences of the form of (26), in which the prepositional phrase is ultimately attached to the nounphrase. However, a series of experiments (Taraban, 1988; Taraban & McClelland, 1988; 1990) has now established several important findings regarding this particular construction. Taraban and McClelland (1988, experiment 1) established three basic points. First, the materials used by Rayner et al. generally had a bias such that the part of the sentence preceding the disambiguating word (revolver or binoculars, in this case) tended to favour the VP attachment of the prepositional phrase. Secondly, other materials are easily constructed in which this attachment preference is reversed. Thirdly, studies of on-line processing using the word-by-word reading task developed by Just, Car-

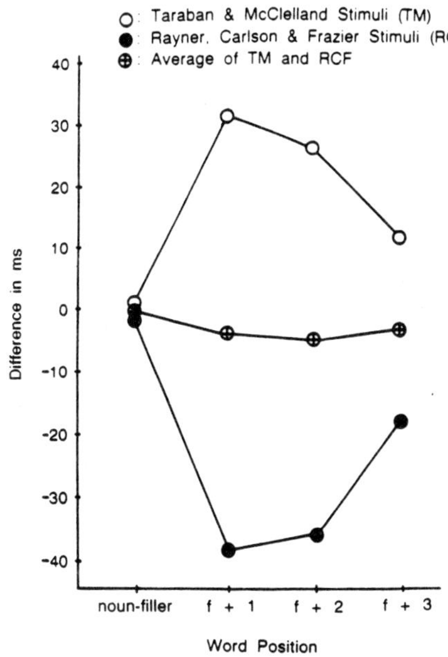

FIG. 8 Reading time advantage (negative numbers) or disadvantage (positive numbers) for sentences requiring a verbphrase attachment of a prepositional phrase compared to matched sentences requiring a nounphrase attachment. Rayner et al.'s (1983) stimuli are biased so that subjects expect the PP to attach to the VP. Taraban and McClelland's stimuli lead subjects to expect the PP to attach to the preceding NP.

penter, and Woolley (1982) revealed that the finding reported by Rayner et al. (1983) only holds with the VP-attachment-biased materials, and is reversed with the NP-biased-materials (Fig. 8). With VP-attachment-biased materials (Rayner et al.'s materials), there is a reading time advantage for noun-fillers that accords with the VP attachment bias, which totals about 100 msec and is distributed over the three words following the noun-filler. However, with NP-attachment-biased materials (Taraban and McClelland's sentences), there is an approximately equal and opposite pattern; averaging the two types of materials, there is virtually no overall advantage for either type of attachment. Thus, the study indicates that content, rather than any general syntactic preference, appears to determine initial attachment preferences in this kind of construction.

Another experiment (Taraban & McClelland, 1990) addressed the source of the content-based influences on processing of the prepositional phrase. One possibility that is often considered is the idea that the verb may provide a basis for expectations about possible arguments that might influence the course of processing; these expectations could still be attributed to the workings of an autonomous syntactic process which nevertheless consulted syntactic information in the lexicon. In this experiment, Taraban and McClelland demonstrated, however, that the content of the object NP also influenced performance. For example, in sentence (27),

27. The dictator viewed the masses from the . . .
28. The dictator viewed the petition from the . . .

subjects expected a locative PP, attaching to the verb, indicating the place from which the viewing was to occur; whereas in (28), they expected a source of the petition, attaching to the object NP. When these expectations were violated, there was a slowdown in processing.

The experiments by Taraban and McClelland demonstrate that the content of the main verb, as well as that of the post-verbal object NP, can influence on-line processing decisions about PP attachment. They do not address whether or not the content of the *subject* nounphrase can also influence on-line parsing decisions, although it is known from Oden (1978) that it can influence the choice of the ultimate attachment. However, work reported by Tanenhaus, Carlson, and Trueswell (this issue) suggests that the semantic characteristics of the subject *can* influence on-line processing decisions in structures similar to (23) and (24) (see Tanenhaus et al. for further details). Thus, it would appear that evidence is accumulating in favour of the view that all parts of a sentence can influence on-line processing decisions about every other part.

Another of Taraban and McClelland's (1988) experiments considered the possibility that the disruption in processing that is occurring in these sentences is due to specific expectations for particular fillers rather than expectations concerning the role and/or attachment of the prepositional phrases. Though a small effect for particular fillers was found, the largest effect appeared to be due to violations of expectations for the role of the prepositional phrase. Violations of expected attachment had no further disruptive effect over and above that attributable to the inevitable concomitant violation of the subject's role expectations (see Taraban & McClelland, 1988, for details). These findings are certainly consistent with the SG model, in that there is no separate representation of the syntactic form of a sentence; there is, instead, direct processing into a representation which can be used to answer questions about the roles of the participants in the event that is described by the sentence.

In summary, the evidence from Taraban and McClelland's PP attachment studies seems consistent with the view that content can indeed play a role in setting up expectations for the roles played by the objects of prepositional phrases, and that these expectations can govern the initial processing of these phrases as they are encountered on-line in sentence processing. Tanenhaus et al.'s findings indicate that the effects of content are not restricted to lexical information that might be stored directly with heads of phrases. Though it is very clear that syntax often exerts an overriding influence, there is no reason to suppose on the basis of the studies reviewed here that it occupies a privileged or autonomous position in the initial processing of sentences. Instead, it appears that content as well as syntax can influence initial attachment and role assignment preferences.

Further arguments against the autonomy of syntax come from the research of Crain and Steedman (1985), Altmann and Steedman (1988), and Altmann (1988). These papers argue that attachment decisions can be governed by referential processes triggered by context presented prior to the sentence containing the ambiguity. Taken together with Taraban and McClelland's results, these results help paint a general picture in which syntax is far from autonomous.

Altmann and Steedman (1988) point out that the findings on attachment ambiguity resolution are consistent with a view they call "weak interactivity", in which a syntactic module constructs all possible parses and the candidate that best satisfies all of the constraints is selected by subsequent processes sensitive to content, referential coherence, etc. They point out that such a weak interactivity account is probably not distinguishable empirically from plausible versions of strongly interactive accounts, in which conceptual/referential modules in the language processing system instruct modules specialised for syntactic processing.

The view taken here goes beyond even strongly interactive accounts, in proposing that the syntactic and conceptual aspects of processing are in fact inextricably intertwined. Perhaps this view might best be called an integrative as opposed to an interactive account. Interactivity suggests separate systems that exert simultaneous mutual influence (cf. McClelland, 1987; Rumelhart & McClelland, 1981), even though they construct separate representations of different kinds of information. In the present approach, there is but a single integrated system in which syntactic and other constraints are combined in the connection weights, to influence the construction of a single representation reflecting the influences of syntactic, semantic, and lexical constraints.

Neuropsychological Dissociations

This integrative approach is actually quite different from the position one of us has taken in previous publications (McClelland, 1987). We have adopted it here, not out of any strong *a priori* commitment, but because it has turned out to work well in capturing the phenomena considered in this paper. Indeed, the notion that there is a separate module for syntax is so ingrained in theoretical treatments of language processing, that it is difficult even for us to be fully comfortable with abandoning it. But, the successes of the SG model in dealing with some of the central difficulties facing conventional approaches, coupled with the fact that the empirical evidence is beginning to favour at least some form of an interactive account, makes us feel that it is worthwhile to see if indeed there is any real basis for this very general acceptance of some form of modularity.

In this connection, it is worth considering evidence from neuropsychology, because some of the most often-cited evidence for the view that there are separate processing systems for syntactic and conceptual information come from neuropsychological dissociations. It is generally claimed, for example, that Wernicke's aphasics have a general deficit in the comprehension of word and sentence meaning, which interferes with their understanding of all sentences regardless of their syntactic complexity, whereas Broca's aphasics have a specific deficit in the ability to make use of syntactic information for comprehension. Such dissociations invite a modularist approach, in which one part of the system is specialised for the use of content information and the other for the use of syntactic cues in comprehension. Could such findings possibly be consistent with the framework considered here, in which syntactic and content-based influences on processing are inextricably intertwined in the structure of the language processing mechanism?

In fact, the notion that the difference between Wernicke's and Broca's aphasics can be characterised in terms of syntax and semantics is being called into question from several different vantage points. First, Milberg, Blumstein, and Dworetzky (1988) have recently reported that both Wernicke's and Broca's aphasics differ from normals in lexical access, though the differences are complementary. Normals show a graded decrement in priming as primes are increasingly distorted, but Broca's aphasics show priming only when the prime is undistorted, and Wernicke's aphasics show priming over a wider range of distortion than normals. This suggests that Wernicke's aphasics may be suffering from something akin to undamped activation, whereas Broca's aphasics are suffering from overdamping.

Other studies suggest that Broca's and Wernicke's aphasics both show comprehension deficits, and that the deficts differ more between aphasics who speak different languages than they differ between different types of aphasics who speak the same language. For example, Bates, Friederici, Miceli, and Wulfeck (1985) studied groups of Broca's aphasics, Wernicke's aphasics, and normal controls who were native speakers of each of three different languages—English, German and Italian. They found that within each language, Broca's and Wernicke's aphasics both showed deficits in the use of morphological cues, and that the degree of preservation of the use of these cues correlated with the extent of reliance on these cues in the speaker's language. Italians rely much more on agreement and much less on word order than English speakers, and the Italian aphasics showed the least impairment in the use of subject–verb agreement to mark agency, whereas English aphasics showed the greatest impairment. German is intermediate between the two languages in the extent of normal reliance on word order *vs* agreement cues, and showed an intermediate degree of disruption of the use of agreement with damage. The findings of this study are consistent with the idea that both aphasic groups show the greatest deficits in the use of cues that are relatively weaker in their native language (Bates & Wulfeck, in press; McDonald and MacWhinney, in press), and tend to run counter to the notion that Broca's and Wernicke's aphasia differentially impact mechanisms specific to syntactic and semantic aspects of comprehension, respectively.

We do not mean to suggest that there is no basis at all for the idea that there may be specific dissociations of aspects of linguistic knowledge that call into question the idea that content and syntactic constraints are as fully integrated as they are in the approach that we have taken. There are several studies which support the idea that there are particular deficits in the use of closed-class words that are restricted to Broca's and not to Wernicke's aphasics, which have yet to be reconciled with the type of account suggested by Milberg et al.'s findings, as well as other evidence which has been taken as favouring the existence of autonomous syntactic structures (Caplan & Hildebrandt, 1988). Our only claim here is that the neuropsychological evidence is not completely clear-cut, and there is room for a consideration of the idea that there may indeed be a single processing system that is simply thrown out of regulation in slightly different ways in Broca's and Wernicke's aphasics. The model we have proposed does not of course offer any insight into this differential disruption, but the model is compatible with the idea that there is a single system which uses syntax and content together to guide the language comprehension process.

FUTURE DIRECTIONS

In this paper, we have described an alternative to traditional models of language processing. We have tried to indicate how this alternative may allow us to solve many of the problems facing traditional approaches, and how it may provide different ways of conceptualising basic aspects of the problem of comprehension. We have also indicated that many of the arguments against the type of approach we have taken can be countered. Of course, the facts are not all in, but given what is known at this time the approach seems to us to be at least as viable as any other that we know of. The model we have offered is far from the final word, and many problems need to be addressed. Our only goal has been to suggest that there may be some basis for optimism that further development of the approach might be successful.

There are several further steps that need to be taken. First, we need to find ways of improving the rate of learning; as things stand, learning is unduly slow, especially given the small size of the corpora that we have used in our training experiments. Secondly, we need to extend the framework to force the construction of representations that can answer more sophisticated questions than merely the completion of role–filler pairs. As previously noted, the role–filler completion task that we have used here has several limitations; the role–filler pair language is insufficiently structured, and the localist representation of concepts lacks the reliance on distributed representations which is one of the strengths of the PDP framework. Thirdly, our long-term goal is to move in the direction of capturing the influence of broader, extra-sentential context on sentence processing. Ultimately, the approach will stand or fall on its ability to capture the pervasive influences of these extra-sentential factors.

REFERENCES

Allen, R. B. (1987). Several studies on natural language and back-propagation. *Proceedings of the IEEE First Annual International Conference on Neural Networks*, Vol. II, 287–298. Boston.

Allen, R. B. (1988). Sequential connectionist networks for answering simple questions about a microworld. *Proceedings of the Tenth Annual Conference of the Cognitive Science Society*, pp. 489–495. Montreal.

Altmann, G. (1988). Ambiguity, parsing strategies, and computational models. *Language and Cognitive Processes*, *3*, 73–97.

Altmann, G. & Steedman, M. (1988). Interaction with context during human sentence processing. *Cognition*, *30*, 191–238.

Bates, E. & Wulfeck, B. (in press). Crosslinguistic studies of aphasia. In B. MacWhinney & E. Bates (Eds), *The crosslinguistic study of sentence processing*. New York: Cambridge University Press.

Bates, E., Friederici, A., Miceli, G., & Wulfeck, B. (1985). Sentence comprehension in aphasia: A cross-linguistic study. Manuscript, University of California, San Diego.

Bever, T. G. (1970). The cognitive basis of linguistic structures. In J. R. Hayes (Ed.), *Cognition and the development of language*. New York: John Wiley.

Caplan, D. & Hildebrandt, N. (1988). *Disorders of syntactic comprehension*. Cambridge, Mass.: MIT Press.

Chomsky, N. (1988). Lecture presented at the University of Pittsburgh, Fall, 1988.

Clark, H. H. & Clark, E. V. (1977). *Psychology and language: An introduction to psycholinguistics*. New York: Harcourt Brace Jovanovich.

Crain, S. & Steedman, M. J. (1985). On not being led up the garden path: The use of context by the psychological parser. In D. Dowty, L. Karttunen, & A. Zwicky (Eds), *Natural language parsing: Psychological, computational, and theoretical perspectives*. Cambridge: Cambridge University Press.

Elman, J. L. (1988). Finding structure in time. CRL Technical Report 8801. Center for Research in Language, University of California, San Diego.

Elman, J. L. (1989). Representation and structure in connectionist models. CRL Technical Report 8903. Center for Research in Language, University of California, San Diego.

Elman, J. L. & McClelland, J. L. (1986). Exploiting the lawful variability in the speech wave. In J. S. Perkell & D. H. Klatt (Eds), *Invariance and variability of speech processes*. Hillsdale, N.J.: Lawrence Erlbaum Associates Inc.

Erickson, T. D. & Mattson, M. E. (1981). From words to meaning: A semantic illusion. *Journal of Verbal Learning and Verbal Behavior*, *20*, 540–551.

Ferreira, F. & Clifton, C. (1986). The independence of syntactic processing. *Journal of Memory and Language*, *25*, 348–368.

Fillmore, C. (1968). The case for case. In E. Bach & R. T. Harms (Eds), *Universals in linguistic theory*. New York: Holt, Rinehart and Winston.

Fodor, J. A. & Pylyshyn, Z. W. (1988). Connectionism and cognitive architecture: A critical analysis. *Cognition*, *28*, 3–71.

Frazier, L. (1986). Theories of sentence processing. In J. Garfield (Ed.), *Modularity in knowledge representation and natural language processing*. Cambridge, Mass.: MIT Press.

Gleitman, L. R. & Wanner, E. (1982). Language acquisition: The state of the state of the art. In E. Wanner & L. R. Gleitman (Eds), *Language acquisition: The state of the art*. Cambridge: Cambridge University Press.

Hinton, G. E. (1986). Learning distributed representations of concepts. *Proceedings of the Eighth Annual Conference of the Cognitive Science Society*, Amherst, Mass.

Hinton, G. E., McClelland, J. L., & Rumelhart, D. E. (1986). Distributed representations. In D. E. Rumelhart, J. L. McClelland, & the PDP Research Group (Eds), *Parallel distributed processing: Explorations in the microstructure of cognition*, Vol. I. Cambridge, Mass.: Bradford Books.

Just, M. A., Carpenter, P. A., & Wooley, J. D. (1982). Paradigms and processes in reading comprehension. *Journal of Experimental Psychology: General, 111*, 228–238.

Kawamoto, A. H. (1985). Dynamic processes in the (re)solution of lexical ambiguity. Doctoral dissertation, Department of Psychology, Brown University.

Kawamoto, A. H. (1988). Distributed representations of ambiguous words and their resolution in a connectionist network. In S. L. Small, G. W. Cottrell, & M. K. Tanenhaus (Eds), *Lexical ambiguity resolution: Perspectives from psycholinguistics, neuropsychology, and artificial intelligence*. San Mateo, Calif.: Morgan Kaufmann.

Marcus, M. P. (1980). *A theory of syntactic recognition for natural language*. Cambridge, Mass.: MIT Press.

McClelland, J. L. (1979). On the time relations of mental processes: An examination of systems of processes in cascade. *Psychological Review*, *86*, 287–330.

McClelland, J. L. (1987). The case for interactionism in language processing. In M. Coltheart (Ed.), *Attention and performance XII: The psychology of reading*, pp. 1–36. London: Lawrence Erlbaum Associates Ltd.

McClelland, J. L. (in press). Parallel distributed processing: Implications for cognition and development. In R. Morris (Ed.), *Parallel distributed processing: implications for psychology and neurobiology*. Oxford: Oxford University Press.

McClelland, J. L. & Elman, J. L. (1986). An architecture for parallel processing in speech recognition: The TRACE model. In M. R. Schroeder (Ed.), *Speech recognition*. Basel: S. Krager AG.

McClelland, J. L. & Kawamoto, A. H. (1986). Mechanisms of sentence processing: Assigning roles to constituents. In J. L. McClelland, D. E. Rumelhart, & the PDP Research

Group (Eds), *Parallel distributed processing: Explorations in the microstructure of cognition*, Vol. II. Cambridge, Mass.: Bradford Books.

McClelland, J. L. & Rumelhart, D. E. (1981). An interactive activation model of context effects in letter perception, Part 1: An account of basic findings. *Psychological Review*, *88*, 375–407.

McDonald, J. & MacWhinney, B. (in press). Maximum likelihood models for sentence processing. In B. MacWhinney & E. Bates (Eds), *The crosslinguistic study of sentence processing*. New York: Cambridge University Press.

Miikkulainen, R. & Dyer, M. G. (1989). A modular neural network architecture for sequential paraphrasing of script-based stories. Technical Report UCLA-AI-89-02. University of California, Artificial Intelligence Laboratory, Computer Science Department, Los Angeles.

Milberg, W., Blumstein, S., & Dworetzky, B. (1988). Phonological processing and lexical access in aphasia. *Brain and Language*, *34*, 279–293.

Oden, G. (1978). Semantic constraints and judged preference for interpretations of ambiguous sentences. *Memory and Cognition*, *6*, 26–37.

Rayner, K., Carlson, M., & Frazier, L. (1983). The interaction of syntax and semantics during sentence processing: Eye movements in the analysis of semantically biased sentences. *Journal of Verbal Learning and Verbal Behavior*, *22*, 358–374.

Rumelhart, D. E. & McClelland, J. L. (1981). Interactive processing through spreading activation. In C. Perfetti & A. Lesgold (Eds), *Interactive processes in reading*. Hillsdale, N.J.: Lawrence Erlbaum Associates Inc.

Rumelhart, D. E. & McClelland, J. L. (1982). An interactive activation model of context effects in letter perception, Part II: The contextual enhancement effect and some tests and extensions of the model. *Psychological Review*, *89*, 60–94.

Rumelhart, D. E., Hinton, G. E., & Williams, R. J. (1986a). Learning internal representations by error propagation. In D. E. Rumelhart, J. L. McClelland, & the PDP Research Group (Eds), *Parallel distributed processing: Explorations in the microstructure of cognition*, Vol. I. Cambridge, Mass.: MIT Press.

Rumelhart, D. E., Smolensky, P., McClelland, J. L., & Hinton, G. E. (1986b). Parallel distributed processing models of schemata and sequential thought processes. In J. L. McClelland, D. E. Rumelhart, & the PDP Research Group (Eds), *Parallel distributed processing: Explorations in the microstructure of cognition*, Vol. II. Cambridge, Mass.: Bradford Books.

St. John, M. F. (1988). Hitting the right pitch: A meta-analysis of the processing of ambiguous words in context. Manuscript.

St. John, M. F. & McClelland, J. L. (1987). Reconstructive memory for sentences: A PDP approach. Paper presented to the Ohio University Inference Conference, *Proceedings Inference: OUIC 86*. University of Ohio, Athens, Ohio.

St. John, M. F. & McClelland, J. L. (in press). Learning and applying contextual constraints in sentence comprehension. *Artificial Intelligence*.

Schank, R. C. (1981). Language and memory. In D. A. Norman (Ed.), *Perspectives on cognitive science*. Norwood, N. J.: Ablex.

Servan-Schreiber, D., Cleeremans, A., & McClelland, J. L. (1988). Encoding sequential structure in simple recurrent networks. CMU-CS-88-183. Carnegie Mellon University, Computer Science Department, Pittsburgh.

Swinney, D. A. (1979). Lexical access during sentence comprehension: (Re)consideration of context effects. *Journal of Verbal Learning and Verbal Behavior*, *18*, 645–659.

Tanenhaus, M. K., Leiman, J. M., & Seidenberg, M. S. (1979). Evidence for multiple stages in the processing of ambiguous words in syntactic contexts. *Journal of Verbal Learning and Verbal Behavior*, *18*, 427–440.

Taraban, R. (1988). Content-based expectations: One source of guidance for syntactic attachment and thematic role assignment in sentence processing. Ph.D. dissertation, Carnegie Mellon University, Pittsburgh.

Taraban, R. & McClelland, J. L. (1988). Constituent attachment and thematic role assignment in sentence processing: Influences of content-based expectations. *Journal of Memory and Language*, *27*, 597–632.

Taraban, R. & McClelland, J. L. (1990). Parsing and comprehension: A multiple-constraint view. In D. Balota, G. B. Flores d'Arcais, & K. Rayner (Eds), *Comprehension processes in reading*. Hillsdale, N.J.: Lawrence Erlbaum Associates Inc.

Touretzky, D. S. (1988). Connectionism and PP attachment. In D. Touretzky, G. Hinton, & T. Sejnowski (Eds), *Proceedings of the 1988 Connectionist Mosels*. San Mateo, Calif.: Morgan Kaufmann.

Touretzky, D. S. & Geva, S. (1987). A distributed connectionist representation for concept structures. Paper presented to the 9th Annual Conference of the Cognitive Science Society, Seattle.

Touretzky, D. S. & Hinton, G. E. (1988). A distributed connectionist production system. *Cognitive Science*, *12*, 423–466.

van Gelder, T. (in press). Compositionality: Variation on a classical theme. *Cognitive Science*.

LANGUAGE AND COGNITIVE PROCESSES, 1989, *4*, (3/4) SI 337–368

Computational Models of Incremental Semantic Interpretation

Nicholas J. Haddock
Information Systems Centre, Hewlett-Packard Laboratories, Bristol, and Department of Artificial Intelligence and Centre for Cognitive Science, University of Edinburgh, Edinburgh, U.K.

This paper provides a tutorial introduction to the computational problem of "incremental" semantic interpretation: the problem of computing the semantic interpretation of a sentence on a word-by-word basis as the sentence is read from left to right. We also consider the way in which incremental interpretation can guide the syntactic processing, and pay particular attention to the use of referential information during parsing. We address these issues in terms of the computational models of Bobrow and Webber (1980a,b), Winograd (1972), Mellish (1985), and Haddock (1988). In each case, we ask two questions: First, to what extent does the program embody an incremental process of semantic interpretation? Secondly, how does this process help resolve syntactic ambiguities encountered by the parser? Here we will relate the behaviour of the models to the psychological theory of ambiguity resolution offered by Crain and Steedman (1985). In the context of this review, we identify some of the specific problems involved in incremental interpretation, and compare the computational techniques which have been applied to these problems.

INTRODUCTION

Our intuitions about natural language comprehension strongly suggest that the process of understanding a spoken or written sentence is a continuous one, carried out in small, gradual steps as each word is heard or read. We

Requests for reprints should be addressed to Nicholas J. Haddock, Hewlett-Packard Laboratories, Filton Road, Stoke Gifford, Bristol BS12 6QZ, U.K.

This paper is based on research carried out at the Department of Artificial Intelligence and Centre for Cognitive Science, University of Edinburgh, with the financial support of a Science and Engineering Research Council Research Studentship.

I would like to thank Mark Steedman, Chris Mellish, Henry Thompson, and Bonnie Webber for advice and encouragement, and Gerry Altmann and two anonymous reviewers for detailed comments on an earlier draft of the manuscript.

might therefore think of the comprehension process as being "incremental", in that an utterance seems to acquire its meaning bit by bit rather than in one go when it has come to an end. A number of psychological experiments indicate that such incremental semantic interpretation is indeed a feature of human sentence processing.

Given the evidence in favour of incremental interpretation, it is fitting to ask how far computational linguists have got in building explicit models of this process. The present paper aims to provide a tutorial introduction to some of the computational issues involved in this endeavour. We start by briefly reviewing the psycholinguistic motivation for our study, and with this in mind identify the angles from which we will approach the literature. The paper then considers several computational models of on-line semantic interpretation, and in doing so identifies some of the techniques which have been applied to the problem of incremental interpretation. The concluding section discusses the linguistic and computational challenge's which have yet to be faced by this enterprise.

Psychological Motivation

A number of psychological inquiries provide support for the view that people understand sentences incrementally. These include studies of the word-by-word, real-time nature of comprehension (Marslen-Wilson, 1975; 1987; Marlsen-Wilson & Tyler, 1980; Tanenhaus, Carlson, & Seidenberg, 1985; Tyler & Marslen-Wilson, 1977); the immediacy of reference resolution (Garrod & Sanford, 1985; Shillcock, 1982), and the early contextual disambiguation of ambiguous nouns (Swinney, 1979). Such evidence provides a general incentive for the present computational exercise. Moreover, our study has been particularly influenced by the empirical investigations of Crain and Steedman (1985) and Altmann and Steedman (1988) into the role of incremental interpretation in resolving syntactic ambiguity.

Following Crain and Steedman (1985), Altmann and Steedman (1988) consider globally ambiguous sentences like (1), in which the PP *with the gladiolus* may modify the VP *tickled the man* or the NP *the man*:

1. She tickled the man with the gladiolus

It is not clear how the human sentence processor resolves such ambiguities. Sentence processing might be guided by structural factors, such as those of Kimball (1973), Frazier and Fodor (1978), and Ford, Bresnan, and Kaplan (1982). For example, Frazier's (1978) strategy of "Minimal Attachment" predicts that the VP-modifying reading of (1) is preferred—where the gladiolus does the tickling—because this analysis is syntactically less complex than the NP-modifying analysis. In contrast, Altmann and Steedman

(1988) argue that the preference is dependent on the context of the discourse in which the sentence is uttered. For instance, their principle of "Referential Support" predicts that if there is more than one man under discussion, and one of them is associated with a gladiolus, the NP-modifying analysis of (1) is preferred. They propose that the VP-modifying reading is disregarded because under this reading the definite, object NP *the man* fails to refer uniquely; the NP-modifying reading is chosen instead because a unique referent can be determined for the complex NP *the man with the gladiolus*.

The debate over the human preference data is by no means resolved, but for the purposes of the present paper we will relate our discussion of computational models to the theory of sentence processing offered by Crain, Altmann, and Steedman. In their model, the psychological parser interacts with the referential context on a word-by-word basis, choosing between the available syntactic alternatives according to their interpretations in the context.

Computational Issues

In the light of these remarks, our review of computational models will concentrate on the following two aspects of on-line interpretation.

Incremental Interpretation. Our foremost concern will be in the way semantic representations are formed. Here we will be looking for an incremental construction process, where a processor gradually accumulates semantic information as an input sentence is read from left to right. One way of determining the degree to which a given process is incremental, is to consider how soon the semantics of an incoming word is related to the semantics of the entire preceding sentence fragment.

Interaction. We may also analyse a scheme of semantic interpretation in terms of its interaction with the syntactic processor. In particular, how do the available interpretations help resolve structural ambiguities as they are discovered by the parser? Here, in broad terms, we will compare each model to the psychological theory of sentence processing offered by Crain, Altmann, and Steedman.

Overview of the Field

There is a wealth of work illustrating how various kinds of semantic information can be manipulated during parsing. From our point of view, it will be useful to distinguish between those models which involve interactions with temporary but specific knowledge about the current conversational or physical context (such as the particular referents under discussion), and those models which only involve a more general, commonsense knowledge about what is plausible in the world (such as the knowledge which tells us that it is more likely for doctors to cure patients than the reverse). Following the results of Crain, Altmann, and Steedman, which suggest that the immediate referential context takes precedence over general world knowledge in resolving local ambiguities, we will devote most attention to the systems which explicitly include on-line referential processing. For a broader discussion of the role of semantics in parsing, the reader is referred to Ritchie's (1983) survey article.

The majority of systems have concentrated on the deployment of *context-independent* semantic and world knowledge during sentence processing. Woods (1973), Ford et al. (1982), Milne (1982), and Pazzani (1984) advocate the use of shallow, sense-semantic information stemming from individual lexical items (e.g. to check that the agent of the verb *drive* is animate), whereas Bobrow and Webber (1980b), Lytinen (1984), Waltz and Pollack (1985), Wilks, Huang, and Fass (1985), Lesmo and Torasso (1985), Charniak (1986), Dahlgren and McDowell (1986), Palmer et al. (1986), Hirst (1987), and Jacobs (1987) employ a variety of more general knowledge to guide the process of syntactic analysis. Some models, such as those of Riesbeck (1975), Burton (1976), and Tomabechi (1987), do away with a distinct syntactic level altogether, making information about word order and constituency more or less implicit in the interpretation process. We will discuss just one example of the use of discourse-independent, general knowledge during parsing—Bobrow and Webber's PSI-KLONE system.

Less work has been directed at the involvement of pragmatic elements in the parsing process, although Gehrke (1983) discusses how a processor may incrementally determine a speaker's intentions in the context of an ongoing dialogue. Weischedel (1979) shows how the presuppositions and entailments of a sentence may be computed as it is parsed, but his inference procedures are limited to the structural aspects of the sentence and do not relate to the local context. More relevant from the present point of view are the models of Winograd (1972), Mellish (1985), Hirst (1987), Charniak and Goldman (1988), and Haddock (1988), which all process referential information during syntactic parsing. Here we will discuss the work of Winograd, Mellish, and Haddock in detail, and touch on the rest as the paper progresses.[1]

---

[1]Schubert (1984; 1986) also describes a program in which syntactic, semantic, and pragmatic factors all contribute to the disambiguation of a syntactically ambiguous sentence, but his model is too briefly described to comment on here.

The following sections, therefore, review four models of linguistic processing according to the criteria we set down in the previous section. We begin with an early and innovative example of incremental semantic interpretation which proceeds without the help of local knowledge about the discourse, the PSI-KLONE system.

INCREMENTAL AND INTERACTIVE SENSE-SEMANTICS

This section discusses the PSI-KLONE program developed by Bobrow and Webber (1980a,b),[2] a program which maintains the formal distinction between syntax and semantics, but allows them to interact in an incremental fashion during sentence processing. Bobrow and Webber's model is an appropriate one with which to start our review, because they emphasise the notion of "incremental description refinement". This is a general class of algorithms which they consider to be suitable for incremental processing, and we will come across two members of this class during the course of the paper. The first of these is Bobrow and Webber's own method of incrementally determining the sense of a verb in the context of the enclosing sentence. We describe this process below, explain its relationship to incremental description refinement, and discuss the kind of feedback it provides to the parser.

Incremental Interpretation

PSI-KLONE consists of an ATN-based syntactic parser[3] which engages in a dialogue of requests and responses with a semantic interpreter as an input sentence is scanned from left to right. As an arc in the ATN is traversed, it may transmit a "request" to the semantic component, typically in the form of an instruction to interpret partially the constituent being parsed. The semantic component will respond either with an updated version of the sentence's interpretation, or with a failure message indicating that the proposed syntactic move is implausible on semantic grounds. If such a failure message is received, the parser abandons that particular path through the ATN and backs up in the normal way. [Bobrow and Webber view this processing architecture in terms of Woods' (1980) Cascaded ATN model of interaction, although they do not describe the relationship in detail. However, Woods (1980, pp. 9–11) shows how aspects of PSI-

[2]See also Bates, Bobrow, and Webber (1981), Brachman (1979), and Sondheimer, Weischedel, and Bobrow (1984).

[3]For a general presentation of the Augmented Transition Network (ATN) grammar formalism, see Woods (1970).

KLONE's interactive semantic processing can be formulated in terms of his ATN-based syntactic/semantic cascade.]

Each message from the ATN to the semantic component takes the form of a triple

(M, L, C)

where M ("matrix") represents the half-built constituent currently being parsed, C is a parsed and interpreted subconstituent, and L is the syntactic label which is proposed to link C to M. Thus, in parsing

2. John ran the race

a message is sent after reading *ran*, proposing that an animate NP, *John*, is the subject of the main clause. In this case, the (M, L, C) triple would contain the following information:[4]

(M = <a CLAUSE whose main verb is *ran*>,
L = SUBJECT,
C = <an ANIMATE NP>)

Note that the above triple includes both syntactic and semantic information, because *John* has already been interpreted by this same process of syntactic "proposals" at a lower level in the ATN. The semantic component assesses the general plausibility of the request by trying to relate the proposed syntactic label to a thematic role in one of its stored semantic case frames. For example, it might relate the above subject label to the semantic role of agent, because *John* is an animate description and is in the subject position, and because one case frame for running requires an animate-type agent. The semantic component then updates the matrix structure M with this information and returns it to the parser for use in later transmissions.

In essence, then, PSI-KLONE checks the semantic plausibility of a proposal—which contains both syntactic and semantic information—by determining its consistency with some semantic case frame. Interestingly, the system represents the set of syntactic/semantic proposals that can be interpreted (i.e. mapped into a case frame) in the intensional format provided by KL-ONE, a formalism for representing generic knowledge (Brachman & Schmolze, 1985). This allows the set of syntactic/semantic shapes to be taxonomically organised in a lattice which specifies the way they share information.

By way of an example, Fig. 1 illustrates the central links in a KL-ONE lattice specifying the connections between the various interpretable clauses

[4]As in all such examples throughout this paper, the authors' original notation is simplified for the purposes of exposition.

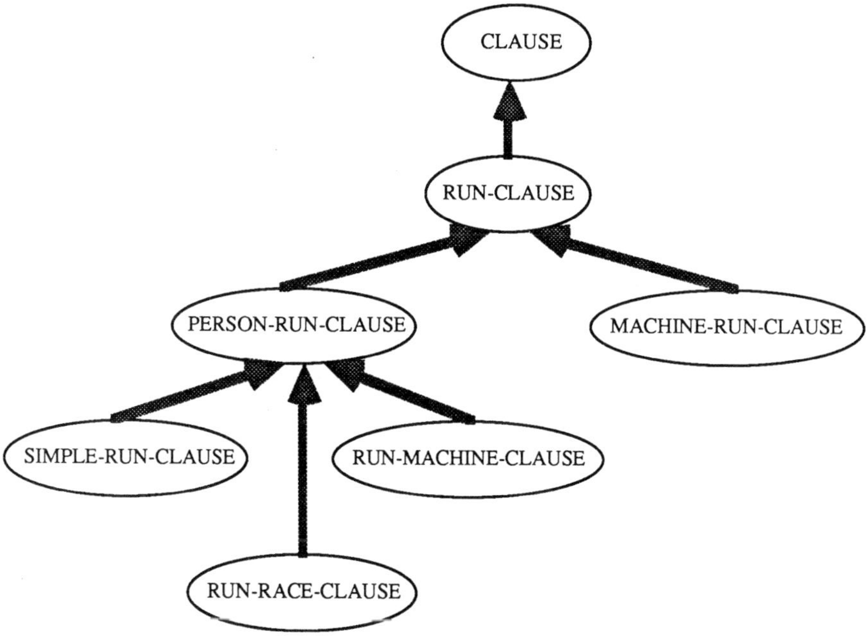

FIG. 1 How recognisable *run* clauses relate to each other in KL-ONE (adapted from Bates et al., 1981, p. 107).

about running.[5] In addition, each node in the lattice is associated with certain linguistic roles, and any node which it subsumes inherits these same roles in order to facilitate the structure-sharing. In Fig. 1, for example, the CLAUSE node would be linked to an obligatory subject role, an obligatory head role, and an optional object role (these roles are not included in the figure because of their pictorial complexity). The taxonomy also indicates the types of linguistic object that may fill these roles; stating that the sentential subject must be an NP, that the clausal head should be a verb, and so on. Because the CLAUSE node subsumes the RUN-CLAUSE node, the RUN-CLAUSE node inherits all of these expected features. But, in addition, it expects its head to be the verb *run*. So the RUN-CLAUSE node characterises a more specific shape than the CLAUSE node. In turn, RUN-CLAUSE subsumes PERSON-RUN-CLAUSE and MACHINE-RUN-CLAUSE, and each of these places further restrictions on the attributes of an interpretable running clause.

[5]In fact, the network in Fig. 1 specifically constitutes a *tree*, rather than a *lattice*, but we will continue to use the latter term as in general KL-ONE permits a node to have multiple parents.

Thus a sentence is recognised as a PERSON-RUN-CLAUSE only if its subject NP is an animate type of NP. In contrast, MACHINE-RUN-CLAUSE expects a machine-type NP as subject (as in *The computer ran the program*).

Within this framework, the matrix M and subconstituent C in a proposal can be understood as pointers to specific nodes in a taxonomy. PSI-KLONE's decision to accept or reject a proposal from the ATN thus depends simply on whether or not the proposal can be located within the taxonomy. If the proposed syntactic/semantic shape satisfies the role restrictions of some clausal node in the lattice, then it is assumed to be interpretable, and actions associated with the node can build the appropriate case frame when it is required. The important point is that the set of allowable syntactic/semantic shapes is represented intensionally, meaning that PSI-KLONE can develop incrementally the details of a particular clausal matrix by moving from node to node in the lattice as the ATN arcs are traversed.

Consider the sentence in (3), for instance:

3. John ran the drill press.

In isolation, the sense of the verb *ran* is ambiguous: According to Fig. 1, it may relate to the running of a machine or the running of a person. But PSI-KLONE's taxonomic representation of linguistic sense allows the ambiguity to be resolved incrementally, as the sentence is read. After determining that *John* is an animate type of NP, the parser reads the next word and proposes that *run* is the head of a CLAUSE. The verb satisfies the restrictions which apply to the head role of a RUN-CLAUSE and so creates an instance of this generic node. The parser can now make another proposal, to the effect that *John* should fill the subject slot in the newly created instance of RUN-CLAUSE. The semantic interpreter accepts this, now linking the matrix to the PERSON-RUN-CLAUSE, as the subject is animate. Finally, the object NP *the drill press* is recognised. This distinguishes between the three specialisations of PERSON-RUN-CLAUSE, making the sentence a RUN-MACHINE-CLAUSE. Because all the roles pertaining to this node are now filled, a complete semantic representation is built, on the basis of the type of description that has been recognised.

The point of interest in this example is in the way PSI-KLONE incrementally refines the sense of the verb *run* by gradually progressing down the inheritance lattice as information becomes available from the parser. This seems a very natural form of incremental processing. Intermediate results influence the interpretations of subsequent words and, correspondingly, each word makes the intermediate interpretation more specific. Importantly, later processing in the string cannot *change* earlier decisions; it can only make an earlier representation more specific. Here, then, incremental processing consists of gradually refining a set of possibilities by, at each stage, moving from a certain node in the lattice to one of the nodes which it subsumes.

Bobrow and Webber (1980b, p. 319) characterise their refinement mechanism as an instance of a general class of incremental process, which they call Incremental Description Refinement:

> *Incremental Description Refinement* (IDR) is the process of:
> - Determining the set of descriptions compatible with an object known to have a given set of properties.
> - Refining the set of descriptions as more properties are learned.

In the domain of syntactic/semantic shapes, an "object" is some linguistic constituent, and the compatible descriptions are represented by nodes in the lattice. If PSI-KLONE's refinement operation has reached a given node in the lattice, the currently applicable set of compatible descriptions are just those terminal nodes subsumed by this node.

Interaction

Bobrow and Webber also apply their model to the problem of syntactic ambiguity. Consider, for example, a sentence fragment of the form in (4):

4. Smith sent NP . . .

(4) contains a local structural ambiguity: The NP may be the direct object of the verb (as in *Smith sent a message to Bill*) or the indirect object (as in *Smith sent Bill a message*). Subsequent syntactic information should resolve the ambiguity, but by considering the semantics of the NP in (4), PSI-KLONE may be able to dispose of one of the readings immediately. So if the fragment in question is

5. Smith sent a message . . .

PSI-KLONE can reject the syntactic reading in which *a message* is treated as the indirect object of *sent*, because it is generally implausible for a message to be sent anything. This kind of syntactic disambiguation is an instance of what Crain and Steedman (1985) call the "Principle of A Priori Plausibility":

> *The Principle of A Priori Plausibility*
>
> If a reading is more plausible in terms either of general knowledge about the world, or of specific knowledge about the universe of discourse, then, other things being equal, it will be favoured over one that is not.

PSI-KLONE will accept a proposal from its parser only if it can be related to one of its stored semantic case frames, which, in the terms of the above principle, represent "general knowledge about the world".

However, PSI-KLONE does not access knowledge of the more specific, discourse-related kind. Crain and Steedman claim that if general knowledge about the world and specific knowledge about the discourse ever give conflicting advice about the plausibility of an analysis, the specific knowledge takes precedence. This claim is further borne out by the data presented by Altmann and Steedman. It therefore seems appropriate that we now turn our attention to those models which do utilise such knowledge, and, in particular, consider how reference evaluation has been combined with the parsing process.

INTERACTIVE REFERENCE-SEMANTICS

Winograd (1971; 1972; 1973) provides an early example of on-line referential processing in his SHRDLU program. Although the program's method of reference evaluation does not embody any relevant form of incrementation, we will see how the results of reference evaluation can interact with a syntactic processor to resolve certain structural ambiguities.

Incremental Interpretation

SHRDLU, a simulated robot, operated in a simulated toy "blocks world", consisting of a box, and some blocks and pyramids. The blocks world is straightforwardly represented as a "database", or list of facts, such as the following (adapted from Winograd, 1973, p. 168):

6. (IS B1 BOX)
   (IS B2 PYRAMID)
   (IS B3 BLOCK)
   (IS B4 BLOCK)
   (COLOUR-OF B2 BLUE)
   (COLOUR-OF B3 RED)
   (COLOUR-OF B4 BLUE)
   (CONTAIN B1 B2)

The above fragment of knowledge expresses the fact that B1 is a box, that it contains a pyramid, B2, and so on.

SHRDLU interprets an input sentence by translating it into a program (in the problem-solving language Planner), and then executing the program with respect to its current set of blocks world facts. The question in (7a), for instance, might be translated into the procedure call of (7b):

7a. Does the box contain the red block?
b. (PROVE (CONTAIN B1 B3))

The system thus translates the yes/no question into the goal of proving that the box, B1, contains the red block, B3; and its response to the user will depend on whether the proposition can be proved. It can carry out such proofs by checking that the database includes the fact (CONTAIN B1 B3), or perhaps by seeing whether B1 contains some other object which, in turn, contains B3. In a similar way, natural language commands are interpreted as calls to procedures which can execute actions in the blocks world. So the instruction *Pick up a big blue block* might translate as (GRASP B4)—an instruction which, when executed, simulates the appropriate robot action.

Notice that in procedure calls such as (7b), SHRDLU has already determined the referents of *the box* and *the red block*. In fact, referring expressions are evaluated in the same deductive manner as questions and commands. In the case of *the red block*, SHRDLU first assembles a procedure from the senses of the words in the NP:

8a. the red block
b. (FIND 1 ?X s.t. (PROVE (IS ?X BLOCK))
(PROVE (COLOUR-OF ?X RED)))

Here the variable ?X stands in place of the referent of the expression; the clauses (PROVE (IS ?X BLOCK)) and (PROVE (COLOUR-OF ?X RED)) stem from *block* and *red*, respectively; and the enclosing instruction to FIND 1 ?X is designed to capture the uniqueness intended by the use of the definite article. Once complete, this procedure is evaluated by searching in the database for all instances of ?X for which the twin properties (IS ?X BLOCK) and (COLOUR-OF ?X RED) are true. If just one entity fits the description (also considering information about the recent dialogue), then ?X is bound to this value; if no entities or more than one can be found, the procedure fails and SHRDLU reports the error. So with the database of (6), the routine would succeed and bind ?X to B3.

Our present interest in Winograd's program concerns the way such reference evaluation is intermingled with syntactic processing. As the parser finds a complete NP in the string, it calls the semantic component to build an appropriate deductive procedure. This procedure is immediately evaluated to determine the contextually relevant referent for the NP, and this can provide useful feedback to the parser, as we will see below. However, the process of reference evaluation, in itself, is not incremental. Routines like (8b) are designed to be evaluated, instantaneously and completely, at a single point in parsing. For SHRDLU, this is when the corresponding noun phrase is syntactically closed. Given that English grammar permits NPs to be arbitrarily long, reference evaluation may be delayed indefinitely—thus postponing potentially helpful advice to the parser. (Note that this is not true for all forms of semantic interaction in Winograd's program. In particular, "semantic markers", which provide a shallow form of sense-semantic checking, are applied incrementally as a constituent is parsed.)

Interaction

Let us now turn to the role of such interpretation in the parsing process. The success of procedures like (8b) influences the direction taken by the parser: If a referent cannot be found (or if too many can be found), the parser tries an alternative syntactic reading of the string. This strategy helps resolve ambiguities in the closure of definite noun phrases in sentences like (9):

9a. Put [the blue pyramid on the block]$_{NP}$ [in the box]$_{PP}$
b. Put [the blue pyramid]$_{NP}$ [on the block in the box]$_{PP}$

If the database shows there to be a blue pyramid on the block and, furthermore, this is uniquely identifiable either by virtue of being the only one or having been recently mentioned, then analysis (a) is adopted. However, if no referent can be found, analysis (b) is chosen—providing the blocks world contains a single blue pyramid and a single block in the box. It can be seen that this aspect of SHRDLU's context-sensitive behaviour accords with Crain and Steedman's (1985) later "Principle of Referential Success", a special case of the earlier Principle of A Priori Plausibility:

> *The Principle of Referential Success*
>
> If there is a reading which succeeds in referring to an entity already established in the hearer's mental model of the domain of discourse, then it is preferred over one that does not.

For an ambiguous sentence like (9), SHRDLU's parser apparently first investigates the reading with the *longest* possible object NP.[6] Thus, in the case of (9), only once *the blue pyramid on the block* has been parsed as an NP, will the mechanisms for semantic evaluation intervene and pass judgement on the analysis. Later in the paper, when discussing Haddock's (1988) approach to incremental interpretation, we will see how this attachment decision can be made at an earlier point in sentence processing.

Hirst (1987; 1988) has more recently demonstrated how referential information can be brought to bear on syntactic ambiguity, following Winograd, and Crain and Steedman. His program resolves attachment ambiguities potentially earlier in the string than SHRDLU, as his disambiguation procedure is invoked as soon as the shortest possible PP has been

[6]This observation is based on the example in Winograd (1973, p. 182).

found, whereas SHRDLU initially looks for the longest possible complex NP. Moreover, he illustrates how referential feedback might be combined with other strategies for disambiguation, such as the aforementioned "Minimal Attachment". Further discussion of this work can be found in Haddock (1988).

INCREMENTAL REFERENCE-SEMANTICS

The work of Mellish (1981; 1982; 1983; 1985) is explicitly addressed to the problem of incremental reference evaluation, a problem which Winograd did not directly confront. Mellish's approach provides our second example of incremental description refinement (IDR), though in the domain of reference evaluation rather than Bobrow and Webber's sense-semantic refinement. Mellish thus shares Bobrow and Webber's interest in intrinsically incremental semantic processes, and considers how referential information can be derived from a sentence as early as possible during a left-to-right syntactic analysis.

Incremental Interpretation

Why should Mellish want to provide an IDR process for reference evaluation? To set the scene, recall that Winograd's program evaluates the reference of a definite noun phrase when it has been read and parsed in its entirety. No reference evaluation is done before this point, and none is done afterwards; thus the phrase is expected to refer successfully once it is syntactically closed. Mellish questions this rigid view of reference evaluation, claiming that there is no fixed point in sentence processing at which we can guarantee to be able to resolve the reference of an NP. Instead, he argues that the reference of an NP is dependent on the linguistic and non-linguistic context created by the enclosing sentence, previous sentences, and possibly even subsequent ones. Therefore, he argues, if reference resolution is to occur at all during syntactic analysis, it *must* be done in an incremental fashion. Mellish thus sets about developing an inherently vague representation for references that can be incrementally refined as the text makes the disambiguating information available. His program deals with a variety of singular and plural referring expressions in this context, though in what follows we will be concerned mainly with the treatment of singular definite reference.

The program's overall process of semantic analysis is driven by a Definite Clause Grammar (DCG; see Pereira & Warren, 1980)—a grammar, written as a Prolog program, with a direct procedural interpretation as a top-down parser, and similar in many respects to an ATN. Semantic operations, built up from definitions in the lexicon, are invoked whenever

TABLE 1
Order of Semantic Evaluation by Mellish's Program (from Mellish, 1985, p. 35)

A *particle*	*of mass*	*b*	*rests on*	the	*smooth*	*table*
(1)	(2)	(3)	(6)		(5)	(4)

the parser finds a major syntactic constituent. This leads to an order of semantic evaluation which Mellish (1985, p. 35) exemplifies with the following sentence (Table 1):

10. A particle of mass b rests on the smooth table

The type of semantic evaluation involved at each of the points in Table 1 depends on whether the corresponding linguistic material is seen as providing *given* or *new* information (cf. Halliday, 1967), in contrast to Winograd's program, which assumes all NPs refer to given, known entities. However, in order to avoid the immensely complex issue of determining the informational status of a fragment of a sentence, the program assumes all definite NPs are given, and all indefinite NPs and verbal constituents at the main clause level are new. Therefore, in the sentence in (10), the indefinite *a particle of mass b* is taken to introduce a new, specific particle into the context; this is modelled by creating an instance of a particle, giving it a name, say PARTICLE1, and adding this to the program's database. The definite NP *the smooth table*, on the other hand, is assumed to refer to some table already present in the context; and in this case the program starts to resolve the reference by collecting together a set of candidate entities from its database.

How are definite references resolved by the program? Mellish sees semantic interpretation as a process of satisfying the "constraints" which must hold if a sentence is to make sense, and reference resolution simply comes about as a by-product of this more global procedure of constraint satisfaction. These constraints—which may come from the general context, the sentence, and the noun phrase itself—gradually accumulate as the sentence is parsed; and as the constraints are imposed, the number of candidate referents which satisfy them shrinks.

The program can derive two sorts of constraint from a text, and these are both useful in evaluating references. In evaluating the reference of *the smooth table* in (10), for example, it derives the constraints

smooth(X) & table(X)

from the NP, meaning that whatever the referent X is, it must be smooth and it must be a table. These constraints can be applied to entities in the database to pick out just those objects that fit the description—they are of the same variety as Winograd's (PROVE (IS ?X BLOCK)) deductive procedure calls. Whereas these constraints arise from *given* information, a second source of constraint can be derived from both the *new* and *given* information in the sentence. This concerns knowledge about the physical possibilities of the world, which can act as a "semantic check" on all information expressed in the sentence. For example, a general physical constraint stems from the verb group in (10): The referent X of *the smooth table* must be something which, in principle, can support a particle. Thus X will also be subject to the constraint:

can_support(particle,X)

which is a precondition for the meaningfulness of the sentence as a whole.

Given these sources of constraints, Mellish formalises the actual process of reference resolution in terms of a form of constraint satisfaction known as "network consistency" (see Mackworth, 1977; 1987; Waltz, 1975). As Mellish demonstrates, we can do this by representing a partially evaluated reference by a symbol, such as ref(3). And with each such symbol we associate a candidate set of potential referents from the context. To begin with, this candidate set will contain all those discourse entities consistent with the initial constraints on the reference. But as constraints on the reference accumulate, the candidate entities no longer consistent with the constraints are eliminated or "filtered" out of the set.

The candidate set may, eventually, reduce to a single element, in which case the reference has been fully resolved. Or the imposition of some constraint may actually eliminate every entity from a certain candidate set, meaning that the syntactic analysis which derived the constraints is inconsistent with the program's view of the world. In such cases, the parser is forced to abandon the analysis and backtrack to a previous choice point, retracting constraints as it goes.

We should note that such constraint satisfaction algorithms are network-based, in that the constraints are linked together in a network as they accumulate. The network provides explicit connections between the references that are directly related to each other. This means that whenever a discourse entity is eliminated from a particular candidate set, the effects can be "propagated" through the network to any related references, in case their candidate sets have to be revised too.

To appreciate the workings of this and other aspects of Mellish's reference procedure, consider the example in (11), from Mellish (1985, pp. 49–52):

11. A uniform rod is supported by a string attached to *its* ends.

We will focus on the problem of determining that *it* refers to the rod, and not the string. Supposing that this sentence occurs at the beginning of a text, by the time the program reads *its*, it will be aware of two entities: a uniform rod, ROD1, and a string, STRING1. Symbolising the reference of *it* as ref(1), the program therefore creates an initial candidate set consisting of just these elements, {ROD1, STRING1}, and associates this with ref(1).

The next step is to apply the meaning of *ends* to ref(1). First of all, this entails checking that both candidates for ref(1) can, in principle, have ends. They both pass the test, and the program now starts to resolve the reference of *ends* by imposing the following constraints:

leftend(ref(1),ref(2))
rightend(ref(1),ref(3))

These constraints introduce two more undetermined references: the left-end, ref(2), and the right-end, ref(3), of whatever ref(1) is. Because the system can infer that ROD1 and STRING1 both have left- and right-ends, ref(2) and ref(3) initially each have two candidates. At this point, then:

ref(1) is one of {ROD1, STRING1}
ref(2) is one of {ROD1-leftend, STRING1-leftend}
ref(3) is one of {ROD1-rightend, STRING1-rightend}

The program now turns to the new information that STRING1 is *attached to* the ends of ref(1), and so begins to assert the appropriate new propositions in the database. One precondition relating to such assertions is designed to reflect the fact that it is pragmatically odd to speak of a physical object being attached to its *own* ends. Thus as each attachment proposition is added to the database, a precondition of separability is checked. First, therefore, the program imposes the preconditional constraint:

separable(STRING1,ref(2))

In attempting to satisfy this, the program sequentially instantiates ref(2) with the two potential referents in its candidate set. The constraint holds were ref(2) = ROD1-leftend but not where ref(2) = STRING1-leftend, because an object is not considered separable from itself. The string's left-end is therefore removed from the candidate set of ref(2), meaning that now:

ref(2) is one of {ROD1-leftend}

The effects of this refinement must now be propagated to any other unresolved references related to ref(2). Given that ref(2) is related to ref(1) by the leftend constraint, the program must ensure that all candidates for ref(1) remain consistent with the filtered set for ref(2). At this point, STRING1 is eliminated as a candidate for ref(1), because it does not have a left-end in the set for ref(2). So now:

ref(1) is one of {ROD1}

Because ref(1) has changed, ref(3) must be reconsidered. This, in turn, resolves the reference of the right-end:

ref(3) is one of {ROD1-rightend}

Hence, once the second precondition of separability,

separable(STRING1, ref(3))

is imposed, it is trivially satisfied. The program maintains consistency in this manner as it parses the remainder of the sentence; ROD1 will satisfy these further constraints and so will be accepted as the referent of *it*.

This process of progressive constraint satisfaction seems a natural form of incremental description refinement. In terms of Bobrow and Webber's (1980b) definition of IDR, we can regard a reference symbol like ref(3) as an "object". A candidate set of discourse entities can be seen as a "set of descriptions", and each such set is refined as constraints or "properties" are learned.[7] PSI-KLONE's taxonomy-based processing and network consistency are thus similar mechanisms, in that they both operate with representations that can be incrementally refined. They are different in that the former represents the space of interpretations *intensionally*, whereas the latter represents the space *extensionally*. Correspondingly, in the first system, incremental refinement consists of stepping to a more specific intensional representation, whereas in the second it involves removing an element from an enumerated set of alternatives.

Mellish has thus identified network consistency among constraints as an IDR process which is suitable for reference evaluation. However, there is more to the problem of incremental interpretation than determining a process which can interpret incoming semantic information in a step-by-step fashion. One must also ensure that the semantic information is extracted from the sentence in a truly left-to-right order. Here Mellish (1985, p. 32) acknowledges that his constraint-based process of semantic interpretation does not directly follow the left-to-right scan of a sentence. Table 1 shows that verbs are processed after their arguments, meaning that a noun phrase subject is only combined with an adjacent right-hand verb once all other arguments to the right of the verb have been found. This strategy contradicts our intuitions about incremental interpretation and

---

[7]For the purposes of exposition, this interpretation of network consistency in terms of IDR is slightly at variance with Bobrow and Webber's (1980b) own interpretation of the mechanism, where the reference symbols would be viewed collectively, as a single object to be processed.

predicts, for example, that the semantic disagreement of subject and main verb in

12. # [A fixed pulley]$_{NP}$ [believes]$_{V}$ [the two small particles]$_{NP}$.

is not noticed until reading the full-stop (at which point the parser would attempt to combine the representation for the verb with those for its subject and object NPs). In general, Mellish's system processes linguistic functions after their linguistic arguments; when a verb, preposition or adjective is read, its semantic interpretation is not immediately incorporated into the interpretation of the preceding fragment of sentence. Thus, while the progressive steps of the semantic interpreter constitute incremental description refinement, these steps are not in a one-to-one correspondence with the steps of the processor which reads the input string from left to right. We will return to this issue from the general perspective of syntactic processing in the section on "The Syntactic Problem of Incremental Interpretation".

Interaction

Mellish's work does not explicitly address the problem of syntactic ambiguity resolution. This is partly due to the treatment of definite noun phrases like *the smooth table*: Although the interpretations of *smooth* and *table* are evaluated during parsing, and thus in principle may guide the syntactic search, the condition of uniqueness arising from the definite determiner is not enforced at all during sentence processing. Thus Mellish's system does not incorporate the kind of interaction found in Winograd's program, where the ability to determine a *unique* referent for a definite NP influences the analysis of an ambiguous PP modifier.

THE SYNTACTIC PROBLEM OF INCREMENTAL INTERPRETATION

Before moving on to our final model, it is worth elaborating on the technical problem encountered above. Even if the underlying interpretation mechanism is designed to accept information in stages, how can we ensure that it has passed semantic information in an appropriate left-to-right order? We can begin to understand this issue by observing that most schemes of semantic interpretation, including those discussed here, are *syntactically driven*. Overall control tends to lie with the parser, which is responsible for finding syntactic constituents in the input string. Once a syntactic constituent is identified, its semantic interpretation is computed and stored with the syntactic category or structure representing that constituent. More specifically, the parsing operation of forming a syntactic constituent from syntactic subconstituents is used to trigger an isomorphic process at the semantic level, which produces a semantic interpretation for the syntactic constituent directly from the interpretations of its syntactic subconstituents. It is thus common to adopt the *rule-to-rule hypothesis* formalised in Montague (1973), and so assume that the rules of syntax are in a one-to-one correspondence with the rules of semantics.

If we do indeed assume some variety of rule-to-rule compositional semantics, and we further assume that the process of semantic interpretation is driven by the syntax rather than the semantics, then the capacity of a given system for *left-to-right* incremental interpretation is simply a question of grammar. As Altmann and Steedman (1988) point out, a grammar which produces left-branching phrase-structure trees, of the form in (13), should be most conducive to incremental semantics (in 13, N represents a non-terminal category, whereas T represents a terminal category):

13.

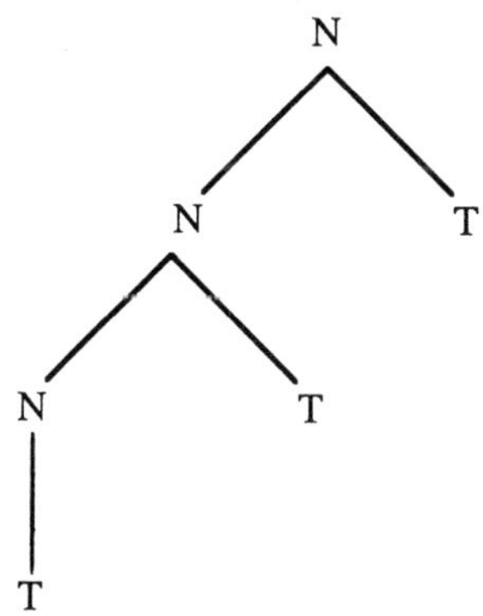

If an input sentence can be analysed as (13), then, in a left-to-right pass through the string, a new syntactic constituent N can be formed when each word is read. In accordance with the rule-to-rule assumption, this means that a semantic interpretation can be provided for each left-hand substring of the sentence, thereby effecting an incremental interpretation. In contrast, with a grammar which produces right-branching structures of the form in (14),

14.

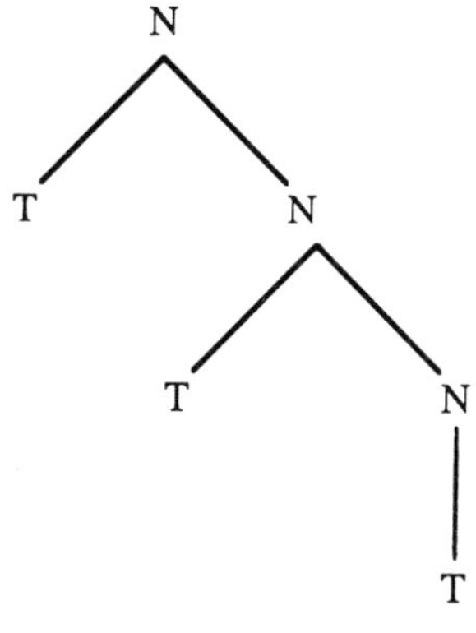

the rule-to-rule hypothesis implies that semantic interpretation must be delayed until the end of the sentence is reached. At this point, a processor can recurse back through the sentence, building syntactic and semantic representations from right to left.

But, of course, English is widely held to be a principally right-branching language, dominated by structures such as (15):

15.

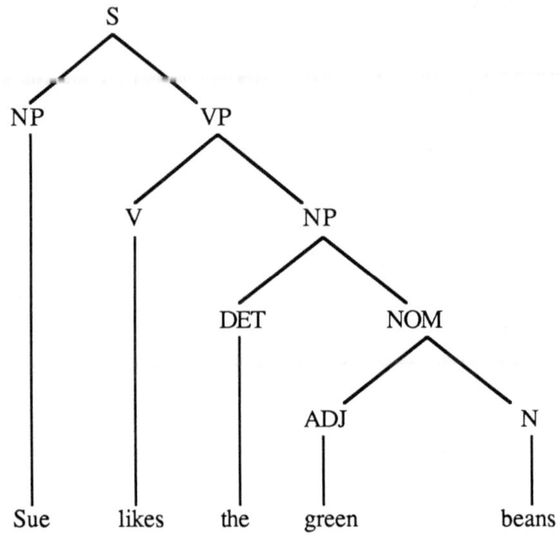

So it is not surprising that a computational model which employs a more or less standard theory of grammar, such as Mellish's, fails to implement properly a left-to-right incremental semantics.

There are at least two possible ways out of this apparent dilemma. The first is to relax the one-to-one correspondence between syntax and semantics, allowing the semantics to proceed more incrementally than the grammar rules themselves suggest. Indeed, Bobrow and Webber's system contains elements of this approach. First, they flatten the structure of main clauses: The syntactic structure implicit in their ATN does not include a VP node, and instead implies the following analysis of (15):

16.

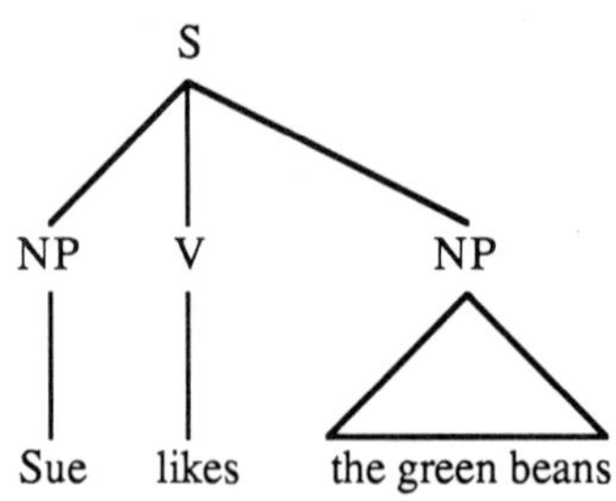

The procedural, non-compositional aspects of PSI-KLONE's ATN are then exploited to check the consistency of the concept *Sue likes*, even though it is not recognised as a syntactic constituent. Charniak and Goldman (1988, p. 88) also appear to adopt this strategy for incremental interpretation. Their rules for main clause analysis relate the subject semantics to the head verb semantics, before the rest of the VP is analysed, but do not treat the subject–verb combination as a syntactic constituent in its own right. The obvious penalty of this general approach is the perspicuity which may be lost in untying syntax and semantics. However, Fenstad et al. (1985) and Halvorsen (1986; 1987) suggest that it is possible to relax the rule-to-rule assumption in a principled fashion, and clearly any moves in this direction may have important implications for incremental interpretation.

An alternative course of action is illustrated by Haddock's (1988) approach to incremental interpretation. In this model, we retain the assumption that the process of forming syntactic and semantic constituents should proceed in a compositional, rule-to-rule manner. And we also continue to assume that the process of semantic interpretation is driven by syntactic rules. But the model differs from other approaches in assuming a theory of grammar that does not yield conventional surface structures for English. As the next section explains, Steedman's extended version of categorial grammar provides *left*-branching analyses for many constructions often held to be *right*-branching, so making it directly compatible with the hypothesis of incremental interpretation.

INCREMENTAL AND INTERACTIVE REFERENCE-SEMANTICS

This section considers recent work by the author on incremental reference evaluation. Haddock (1988; see also 1987) addresses noun phrases which refer to known contextual entities, as in Winograd's program, and follows Mellish in employing a network-based process of constraint satisfaction to evaluate their extensions. The model improves on Mellish's work in two important respects. First, the incorporation of Steedman's Combinatory Categorial Grammar (Ades & Steedman, 1982; Steedman, 1985; 1987a,b) permits a far greater degree of *left-to-right* incremental interpretation. Secondly, the model provides a treatment of the uniqueness presupposed by a definite NP, in terms of the underlying network consistency procedure. This allows the kind of ambiguity resolution pioneered by Winograd to be performed at an earlier stage in sentence processing. In what follows, we provide an informal introduction to the role of the categorial syntax in the model, and the role of the incremental reference process in guiding the parser. The following description is simplified in a number of respects, and the reader is referred to Haddock (1988) for a full exposition of the framework.

Incremental Interpretation

Like all categorial grammars, Combinatory Categorial Grammar (CCG) consists of two components. The first is a lexicon linking words to categories. The lexicon associates arguments, such as nouns, with atomic categories. Therefore, an entry for the noun *cake* will relate it to the atomic category N. Functions, on the other hand, are written as complex categories indicating syntactic mappings. For example, determiners are seen as functions mapping Ns to NPs. Therefore, the definite article *the* is defined as an NP/N, meaning that it combines with an N on its right to form an NP.

The second component of CCG consists of rules for combining functions and arguments, and, of these, the rule of *function application* is common to all categorial grammars. Here we will be concerned with *forward function application*, which combines a function of category X/Y with an adjacent right-hand argument of category Y to yield X:

17. X/Y Y ⟹ X

The rule in (17) can combine the category for *the*, NP/N, with the category for *cake*, N, to produce an NP.

Steedman supplements the rule of application with other "combinatory" operations, and some of these turn out to be especially relevant to the issue of incremental processing. In particular, a rule of *function composition* gives syntactic status to "incomplete" constituents, such as *you can believe that I like*. By way of an example, consider the composition of the determiner *the* with the adjective *red*, an N/N. Function composition rewrites these two words as follows:

18. NP/N N/N ⟹ NP/N

This treats the fragment *the red* as a function which takes an N on its right to produce an NP. The rewrite in (18) is an instance of *forward function composition*, which composes a left-hand function of category X/Y with an adjacent right-hand function of category Y/Z, to yield a new, composite function of category X/Z (19):

19. X/Y Y/Z ⟹ X/Z

These rules allow the following left-branching analysis of the noun-phrase *the red table*:

20.

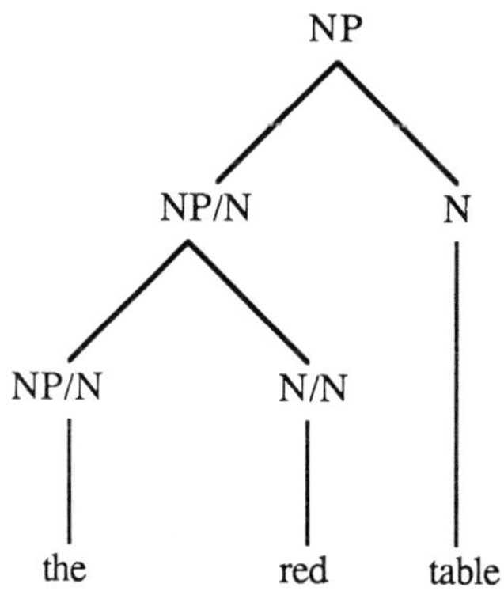

Here *the* and *red* are composed into the function category NP/N, which then applies to the head noun to complete the NP. In the model of incremental interpretation, analyses such as (20) are realised by a non-deterministic parser which reads the input string from left to right, making combinations as soon as the grammar rules permit. Typically, the rule of composition allows a combination to be made as each word is encountered. As we will see below, semantic constraints are associated with each rule and lexical entry in the grammar, and these are evaluated in the referential context in tandem with the process of syntactic analysis. Because the semantics is accessed immediately, there is no need to build phrase-structure trees at all. In common with other models of on-line interpretation, the job of the parser is simply to direct the process of building semantic representations. Trees such as (20) thus represent the derivational history of an analysis, rather than structures which are manipulated explicitly during processing.[8]

The usefulness of function composition for semantic interpretation has been demonstrated by Hinrichs and Polanyi (1986) and Pulman (1986). Hinrichs and Polanyi directly import a version of CCG to help produce partial semantic interpretations for syntactically incomplete utterances,

---

[8]Note that the grammar also permits a second, right-branching analysis of (20), which combines from the right using function application alone. There are two points to be made about such alternative analyses. The first is that, despite the syntactic differences, they are semantically equivalent (given certain assumptions about the nature of semantic interpretations; see Steedman, 1987b, pp. 416–417). We can therefore exploit the potential of functional composition for incremental processing without prejudicing the final semantic outcome. Secondly, such "spurious" ambiguity has important implications for the design of the parser. However, we will not pursue these issues here, and the reader is referred to Wittenburg (1986; 1987), Pareschi and Steedman (1987), Haddock (1988), and Morrill and Hepple (1989) for further discussion.

such as those which can be combined with deictic gestures in ordinary interactive discourse. Pulman augments a conventional phrase-structure grammar with a processing operation which discards syntactic information from time to time during parsing (called "Clear"), using this to model memory limitations in human sentence processing. However, the semantic component of this operation corresponds to function composition, which, as Pulman demonstrates, makes his model capable of incremental interpretation.

Our own interest is in the incremental evaluation of noun phrase reference. How can a scheme of constraint-based semantic evaluation be driven by a system of combinatory grammar? Suppose we associate a constraint with each nominal word and a semantic variable with its category. The noun *table* could have the following entry in the lexicon:

21. table := N_{e_3} : [table(e_3)]

Table is defined (":=") as being an N linked to the variable e_3. The identity of this variable is arbitrary; all that matters is that each word in the string is given novel semantic variables, to avoid unintended name clashes. The definition above associates a constraint with the noun, indicating that any value assumed by e_3 must denote a table in the context. The constraint will be evaluated when the word is read by the parser, and a set of candidates for e_3 computed accordingly. Semantic variables such as e_3 thus play a similar role in this model to symbols like ref(3) in Mellish's system.

Function categories differ only in that they are coupled to *mappings* between variables. For example, the adjective *red* appears as (22) with semantics attached:

22. red := N_{e_2}/N_{e_2} : [red(e_2)]

This simply states that the variable associated with the head noun is the same as the one associated with the modified noun, e_2. This ensures that the constraint arising from the adjective, *red(e_2)*, will ultimately restrict the same set of candidates that apply to the noun.

The combination rules of the grammar have responsibility for relating these representations to each other. For instance, if the above adjective and noun are to be combined by forward application, the variables e_2 and e_3 should be identified, because we will want them to represent the same extension. Thus, in addition to the usual cancellation in the syntax, the rules of application and composition must *equate* semantic variables. This is achieved by imposing a constraint of equality on the variables concerned, so that the application of *red* to *table* appears as the reduction in (23):

23. $N_{e_2}/N_{e_2}\ N_{e_3} \Longrightarrow N_{e_2}$: [$e_2 = e_3$]

At the level of reference evaluation, the constraint $e_2 = e_3$ is interpreted by intersecting the associated candidate sets and propagating the effects among the related constraints.

Finally, the definite determiner is defined in (24):

24. the := NP_{e_1}/N_{e_1} : [unique(e_1)]

The constraint arising from a definite article, *unique(e_1)*, is different in kind to those arising from nouns, adjectives, and the like. It is interpreted as follows:

25. unique(e_i) iff the candidate set for e_i is a singleton

So *unique(e_i)* holds when the candidate set for e_i contains just one element. Whereas a constraint like *red(e_i)* is a predicate over the individual contextual entities which make up the set for e_i, *unique(e_i)* is a predicate over the set as a whole. As such, *unique(e_i)* is a "meta-constraint": It makes a check on the degree to which a given candidate set is constrained. There is another aspect of (24) which distinguishes it from the rest. Whereas *red(e_i)* has its effect as soon as the word *red* is read, the constraint in (24) is only enforced when the NP corresponding to the variable e_i is syntactically closed. For this reason we call the constraint in (24) a *closure constraint*.

Let us now consider a simple example. We will trace through the incremental evaluation of the noun phrase in (26):

26. the red table

in the following context:

27.	table(T1)	red(T1)
	table(T2)	blue(T2)
	chair(C1)	red(C1)

(27) characterises a situation in which there are two tables, T1 and T2, and a chair, C1. The chair and one of the tables, T1, are red, whereas the other table is blue.

Table 2 summarises the successive states of the system as it reads each of the three words and makes a combination with the previous constituent. The first move in processing the phrase is to read the category of the initial determiner, NP_{e_1}/N_{e_1}, and consider its constraint. This simply asserts that e_1 is expected to have a single candidate when the NP is closed. [Because *unique(e_1)* is a closure constraint, it is labelled with an asterisk in (a).] The second word is now read, as defined in (22). This places the constraint *red(e_2)* on the variable e_2, which is at present unconnected to e_1. The constraint determines two candidate values for e_2 (T1 and C1) corresponding to the two red entities in the context. The categories for the determiner and adjective are now combined, using composition. This cancels N_{e_1} and N_{e_2}, producing the category in (b). A constraint of equality arises from the

TABLE 2
Incremental Evaluation of *the red table*

	Category	*Constraints*	*Extensions*
a.	NP_{e_1}/N_{e_1}	*unique(e_1)	
b.	NP_{e_1}/N_{e_2}	red(e_2) $e_1 = e_2$	e_1 : {T1,C1}
c.	NP_{e_1}	table(e_3) $e_2 = e_3$	e_1 : {T1}

reduction, meaning that e_1 and e_2 are treated as alternative names for the same set.

Finally, the noun introduces the category N_{e_3} and adds the constraint *table(e_3)*. This initially produces a candidate set containing the two tables, T1 and T2, for e_3. The rule of function application then combines *the-red* with *table*, which closes the phrase and yields the final cateogry in (c). Identifying e_2 (= e_1) with e_3 forces the intersection of {T1,C1} and {T1,T2}, producing the final candidate set for the expression, {T1}. At this point the closure constraint *unique(e_1)* is enforced, because the NP has been closed by the application to *table*. And, because the candidate set contains just one element, the check for uniqueness succeeds.

Interaction

The above example should give the flavour of the syntax-driven process of evaluation. In this section, we consider how the on-line reference process may influence the parsing of an ambiguous sentence like (28):

28. The girl saw the boy with the telescope.

Recall that Winograd's program would parse the string *the boy with the telescope* as a complex NP before invoking reference routines to check the analysis. Altmann (1986; 1987) points out that the attachment decision can be made earlier, immediately after processing the simple NP *the boy*. In particular, if the context includes more than one boy, then it is clear at this point that the subsequent material should be taken as a modifier for *the boy*, for in isolation it does not refer uniquely (cf. Altmann's, 1986, "Principle of Referential Failure"[9]). The present model can indeed disambiguate the sentence at this early stage, due to the interaction of closure constraints with the parser.

---

[9]Note that Altmann and Steedman (1988) replace both this principle and Crain and Steedman's (1985) Principle of Referential Success under a "Principle of Referential Support".

To see how this comes about, we must look a little more closely at the treatment of noun phrases. After reading the noun *boy* in (28), the parser will attempt to develop two analyses of the fragment *the boy*. The first, which we have already encountered, regards the fragment as a simple NP. This is appropriate when the subsequent PP should be seen as a VP-modifier. The second analysis, which we will write as NP/PP, explicitly subcategorises for a PP modifier for the noun *boy*, and so is appropriate for the complex NP reading. The parser will explore these alternatives in parallel, each associated with its own referential constraints and extensions. The analyses are semantically similar in that they both determine a candidate set of boys. However, they differ in that the former, simple NP reading assumes that the NP *the boy* is closed, and so enforces its closure constraint on the set of boys. In contrast, the latter analysis leaves the NP open, and hence does not evaluate its closure constraint at this stage. Thus, if there are two boys in the context, the simple NP analysis will be dropped, because it attempts to discharge the constraint of uniqueness, and this cannot be satisfied. But the NP/PP reading persists, meaning that the subsequent material must be taken as a modifier of the noun rather than the verb. Hence, the incremental and interactive process of reference evaluation allows the attachment decision to be made before the modifier is even read.

CONCLUSION

This paper has been oriented around the three interrelated issues of incremental interpretation, syntactic interaction, and reference. Given these specific interests, we can observe a certain progression in the models considered above. Bobrow and Webber provide a mechanism for the incremental computation of linguistic sense, and show how it may filter out developing syntactic analyses. However, the psychological evidence suggests that local contextual information takes priority over general commonsense knowledge in guiding the parser, and we accordingly moved on to the involvement of referential elements. Winograd demonstrates the role of definite reference in resolving attachment ambiguities, but although his process of reference evaluation is invoked on-line to the parser, it is not incremental in itself. In contrast, Mellish proposes a mechanism for incremental reference evaluation, but does not apply it to the problem of syntactic ambiguity. Haddock's model can thus be seen as a natural combination of these two earlier referential systems, building on Mellish's incremental refinement so that it can be used for Winograd-style interaction. This final model also attains a much greater degree of left-to-right interpretation than is found in the earlier work.

During the course of this exposition, we have elaborated on what it means for a system to perform incremental interpretation. We adopted Bobrow and Webber's proposal to view the underlying interpretation process in terms of incremental description refinement, and discussed two such IDR processes. Bobrow and Webber's taxonomic lattice refinement allows for the progressive disambiguation of linguistic sense, while the network consistency process used by Mellish and Haddock provides progressive disambiguation at the level of reference. Within some systems, for example those of Mellish and Haddock, it is useful to distinguish between the underlying semantic interpretation process and the process of extracting semantic information from the input string as it is read. Both Mellish and Haddock base the former process on network consistency, and drive the latter process by the syntax. However, because Haddock's system forms syntactic and semantic constituents according to a left-branching grammar, it is more successful in deriving information in a purely left-to-right order.

There are many areas where further work is required. Haddock's (1988) framework has only been applied to singular, definite noun phrases which refer to contextual entities already known to the hearer. Mellish (1985) considers a variety of other expressions, including plural definite and indefinite NPs which introduce new information to the database. Other forms of reference, such as the attributive rather than the referential use of a definite NP, have not been addressed at all in terms of incremental interpretation. And the general issue of quantifier scoping requires thorough investigation in this paradigm. This is an interesting problem, because standard techniques for expressing and resolving scope ambiguities depend on a global analysis of sentence structure. The alternative approach offered by Hobbs (1983), which is geared towards scope-neutral semantic representations, may be more relevant to the problem of incrementally processing scope ambiguities.

Another topic worth mentioning is the given/new distinction, and in particular the problem of determining whether a certain fragment of semantics is given or new with respect to the discourse context. This is a challenging problem for an incremental semantics, because the informational status of low-level constituents may depend on more global aspects of the sentence. It would be appropriate to investigate this issue in terms of interaction with the syntactic processor, for Crain and Steedman (1985) argue that when a definite NP fails to refer to a known entity, the psychological parser favours the reading which carries "the fewer unsupported presuppositions" (cf. their "Principle of Parsimony"). The program of Hobbs et al. (1988) provides a broad computational correlate of this principle, by preferring the syntactic analysis which introduces the fewest new entities to the context. What remains to be done, in the interests of psychological modelling, is to show how such a strategy may be manifested in terms of on-line, incremental interpretation.

REFERENCES

Ades, A. & Steedman, M. J. (1982). On the order of words. *Linguistics and Philosophy*, *4*, 517–558.

Altmann, G. T. M. (1986). Reference and the resolution of local ambiguity: Interaction in human sentence processing. Ph.D. Thesis, University of Edinburgh.

Altmann, G. T. M. (1987). Modularity and interaction in sentence processing. In J. Garfield (Ed.), *Modularity in knowledge representation and natural language processing*, pp. 428–444. Cambridge, Mass.: MIT Press.

Altmann, G. T. M. & Steedman, M. J. (1988). Interaction with context during human sentence processing. *Cognition*, *30*, 191–238.

Bates, M., Bobrow, R., & Webber, B. (1981). Tools for syntactic and semantic interpretation. Annual Report No. 4785, Bolt, Beranek and Newman Inc., Cambridge, Mass.

Bobrow, R. J. & Webber, B. L. (1980a). PSI-KLONE: Parsing and semantic interpretation in the BBN natural language understanding system. In *Proceedings of the Canadian Society for Computational Studies of Intelligence*, pp. 131–142, University of Victoria, Victoria.

Bobrow, R. J. & Webber, B. L. (1980b). Knowledge representation for syntactic/semantic processing. In *Proceedings of the First Annual National Conference on Artificial Intelligence*, pp. 316–323. Stanford, Calif.

Brachman, R. J. (1979). Taxonomy, descriptions, and individuals in natural language understanding. In *Proceedings of the 17th Annual Meeting of the Association for Computational Linguistics*, pp. 33–38, University of California at San Diego, La Jolla, Calif.

Brachman, R. J. & Schmolze, J. G. (1985). An overview of the KL-ONE knowledge representation system. *Cognitive Science*, *9*, 171–216.

Burton, R. R. (1976). Semantic grammar: An engineering technique for constructing natural language understanding systems. BBN Report No. 3453, Bolt, Beranek and Newman Inc., Cambridge, Mass.

Charniak, E. (1986). A neat theory of marker passing. In *Proceedings of the 5th Annual Meeting of the American Association for Artifical Intelligence*, pp. 584–588. Philadelphia, Pa.

Charniak, E. & Goldman, R. (1988). A logic for semantic interpretation. In *Proceedings of the 26th Annual Meeting of the Association of Computational Linguistics*, pp. 87–94, State University of New York at Buffalo, Buffalo, N.Y.

Crain, S. & Steedman, M. J. (1985). On not being led up the garden path: The use of context by the psychological parser. In D. Dowty, L. Karttunen, & A. Zwicky (Eds), *Natural language parsing: Psychological, computational, and theoretical perspectives*. Cambridge: Cambridge University Press.

Dahlgren, K. & McDowell, J. (1986). Using commonsense knowledge to disambiguate prepositional phrase modifiers. In *Proceedings of the 5th Annual Meeting of the American Association for Artificial Intelligence*, pp. 589–593. Philadelphia, Pa.

Fenstad, J. E., Halvorsen, P., Langholm, T., & Benthem, J. (1985). Equations, schemata and situations: A framework for linguistic semantics. Report No. CSLI-85-29, Center for the Study of Language and Information, Stanford University, Stanford, Calif.

Ford, M., Bresnan, J., & Kaplan, R. M. (1982). A competence-based theory of syntactic closure. In J. Bresnan (Ed.), *The mental representation of grammatical relations*. Cambridge, Mass.: MIT Press.

Frazier, L. (1978). On comprehending sentences: Syntactic parsing strategies. Ph.D. Thesis, University of Connecticut. Indiana University Linguistics Club.

Frazier, L. & Fodor, J. D. (1978). The sausage machine: A new two-stage parsing model. *Cognition*, *6*, 291–325.

Garrod, S. C. & Sanford, A. J. (1985). On the real-time character of interpretation during reading. *Language and Cognitive Processes*, *1*, 43–59.

Gehrke, M. (1983). Syntax, semantics and pragmatics in concert: An incremental, multi-level approach in reconstructing task-oriented dialogues. In *Proceedings of the Eighth International Joint Conference on Artificial Intelligence*, pp. 721–723, Karlsruhe.

Haddock, N. J. (1987). Incremental interpretation and combinatory categorial grammar. In *Proceedings of the Tenth International Joint Conference on Artificial Intelligence*, pp. 661–663, Milan.

Haddock, N. J. (1988). Incremental semantics and interactive syntactic processing. Ph.D. Thesis, University of Edinburgh.

Halliday, M. A. K. (1967). Notes on transitivity and theme in English: Part two. *Journal of Linguistics*, *3*, 199–244.

Halvorsen, P. (1986). Natural language understanding and Montague Grammar. *Computational Intelligence*, *2*, 54–62.

Halvorsen, P. (1987). Situation semantics and semantic interpretation in constraint-based grammars. Report No. CSLI-87-101, Center for the Study of Language and Information. Stanford University, Stanford, Calif.

Hinrichs, E. & Polanyi, L. (1986). Pointing the way. In *Papers from the Parasession on Pragmatics and Grammatical Theory at the Twenty-Second Regional Meeting of the Chicago Linguistic Society*, pp. 298–314, Chicago.

Hirst, G. (1987). *Semantic interpretation and the resolution of ambiguity*. Cambridge: Cambridge University Press.

Hirst, G. (1988). Semantic interpretation and ambiguity. *Artificial Intelligence*, *34*, 131–177.

Hobbs, J. R. (1983). An improper treatment of quantification in ordinary English. In *Proceedings of the 21st Annual Meeting of the Association for Computational Linguistics*, pp. 57–63, Massachusetts Institute of Technology, Cambridge, Mass.

Hobbs, J. R., Stickel, M., Martin, P., & Edwards, D. (1988). Interpretation as abduction. In *Proceedings of the 26th Annual Meeting of the Association for Computational Linguistics*, pp. 95–103. State University of New York at Buffalo, Buffalo, N.Y.

Jacobs, P. S. (1987). A knowledge framework for natural language analysis. In *Proceedings of the Tenth International Joint Conference on Artificial Intelligence*, pp. 675–678, Milan.

Kimball, J. (1973). Seven principles of surface structure parsing in natural language. *Cognition*, *2*, 15–47.

Lesmo, L. & Torasso, P. (1985). Weighted interaction of syntax and semantics in natural language analysis. In *Proceedings of the Ninth International Joint Conference on Artificial Intelligence*, pp. 772–778, University of California at Los Angeles, Los Angeles, Calif.

Lytinen, S. L. (1984). The organization of knowledge in a multi-lingual, integrated parser. Ph.D. Thesis, Computer Science, Yale University.

Mackworth, A. K. (1977). Consistency in networks of relations. *Artificial Intelligence*, *8*, 99–118.

Mackworth, A. K. (1987). Constraint satisfaction. In S. Shapiro (Ed.), *The encyclopedia of artificial intelligence*, Vol. 1, pp. 205–211. New York: John Wiley.

Marcus, M. P. (1980). *A theory of syntactic recognition for natural language*. Cambridge, Mass.: MIT Press.

Marslen-Wilson, W. D. (1975). Sentence perception as an interactive parallel process. *Science*, *189*, 226–228.

Marslen-Wilson, W. D. (1987). Functional parallelism in spoken word recognition. *Cognition*, *25*, 71–102.

Marlsen-Wilson, W. & Tyler, L. K. (1980). The temporal structure of spoken language understanding. *Cognition*, *8*, 1–74.

Mellish, C. S. (1981). Coping with uncertainty: Noun phrase interpretation and early semantic analysis. Ph.D. Thesis, University of Edinburgh.

Mellish, C. (1982). Incremental evaluation: An approach to the semantic interpretation of noun phrases. Cognitive Science Research Paper No. 1, Cognitive Studies Programme, University of Sussex, Brighton.

Mellish, C. S. (1983). Incremental semantic interpretation. In K. Sparck-Jones and Y. A. Wilks (Eds), *Automatic natural language parsing*. Chichester/New York: Ellis Horwood/Wiley.

Mellish, C. S. (1985). *Computer interpretation of natural language descriptions*. Chichester: Ellis Horwood.

Milne, R. W. (1982). Predicting garden path sentences. *Cognitive Science*, *6*, 349–373.

Montague, R. (1973). The proper treatment of quantification in ordinary English. In J. Hintikka, J. M. E. Moravcsik, & P. Suppes (Eds), *Approaches to natural language*. Dordrecht: Reidel.

Morrill, G. & Hepple, M. (1989). Parsing and derivational equivalence. In *Proceedings of the 4th Conference of the European Chapter of the Association for Computational Linguistics*, pp. 10–18, University of Manchester Institute of Science and Technology, Manchester.

Palmer, M. S., Dahl, D. A., Schiffman, R. J., Hirschman, L., Linebarger, M., & Dowding, J. (1986). Recovering implicit information. In *Proceedings of the 24th Annual Meeting of the Association for Computational Linguistics*, pp. 10–19, Columbia University, New York, N.Y.

Pareschi, R. & Steedman, M. J. (1987). A lazy way to chart-parse with extended categorial grammars. In *Proceedings of the 25th Annual Meeting of the Association for Computational Linguistics*, Stanford University, Stanford, Calif.

Pazzani, M. J. (1984). Conceptual analysis of garden-path sentences. In *Proceedings of the 10th International Conference on Computational Linguistics and the 22nd Annual Meeting of the Association for Computational Linguistics*, pp. 486–490, Stanford University, Stanford, Calif.

Pereira, F. C. N. & Warren, D. H. D. (1980). Definite clause grammars for language analysis—A survey of the formalism and a comparison with augmented transition grammars. *Artificial Intelligence*, *13*, 231–278.

Pulman, S. G. (1986). Grammars, parsers, and memory limitations. *Language and Cognitive Processes*, *1*, 197–225.

Riesbeck, C. K. (1975). Computational understanding. In R. Schank & B. L. Nash-Webber (Eds), *Theoretical issues in natural language processing*. Cambridge, Mass.: MIT Press.

Ritchie, G. D. (1983). Semantics in parsing. In M. King (Ed.), *Parsing natural language*. London: Academic Press.

Schubert, L. K. (1984). On parsing preferences. In *Proceedings of the 10th International Conference on Computational Linguistics and the 22nd Annual Meeting of the Association for Computational Linguistics*, Stanford University, Stanford, Calif.

Schubert, L. K. (1986). Are there preference trade-offs in attachment decisions? In *Proceedings of the 5th Annual Meeting of the American Association for Artificial Intelligence*, pp. 601–605, Philadelphia, Pa.

Shillcock, R. (1982). The on-line resolution of pronominal anaphora. *Language and Speech*, *25*, 385–402.

Sondheimer, N. K., Weischedel, R. M., & Bobrow, R. J. (1984). Semantic interpretation using KL-ONE. In *Proceedings of the 10th International Conference on Computational*

Linguistics and the 22nd Annual Meeting of the Association for Computational Linguistics, pp. 101–107, Stanford University, Stanford, Calif.

Steedman, M. (1985). Dependency and coordination in the grammar of Dutch and English. *Language*, *61*, 523–568.

Steedman, M. J. (1987a). Combinatory grammars and human language processing. In J. Garfield (Ed.), *Modularity in knowledge representation and natural language processing*. Cambridge, Mass.: Bradford/MIT Press.

Steedman, M. (1987b). Combinatory grammars and parasitic gaps. *Natural Language and Linguistic Theory*, *5*, 403–439.

Swinney, D. A. (1979). Lexical access during sentence comprehension: (Re)consideration of context effects. *Journal of Verbal Learning and Verbal Behavior*, *18*, 645–660.

Tanenhaus, M. K., Carlson, G. N., & Seidenberg, M. S. (1985). Do listeners compute linguistic representations? In D. R. Dowty, L. Karttunen, & A. M. Zwicky (Eds), *Natural language parsing: Psychological, computational and theoretical perspectives*, pp. 359–408. Cambridge: Cambridge University Press.

Tomabechi, H. (1987). Direct memory access translation. In *Proceedings of the Tenth International Joint Conference on Artificial Intelligence*, pp. 722–725, Milan.

Tyler, L. & Marslen-Wilson, W. D. (1977). The on-line effects of semantic context on syntactic processing. *Journal of Verbal Learning and Verbal Behavior*, *16*, 683–692.

Waltz, D. (1975). Understanding line drawings of scenes with shadows. In P. H. Winston (Ed.), *The psychology of computer vision*, pp. 19–91. New York: McGraw-Hill.

Waltz, D. & Pollack, J. (1985). Massively parallel parsing: A strongly interactive model of natural language interpretation. *Cognitive Science*, *9*, 51–74.

Weischedel, R. M. (1979). A new semantic computation while parsing: Presupposition and entailment. In C. Oh & D. Dineen (Eds), *Syntax and semantics II: Presupposition*, pp. 155–182. London: Academic Press.

Wilks, Y., Huang, X., & Fass, D. (1985). Syntax, preference and right attachment. In *Proceedings of the Ninth International Joint Conference on Artificial Intelligence*, pp. 779–784. University of California at Los Angeles, Los Angeles, Calif.

Winograd, T. (1971). Procedures as a representation for data in a computer program for understanding natural language. Technical Report No. MAC TR-84, Artificial Intelligence Laboratory, Massachusetts Institute of Technology, Cambridge, Mass.

Winograd, T. (1972). *Understanding natural language*. Edinburgh: Edinburgh University Press.

Winograd, T. (1973). A procedural model of language understanding. In R. C. Schank & K. Colby (Eds), *Computer models of thought and language*. San Fransisco: W. H. Freeman.

Wittenburg, K. W. (1986). Natural language parsing with combinatory categorial grammar in a graph-unification-based formalism. Ph.D. Thesis, Department of Linguistics, University of Texas.

Wittenburg, K. (1987). Predictive combinators: A method for efficient processing of combinatory categorial grammar. In *Proceedings of the 25th Annual Meeting of the Association for Computational Linguisitics*, Stanford University, Stanford, Calif.

Woods, W. A. (1970). Transition network grammars for natural language analysis. *Communications of the ACM*, *13*, 591–606.

Woods, W. (1973). An experimental parsing system for transition network grammars. In R. Rustin (Ed.), *Natural language processing*, pp. 111–154. New York: Algorithmics Press.

Woods, W. (1980). Cascaded ATN grammars. *American Journal of Computational Linguistics*, *6*, 1–12.

Subject Index